COMMUNICATION STUDIES:
THE ESSENTIAL RESOURCE

Andrew Beck, Peter Bennett and Peter Wall

Routledge
Taylor & Francis Group

LONDON AND NEW YORK

First published 2004
by Routledge
11 New Fetter Lane, London EC4P 4EE

Simultaneously published in the USA and Canada
by Routledge
29 West 35th Street, New York, NY 10001

Routledge is an imprint of the Taylor & Francis Group

Selection and editorial matter © Andrew Beck, Peter Bennett, and Peter Wall

Typeset in Bell Gothic and Novarese by M Rules
Printed and bound in Great Britain by
TJ International Ltd, Padstow, Cornwall

British Library Cataloguing in Publication Data
A catalogue record for this book is available from the British Library

Library of Congress Cataloging in Publication Data
Communication studies : the essential resource / [edited by] Andrew
Beck, Peter Bennett, and Peter Wall.
    p. cm.
Includes bibliographical references and index.
1. Communication. I. Beck, Andrew, 1952- II. Bennett, Peter, 1961-
III. Wall, Peter.
 P91.25.C615 2003
 302.2—dc22

                                        2003018599

ISBN 0–415–28792–8 (hbk)
ISBN 0–415–28793–6 (pbk)

▼ COMMUNICATION STUDIES:
THE ESSENTIAL RESOURCE

Communication Studies: The Essential Resource is a collection of resource material for all those studying communication at university and pre-university level. *The Resource* brings together a wide array of material ranging from academic articles to film scripts to websites to illustrate key topics in Communication Studies. Each extract is introduced and contextualised by the editors, and followed by suggestions for further activities and reading, to help kick-start students' autonomy.

Individual sections address:

- texts and meanings in communication
- themes in personal communication
- communication practice
- culture, communication and context
- debates and controversies in communication.

Edited by the same teachers and examiners who brought us *Communication Studies: The Essential Introduction*, this volume is an ideal companion or standalone resource to help students engage critically with communication texts.

Key features include:

- suggested further activities at the end of each extract
- a glossary of key terms
- comprehensive references including web resources, television programmes, books and films.

Andrew Beck is Principal Lecturer in Applied Communication at Coventry University, and editor of *Cultural Work* (2002). **Peter Bennett** is Head of Communications at Rowley Regis Centre of Dudley College and is Chief Examiner for AQA Communication Studies. **Peter Wall** is Chair of Examiners for AQA Media and Communication Studies, co-editor of *Media Studies: the Essential Resource* (2003) and author of *Media Studies for GCSE* (2002).

Praise for *Communication Studies: The Essential Introduction*

'Students and teachers alike will warmly welcome this book. It addresses the needs of AS students in a lively, pragmatic, intelligent, and above all, accessible way, and is written by authors who understand fully the needs of their audience. A must for any AS student!' Patrick Russell, *George Abbot School, Guildford, UK*

'Well written, organised and inventive, it sets standards by which future textbooks will be judged.' Laurence Alster, *Times Educational Supplement*

Other books for Media and Communication Studies

AS Communication Studies: The Essential Introduction
Andrew Beck, Peter Bennett, Peter Wall

AS Media Studies: The Essential Introduction
Philip Rayner, Stephen Kruger, Peter Wall

Media Studies: The Essential Resource
Philip Rayner, Stephen Kruger, Peter Wall

▼ CONTENTS

PART 4: CULTURE, COMMUNICATION AND CONTEXT   177

▼ ACKNOWLEDGEMENTS

The following were reproduced with kind permission. While every effort has been made to trace copyright holders and obtain permission, this has not been possible in all cases. Any omissions brought to our attention will be remedied in future editions.

1 *Beginning Theory*, by Peter Barry. Manchester University Press, 2002. Reproduced by kind permission of Manchester University Press and the author.

2 *Ways of Seeing*, by John Berger. London, BBC/Penguin, 1972. Reproduced by permission of Penguin Ltd and Penguin Group USA, Inc. René Magritte, *La Clef des songes*, 1930, oil on canvas, private collection. © Photothèque R Magritte – ADAGP Paris, DACS, London 2003.

3 Ludwig Wittgenstein, *Philosophical Grammar*, translated by A Kenny, Blackwell, 1969.

4 Robert Eaglestone, *Doing English*, Routledge, 2000.

5 Terence Hawkes, *Structuralism and Semiotics*, Routledge, 1992.

6 Umberto Eco, *The Role of the Reader*, Indiana University Press, 1984.

7 John Fiske, *Introduction to Communication Studies*, Routledge, 1982.

8 Pierre Guiraud, *Semiotics*, Routledge & Kegan Paul, 1975.

9 *Elements of Semiology*, by Roland Barthes, published by Jonathan Cape. Reprinted by permission of The Random House Group, Ltd.

10 'Semiotics and the Study of Occupational and Organisational Cultures', by Stephen Barley, as published in *Administrative Science Quarterly*, Issue No. 28, 1983. Reproduced by permission of Cornell University Press.

11 Denis McQuail and Sven Windahl, *Communication Models for the Study of Mass Communication,* Longman, 1993. © Denis McQuail and Sven Windahl, reprinted by permission of Pearson Education Limited and the authors.

12 John Morgan and Peter Welton, *See What I Mean?* © 1992, John Morgan and Peter Welton. Reprinted by permission of Hodder Arnold.

13 *Keywords*, by Raymond Williams, published by Fontana. Reprinted by permission of The Random House Group, Ltd.

14 *Mythologies* by Roland Barthes, published by Jonathan Cape. Reprinted by permission of The Random House Group, Ltd.

15 David Lodge, *Write On*, Penguin, 1988. Originally published in 'New Society' 1982, reprinted in *Write On* Martin Secker & Warburg 1986.

16 Reproduced by permission of Helen Hackett and the AQA.

17 *American Psycho*, by Bret Easton Ellis, published by Macmillan, London, 1991. Reprinted by permission of Rogers, Coleridge & White and ICM.

18 Mary Ragan, <http://www.mindspirit.org>, 2002.

19 Mick Underwood,<http://www.cultsock.ndirect.co.uk>, 2002.

20 Sigmund Freud, *The Psychopathology of Everyday Life*, Penguin, 1974.

21 Peter Tolan, Harold Ramis and Kenneth Lonergan, *Analyze This*, Roadshow Pictures, NPV Entertainment, Face Productions, Tribeca Productions, Baltimore/Spring Creek Pictures, 1999.

22 Stephen Pinker, *The Language Instinct*, Penguin, 1994.

23 *The Presentation of the Self in Everyday Life* by Erving Goffman, © 1959 by Erving Goffman. Used by permission of Doubleday, a division of Random House, Inc.

24 Richard Dimbleby and Graeme Burton, *Between Ourselves* © 1988, Richard Dimbleby and Graeme Burton. Reprinted by permission of Hodder Arnold.

25 Andrew Ellis and Geoffrey Beattie, *The Psychology of Language and Communication*, copyright © 1986 by Andrew Ellis and Geoffrey Beattie. Reproduced by permission of Lawrence Erlbaum Associates.

26 Michael Argyle, *The Psychology of Interpersonal Behaviour*, Penguin, 1972

27 Desmond Morris, *Body Talk: A World Guide to Gestures*, Penguin, 1994. Reproduced by permission of the author.

28 Peter Hartley, *Interpersonal Communication*, Routledge, 1999.

29 Eric Berne, from 'Away from a Theory of the Impact of Interpersonal Interaction on Non-Verbal Participation' from the *Transactional Analysis Journal*, Vol. 1, No. 1, January 1971, pp. 6–13.

30 pp. 15–17, 125–8 from *That's Not What I Meant* by Deborah Tannen. Copyright © 1986 by Deborah Tannen. Reprinted by permission of HarperCollins Publishers Inc.

31 Liz Lochhead, from *The Funny Side*, by Wendy Cope. Faber, 1988.

32 Stephen Pinker, *The Language Instinct*, Penguin, 1994.

33 'City of Glass' in Paul Auster, *New York Trilogy*, Faber, 1998.

34 Mark Jones, from the *Evening Standard* 15 June, 2001, p. 13.

ACKNOWLEDGEMENTS

35 'The Last Word in Texting', *Daily Mail* reporter, *The Daily Mail*.

36 Peter Hartley, *Group Communication*, Routledge, 1997.

37 Gerald Cole, *Management: Theory and Practice*, DP Publications, 1984.

38 Carl Sagan and Frank Drake, NASA, 1973.

39 Keith Punch, *Introduction to Social Research*, Sage, 1998. © 1998, Keith Punch. Reprinted by permission of Sage Publishing Ltd.

40 Liesbet van Zoonen, *Feminist Media Studies*, Sage, 1994. © 1994, Liesbet van Zoonen. Reprinted by permission of Sage Publishing Ltd.

41 British Psychological Society, *Code of Conduct, Ethical Principles and Guidelines*, BPS, November 2000.

42 Angus Kennedy, *The Rough Guide to the Internet, 8th Edition*, Rough Guides, 2003.

43 Winford Hicks, Sally Adams, Harriett Gilbert, *Writing for Journalists*, Routledge, 2002.

44 George Orwell, *Inside the Whale and Other Stories*, Penguin, 2001.

45 Plain English Campaign, <http://www.plainenglish.co.uk>.

46 *How Proust Can Change Your Life*, by Alain de Botton, © 1997 by Alain de Botton. Used by permission of Macmillan, London, UK, and Pantheon Books, a division of Random House, Inc.

47 Ernest Hemingway, *By-Line*, Penguin, 1967.

48 Newcastle University Classics Department, 2002.

49 Dale Carnegie, *The Quick and Easy Way to Effective Speaking*, World's Work Ltd, 1962.

50 Jacquie L'Etang and Magda Pieczka, *Critical Perspectives in Public Relations*, Thomson Business Press, 1996.

51 *Ringolevio: A Life Played For Keeps*, by Emmett Grogan. © 1972 by Eugene Leo Michael Emmett Grogan. By permission of Little, Brown and Company.

52 Alan Bryman, *Social Research Methods*, Oxford University Press, 2001.

53 John Cleese and Polly Booth, *Fawlty Towers*, (Episode entitled 'Communications Problems'), BBC2, 19 February 1979, BBC2.

54 Dick Hebdige, *Subculture: The Meaning Of Style*, Methuen, 1979. Reprinted courtesy of Taylor & Francis Books, Ltd.

55 Raymond Williams, *Keywords,* Fontana, 1983.

56 Matthew Arnold, *Culture and Anarchy*, John Murray, 1869.

57 *Communications* by Raymond Williams, published by Chatto & Windus. Reprinted by permission of The Random House Group Ltd.

58 Melvyn Bragg, 'They Want Us to Choose Between the Beatles and Beethoven. Why Can't We Have Both?' *Guardian*, 12 September 2000, © Melvyn Bragg, 2000.

59 DJ Taylor, 'It's only Mick and Keef but We Like Them', *Independent on Sunday,* 18 September 2002.

60 Robert Eaglestone, *Doing English*, Routledge, 2000.

61 Paul Taylor, *Investigating Culture and Identity*, Collins Educational, 1997.

62 Jonathan Hale, *Building Ideas: An Introduction to Architectural Theory*, MIT Press, 1998.

63 Ernst Fischer, *Marx In His Own Words*, Penguin, 1970.

64 David Lodge, *Nice Work*, Penguin, 1988. © 1988, David Lodge.

65 Germaine Greer, *The Female Eunuch*, Flamingo, 2003.

66 Yvonne Tasker, *Cultural Work* (ed. Andrew Beck), Routledge, 2003.

67 *Sex, Art and American Culture*, by Camille Paglia, © 1992 by Camille Paglia. Used by permission of Vintage Books, a division of Random House, Inc.

68 John Lechte, *Fifty Key Contemporary Thinkers*, Routledge, 1994.

69 Alan Bryman, *Social Research Methods*, Oxford University Press, 2001.

70 Jean Baudrillard, *Simulations*, Semiotext(e), 1983.

71 *Orientalism*, by Edward W Said, © 1978 by Edward W Said. Used by permission of Pantheon Books, a division of Random House, Inc.

72 Anthony P Cohen, *The Symbolic Construction of Community*, Routledge, 1992.

73 Gunther Kress and Theo van Leeuwen, *Reading Images: The Grammar of Visual Design*, Routledge, 1996.

74 Mike Davis, *City of Quartz: Excavating the Future in Los Angeles.* © 1990, Mike Davis. Reprinted by permission of Verso.

75 Georg Simmel, *Simmel on Culture*, Sage, 1997. © 1997, Georg Simmel. Reprinted by permission of Sage Publishing Ltd.

76 Margaret Visser, *The Way We Are,* Penguin, 1997.

77 David Fickling, *London Metro*, 10 February, 2001.

78 Susan Jeffords, *Hard Bodies: Hollywood Masculinity in the Reagan Era,* Copyright © 1994, by Susan Jeffords. Reprinted by permission of Rutgers University Press.

79 Janice Winship, *Looking On* (ed. Rosemary Betterton), Pandora, 1987.

80 Julie Burchill, Review of 'Heavier Than Heaven', *Guardian*, 22 September 2001. © the *Guardian*.

81 Ellis Cashmore, *Beckham*, Polity Books. © 2002 Ellis Cashmore. Reprinted by permission of Blackwell Publishing.

82 John Fiske, *Reading the Popular*, Routledge, 1989.

83 JG Ballard, *Running Wild*, Flamingo, 1997.

84 Iain Chambers, *Popular Culture: The Metropolitan Experience*, Routledge, 1986.

85 Colin Cherry, *On Human Communication*, © 1996 by Colin Cherry. Reprinted by permission of MIT Press.

86 Raymond Williams, *Communications*, Penguin, 1962.

87 Judith Williamson, *Consuming Passions*, Marion Boyars, 1986.

88 Denis MacQuail and Sven Windahl, *Communication Models for the Study of Mass Communication,* Longman, 1993. © Denis McQuail and Sven Windahl, reprinted by permission of Pearson Education Limited and the authors.

89 John Lye, *Jakobson's Communication Model*. <http://www.brocku.ca/commstudies/courses/2F50/jakobson.html>.

90 Marshall McLuhan, *Understanding Media*, Routledge, 1964.

91 George Ritzer, *The McDonaldization of Society*, Sage, 1983. © 1983, George Ritzer. Reprinted by permission of Sage Publishing Ltd.

92 Raymond Williams, Inaugural professorial lecture at Cambridge University, 29 October 1974, reprinted in Raymond Williams, *On Television*, Routledge, 1989.

93 *Technopoly: The Surrender of Culture to Technology*, by Neil Postman, Copyright © by Neil Postman. Used by permission of Alfred A Knopf, a division of Random House, Inc.

94 Kate Kellaway, *Observer*, 8 April 2001. © *Observer*.

95 Sam Sifton, *Independent Magazine*, 3 November 2001.

96 Charles Cheung, from *Web.Studies*, Arnold, 2000. © 2000 by Charles Cheung. Reprinted by permission of Hodder Arnold.

97 Basil Bernstein, *Class, Codes and Control*, Routledge 1971.

98 Michael Moore, *Stupid White Men,* Penguin, 2002.

99 Anthony P Cohen, *The Symbolic Construction of Community*, Routledge, 1992.

100 Humbert Wolfe, 'The British Journalist', from *The Uncelestial City*, New York, Alfred Knopf, 1930.

▼ BEGINNINGS (AND ENDS)

Sloppy is a beautiful reader of a newspaper. He do the Police in different voices.

(Dickens 1971: 246)

Introductions to books are most often examples of what Roman Jakobson called meta-lingual communication, that is, communication about communication itself. Like those (not really) extras with blockbuster films on DVD (the 'Making of' documentary, the episode from the 1959 television series in which the lead actor played a very minor role) they take up a little of your time to talk about themselves, not only what but how, while you'd rather be moving on to the main feature. They are about the book while also in it – a part of it as well as apart from it.

They are not even, in any real sense, the places where books start. They are more often, like the one you are now reading, places where books end. This is almost especially the case with a book like this one which is, after all, a collection of introduced extracts, where every piece is a potential starting point and where the introduction serves to shut them all up for a while, like the act of calling horses to the stalls at a big race. Whichever one did come first, they are all nevertheless returned to their places. It's also the case that the introduction to any book, like any well-crafted essay, is invariably the last text to be written. How else could authors announce their book's contents with any degree of confidence and authority?

In fact the genuine starting points of texts, the fabled first lines, almost inevitably end up submerged in the finished text and this is as true for fiction as it is for academic texts like this one. Mary Shelley was only eighteen when she wrote the promising first lines of what would ultimately be *Frankenstein*:

> It was a dreary night in November that I beheld the accomplishment of my toils. With an anxiety that almost amounted to agony, I collected the instruments of my life around me, that I might infuse a spark of being into the lifeless thing that lay at my feet. It was already one in the morning. The rain pattered dismally against the panes and the candle was nearly burnt out, when, by the glimmer of the half-extinguished light, I saw the dull yellow eye of the creature open. It breathed hard and a convulsive motion agitated his limbs.

> How can I describe my emotions at this catastrophe, or how delineate the wretch whom with such infinite pains and care I have endeavoured to form? His limbs were in proportion, and I had selected his features as beautiful. Beautiful! – Great God! His yellow skin scarcely covered the work of muscles and arteries beneath. His hair was a lustrous black, and flowing. His teeth of a pearly whiteness. But these luxuriances only formed a more horrid contrast with his watery eyes, that seemed

almost of the same colour as the dun white sockets in which they were set, his shriv-
elled complexion and straight black lips.

(Shelley 1994: 55)

When the novel was finally published these had become the first lines of Chapter 5 and the
novel's first lines became these far less dramatic comments from the novel's first narrator, the would-be explorer Walton: 'You will rejoice to hear that no disaster has
accompanied the commencement of my enterprise which you have regarded with such evil
forebodings' (Shelley 1994: 5).

Less dramatic they may be but it is somewhat worrying that both of these starts have
some merits as introductions to this Resource, this collection of severed and extracted
parts to which this introduction is attempting to 'infuse a spark of being'.

Perhaps it is fitting that this introduction is itself fast becoming an odd collection of other
people's starts, for this book is unashamedly a 'rattle bag'. It constitutes a noisy collection of provocations and opinions: it is a conversation of extracts, disputing, debating and
occasionally agreeing. In England's Black Country, that scrap of industrial land on which
Tolkien modelled 'the land of Mordor where the shadows lie', it would be called codge-
modge, an unsightly collection of things that nevertheless combine to do a job: to block
a hole, to hold something up, or in this case to inform a debate. Within the language of
Communication Studies you will see the act of taking items from diverse sources and
welding them together to make something new referred to as *bricolage*, which is French
for much the same thing and yet has a completely different resonance and register. Indeed
the term *bricolage* was itself appropriated by structural anthropologists who noted that
French itinerant workers who turned their hand to any job of work, who combined all
manner of skills to earn enough money to get them to the next day and the next destination, were referred to as *bricolateurs*. The house of Communication Studies is full of halls
which echo with sounds heard, half-heard, and heard again, albeit in new combinations.

These resonances are the stuff of Communication Studies: matters of language, matters of
register, even matters of media (which Marshall McLuhan was offering as 'the message' as
far back as 1964). If communication was a collective noun it would surely refer to a collection of opinions and this book simply would be subtitled *A Communication*. The process
is endless, for even as this narrative, this introduction, is being written so it is exchanging
opinions and negotiating its communication, according to such vital variables as:

- the status of its senders
- the aesthetic appeal of its cover
- the implied authority of its cover price
- the circumstances in which it is being read.

This may be your own copy of the book or a college textbook or a library book or an as-
yet-unsold copy in a bookshop. You may recognise the authors' names because you have
used them before perhaps, in preparation for a public examination, and consider them a
reliable brand (or not!).

In an early draft of *Communication Studies: The Essential Introduction* we produced
writing which was prompted by these words of Raymond Williams:

We need to say what many of us know in experience: that the struggle to learn, to describe, to understand, to educate is a central and necessary part of our humanity. This struggle is not begun, at second hand, after reality has occurred. It is in itself a major way in which reality is formed and changed . . . Communication begins in the struggle to learn and describe.

(Beck, Bennett and Wall 2002: 54)

In the contexts of beginnings and ends it's worth noting that (1) in the published text this ended up on page 54, most certainly not the beginning; (2) Williams's words are in themselves a cry to take up arms in the fight for a new conception of education as a whole, never mind the emerging discipline of Communication Studies; and (3) if you inflect Williams's words with some of the sentiments contained between these covers you might end up questioning why it should be the case that Williams's take on what constituted Communication Studies is so very different from other founding fathers of the discipline and why it should be the case that all these founding fathers were just that – fathers. Williams's beginnings are not necessarily ours . . . maybe his ends are our beginnings.

So in that sense, gentle reader, don't be surprised if this book doesn't add up, if it doesn't deliver the one big argument. Indeed, once you've wrangled some key notions of postmodernism into your own rattle bag of concepts you will appreciate that such a task is maybe not only impossible but also undesirable in the twenty-first century. What you will read here are embodiments and enactments of both the desire to communicate and at the same time to understand what it is we are doing.

So why are we doing Communication Studies? And why are we exhorting you to read so many writers with so many different positions? Well, in the first case this is because, as Peter Hartley points out in the introduction to his excellent and unpretentious text *Interpersonal Communication,* communication is 'an important part of everyday life'. In fact most of the first two paragraphs is worth considering in this respect:

> If you have picked up this book to flick through the contents, then I probably do not need to convince you that face-to-face communication between people is an important part of everyday life. Our relationships at work, home and at play are critical to our psychological well-being. My telephone company is also convinced of this – it quotes a recent survey which 'showed that 60% of the British public would like to be better at communicating with their friends and family'. Of course you might not be surprised that a communications company wishes to promote the fact that 'it's good to talk', but we can find plenty of evidence from other sources to support its views on the value of communication.
>
> The way we communicate also influences our life opportunities in situations such as job or course interviews. The importance of interactive or interpersonal skills at work is frequently emphasised and this has led to a corresponding increase in training, seminars, workshops and publications which focus on these skills, across a *very* wide range of organisations.

(Hartley 1999: 1)

Moreover, Hartley goes on to ask some very direct questions about communication text-books which will likely prove useful: 'We cannot change our interpersonal behaviour just by reading a book. So what is the value of a textbook like this, apart from helping some students get through their course assignments? Can a book like this make any difference to your everyday situation?' (Hartley 1999: 2).

Now partly this book has an easy response to this challenge because it is not straight-forwardly a textbook but rather a book of texts, in the main all extracts from longer texts. For sure the extracts are sequenced; in the way in which they read this could be called a narrative. It also has a structure, indeed it has more than one structure. Read one way the book is divided into five parts that largely correspond to the six modules of the AQA A Level in Communication Studies. Read another way it starts by offering the reader some tools with which to begin doing Communication Studies; it then moves to offer key writers' attempts to do Communication Studies; it provides the reader with a bag of tools with which to do their own Communication Studies; then it takes the argument out into the streets to wrestle with big theory in broad daylight; and finally it kicks over the whole carefully constructed edifice by questioning the very territory and very disciplinarity of Communication Studies itself. It also provides all its extracts with numbers; the very act of numbering extracts generates all kinds of connotations it would be foolish to ignore. The hitherto unspoken secret behind our whole edifice is that maybe what you are about to be entertained by is a massive act of ventriloquism. That is, we will do Communication Studies in different voices – just as Sloppy did the Police in different voices. And so it's here that you maybe get the point of the epigraph from Dickens at the head of this intro-duction of sorts. Sometimes writers offer a hint in the form of a quotation from another writer at the beginning of a text and only make the allusion into a reality many pages later. And sometimes it's difficult to know whether it's the ventriloquist or the dummy that's doing the talking.

However in other ways the design principle of the book is healthily random. It is very much a meta-selection, a selection which talks of and encourages other selections, both from this material and beyond. The extracts are ultimately separate so that they can be individually selected and infinitely combined. There are 100 of these for no better reason than knights are given a year and a day to complete quests. There could be other reasons but there is no better reason. This is a chart, a hot 100, but also a map with at least 100 contours, a list but also a metaphor, a technique. Even this introduction is largely a selec-tion from others, call them alternatives.

As we draw this section of our introduction to a close perhaps we should try to remind ourselves of what it is we are trying to do. The following was written in 1949 by Marion Hope Parker as an introduction to *Language and Reality: A Course In Contemporary Criticism*. Despite its occasional echoes of a bygone age in its language, it remains remarkably fresh and stands as a pretty good introduction to the course in contemporary criticism you are about to begin:

> This book is designed not only for those with a specialised interest in language but for those with a special interest in life. Every man ought to be a student, but every man must be a critic or else rapidly and recognisably become something less than a man.

We live in an age of emotion when reading has made thinking particularly difficult and the liberty to think is insecure. Though no country, ancient or modern, has completely achieved democracy we have been fighting recently lest our idea of it should be taken away. This is what is sometimes known as fighting for one's rights; it might also be known, perhaps no less convincingly, as fighting for one's wrongs, since it is the defence of principles by which alone practice may be judged wrong – or right. It remains today what it has always to some extent been for us – a mental battle against great odds.

(Parker 1949: vii–viii)

Just as with Raymond Williams's word this is another call to take up arms in the fight to see things clearly, to return to where we started, and to see things afresh. We will go back to our roots, we will return to our beginnings, and we will know them anew. You will, just as we have in the making of this book, create your own beginnings and ends: you will dip into the book, you will extract at random, you will read whole sequences in the order in which they are presented, and you will use a combination of contents table, references, and index to create your own new structure of the structure which is fixed only on the page.

In my beginning is my end.

(Eliot 1936: 196)

HOW TO USE THIS BOOK

Given the tentative way in which we have approached communicating about this book's structure maybe it's a little confusing to offer you a guide to how to use the book. But there are a number of quite uncontroversial things that it's useful for you to know. The book is built out of 100 extracts. These extracts are clustered into five parts. Each extract is introduced with two questions (and two answers): WHAT'S THE TOPIC? (we answer this question by telling you as briefly as possible what the topic, the focus, of the extract is) and WHAT'S THE TEXT? (we answer this question by giving you the title of the work from which the extract is drawn). We don't give you each work's full publishing details – these appear at the back of the book in the References section. At the end of each extract (apart from the very first) there appears a third question WHAT'S NEXT? (and we answer this by giving you some self-development activity to do: this is designed to reinforce the reading of the extract by making you do something else, whether it's thinking, writing, planning, researching, sketching, or doing more reading. Many of the extracts, introductions and activities contain brief references to other texts; full details of all of these texts appear in the References section at the back of the book (whether the texts are newspaper or magazine articles, chapters in books, whole books, films, records, television programmes, or websites).

As a guide many of the early extracts (certainly in Parts 1, 2 and 3) are fairly brief, but the introductions and commentaries are quite long. As the book goes on the extracts tend to get longer and the introductions and commentaries tend to get briefer. (Like any generalisation this is not always the case.) We hope that this form of organisation will give you plenty of handholds to help you through the early parts of the book but that, suitably emboldened, you will be able to cope with the later parts of the book with only the smallest of safety nets. As we've said before you can work through this collection any way you want: we've provided you with a contents table, with a bank of references, with an index. The rest is up to you.

Before we end it's important that we acknowledge the help of some people in particular who have helped us on our way with this book. Take a bow – David Alexander, Will Barton Catmur, Betty Bodsworth, Lynne Kennedy, and Jerry Slater: we're always touched by your presence.

Andrew Beck, Peter Bennett, Peter Wall
Leamington Spa, Stourbridge, Wakefield, February 2003

I don't dig this brooding analytical stuff. I just danced; and I just acted.

(Fred Astaire)

▼ 1 WHAT'S THE TOPIC? Approaching theory
WHAT'S THE TEXT? Peter Barry *Beginning Theory*

Experienced and confident students of Communication Studies assert that it is misleading to distinguish between theory and practice. Nevertheless many commentators find such a distinction useful. One way of characterising the discipline is that it consists of practices which are informed by theory. As Communication Studies students we subject the world of communication to various kinds of analysis prompted, guided and shaped by those theoretical pioneers who have gone before. Given the multi-disciplinary character of the subject this results in our drawing on the broadest range of useful theoretical work: philosophical, linguistic, anthropological, psychological, sociological, aesthetic. Because the discipline draws on work originally written in languages other than English we are thus at the mercy of translators.

This book is a collection (and, necessarily, a selection) of readings which we hope will represent a coming together of theory and practice, in which theory becomes a means of expression, a way through to meanings, a bridge. Often before it becomes this bridge, theory will first function as a barrier – both semantic and psychological. In other words you're put off because you think you can't understand it and then lose confidence as a result of feeling stupid. Peter Barry, writing specifically for students of literature, addresses this in the introduction to his book *Beginning Theory*. This is good advice for all prospective students on an Arts, Humanities, or Social Sciences programme, and it's particularly useful for Communication Studies students.

I want to assure you at the outset that the doubts and uncertainties you will have about this material are probably *not* due to:

1. any supposed mental incapacity of your own, for example, to your not having 'a philosophical mind', or not possessing the kind of X-ray intellect which can penetrate jargon and see the sense beneath, or

2. the fact that your schooling did not include intensive tuition in, say, linguistics or philosophy, or

3. the innate and irreducible difficulty of the material itself (a point we will come back to).

Rather, nearly all the difficulties you will have will be the direct result of the way theory is written, and the way it is written about. For literary theory, it must be emphasised, is not innately difficult. There are very few inherently complex ideas in existence in literal theory. On the contrary, the whole body of work known collectively as 'theory' is based upon some dozen or so ideas, none of which are in themselves difficult. . . . What *is* difficult, however, is the language of theory. Many of the major writers on theory are French, so that much of what we read is in translation, sometimes of a rather clumsy kind. Being a Romance language, French takes most of its words directly from Latin, and it lacks the reassuring Anglo-Saxon layer of vocabulary which provides us with so many of our brief, familiar, everyday terms. Hence, a close English translation of a French academic text will contain a large number of longer Latinate words, always perceived as a source of difficulty by English-speaking readers. Writing with a high proportion of these characteristics can be off-putting and wearying, and it is easy to lose patience.

But the frame of mind I would recommend at the outset is threefold. *Firstly*, we must have some *initial* patience with the difficult surface of the writing. We must avoid the too-ready conclusion that literary theory is just meaningless, pretentious jargon (that is, that the theory is at fault). *Secondly*, on the other hand, we must, for obvious reasons, resist the view that we ourselves are intellectually incapable of coping with it (that is, that we are at fault). *Thirdly*, and crucially, we must not assume that the difficulty of theoretical writing is *always* the dress of profound ideas – only that it *might* sometimes be, which leaves the onus of discrimination on us. To sum up this attitude: we are looking, in literary theory, for something we can use, not something which will use us. We ought not to issue theory with a blank cheque to spend our time for us. (If we do, it will certainly spend more than we can afford.) Do not, then, be *endlessly* patient with theory. Require it to be clear, and expect it, in the longer term, to deliver something solid. Don't be content, as many seem to be, just to see it as 'challenging' conventional practice or 'putting it in question' in some never quite specified way. Challenges are fine, but they have to amount to something in the end.

(Barry 2002: 6–8)

One line leaps out as a perfect introduction to something that purports to be 'the essential resource': 'We are looking . . . for something we can use, not something that will use us'. Let this be true of both you and us.

▼ 2 WHAT'S THE TOPIC? Perception, perspective, and the character of images
WHAT'S THE TEXT? John Berger *Ways of Seeing*

In *Bean: The Ultimate Disaster Movie* Rowan Atkinson's hapless character is mistaken for a leading English art expert at an American gallery (in fact he is merely a security guard). At the end of the film he is required to give a lecture to celebrate the fact that the gallery has acquired the famous American painting 'Whistler's Mother'. The audience, knowing Bean's near incapacity with words, can see no way out for him: he will be exposed. However, to much applause, he begins by explaining, 'I sit and look at the paintings'. (An earlier generation of filmgoers had witnessed something similar with Chance the Gardener, the Peter Sellers character, in Hal Ashby's 1979 film of Jerzy Kosinski's novel *Being There*, where Chance's banal utterances are taken for profound philosophy.)

Beyond the irony are the opening questions of any textual analysis:

- what are we seeing?
- how is it organised? and,
- what is important?

John Berger's book *Ways of Seeing* begins by addressing some of these issues. Berger is mainly concerned with those special pieces of communication to which we give the collective title 'Art' but his approach is extremely useful to any student of communication. The first of the seven essays which comprise the book begins with a provocative assertion: 'Seeing comes before words. The child looks and recognises before it can speak'. This is a provocative statement, one that many psychologists would want to refute. Indeed, there is much speculation as to whether seeing comes before words just as much as whether the spoken word precedes the written. Taking his lead from Korzybski's concept of General Semantics William S Burroughs reflects (in the introduction to 'The Book of Breeething'): 'It is generally assumed that the spoken word came before the written word. I suggest that the spoken word as *we* know it came *after* the written word' (1979: 65). What Berger offers is a contribution to the debate as to what is communication and where communication starts. Berger puts seeing at the centre of this discussion; other commentators beg to differ.

> Seeing comes before words. The child looks and recognises before it can speak.

But there is also another sense in which seeing comes before words. It is seeing which establishes our place in the surrounding world; we explain that world with words, but words can never undo the fact that we are surrounded by it. The relation between what we see and what we know is never settled. Each evening we *see* the sun set. We *know* that the earth is turning away from it. Yet the knowledge, the explanation, never quite fits the sight. The Surrealist painter Magritte commented on this always-present gap between words and seeing in a painting called *The Key of Dreams*.

The way we see things is affected by what we know or what we believe. In the Middle Ages when men believed in the physical existence of Hell the sight of fire must have meant something different from what it means today. Nevertheless their idea of Hell owed a lot to the sight of fire consuming and the ashes remaining – as well as to their experience of the pain of burns.

When in love, the sight of the beloved has a completeness which no words and no embrace can match: a completeness which only the act of making love can temporarily accommodate.

Yet this seeing which comes before words, and can never be quite covered by them, is not a question of mechanically reacting to stimuli. (It can only be thought of in this way if one isolates the small part of the process which concerns the eye's retina.) We only see what we look at. To look is an act of choice.

As a result of this act, what we see is brought within our reach – though not necessarily within arm's reach. To touch something is to situate oneself in relation to it. (Close your eyes, move round the room and notice how the faculty of touch is like a static, limited form of sight.) We never look at just one thing; we are always looking at the relation between things and ourselves. Our vision is continually active, continually moving, continually holding things in a circle around itself, constituting what is present to us as we are.

Soon after we can see, we are aware that we can also be seen. The eye of the other combines with our own eye to make it fully credible that we are part of the visible world.

If we accept that we can see that hill over there, we propose that from that hill we can be seen. The reciprocal nature of vision is more fundamental that that of spoken dialogue. And often dialogue is an attempt to verbalize this – an attempt to explain how, either metaphorically or literally, 'you see things', and an attempt to discover how 'he sees things'.

In the sense in which we use the word in this book, all images are man-made.

An image is a sight which has been recreated or reproduced. It is an appearance, or a set of appearances, which has been detached from the place and time in which it first made its appearance and preserved – for a few moments or a few centuries. Every image embodies a way of seeing. Even a photograph.

For photographs are not, as is often assumed, a mechanical record. Every time we look at a photograph, we are aware, however slightly, of the photographer selecting that sight from an infinity of other possible sights. This is true even in the most casual family snapshot. The photographer's way of seeing is reflected in his choice of subject. The painter's way of seeing is reconstituted by the marks he makes on the canvas or paper. Yet, although every image embodies a way of seeing, our perception or appreciation of an image depends also upon our own way of seeing. (It may be, for example, that Sheila is one figure among twenty; but for our own reasons she is the one we have eyes for.)

Images were first made to conjure up the appearances of something that was absent. Gradually it became evident that an image could outlast what it represented; it then showed how something or somebody had once looked – and thus by implication how the subject had once been seen by other people. Later still the specific vision of the image-maker was also recognised as part of the record. An image became a record of how X had seen Y. This was the result of an increasing consciousness of individuality, accompanying an increasing awareness of history.

(Berger 1972: 7–10)

[handwritten margin note: Eg, Fire = Hell?]

Berger reinforces some important points concerning images. These are also true more generally of all texts. The following might be seen as central to all analytical work on Communication texts where 'text' and 'image', in Berger's 1972 formulation, are virtually interchangeable:

- 'all images are man-made' (that is they are all conscious human constructions)
- 'an image is a sight which has been recreated or reproduced' (the means of and control over this reproduction is a significant issue in Communication Studies)
- 'it is an appearance, or a set of appearances which has been detached from the place and the time in which it first made its appearance and preserved – for a few moments or a few centuries' (images [and all texts] are 'stores' – of experience, of occasion, of information)
- 'every image embodies a way of seeing' (this is partly what, as Communication Studies students, we call the 'mode of address', the way a particular text encourages us to look at it, and to look at it in a certain fashion).

[handwritten note: How it interpellates depending on target market.]

➤ Spend some time looking at images of landscapes (representative paintings, photographs, scenes from films, scenes from television programmes) and consider how far they embody a 'way of seeing'. Then go and look at a landscape, townscape or cityscape near where you live. Try to decide what are the differences between looking at it, looking at images of it, and making images of it.

➤ Make a list of the words that we commonly use to describe landscapes (e.g. picturesque, breathtaking, dramatic, industrial, bleak) and suggest the visual features of the landscape that create these descriptions. Does seeing always come before words?

➤ Read Mary Anne Staniszewski's *Seeing is Believing: Creating the Culture of Art* (1995), London and New York: Penguin.

▼ ## 3 WHAT'S THE TOPIC? Language and the world
WHAT'S THE TEXT? Ludwig Wittgenstein
Philosophical Grammar

The philosopher Ludwig Wittgenstein was concerned about the ways in which the language that we use conditions and limits our understandings of the world. In his *Philosophical Grammar* he painstakingly attempts to arrive at a set of 'rules' for the study of meaning and understanding. In each case he comes face to face with language as a significant limitation; he concluded that 'the limits of my language are the limits of my world'. Put simply, it might be the case that our experience of real life in all of its glory and detail may be significantly determined by the language that we use to explain and to describe it. Here he is addressing what is meant by understanding.

How can one talk about 'understanding' and 'not understanding' a proposition? Surely it is not a proposition until it's understood?

Does it make sense to point to a clump of trees and ask 'Do you understand what this clump of trees says?' In normal circumstances, no; but couldn't one express a sense by an arrangement of trees? Couldn't it be a code?

One would call 'propositions' clumps of trees one understood; others, too, that one didn't understand, provided one supposed the man who planted them had understood them.

'Doesn't understanding only start with a proposition, with a whole proposition? Can you *understand* half a proposition?' – Half a proposition is not a whole proposition. – But what the question means can perhaps be understood as follows. Suppose a knight's move in chess was always carried out by two movements of the piece, one straight and one oblique; then it could be said 'In chess there are no half knight's moves' meaning: the relationship of half a knight's move to a whole knights move is not the same as that of half a bread roll to a whole bread roll. We want to say that it is not a difference of degree.

It is strange that science and mathematics make use of propositions, but have nothing to say about understanding those propositions.

2 We regard understanding as the essential thing, and signs as something inessential. – But in that case, why have the signs at all? If you think that it is only so as to make ourselves understood by others, then you are very likely looking on the signs as a drug which is to produce in other people the same condition as my own.

Suppose that the question is 'what do you mean by that gesture?' and the answer is 'I mean you must leave'. The answer would not have been more correctly phrased: 'I mean what I mean by the sentence "you must leave".'

In attacking the formalist conception of arithmetic, Frege says more or less this: these petty explanations of the signs are idle once we *understand* the signs. Understanding would be something like seeing a picture from which all the rules followed, or a picture that makes them all clear. But Frege does not seem to see that such a picture would itself be another sign, or a calculus to explain the written one to us.

What we call 'understanding a language' is often like the understanding we get of a calculus when we learn its history or its practical application. And there too we meet an easily surveyable symbolism instead of one that is strange to us. – Imagine that someone had originally learnt chess as a writing game, and was later shown the 'interpretation' of chess as a board game.

In this case 'to understand' means something like 'to take in as a whole'.

If I give anyone an order I feel it to be quite enough to give him signs. And if I am given an order, I should never say: 'this is only words, and I have got to get behind the words'. And when I have asked someone something and he gives me an answer I am content – that was just what I expected – and I don't raise the objection: 'but that's a mere answer.'

But if you say: 'How am I to know what he means, when I see nothing but the signs he gives?' then I say: 'How is *he* to know what he means, when he has nothing but the signs either?'

What is spoken can only be explained in language, and so in this sense language itself cannot be explained.

Language must speak for itself.

(Wittgenstein 1969: 39–40)

Wittgenstein is addressing, at a fairly refined level, the essential issue of textual analysis – the relationship between a text and its meanings. The problem for Wittgenstein resides in the fact that meaning is reduced to and by signs, particularly linguistic signs. In other words we tend to express the meaning of one set of signs in terms of the meaning of a second set of signs. This example demonstrates this problem usefully:

- 'What do you mean by that gesture?' (practically, 'what does that gesture mean?' but for gesture we can substitute 'picture', 'word', or 'smile')
- 'I mean you must leave' (which is then clarified by Wittgenstein as: 'I mean what I mean by the sentence "you must leave"').

This is partly another way of addressing Berger's assertion that 'seeing . . . comes before words, and can never be quite covered by them' or more poignantly 'the sight of the beloved has a completeness which no words . . . can match'. As a philosopher Wittgenstein is rather more concerned with the theory of language and his conclusion is ruthless: 'language itself cannot be explained' and yet it is simultaneously pragmatic: 'language must speak for itself'.

WHAT'S NEXT?

- ➤ Consider the different kinds of understanding that might be had from
  - observing a supposedly 'natural' landscape (like woodland or open fields)
  - observing a theoretically constructed landscape (like a local park or a housing development or an industrial estate)
  - observing a photographic or video representation of one of the above
  - observing a drawn or painted version of one of the above
  - making a representation of a 'natural' or 'artificial' landscape.
- ➤ Read JL Austin's *How To Do Things With Words* (1962), Oxford: Oxford University Press.

▼ 4 WHAT'S THE TOPIC? Approaching reading
WHAT'S THE TEXT? Robert Eaglestone *Doing English*

We have been looking at a number of extracts which collectively suggest that the way in which we have traditionally thought about how we see (perception) and how we use language (communication) need reassessing. This shift in position could be explained away by saying that what was being talked about were objects from everyday life, that they are not things which we ordinarily study and that, because of this, we have been caught off our guard, we have fallen prey to misconceptions in a casual fashion. The implication being that when we engage in the formal study of something we will be fully aware and will not be caught unawares. But the following extract from Robert Eaglestone's *Doing English* is prompted by the notion that even when we are intellectually on our toes we could well be labouring under similar misconceptions. Reading, Eaglestone argues, is not the act of mere looking, or even uncovering what the author intended, but an act of personal selection and interpretation. Although Eaglestone (like Barry in Extract 1 above) is talking about the reading of literary texts as students of Communication Studies we suggest that his admonitions apply to all texts.

Understanding literature isn't a natural process and we have to use certain tools to find meaning in a text, whether we realise we are doing so or not. What you make of a novel, a poem or play is exactly that: what you *make* of it. Another way of expressing this is to say that to read a literary text, to think about it, or to write about it in any way, is to undertake *an act of interpretation*. When you interpret text it means that you find some things important and not others, or that you focus on some ideas and questions and exclude others. Rather than reading in a vacuum, we take our ideas, our tendencies and preferences – *ourselves* – to a text. This means that 'reading' and 'interpreting' mean almost the same . . . It is because of the importance of interpretation that I have used the word 'text' regularly throughout this book. Apart from being shorter to write than 'novel, poem or play', it emphasises that reading is an act of interpretation – texts are things that are interpreted. (The word 'text' also makes it clear that it's not only literature that is interpreted; so are people's actions, television and music, for example. News is interpreted both when it is watched, heard or read, and when it is put together by journalists.)

Because interpretation doesn't happen in a vacuum, *no interpretation is neutral or objective*. Whenever you interpret a novel, poem or play (or anything else for that matter: TV soap, advert, film) your interpretation is shaped by a number of *presuppositions*. These are the 'taken for granted' ideas, tendencies and preferences you carry with you and, like the glasses that you can't take off, you always tend to read through them. On a surface level, your interpretation will be affected by the *context* in which you read and the expectations you have of the text. For example, if you read a novel about World War II for a history project, you'll think about it in a different way from how you would look at it if you were to read it for fun. At a deeper level, you bring with you presuppositions about yourself, other people and the world, which you may take so much for granted that you don't even realise you have them. At this level everyone has different presuppositions because – simply – people are different, to a greater or lesser degree, and have been shaped by different experiences. People from different backgrounds, sexes, sexualities, religions, classes and so on will be struck by different things in any text. Everything you have read and experienced previously affects how you interpret now. This idea can be summed up by saying that everyone is 'located' in the world. Just as you can't jump higher than your shadow, you can't escape your location in the world.

(Eaglestone 2000: 20–1)

To see is to select and to interpret. To read is always an act of interpretation. Our gender, ethnicity, geographical location, religious beliefs, age, family position, income, will all affect how we approach reading and will help determine what we take away from any given reading. Reading is not neutral; it is always an act of interpretation. Some of the ways in which we select and interpret texts will be determined by essential factors over which we have little or no control; this tends to be the case when we are young. But as we mature we can exercise more and more control over, and choice in, how we guide and inform our selections and interpretations.

WHAT'S NEXT?

- ➤ Read Terry Eagleton's *Literary Theory: An Introduction* (1983) Oxford: Blackwell.
- ➤ Prepare a checklist of those positions (as identified by Eagleton) which you can adopt to interpret texts. (Hopefully this will correspond to work you'll encounter in Extracts 40, 63, and 65 of this book.)

5 WHAT'S THE TOPIC? Structuralism
WHAT'S THE TEXT? Terence Hawkes
Structuralism and Semiotics

Although many of the perspectives and methods that have come to be held as fundamen-tal to Communication Studies had currency and status in mainland Europe for much of the first half of the twentieth century it was only in the late 1960s that these ideas made the successful journey to the United Kingdom and the USA. Given the absorption of many of the principles and practices of semiotics (as evidenced by Guiraud, Barthes, and Barley [which appear as Extracts 8, 9, and 10 in this book]) into contemporary experiences of everyday life and representations it's now quite difficult to imagine the impact that texts such as Peter Wollen's *Signs and Meanings in the Cinema* had when it was first published in 1969. Not only were the ideas of semiotics and structuralism taken up by communica-tions professionals but they were also taken up by the academic world. In some cases the revolutionary impact of these perspectives was too much for the Academy. David Lodge sets his 1988 novel *Nice Work* in the world of the late 1980s' British university system. As background to the material practices of key characters in the novel, Lodge brilliantly sketches the scene at Cambridge University in the late 1970s/early 1980s before making barely disguised reference to the sacking of Colin MacCabe from his Cambridge University teaching post on account of his promoting 'new' ideas such as structuralism:

> Intellectually it was an exciting time to be a research student in the English Faculty. New ideas imported from Paris by the more adventurous young teachers glittered like dustmotes in the Fenland air: structuralism and poststructuralism, semiotics and deconstruction, new mutations and graftings of psychoanlaysis and Marxism, linguistics and literary criticism. The more conservative dons viewed these ideas and their proponents with alarm, seeing in them a threat to the traditional values and methods of literary scholarship. Battle was joined, in seminars, lectures, commit-tee meetings and the review pages of scholarly journals. It was a revolution. It was civil war. . . . Then in 1981 all hell broke loose in the Cambridge English Faculty. An extremely public row about the denial of tenure to a young lecturer associated with the progressive party opened old wounds and inflicted new ones on this already thin-skinned community. . . . For a few weeks the controversy featured in the national and even international press, up-market newspapers carrying spicy stories about the leading protagonists and confused attempts to explain the difference between struc-turalism and poststructuralism to the man on the Clapham omnibus.

(Lodge 1988: 46–8)

The newness of these perspectives cannot be underestimated or overemphasised. Nor is it wise to play down the continuing impact such perspectives continue to exert over work within academic circles; as Robert Eaglestone puts it in *Doing English*: 'change doesn't come easily . . . in the last twenty or thirty years [these new ideas] have caused terrible arguments and divisions between students and teachers . . . in schools, colleges and uni-versities all over the English-speaking world' (Eaglestone 2000: 27).

In his book *Structuralism and Semiotics* Terence Hawkes provides a comprehensive guide to that then-new thinking about perception, reality and representation. In the extract below he provides a workable description of a much used and much misunderstood term *structuralism*. First he locates structuralism very clearly by describing it as 'a way of thinking about the world' to which we might add 'of Communication'. He then talks about that new perception which focuses on relationships rather than components in the communication process. As such is a very useful basis for the analysis of a wide range of texts and situations.

It follows that structuralism is fundamentally a way of thinking about the world which is predominantly concerned with the perception and description of structures, as defined above. As a developing concern of modern thinkers since Vico, it is the result of a momentous historic shift in the nature of perception, which finally crystallized in the early twentieth century, particularly in the field of the physical sciences, but with a momentum that has carried through to most other fields. The 'new' perception involved the realization that despite appearances to the contrary, the world does not consist of independently existing objects, whose concrete features can be perceived clearly and individually, and whose nature can be classified accordingly. In fact, every perceiver's *method* of perceiving can be shown to contain an inherent bias which affects what is perceived to a significant degree. A wholly objective perception of individual entities is therefore not possible: any observer is bound to *create* something of what he observes. Accordingly, the *relationship* between observer and observed achieves a kind of primacy. It becomes the only thing that *can* be observed. It becomes the stuff of reality itself. Moreover the principle involved must invest the whole of reality. In consequence, the true nature of things may be said to lie not in things themselves, but in the relationships which we construct, and then perceive, *between* them.

This new concept, that the world is made up of relationships rather than things, constitutes the first principle of that way of thinking which can properly be called 'structuralist'. At its simplest, it claims that the nature of every element in any given situation has no significance by itself, and in fact is determined by its relationship to all the other elements involved in that situation. In short, the full significance of any entity or experience cannot be perceived unless and until it is integrated into the *structure* of which it forms a part.

It follows that the ultimate quarry of structuralist thinking will be the permanent structures into which individual human acts, perceptions, stances fit, and from which they derive their final nature. This will finally involve what Fredric Jameson has described as 'an explicit search for the permanent structures of the mind itself, the organizational categories and forms through which the mind is able to experience the world, or to organize a meaning in what is essentially in itself meaningless'.

(Hawkes 1992: 17–18)

One of the abiding themes of the first part of this book is a version of the theme of inherent bias (which has been prominent in the last two extracts). Hawkes takes this as far as it will go. Hawkes suggests that the bias occurs even as early as 'every perceiver's method of perceiving'. In simple terms we must be aware that how we approach Communication texts is not without problems. Methodology is just as much in need of a critical evaluation as the material on which we use it. It may be true that we see whatever we want to see.

WHAT'S NEXT?

> ➤ Take a television soap opera with which you are familiar. Make a note of as many of the characters as you can. Describe the relationships between the characters in terms of such factors as power, sexual attraction, hate, indebtedness, fear, or love, and express this in diagrammatic form. How does your diagram differ from, say, a family tree or a biographical sketch of the characters you might find in a television guide?

▼ 6 WHAT'S THE TOPIC? Applying structuralist analysis
WHAT'S THE TEXT? Umberto Eco *The Role of the Reader*

Early structuralist writers adhered to the notion that what we often take to be important is merely superficial and that in so doing we ignore the more significant (both figuratively and literally deeper) structure. Writers whose work informed early structuralist writing included Claude Lévi-Strauss (one of whose key works is the structuralist analysis of South American Indian myths) and Vladimir Propp (who analysed story structure and characters in Russian folk tales). All structuralist work is informed by a sense in which it didn't matter on what you turned the microscope because what would be discovered underneath the surface were the same fundamental structures. And it didn't matter whether what was structurally analysed was a classic myth drawn from antiquity or a story ripped from the pages of a contemporary comic. In that spirit we now offer an extract from a detailed analytical piece by Umberto Eco analysing the James Bond novels of Ian Fleming. Eco begins his structuralist analysis of the Bond novels by identifying sets of oppositions which underlay the whole series of books.

The novels of Fleming seem to be built on a series of oppositions which allow a limited number of permutations and interactions. These dichotomies constitute invariant features around which minor couples rotate as free variants. I have singled out fourteen couples, four of which are opposing characters, the others being opposing values, variously personified by the four basic characters:

(1)   Bond – M;
(2)   Bond – Villain;
(3)   Villain – Woman;
(4)   Woman – Bond;
(5)   Free World – Soviet Union;
(6)   Great Britain – Non-Anglo-Saxon Countries;
(7)   Duty – Sacrifice;
(8)   Cupidity – Ideals;
(9)   Love – Death;
(10)   Chance – Planning;
(11)   Luxury – Discomfort;
(12)   Excess – Moderation;
(13)   Perversion – Innocence;
(14)   Loyalty – Disloyalty.

These pairs do not represent 'vague' elements but 'simple' ones that are immediate and universal, and, if we consider the range of each pair, we see that the variants allowed in fact include all the narrative devices of Fleming.

Bond–M is a dominated–dominant relationship which characterizes from the beginning the limits and possibilities of the character of Bond and which sets events moving. Psychological and psychoanalytical interpretations of Bond's attitude towards M have been discussed in particular by Kingsley Amis. The fact is that, even in terms of pure fictional functions, M represents to Bond the one who has a global view of the events, hence his superiority over the 'hero' who depends on him and who sets out on his various missions in conditions of inferiority to the omniscient chief. Frequently, his chief sends Bond into adventures the upshot of which he had discounted from the start. Bond is thus often the victim of a trick – and it does not matter whether things happen to him beyond the calculations of M. The tutelage under which M holds Bond – obliged against his will to visit a doctor, to undergo a nature cure (*Thunderball*), to change his gun (*Dr. No*) – makes so much the more insidious and imperious his chief's authority. We can, therefore, see that M represents certain values such as Duty, Country, and Method (as an element of programming contrasting with Bond's own inclination to rely on improvisation). If Bond is the hero, hence in possession of exceptional qualities, M represents Measure, accepted as a national virtue. But Bond is not so exceptional as a hasty reading of the books (or the spectacular interpretation which films give of the books) might make one think. Fleming always affirmed that he had thought of Bond as an absolutely ordinary person, and it is in contrast with M that the real stature of 007 emerges, endowed with physical attributes, with courage and fast reflexes, but possessing neither these nor other qualities in excess. It is, rather, as certain moral force, an obstinate fidelity to the job – at the command of M, always present as a warning – that allows him to overcome superhuman ordeals without exercising any superhuman faculty.

The Bond–M relationship presupposes a psychological ambivalence, a reciprocal love–hate. At the beginning of *The Man with the Golden Gun*, Bond, emerging from a lengthy amnesia and having been conditioned by the Soviets, tries a kind of ritual parricide by shooting at M with a cyanide pistol; the gesture chosen loosens a longstanding series of narrative tensions which are aggravated every time M and Bond find themselves face to face.

Having explored the fundamental relationship between Bond and M (number 1 on his list) Eco then proceeds to work through a detailed analysis of the key villains in Fleming's novels (number 2 on his list). We rejoin him as he begins to look at those later sets of oppositions which Bond's actions in the novels embody, that is Eco uncovers the structures common to narratives of the James Bond books (numbers 3 through 14 on his list).

To the typical qualities of the Villain are opposed the Bond characteristics, particularly Loyalty to the Service, Anglo-Saxon Moderation opposed to the excesses of the halfbreeds, the selection of Discomfort and the acceptance of Sacrifice opposed to the ostentatious Luxury of the enemy, the genial improvisation (Chance) opposed to the cold Planning which it defeats, the sense of an Ideal opposed to Cupidity (Bond in various cases wins from the Villain in gambling, but as a rule returns the enormous winnings to the Service or to the girl of the moment, as occurred with Jill Masterson). Some oppositions function not only in the Bond–Villain relationship but also in the behaviour of Bond. Thus Bond is normally loyal but does not disdain overcoming a cheating enemy by a deceitful trick and blackmailing him (see *Moonraker* or *Goldfinger*). Even Excess and Moderation, Chance and Planning are opposed in the acts and decisions of Bond. Duty and Sacrifice appear as elements of internal debate each time Bond knows he must prevent the plan of the Villain at the risk of his life, and in those cases the patriotic ideal (Great Britain and the Free World) takes the upper hand. He calls also on the racist need to show the superiority of the Briton. Also opposed in Bond are Luxury (the choice of good food, care in dressing, preference for sumptuous hotels, love of the gambling table, invention of cocktails, and so on) and Discomfort (Bond is always ready to abandon the easy life – even when it appears in the guise of a Woman who offers herself – to face a new aspect of Discomfort, the acutest point of which is torture).

We have discussed the Bond–Villain dichotomy at length because in fact it embodies all the characteristics of the opposition between Eros and Thanatos, the principle of pleasure and the principle of reality, culminating in the moment of torture (in *Casino Royale* explicitly theorized as a sort of erotic relationship between the torturer and the tortured). This opposition is perfected in the relationship between the Villain and the Woman; Vesper is tyrannized and blackmailed by the Soviets, and therefore by Le Chiffre; Solitaire is the slave of Mr. Big; Tiffany Case is dominated by the Spangs; Tatiana is the slave of Rosa Klebb and of the Soviet government in general; Jill and Tilly Masterson are dominated, to various degrees, by Goldfinger, and Pussy Galore works under his orders; Domino Vitali is subservient to the wishes of Emilio Largo; the English girls of Piz Gloria are under the hypnotic control of Blofeld and the virginal surveillance of Irma Blunt; Honeychile, wandering pure and untroubled on the shores of his cursed island, has a purely symbolic relationship with the power of Dr. No, except that at the end Dr. No offers her naked body to the crabs (she has been dominated by the Villain through the vicarious effort of the brutal Mander and has justly punished Mander by causing a scorpion to kill him, anticipating the revenge of No – who had recourse to crabs); and finally, Kissy Suzuki lives on her island in the shade of the cursed castle of Blofeld, suffering a purely allegorical domination shared by the whole population of the place. In an intermediate position is Gala Brand, who is an agent of the Service but who becomes the secretary of Hugo Drax, and establishes a relationship of submission to him. In most cases the Villain–Woman relationship culminates in the torture the woman undergoes along with Bond; here the Love–Death pair functions also, in the sense of a more intimate erotic union of the two through their common ordeal.

Dominated by the Villain, however, Fleming's woman has already been previously conditioned to domination, life for her having assumed the role of the villain. The general scheme is (i) the girl is beautiful and good; (ii) she has been made frigid and unhappy by severe trials suffered in adolescence; (iii) this has conditioned her to the service of the Villain; (iv) through meeting Bond she appreciates her positive human chances; (v) Bond possesses her but in the end loses her. This curriculum is common to Vesper, Solitaire, Tiffany, Tatiana, Honeychile, and Domino; rather vague as for Gala; equally shared by the three vicarious women of Goldfinger (Jill, Tilly, and Pussy – the first two have had a sad past, but only the third has been violated by her uncle; Bond possessed the first and the third; the second is killed by the Villain; the first is tortured with gold paint; the second and third are Lesbians, and Bond redeems only the third; and so on); more diffuse and uncertain for the group of girls on Piz Gloria (each has had an unhappy past, but Bond in fact possesses only one of them; similarly, he marries Tracy, whose past was unhappy because of a series of unions, dominated by her father, Draco, and who was killed in the end by Blofeld, who realizes at this point his domination and who ends by Death the relationship of Love which she entertained with Bond); Kissy Suzuki's unhappiness is the result of a Hollywoodian experience which has made her chary of life and of men.

In every case Bond loses the woman, either by her own will or by that of another (in the case of Gala, it is the woman who marries somebody else, although unwillingly) and either at the end of the novel or at the beginning of the following one (as happens with Tiffany Case). Thus, in the moment in which the Woman solves the opposition to the Villain by entering with Bond into a purifying–purified, saving–saved relationship, she returns to the domination of the negative. Every woman displays an internal combat between the couple Perversion–Purity (sometimes external, as in the relationship of Rosa Klebb and Tatiana) which makes her similar to the Richardsonian persecuted virgin. The bearer of purity, notwithstanding and despite her perversion, eager to alternate lust with torture, she would appear likely to resolve the contrast between the privileged race and the non-Anglo-Saxon halfbreed; but insofar as the erotic relationship always ends with a form of death, real or symbolic, Bond resumes willy-nilly his purity as an Anglo-Saxon bachelor. The race remains uncontaminated.

(Eco 1981: 147–8, 153–5)

WHAT'S NEXT?

➤ Taking Eco's Bond piece as a model apply a structuralist analysis to an episode of *Friends* or *Buffy the Vampire Slayer*.

➤ How would a structuralist analysis of one episode of *Friends* or *Buffy the Vampire Slayer* be informed or changed or modified by a structuralist reading of a season of *Friends* or *Buffy the Vampire Slayer*?

➤ For another analysis of Bond's relationships with women read Chapter 8 ('James Bond Girls') of Julie Burchill's *Girls On Film* (1986) New York: Pantheon Books.

▼ 7 WHAT'S THE TOPIC? The semiotic and process schools of communication theory
WHAT'S THE TEXT? John Fiske *Introduction to Communication Studies*

Communication Studies as a discipline contains a recognisable body of theoretical work. Within this body of work there are two traditions, what are commonly characterised as schools of thought, schools for short. These constitute two distinct ways of understanding communication both in terms of theory and in terms of practice. What follows is a very succinct clarification of where these schools stand and what they stand for. It is taken from the introduction to Fiske's *Introduction to Communication Studies*, a section entitled 'What is Communication?' Fiske makes a number of useful statements about communication and its study. For example he argues that 'communication is amenable to study' and that 'we need a number of disciplinary approaches to be able to study it'. He also advances a definition of communication as 'social interaction through messages'. It is at this point he begins his survey of the two schools.

> The structure of this book reflects the fact that there are two main schools in the study of communication. The first sees communication as the *transmission of messages*. It is concerned with how senders and receivers encode and decode, with how transmitters use the channels and media of communication. It is concerned with matters like efficiency and accuracy. It sees communication as a process by which one person affects the behaviour or state of mind of another. If the effect is different from or smaller than that which was intended, this school tends to talk in terms of communication failure, and to look to the stages in the process to find out where the failure occurred. For the sake of convenience I shall refer to this as the 'process' school.
>
> The second school sees communication as the *production and exchange of meanings*. It is concerned with how messages, or texts, interact with people in order to produce meanings; that is, it is concerned with the role of texts in our culture. It uses terms like signification, and does not consider misunderstandings to be necessarily evidence of communication failure – they may result from cultural differences between sender and receiver. For this school, the study of communication is the study of text and culture. The main method of study is semiotics (the science of signs and meanings), and that is the label I shall use to identify this approach.
>
> The process school tends to draw upon the social sciences, psychology and sociology in particular, and tends to address itself to *acts* of communication. The

CONTINUED

semiotic school tends to draw upon linguistics and the arts subjects, and tends to address itself to *works* of communication.

Each school interprets our definition of communication as social interaction through messages in its own way. The first defines social interaction as the process by which one person relates himself to others, or affects the behaviour, state of mind or emotional response of another, and, of course, vice versa. This is close to the common sense, everyday use of the phrase. Semiotics, however, defines social interaction as that which constitutes the individual as a member of his culture or society. I know I am a member of western, industrial society because, to give one of many sources of identification, I respond to Shakespeare or 'Coronation Street' in broadly the same ways as do the fellow members of my culture. I also become aware of cultural differences if, for instance, I hear the Soviet critic reading *King Lear* as a devastating attack upon the western ideal of the family as the basis of society, or that 'Coronation Street' shows how the West keeps the workers in their place. Both these readings are possible, but my point is, they are not mine, as a typical member of my culture. In responding to 'Coronation Street' in the more normal way, I am expressing my commonality with other members of my culture. So too, the teenager, in appreciating one particular style of rock music is expressing his identity as a member of a subculture and is, albeit, in an indirect way, interacting with other members of his society.

The two schools also differ in their understanding of what constitutes a message. The process school sees a message as that which is transmitted by the communication process. Many of its followers believe that intention is a crucial factor in deciding what constitutes a message. Thus pulling my earlobe would not be a message unless I deliberately did it as a pre-arranged signal to an auctioneer. The sender's intention may be stated or unstated, conscious or unconscious, but must be retrievable by analysis. The message is what the sender puts into it by whatever means.

For semiotics, on the other hand, the message is a construction of signs which, through interacting with the receivers, produce meanings. The sender, defined as transmitter of the message, declines in importance. The emphasis shifts to the text and how it is 'read'. And reading is the process of discovering meanings that occurs when the reader interacts or negotiates with the text. This negotiation takes place as the reader brings aspects of his cultural experience to bear upon the codes and signs which make up the text. It also involves some shared understanding of what the text is about. We have only to see how different papers report the same event differently to realize how important is this understanding, this view of the world, which each paper shares with its readers. So readers with different social experiences or from different cultures, may find different meanings in the same text. This is not, as we have said, necessarily evidence of communication failure.

The message, then, is not something sent from A to B, but an element in a structured relationship whose other elements include external reality and the producer/reader. Producing and reading the text are seen as parallel, if not identical, processes in that they occupy the same place in this structured relationship. We might model this structure as a triangle in which the arrows represent constant interaction, the structure is not static but a dynamic practice.

(Fiske 1982: 2–4)

WHAT'S NEXT?

➤ Consider how process and semiotic approaches might differently describe:
- communication between a teacher and a student
- a popular television programme
- a poetry reading by a contemporary poet
- an e-mail to a friend describing a time and place to meet
- the communication of a ringing fire alarm.

▼ 8 WHAT'S THE TOPIC? The semiotic or semiological approach
WHAT'S THE TEXT? Pierre Guiraud *Semiology*

Semiotics or semiology is a vital part of the tool kit of Communication Studies (and a number of other disciplines as well). Semiotic terms appear as a matter of course in all manner of textual analyses and one sometimes gets the suspicion that certain semiotic signifiers have drifted too far away from their signified moorings. In that spirit let's look at an extract from Pierre Guiraud's work *Semiology*. It was originally written in French for a series of texts produced for the general reader eager to be informed about a range of topics of contemporary interest.

Semiology is the science which studies sign systems: languages, codes, sets of signals, etc. According to this definition, language is a part of semiology. However, it is generally accepted that language has a privileged and autonomous status, and this allows semiology to be defined as the study of non-linguistic sign systems, which is the definition we shall adopt here.[1]

Semiology was conceived by F. de Saussure as the science which studies the life of signs in society. Here is the much-quoted text (*Cours de linguistique général*, p.33):

> Language is a system of signs that expresses ideas, and is therefore comparable to writing, to the deaf-mute alphabet, to symbolic rites, to codes of good manners, to military signals, etc. It is simply the most important of these systems. *A science that studies the life of signs in society* is therefore conceivable: it would be a part of general psychology; we shall call it semiology (from the Greek *semeion*, 'sign'). Semiology would teach us what signs are made of and what laws govern their behaviour. Since this science does not yet exist, no one can say quite what it will be like, but it has a right to exist and it has a place staked out in advance. Linguistics is only a part of the general science of semiology: the laws discovered by semiology will be applicable to linguistics, and the latter will therefore find itself linked to a well-defined area within the totality of facts in the human sciences.

At roughly the same time, the American C. S. Peirce also conceived of a general theory of signs which he called *semiotics* (from *Philosophical Writings of Peirce*, p.98):

> I hope to have shown that logic in its general acceptation is merely another word for *semiotics*, a quasi-necessary or formal doctrine of signs. In describing the doctrine as 'quasi-necessary', or formal, I have in mind the fact that we observe the nature of such signs as best we can, and, on the basis of fine observations, by a process which I do not hesitate to call Abstraction, we are led to eminently necessary judgments concerning what *must be* the nature of the signs used by the scientific intellect.

Saussure emphasizes the social function of the sign, Peirce its logical function. But the two aspects are closely correlated and today the words semiology and semiotics refer to the same discipline; Europeans using the former term, Anglo-Saxons the latter.[1] Thus, as early as the beginning of this century, a general theory of signs was conceived.

(Guiraud 1975: 1–3)

---

1 *Semiology and semiotics* ('the general study of signs', particularly non-linguistic ones) are not to be confused with *semantics* (the study of the meaning of linguistic signifiers). As for *semasiology* (another word which belongs to linguistic terminology) it is the study of the meaning of words as opposed to *onomasiology* or study of the names which things designated can take. Unfortunately, this terminology is far from being unanimously agreed.

➤ Find out more about Saussure and Peirce. What contributions did they make to the study of signs in society?

▼ ## 9 WHAT'S THE TOPIC? *Langue* and *parole*
WHAT'S THE TEXT? Roland Barthes *Elements of Sociology*

Vital to an understanding of semiological approaches to the meanings of texts is the issue of contexts. As Roland Barthes explains below the problem confronted by Saussure, the Swiss linguist whose work laid the foundations of semiology, is that of 'the multiform and heterogeneous nature of language' (and from language we can extrapolate to any codified communication system). In simple terms language is so varied and various that it only lends itself to systematic analysis with great difficulty. Saussure's significant insight was to recognise two different ways in which language operates:

- as a social institution and social values (the *langue*): this is language as potential and language as a repository of cultural values (attitudes, beliefs, behaviours); and
- as an individual act of selection and actualisation (the *parole* or speech): this is language in action, in performance.

The relationship between *langue* and *parole* is central to a semiotic or semiological approach simply because it underlines the significantly cultural, social and ultimately ideological character of all communication. Again, in simple terms, this is to stress that whenever we use a language, for example English, to communicate what we are in fact doing is buying into a game with its own rules and its own luggage (history, ideology). With each sign selection we make we take on a set of values. (Language is not neutral; interpretation is not neutral; selection is not neutral.)

In working out this famous dichotomy, Saussure started from the multiform and heterogeneous 'nature of language, which appears at first sight as an unclassifiable reality' the unity of which cannot be brought to light, since it partakes at the same time of the physical, the physiological, the mental, the individual and the social. Now this disorder disappears if, from this heterogeneous whole, is extracted a purely social object, the systematised set of conventions necessary to communication, indifferent to the *material* of the signals which compose it, and which is a *language* (*langue*); as opposed to which

CONTINUED

speech (*parole*) covers the purely individual part of language (phonation, application of the rules and contingent combinations of signs).

1.1.2. *The language* (*langue*): A *language* is therefore, so to speak, language minus speech: it is at the same time a social institution and a system of values. As a social institution, it is by no means an act, and it is not subject to any premeditation. It is the social part of language, the individual cannot by himself either create or modify it; it is essentially a collective contract which one must accept in its entirety if one wishes to communicate. Moreover, this social product is autonomous, like a game with its own rules, for it can be handled only after a period of learning. As a system of values, a language is made of a certain number of elements, each one of which is at the same time the equivalent of a given quantity of things and a term of a larger function, in which are found, in a differential order, other correlative values: from the point of view of the language, the sign is like a coin, which has the value of a certain amount of goods which it allows one to buy, but also has value in relation to other coins, in a greater or lesser degree. The institutional and the systematic aspect are of course connected: it is because a language is a system of contractual values (in part arbitrary, or, more exactly, unmotivated) that it resists the modifications coming from a single individual, and is consequently a social institution.

1.1.3. *Speech* (*parole*): In contrast to the language, which is both institution and system, *speech* is essentially an individual act of selection and actualisation; it is made in the first place of the 'combination thanks to which the speaking subject can use the code of the language with a view to expressing his personal thought' (this extended speech could be called *discourse*), – and secondly by the 'psychophysical mechanisms which allow him to exteriorise these combinations.' It is certain that phonation, for instance, cannot he confused with the language; neither the institution nor the system are altered if the individual who resorts to them speaks loudly or softly, with slow or rapid delivery, etc. The combinative aspect of speech is of course of capital importance, for it implies that speech is constituted by the recurrence of identical signs: it is because signs are repeated in successive discourses and within one and the same discourse (although they are combined in accordance with the infinite diversity of various people's speech) that each sign becomes an element of the language; and it is because speech is essentially a combinative activity that it corresponds to an individual act and not to a pure creation.

(Barthes 1973: 17–19)

> ➤ Give examples of the ways in which a language might contain values.
> ➤ In what ways does language resist significant modifications coming from a single individual?

▼ 10 **WHAT'S THE TOPIC? The application of semiotic ideas: metaphor and metonymy WHAT'S THE TEXT? Stephen Barley 'Semiotics and the study of occupational and organisational cultures'**

As Peter Barry best expressed it in *Beginning Theory*, 'we are looking . . . for something we can use' (2002: 8). What better place to look than where it is being used. Stephen Barley's paper represented one of the first attempts to apply semiotic ideas to the analysis of human behaviour in work contexts. It was first published in 1983 in the *Administrative Science Quarterly* where it was unlikely that his audience would have encountered semiotic ideas. To remedy this he offered crisp definitions of key concepts in semiotics. Barley begins with a definition-come-history of semiotics, which he characterises as the study of signs, codes, and culture.

Semiotics is an eclectic and amorphous field that traces its roots to the teachings of Ferdinand de Saussure (1966), the father of modern structural linguistics, and to the pragmatic philosophy of Charles Peirce (1958). Defined as the study of signs or systems of signs, semiotics concerns the principles by which signification occurs. Signification refers both to the processes by which events, words, behaviours, and objects carry meaning for the members of a given community, and to the content they convey. Therefore, semiotics is ultimately the study of how communication is possible, since all communication presumes shared codes. The essence of semiotics is the isolation of systems of signification and the rules that govern their use.

The importance of semiotics as a set of tools for students of communication is easily offered in 'semiotics is ultimately the study of how communication is possible'. What is also offered here and across Barley's work is the extension of semiotic analysis into a broader set of 'systems of signification'. In his case these are sociological and anthropological contexts; in our case it's whatsoever we chose to look at and to read.

In preparation for this widening of perspectives Barley offers a cogent and coherent summary of semiotics as an approach, concentrating on three significant principles:

- metaphor
- metonymy
- opposition.

At the core of semiotics is the notion of the sign. A sign is understood to be the relationship between or the union of a sign-vehicle (an expression or form such as a word, sound, or coloured light) and the signified, the notion or *content* conveyed by the sign vehicle (Barthes, 1967). The link between expression and content is arbitrary in the sense that it is a convention of the group to which the sign's users belong. Arbitrary coupling implies that the same expression can signify alternative contents and that similar contents can be conveyed by different expressions, depending on the conventions one holds. As you drive toward me in your speeding car, I hold up my hand, palm out, intending an expression signifying the content, 'Stop while I cross the street.' From your vantage point behind the wheel, you wonder why I am so brash as to say hello from the middle of the crosswalk and you step on the gas. Obviously, our conventions differ. Both Geertz and the cognitive anthropologists argue that, in studying culture, a researcher's task is to discover the relevant expressions, contents, and rules that bind the two, so as to be able to portray the signs by which members of a culture make sense of their world.

In addition to identifying signs, a semiotic analysis of an interpretive system also considers the processes by which expressions are linked to their contents. Since semioticians are concerned primarily with elucidating operative principles at a level of abstraction congruent with meaning itself, they have preferred to traffic in processes that are specifically interpretive and have, therefore, eschewed historical or functional explanations for how signs signify. Instead, tropes or rhetorical forms are understood to be the processes that generate meaning. In a seminal work, Jacobson and Halle (1956) distinguished metonymy and metaphor as two processes by which signs signify, and upon which coding conventions are built. In anthropology, Leach (1976) has shown how both devices enable members of a culture to construct, maintain and communicate realities. Known for their bare-bones analyses, the ethnosemanticists largely ignore metaphor and metonymy, but emphasise a third semiotic process, opposition, for explicating how semantic systems are structured (see Conklin, 1955; Goodenough, 1956; Lounsbury, 1956, 1969; Frake, 1961). Geertz, on the other hand, claimed that all rhetorical forms are useful for understanding how meaning is spun within a culture.

Metaphor is, of course, not the only stylistic resource upon which ideology draws. Metonymy ('All I have to offer is blood, sweat, and tears'), hyperbole ('The thousand year Reich'), meiosis ('I shall return'), synecdoche ('Wall street'), oxymoron ('Iron Curtain'), personification ('The hand that held the dagger has plunged it into the back of its neighbour'), and all the other figures the classical rhetoricians so painstakingly collected and so carefully classified are utilised over and over again, as are such syntactical devices as antithesis, inversion, and repetition; such prosodic ones as rhyme, rhythm, and alliteration; such literary ones as irony, eulogy and sarcasm . . . as a cultural system, an ideology that has developed beyond the stage of mere sloganeering consists of an intricate structure of interrelated meanings – interrelated in terms of the semantic mechanisms that formulate them – of which the two level organisation of an isolated metaphor is but a feeble representation. (Geertz, 1973: 213).

While Geertz's formulation, if assiduously worked out, would provide a most comprehensive set of semiotic processes for arming culture researchers, for the purposes of this article and the codes it discusses an understanding of the processes of metonymy, metaphor, and opposition will be sufficient.

Signs signify by metonymy when expressions are related to contents by contiguity or juxtaposition. The classic definition of metonymy in rhetoric is: a quality or aspect standing for the entity of which it is an attribute. For example, we use 'crown' to signify 'king' because a crown is a marker associated with a king and his regalia. Another type of metonymy is found in music. The sense of a melody is pure metonymy, since melody arises from the juxtaposition of notes or chords. A single note or chord by itself carried little meaning, but when a note becomes part of a progression of notes, a tune is produced. Hence, only by juxtaposition do notes and chords convey messages. Finally, indices, signs whose expressions are naturally associated with their contents (as smoke stands for fire), signify by metonymy.

Metaphor is signification by similarity or analogy. Similarity between two signs typically arises when both share one or more denotations or connotations. A linguistic metaphor such as 'the ship plowed the sea' invites us to see similarities between plowshares and ships' bows since both have similar physical contours and both cut furrows into the surfaces over which they travel. The metaphor functions even though plows and ships are members of distinctly different technological and semantic domains, the first agricultural and the second nautical. The archetypal sign that functions by metaphor is the 'symbol.' When a crown is used to signify a brand of margarine, it is used metaphorically to suggest that both objects share regal qualities.

The crucial difference between metonymy and metaphor as semiotic processes can be summarised by the following rule of thumb: metonymical signification occurs when expression and content are both part of the same domain or context, whereas metaphorical signification mixes domains or contexts. Note that the term 'domain' can refer either to a semantic context, such as all nautical terms, or to a domain of physical objects and attributes (e.g. actual nautical events and objects). Since the distinction between metonymy and metaphor is central to the codes discussed below, let us consider the distinction in relation to the two uses of 'crown' cited above. By metonymy, 'crown' signifies 'king' because both crown and king are part of the same domain: things regal. However, the use of crown to signify a margarine's qualities is a metaphorical device since the symbol mixes semantic domains: things regal and things culinary. Hence, an icon (such as a sketch or photograph) is metaphorical because it represents, in a different context (marks on paper), a host of attributes of a content belonging to another context (the object of the sketch) (Eco, 1976: 191–217).

Barley ends with a worked-through practical example of analysis, in this case of a subcultural group.

Let me illustrate the process by an example drawn from a subcultural remnant of the 1960s: that of 'Dead heads,' aficionados of the San Francisco rock and roll band, The Grateful Dead. A Dead head, browsing in a candle store, spies on a shelf a candle moulded to resemble a human skull, around whose head are draped red roses. Whereas another person might think, 'that's odd' or 'how disgusting', as a member of a particular subculture, the Dead head immediately recognises 'The skull and roses,' the band's logo. After this comes the thought 'a Dead head made this,' upon whose heels may follow a sense of solidarity and belonging with someone never met. It is precisely such chains of signification that people must learn in order to become thoroughly socialised members of any social group.

A chain of significations is composed of two major parts, the denotative code and the connotative code. The denotative code refers only to contents immediately associated with the sign-vehicles themselves ('The skull and roses') and arises from the semiotic processes of metonymy (roses in contiguous association with a skull), metaphor (life (roses) and death (skull) are somehow similar) and opposition (the rose is not a begonia). The connotative code represents meaning at a more inclusive, reflexive level. Similar connotative codes may generalise across quite different denotative codes (the morphemes 'Lately it occurs to me what a long, strange trip it's been' scrawled across a wall would have elicited the same chain of significations as the candle). A familiar example of how diverse denotative codes can be subsumed by the same connotative code is our sociological proclivity to interpret pins on soldier's lapels and the size and location of a manager's office as indications of a 'status hierarchy.'

The connotative code is particularly germane to semiotic analyses of cultures, for it is in the connotative code that the researcher finds those redundancies of interpretation that bind together the denotative codes undergirding diverse arenas of action and social life. It is on the basis of these redundancies that the researcher can begin to attribute the coherence necessary for claiming that members of a group under study share a perspective rather than simply a code. I shall term such redundancy at the connotative level a theme. Themes imply a 'message' or interpretation that runs through numerous activities and events and thus act as the cultural glue to attributing coherence and consistency to myriad separate actions, events, and objects.

(Barley 1981: 394–5, 395–7, 398–9)

WHAT'S NEXT?

➤ List and analyse the emblems of groups with which you are familiar. Consider some of the following
   ■ sporting groups or teams
   ■ your school or college
   ■ a business or place of employment
   ■ a music-based youth sub-culture.
➤ Look for examples of metaphor and metonymy in advertisements broadcast on prime time television.
➤ Read Roland Barthes, 'Myth today', in *Mythologies* (1972) London: Paladin.

▼ **11 WHAT'S THE TOPIC? Shannon and Weaver's mathematical theory of communication, and linear models of communication**
WHAT'S THE TEXT? Denis McQuail and Sven Windahl *Communication Models for the Study of Mass Communication*

Despite communication being at least as old as the human race formal theorisations about communication as such are a relatively recent (twentieth-century) phenomenon. Working for Bell Laboratories in the 1940s Claude Shannon was attempting to solve technical problems in telecommunications. Rather than approaching these problems technologically he chose to approach them theoretically. He did this by devising what was essentially a problem-solving model. Shannon first published a technical paper on his mathematical theory of communication (as he entitled it) in 1948 and, together with Warren Weaver, published an expanded version of this theory in book form in 1949. Fundamental to *A Mathematical Theory of Communication* was Shannon's coining of the term 'bit', the essential unit of information which represents a clear cut digital differentiation: yes or no; on or off. (He created the term bit by contracting the two words 'binary' and 'digit'.) Laying out the foundations for what became Information Theory Shannon identified the channel of communication and proposed that it could have its bit value calculated. In this way Shannon's elegant theory led to real material practice, without which we would lack compact discs, web pages, and digital radio and television. The mathematical dimensions of Shannon and Weaver's theory were largely ignored by early communication theorists in favour of the adoption of a general diagrammatic model of the process of communication. Here McQuail and Windahl offer a succinct introduction to this fundamental building block of the process school of communication.

Johnson and Klare (1961) say in their review of communication models:

> Of all single contributions to the widespread interest in models today, Shannon's is the most important. For the technical side of communication research, Shannon's mathematical formulations were the stimulus to much of the later effort in this area.

We will not discuss here the mathematical aspects of Shannon's work. Let us just note that he worked for the Bell Telephone Laboratory and that his theories and models primarily applied to its particular field of communication, involving questions such as: Which kind of communication channel can bring through the maximum amount of signals? How much of a transmitted signal will be destroyed by noise while travelling from transmitter to receiver?

These are questions mostly dealt with within the field of information theory. Nevertheless the graphical model, made by Shannon and his co-worker Warren Weaver (1949) has been used analogically by behavioural and linguistic scientists. Technological problems differ of course from human ones, but it is easy to find the traces of the Shannon–Weaver model in a number of later models of human communication.

Communication is here described as a linear, one-way process. The model states five functions to be performed and notes one dysfunctional factor, noise. Graphically, it may be presented as

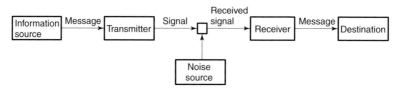

Shannon and Weaver's 'mathematical model' describes communication as a linear, one-way process (Shannon and Weaver 1949).

First in the process is the *information source*, producing a *message* or *a chain of messages* to be communicated. In the next step, the message is formed into *signals* by a *transmitter*. The signals should be adapted to the *channel* leading to the *receiver*. The function of the receiver is the opposite of that of the transmitter. The receiver constructs the message from the signal. The *received message* then reaches the *destination*. The signal is vulnerable in so far as it may be disturbed by *noise*, interference which may occur, for example, when there are many signals in the same channel at the same time. This may result in a difference between transmitted and received signal, which, in its turn, may mean that the message produced by the source and then reconstructed by the receiver and having reached the destination do not have the same meaning. The inability on the part of communicators to realize that a sent and a received message are not always identical, is a common reason why communication fails.

(McQuail and Windahl 1993: 16–17)

In many accounts of the history of Communication Studies linear, process models are often set up to be knocked down by semiotic approaches – in all contexts and all readings. To presume the superiority of semiotics for the analysis of all communication situations and all communication processes is dangerous. For some communication processes a process or linear model is an appropriate and fitting tool for analysis and theorisation.

WHAT'S NEXT?

➤ Identify communication situations which could best be analysed by the Shannon and Weaver model.

▼ 12 WHAT'S THE TOPIC? Feedback and Osgood and Schramm's model of communication WHAT'S THE TEXT? John Morgan and Peter Welton *See What I Mean?*

At first glance this extract from Morgan and Welton's eminently useful textbook *See What I Mean?* seems to be out of place. First they are discussing the dynamics (specifically the role of feedback) of interpersonal communication. Second they are exemplifying a model which, as they themselves point out, 'is clearly better suited to the description of face-to-face interaction than to the more remote processes of the mass media'. But this is to stop short of both the extent and the implications of their arguments. The passage just quoted continues 'but remnants of the same psychological interaction can still be seen in more distant communication' and then makes its further point explicitly: 'while I am looking at a photograph, painting or film, I am interpreting it and formulating some kind of response'. What quickly becomes apparent is the capacity of models to embody arguments about what communication is (and is not). Osgood and Schramm's model may rather more straightforwardly describe conversations between people. It can also go some way to address those essential negotiations that go on between texts and their readers.

FEEDBACK[1] IN INTERPERSONAL COMMUNICATION

The briefest, sparest means of conveying your message is rarely the most effective. You need to consider the psychology of the receiver, who is actively absorbing what you have to say and checking it against previous knowledge. The active listener is constantly evaluating our talk through such questions as:

> Does this make sense?
> Does this person have an axe to grind?
> Do I like this person?
> How does this fit in to what I already know?
> What am I going to say when it comes to my turn?

When two people are engaged in a conversation, they respond continually to each other's statements: while I recite my tale of woe, you will make regular brief responses, either through changes in your facial expression or through interjections: 'Uh-huh, oh really, well I never, oh your poor thing, that's terrible.' Without this kind of feedback, my flow of words will probably dry up; I need to have confirmation that you are still listening and that you understand what I am saying.

There is a well established technique in television and radio whereby the interviewer nods encouragingly at the interviewee in order to prevent any hesitation in the flow of words. Even in a television interview which has taken place in the street or in someone's home, the face of the interviewer will appear from time to time asking questions or nodding encouragement; and yet the economics of television are such that only one camera will have been used. These shots are filmed after the interview and are skilfully edited into the final version to suggest a continuous event. Many of these inserts are of the journalist's head nodding: the effect on the viewer at home is that the veracity of the interviewee's statements is supported by the nodding head of the supposedly impartial interviewer.

Anticipated or actual feedback is an essential factor in the psychology of communication, and one which plays an essential part in Osgood and Schramm's (1954) model:

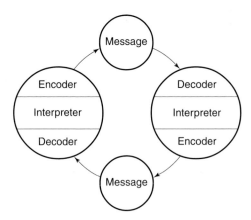

As a representation of interpersonal communication, this has a number of advantages over the account of Shannon and Weaver. First, it makes feedback a central feature of the process, rather than an optional extra added onto a one-directional basic frame-work. Second, it is a dynamic model: it helps to show how a situation can change. In addition, it shows graphically why redundancy is an essential part of the process: since the participants are interpreting each other's signals while they encode their own, they need some spare capacity in the system to leave space for this interpretation to function. Both 'sender' and 'receiver' are modifying their intentions at every point in the exchange.

This model is clearly better suited to the description of face-to-face interaction than to the more remote processes of the mass media, but remnants of the same psychological interaction can still be seen in more distant communication: while I am looking at a photograph, painting or film, I am interpreting it and

CONTINUED

formulating some kind of response, which may be expressed to a companion or completely internalized to form an element in a later communication of my own. Behaviourist psychologists such as Vygotsky have referred to the thought process as 'internalized dialogue', a concept which relates closely to Osgood and Schramm's model. They suggest that young children's thinking grows out of the dialogues which they hold with adults. Problems are solved by an exchange of question, answer and instruction. As time passes, you can hear a child continuing the dialogue in the absence of the adult, but playing both roles. Later the dialogue becomes silent, but is still taking place inside the child's head. Photographers, painters and film-makers, as they plan their compositions, will try to anticipate the interpretative processes of their ultimate audience: this, too, may take the form of an 'internalized' dialogue', where production and anticipated interpretation interact with each other to stimulate the creative process.

For both sender and receiver, feedback is vital. Without it, the sender cannot be sure if the message has even been received, still less whether it has been greeted with disagreement, disbelief, misunderstanding or bored complacency. There is no way of knowing which points to labour, nor which are likely to be key issues for future development. For the receiver, on the other hand, feedback is the means by which dialogue can focus on more fruitful areas and skip less interesting matters.

(Morgan and Welton 1992: 26–8)

---

1   Feedback is the return flow of messages from receiver to sender. It can be either *positive* (supporting or agreeing with the message) or *negative* (criticizing or contradicting the message).

In retrospect it seems clear that there is little to discriminate between Morgan and Welton's 'active listener' and the 'active reader' that we are aspiring to be in textual analysis. The proof of the pudding is in the eating, in the something we can use. In that spirit we can borrow from them what seems a useful set of prompts for textual analysis:

The active listener is constantly evaluating our talk through such questions as:
>   Does this make sense?
>   Does this person have an axe to grind?
>   Do I like this person?
>   How does this fit in to what I already know?
>   What am I going to say when it comes to my turn?

> ➤ Choose a print text (for example, a magazine advertisement) and use the five questions above as the foundations of your critical analysis.
> ➤ What is added to your understanding of the text or your approach to the text by the posing and the answering of these questions?
> ➤ Read Ronald Carter, Angela Goddard, Danuta Reah, Keith Sanger, Maggie Bowring (2001) *Working with Texts*, second edition, London: Routledge.

▼ 13 **WHAT'S THE TOPIC? Culture**
   WHAT'S THE TEXT? Raymond Williams
   Keywords

One of the central differences between the process and semiotic approaches to communication is in process models' excluding data that would locate communication in a specifically cultural context. In the semiotic approach meaning is dependent upon the cultural contexts of sender, receiver and message. On the other hand the process approach plays down the role of culture, save as a potential barrier to communication, semantically and psychologically.

Culture is, as Raymond Williams admits, 'one of the two or three most complicated words in the English language'. Although we will return to the debate about its meaning later in this book (in Part 4) what Williams gives is a feeling for the area. Culture is a significant context in all of the readings which follow and which complete this first part so it's as well to get it straight as culture is what Williams calls a *keyword*.

The complexity of the modern development of the word, and of its modern usage, can then be appreciated. We can easily distinguish the sense which depends on a literal continuity of physical process as now in 'sugar-beet culture' or, in the specialized physical application in bacteriology since the 1880s, 'germ culture'. But once we go beyond the physical reference, we have to recognize three broad active categories of usage. The sources of two of these we have already discussed: (i) the independent and abstract noun which describes a general process of intellectual, spiritual and aesthetic development, from the eighteenth century; (ii) the independent noun, whether used generally or specifically, which indicates a particular way of life, whether of a people, a period, a group, or humanity in general, from Herder and Klemm. But we have also to

CONTINUED

recognize (iii) the independent and abstract noun which describes the works and practices of intellectual and especially artistic activity. This seems often now the most widespread use: culture is music, literature, painting and sculpture, theatre and film. A Ministry of Culture refers to these specific activities, sometimes with the addition of philosophy, scholarship, history. This use, (iii), is in fact relatively late. It is difficult to date precisely because it is in origin an applied form of sense (i): the idea of a general process of intellectual, spiritual and aesthetic development was applied and effectively transferred to the works and practices which represent and sustain it. . . . In English (i) and (iii) are still close; at times, for internal reasons, they are indistinguishable as in Arnold, *Culture and Anarchy* (1867); while sense (ii) was decisively introduced into English by Tylor, *Primitive Culture* (1870), following Klemm. The decisive development of sense (iii) in English was in the late nineteenth century and early twentieth century.

Faced by this complex and still active history of the word, it is easy to react by selecting one 'true' or 'proper' or 'scientific' sense and dismissing other senses as loose or confused. . . . It is clear that, within a discipline, conceptual usage has to be clarified. But in general it is the range and overlap of meanings that is significant. The complex of senses indicates a complex argument about the relations between general human development and a particular way of life, and between both and the works and practices of art and intelligence. It is especially interesting that in archaeology and in *cultural anthropology* the reference to culture or a culture is primarily to *material* production, while in history and *cultural studies* the reference is primarily to *signifying* or *symbolic* systems. This often confuses but even more often conceals the central question of the relations between 'material' and 'symbolic' production, which in some recent argument – cf. my own *Culture* – have always to be related rather than contrasted. Within this complex argument there are fundamentally opposed as well as effectively overlapping positions; there are also, understandably, many unresolved questions and confused answers. But these arguments and questions cannot be resolved by reducing the complexity of actual usage. This point is relevant also to uses of forms of the word in languages other than English, where there is considerable variation. The anthropological use is common in the German, Scandinavian and Slavonic language groups, but it is distinctly subordinate to the senses of art and learning, or of a general process of human development, in Italian and French. Between languages as within a language, the range and complexity of sense and reference indicate both difference of intellectual position and some blurring or overlapping. These variations, of whatever kind, necessarily involve alternative views of the activities, relationships and processes which this complex word indicates. The complexity, that is to say, is not finally in the word but in the problems which its variations of use significantly indicate.

(Williams 1983: 90–2)

➤ Give examples of meanings (i), (ii) and (iii) of culture above.
➤ Williams states that 'the most widespread use' is the idea of culture as 'music, literature painting and sculpture'. What is it that makes these activities 'culture'?

▼ 14 WHAT'S THE TOPIC? Applying semiotics
WHAT'S THE TEXT? Roland Barthes
Mythologies

In 1950s France semiologist Roland Barthes produced a series of readings in which he demonstrated and explored semiotic ideas. He chose not to publish these readings in an academic publication but rather in a popular one. He did this in part to prove his point that semiological analysis could be applied to any thing, any object, any process; just because semiology constituted a different or special way of looking at the world it didn't have to be applied only to special things, objects or processes. Accordingly he took his readings from across the range of popular and high cultural items (from literature to popular television to real life experiences). In the extract below he is considering Joseph L. Mankiewicz's 1953 film of Shakespeare's *Julius Caesar* and in particular the (supposed) meaning to be found in the hairstyles of these Romans.

THE ROMANS IN FILM

In Mankiewicz's *Julius Caesar*, all the characters are wearing fringes. Some have them curly, some straggly, some tufted, some oily, all have them well combed, and the bald are not admitted, although there are plenty to be found in Roman history. Those who have little hair have not been let off for all that, and the hairdresser – the king-pin of the film – has still managed to produce one last lock which duly reaches the top of the forehead, one of those Roman foreheads, whose smallness has at all times indicated a specific mixture of self-righteousness, virtue and conquest.

What then is associated with these insistent fringes? Quite simply the label of Roman-ness. We therefore see here the main-spring of the Spectacle – the *sign* – operating in the open. The frontal lock overwhelms one with evidence, no one can doubt that he is in Ancient Rome. And this certainty is permanent: the actors speak, act, torment themselves, debate 'questions of universal import', without losing, thanks to this little flag displayed on their foreheads, any of their historical plausibility. Their general representativeness can even expand in complete safety, cross the ocean and the centuries, and merge into the Yankee mugs of Hollywood extras: no matter, everyone is reassured, installed in the quiet certainty of a universe without duplicity, where Romans are Romans thanks to the most legible of signs: hair on the forehead.

A Frenchman, to whose eyes American faces still have something exotic, finds comical the combination of the morphologies of these gangster-sheriffs with the little Roman fringe: it rather looks like an excellent music-hall gag. This is because for the French the sign in this case overshoots the target and discredits itself by letting its aim appear clearly. But this very fringe, when combed on the only naturally Latin forehead in the film, that of Marlon Brando, impresses us and does not make us laugh; and it is not impossible that part of the success of this actor in Europe is due to the perfect integration of Roman capillary habits with the general morphology of the characters he usually portrays. Conversely, one cannot believe in Julius Caesar, whose physiognomy is that of an Anglo-Saxon lawyer – a face with which one is already acquainted through a thousand bit parts in thrillers or comedies, and a compliant skull on which the hairdresser has raked, with great effort, a lock of hair.

In the category of capillary meanings, here is a sub-sign, that of nocturnal surprises: Portia and Calpurnia, woken up at dead of night, have conspicuously uncombed hair. The former, who is young, expresses disorder by flowing locks: her unreadiness is, so to speak, of the first degree. The latter, who is middle-aged, exhibits a more painstaking vulnerability: a plait winds round her neck and comes to rest on her right shoulder so as to impose the traditional sign of disorder, asymmetry. But these signs are at the same time excessive and ineffectual: they postulate a 'nature' which they have not even the courage to acknowledge fully: they are not 'fair and square'.

Yet another sign in this *Julius Caesar*: all the faces sweat constantly. Labourers, soldiers, conspirators, all have their austere and tense features streaming (with Vaseline). And close-ups are so frequent that evidently sweat here is an attribute with a purpose. Like the Roman fringe or the nocturnal plait, sweat is a sign. Of what? Of moral feeling. Everyone is sweating because everyone is debating something within himself; we are here supposed to be in the locus of a horribly tormented virtue, that is, in the very locus of tragedy, and it is sweat which has the function of conveying this. The populace, upset by the death of Caesar, then by the arguments of Mark Antony, is sweating, and combining economically, in this single sign, the intensity of its emotion and the simplicity of its condition. And the virtuous men, Brutus, Cassius, Casca, are ceaselessly perspiring too, testifying thereby to the enormous physiological labour produced in them by a virtue just about to give birth to a crime. To *sweat* is to think – which evidently rests on the postulate, appropriate to a nation of businessmen, that thought is a violent, cataclysmic operation, of which sweat is only the most benign symptom. In the whole film, there is but one man who does not sweat and who remains smooth-faced, unperturbed and water-tight: Caesar. Of course Caesar, the *object* of the crime, remains dry since *he* does not know, *he does not think*, and so must keep the firm and polished texture of an exhibit standing isolated in the courtroom.

Here again, the sign is ambiguous: it remains on the surface, yet does not for all that give up the attempt to pass itself off as depth. It aims at making people understand (which is laudable) but at the same time suggests that it is spontaneous (which is cheating); it presents itself at once as intentional and irrepressible, artificial and natural, manufactured and discovered. This can lead us to an ethic of signs. Signs ought to present themselves only in two extreme forms: either openly intellectual and so remote that they are reduced to an algebra, as in the Chinese theatre, where a flag on its own signifies a regiment; or deeply rooted, invented, so to speak, on each occasion, revealing an internal, a hidden facet, and indicative of a moment in time, no longer of a concept (as in the art of Stanislavsky, for instance). But the intermediate sign, the fringe of Roman-ness or the sweating of thought, reveals a degraded spectacle, which is equally afraid of simple reality and of total artifice. For although it is a good thing if a spectacle is created to make the world more explicit, it is both reprehensible and deceitful to confuse the sign with what is signified. And it is a duplicity which is peculiar to bourgeois art: between the intellectual and the visceral sign is hypocritically inserted a hybrid, at once elliptical and pretentious, which is pompously christened '*nature*'.

(Barthes 1973: 26–8)

WHAT'S NEXT?

➤ What are the strengths and weaknesses of Barthes's analysis?
➤ Consider the meanings of hairstyles in another film or television context. What are the rules and what are the meanings presented?

▼ 15 WHAT'S THE TOPIC? Making an active reading of a text
WHAT'S THE TEXT? David Lodge 'Shakin' Stevens Superstar'

One of Roland Barthes's projects was the reading of the sign systems of everyday life. We've just worked through his reading of a then-current everyday sign system, the Romans in Film. Communication Studies needs to maintain a definition of text which is as big as the world itself, if not beyond. In this sense a text is that which consciously presents itself as meaningful, it is a discrete collection (and selection) of signs.

This extends the scope of the subject to all of the significant events of a society and culture: baptisms and marriages, celebratory meals, sporting events, and music festivals. The latter in particular makes for fascinating observations and critiques as fans and artists conspire and compete to be unique and/or original. Originally published in 1982 David Lodge's piece below is dated now in terms of the specific popular music act it looks at but it still provides a useful basis for the analysis of the more generic (not to say structural) performance of popular music.

There is no reason to suppose that, structurally speaking, similar processes are not being played out in the pop world right now. Indeed the process of pop as a religious experience is a very live contemporary phenomenon. (See Julie Burchill's piece on Kurt Cobain (Extract 80 of this book) and consider the ramifications of Vernon Reid entitling a track 'Saint Cobain' on his 1996 album *Mistaken Identity*.)

Lodge interprets what is being offered here as a quasi-religious experience without the depth. But the very fact that the religious dimension is experienced as both lack and absent presence is testimony to the enduring power of the treasure trove of historic signs that contemporary texts draw upon to make their meaning. Simultaneously we experience depth and shallowness in the polysemic texts of contemporary existence.

We have quoted (in the introduction to Extract 5 above) David Lodge's account of the impact of semiotics and structuralism on the British university system in the late 1970s/early 1980s. What is remarkable about Lodge's own work is that – unlike many of his colleagues in English departments – he didn't unthinkingly reject key concepts and practices from this new wave of theory. But as an astute commentator on human foibles he was able to incorporate these concepts and practices into his novels, critical writing and journalism. Thus what follows not only offers an application of once new ways of reading texts but it is also done with a sense of humour, making gentle fun of several targets.

Shakin' Stevens is an amiable and athletic young Welshman who sings rock and roll songs roughly in the style of Elvis Presley. He has sold, at the last count, about seven million LP albums and about ten million singles all around the world. He was recently voted Top Male Vocalist in the British Pop and Rock Awards. He is at present in the middle of a nationwide tour which began with a concert at the Odeon, Birmingham, where I accompanied a party of young teenagers.

At a pop concert, as distinct from a rock, folk or jazz concert, the primary motive of those who attend would appear to be the adoration of the star. It is a quasi-religious occasion, in which spectacle is quite as important as the music, and the worshippers are predominantly pubescent or pre-pubescent girls.

It is often said that rock and roll is essentially Dionysian in spirit. The blatantly sexual hip movements of Presley and his imitators, and the collective hysteria of their fans, certainly encourage such interpretation. But watching Shakin' Stevens, I was more struck by the Christian symbolism permeating the entire event.

All pop concerts begin with a support group. Its function is that of John the Baptist: to herald the star. They must be musically compatible with, but inferior to him. They perform on a bare desert of a stage under stark lights, in front of the curtain behind which an elaborate set is being prepared for the star. The support group for Shakin' Stevens is called The Stargazers, which perhaps suggests the Magi. They are a kind of parody of Bill Haley and the Comets (so were Bill Haley and the Comets, as Oscar Wilde might have said). 'Shakin' Stevens is coming soon,' their lead singer promised a restive audience, and was rewarded with an anticipatory scream – a mere whisper to what was to come.

After an extremely long interval, raising the audience's expectations to fever pitch, the curtain rises on a dimly-lit stage, divided by three sloping ramps, between which the nine-piece band is distributed. The star's first appearance has Old Testament overtones: a shadowy figure stalks down the central ramp, to the accompaniment of portentous chords and drumbeats, and amid flashes and explosions and clouds of smoke. But then the lights come on, flickering in rainbow colours to the beat of the music, and Shakin' Stevens – 'Shaky', as he is affectionately known – comes to the front of the stage, smiling, youthful, friendly, to receive a delirious welcome. The Father transformed into the Son.

The performance itself combines features of both Ministry and Passion. At frequent intervals young girls, watchfully observed by uniformed security guards, step to the front of the auditorium and, stretching up to the stage, beseech their idol to accept bouquets, teddy bears, knickers and paper hearts. By the end of the show, the front of the stage is littered with these votive offerings. Some girls proffer handkerchiefs and scarves with which the star dabs the sweat from his brow before handing them back to these diminutive Veronicas, who return raptly to their seats, clutching the precious relics. A more mature young woman in a red dress manages to get up on to the stage and throws herself enthusiastically upon Shaky, but this Mary Magdalen is quickly collared by the uniformed disciples and hustled away.

Then, as the show approaches its climax, as if in obedience to some intuitive, collective impulse, the fans in the front stalls surge forward, overwhelming the security guards, and stand in a heaving, swaying crowd, pressed up against the edge of the stage, arms raised in worship, fingers splayed imploringly. Two tiny tots are allowed up on to the stage and Shaky crouches to let them sing with him into the mike. ('Suffer little children . . .')

The star jerks and gyrates in ever more energetic and exhausting spasms. He turns cartwheels and on occasion throws himself tragically to the ground. ('And he fell for the first time . . .') Eventually he sings his last number and bids his worshippers goodbye.

The encore is, of course, a well-established convention of concerts, planned and rehearsed before the performance begins, but seldom, I imagine, has it been attended with such religious solemnity as in this case. The stage is left dark and silent for a daringly long time. The audience's applause after the star's exit dies away and they begin to chant and wail, 'We want Shaky! We want Shaky!' Then, at last, faint music is audible, plangent guitar chords and muffled drumbeats. Something strange and supernatural is happening on stage. The central ramp is rising in the air, like the jaws of hell opening, and brilliant beams of light suddenly shine out, dazzling the audience. Out of the darkness and the dazzle comes . . . Shaky! He is risen! Crashing chords, flashing lights, delirious rejoicing – and three encores.

After the Resurrection comes the Ascension. The ramp is lowered again and Shaky slowly climbs it to a platform at the back of the stage, where the backdrop suddenly acquires a mirrored surface, reflecting back to the audience their own image, but at a higher level, so that it seems as if Shaky is returning to a heavenly host, their arms raised in hallelujahs.

At last he is really, finally gone. But in the foyer on the way out you can buy a long white scarf with his image imprinted on it.

(Lodge 1986: 54–6)

WHAT'S NEXT?

➤ List the key words with which Lodge interprets Stevens in terms of a religious event.
➤ What are the differences between the presentation of Pop and that of Rock? Semiotically analyse a music act you have seen live or on video or on television.
➤ Read Philip Auslander *Liveness* (1999) London: Routledge.

▼ 16 WHAT'S THE TOPIC? Analysing a text in a limited period of time
WHAT'S THE TEXT? Helen Hackett *Response to AQA 'A' Level Communication Studies Examination Question*

Of course one of the contexts for analysis is that of a formal examination, in which you will be asked to demonstrate the skills of analysis in a subject-specific manner. One such example is the AQA Communication Studies AS unit two (CMS2) in which candidates are required to respond to two similar (in terms of theme perhaps) texts in ninety minutes.

Task One will typically offer the following general instruction: 'using the techniques of textual analysis explore the ways in which this text is communicating'. In June 2002 the chosen text was a Johnny Bravo cartoon, *Tips t'live by.* The second task, related to a second text, is then usually more specific or perhaps comparative. In June 2002 the second text was *Helen's Teenager Trouble*, a black and white Problem Page photo story from the *Sun* newspaper, and candidates were asked to explore the differences in character between the photo story and the Johnny Bravo comic strip.

This is the text of an essay done under examination conditions by Helen Hackett, a student at King Edward VI College, Stourbridge, England, which is both successful and believable. Its strength is in its knowledge and application of critical reading techniques, which result in an intelligent and rewarding analysis of the *Sun* text.

> The photo story also has a comic strip style to communicating its story, but does this differently through the use of highly motivated iconic images (Peirce) as photographs are used and also not only speech but also thought bubbles to show the feelings and ideas of the people portrayed. The use of the photographs means that Fiske's presentational codes are very applicable with the non-verbal communication of the characters portraying a lot of the story as well as the written narration. The use of the 'finger wag' by Gemma's mother to show disapproval and Gemma's hand on hip posture accentuating the image of 'tart' that she has been given help to give the reader supplementary information. Also facial expression; Gemma's sultry, annoyed look and her mother's worried facial expression, with their 'thoughts' anchoring this.
>
> Applying Lasswell and the Process approach will give some clues about the text:
>
> Who? *The Sun*
> Says what? Teenagers are rebellious
> To whom? Parents and anyone else who reads it
> In which channel? Photographs and text in a photo story
> With what effect? Possibly entertain help or inform

CONTINUED

However the semiotic school is more useful for a closer analysis. The dominant signifiers of the text are Gemma and her parents. The way they are portrayed is through paradigms of dress which add up to the syntagm which is each person (they are also themselves selections which add to the syntagms which is the whole text). The representation of Gemma is of her and all teenagers who she represents as being rebellious and disrespectful, as demonstrated by her facial expression of disgust and her hand on hips. On the other hand the parents are represented as being hard done by. The mother is represented as the one who has to take control and resolve conflict while the father says 'Don't worry' and appears less interested: he is reading *The Sun* (the sender advertising its product). The parents represent all of the parents that the photo story is addressing as its audience and are also meant to be representative of *The Sun*'s readers, as the father is reading *The Sun* where readers of the photo story will be reading it.

The narrative using text conforms to the genre of comic strips, as the Johnny Bravo text did, with bold black writing in capital letters on a white background of speech and thought bubbles. The narrative through the photographs is also set out in the same manner, conforming to conventions with the boxes outlined in black with spaces in between.

Using Barthes' 'orders of signification' we can see at a denotative level (the first order) that there are images of a teenage girl and her parents and the conflict with her mother anchored by the title 'Helen's teenager trouble: day 3' and its use of alliteration. 'Day 3' indicates that this is an ongoing serial like a soap and so the audience is likely to be regular readers of *The Sun*, especially parents of teenagers as they may want advice and could identify with the characters.

At the second order of signification, as already mentioned, the clothing, appearance and NVC have connotations of Gemma being rebellious and disrespectful and her mother being very concerned. Also there are connotations that the mother is in charge of and organises the family. The text supports this and offers the myth that teenagers are rebellious through the stereotypical presentation, portrayal and representation of Gemma. A number of dominant ideological views are supported: the ideology that the average and preferred family has a mother and father and are white is offered whereas this is often not the case in Britain. Also the role of women as mothers in charge of the family and cooking etc. (her mother tells her lunch will be ready).

So the photo story communicates differently by trying to get the reader to identify with the characters rather than laugh at them as in Johnny Bravo. The text's intention is therefore more serious, to offer advice than the entertaining nature of Johnny Bravo.

(Hackett 2002)

The strength of this reading is its ability to use techniques to genuinely interrogate the text. Moreover it does this in an active way by being selective rather than exhaustive in its approach. Helen Hackett never loses sight of the text.

WHAT'S NEXT?

➤ Discuss what else you might have said about the photo story text.

At USC, I took Latin and Romance Languages and mathematics through calculus.
And when I started in movies, they had to teach me to say ain't.

(John Wayne)

▼   17 **WHAT'S THE TOPIC? Self-image and
self-presentation
WHAT'S THE TEXT? Bret Easton Ellis**
American Psycho

Proof of the performance of the self is easy to find. We renew our acquaintance with the
divided self every time we look in the mirror or see our reflection in a shop window. This
is the experience of being both knowing and known, seeing and seen. It is this duality that
allows for discussions about identity and the extent to which that which we call our self
(or selves) is given or negotiated. This again is partly about how we present ourselves,
which selections we make, and how we want to be understood.

The extract below has a dislocated sense of this relationship. The central character,
Patrick Bateman (the American Psycho of the title), is offering us, the reader, a tour of
his apartment and, some would argue, himself. He is obsessed with a kind of commercial
authenticity – 'an original David Onica'; and with technology as a status symbol – 'a thirty
inch digital TV set from Toshiba'. Here image is becoming more important than identity
and the total effect is to present a man whose self-concept is out of balance, whose self-
image and mirror self are at odds with one another.

In the early light of a May dawn this is what the living room of my apartment
looks like: Over the white marble and granite gas-log fireplace hangs an original
David Onica. It's a six-foot-by-four-foot portrait of a naked woman, mostly done
in muted grays and olives, sitting on a chaise longue watching MTV, the backdrop a Martian landscape, a gleaming mauve desert scattered above the
woman's yellow head, and the whole thing is framed in black aluminum steel.
The painting overlooks a long white down-filled sofa and thirty-inch digital TV

set from Toshiba; it's a high-contrast highly defined model plus it has a four-corner video stand with a high-tech digital effects system (plus freeze-frame); the audio includes a super high-band Beta unit and has built-in editing function including a character generator with eight-page memory, a high-band record and playback, and three-week, eight-event timer. A hurricane halogen lamp is placed in each corner of the living room. Thin white venetian blinds cover all eight floor-to-ceiling windows. A glass-top coffee table with oak legs by Turchin sits in front of the sofa, with Steuben glass animals placed strategically around expensive crystal ashtrays from Fortunoff, though I don't smoke. Next to the Wurlitzer jukeboxes is a black ebony Baldwin concert grand piano. A polished white oak floor runs throughout the apartment. On the other side of the room, next to a desk and a magazine rack by Gio Ponti, is a complete stereo system (CD player, tape deck, tuner, amplifier) by Sansui with six-foot Duntech Sovereign 2001 speakers in Brazilian rosewood. A down-filled futon lies on an oakwood frame in the center of the bedroom. Against the wall is a Panasonic thirty-one inch set with a direct-view screen and stereo sound and beneath it in a glass case is a Toshiba VCR. I'm not sure if the time on the Sony digital alarm clock is correct so I have to sit up and then look down at the time flashing on and off on the VCR, then pick up the Ettore Sottass push-button phone that rests on the steel and glass nightstand next to the bed and dial the time number. A cream leather, steel and wood chair designed by Eric Marcus is in one corner of the room, a molded plywood chair in the other. A black-dotted beige and white Maud Sienna carpet covers most of the floor. One wall is hidden by four chests of immense bleached mahogany drawers. In bed I'm wearing Ralph Lauren silk pyjamas and when I get up I slip on a paisley madder robe and walk to the bathroom. I urinate while trying to make out the puffiness of my reflection in the glass that encases a baseball poster hung above the toilet. After I change into Ralph Lauren monogrammed boxer shorts and a Fair isle sweater and slide into silk polka-dot Enrico Hidolin slippers I tie a plastic ice pack around my face and commence with the morning's stretching exercises. Afterwards I stand in front of a chrome and acrylic Washmobile bathroom sink – with soap dish, cup holder, and railings that serve as towel bars, which I bought at Hastings Tile to use while the marble sinks I ordered from Finland are being sanded – and stare at my reflection with the ice-pack still on. Then I squeeze Rembrandt onto a faux-tortoise-shell toothbrush and start brushing my teeth (too hung over to floss properly – but maybe I flossed before bed last night?) and rinse with Listerine. Then I inspect my hands and use a deep-pore cleanser lotion, then an herb-mint facial masque which I leave on for ten minutes which I check my toenails. Then I use the Probright tooth polisher (this in addition to the toothbrush) which has a speed of 4200 rpm and reverses direction forty-six times per second; the larger tufts clean between the teeth and massage the gums while the short ones scrub the tooth surfaces. I rinse again, with Cepacol. I wash the facial massage off with a spearmint face scrub. The shower has a universal all-directional shower head that adjusts within a thirty-inch vertical range. It's made from Australian gold-black brass and covered with a white enamel finish. In the shower I use first a water-activated gel cleanser, then a honey-almond body scrub, and on the face an exfoliating gel scrub. Vidal Sassoon shampoo is especially good at getting rid of the coating of dried perspiration, salts, oils, airborne pollutants and dirt that can weigh down hair and flatten it to the scalp which can make you look older. The conditioner is also good – silicone technology permits conditioning benefits without weighing down the hair which can also make you look older. On weekends or before a date I prefer to use the Greune Natural Revitalizing Shampoo, the conditioner and the Nutrient Complex. These are formulas that contain D-panthenol, a vitamin-B-complex factor; polysorbate 80, a cleansing agent for the scalp; and natural herbs. Over the weekend I plan to go over to Bloomingdale's or Bergdorf's and on Evelyn's advice pick up a Foltene European Supplement and Shampoo for thinning hair which contains complex carbohydrates that penetrate the hair shafts for improved strength and shine. Also the Vivagen Hair Enrichment Treatment, a new Redken product that prevents mineral deposits and prolongs the life cycle of hair. Luis Carruthers recommended the Aramis Nutriplexx system, a nutrient complex that helps increase circulation. Once out of the shower and towelled dry I put the Ralph Lauren boxers back on and before applying the Mousse A Raiser, a shaving cream by Pour Hommes, I press a hot towel against my face for two minutes to soften abrasive beard hair. Then I always slather on a moisturizer (to my taste, Clinique) and let it soak in for a minute. You can rinse it off or keep it on and apply a shaving cream over it – preferably with a brush, which softens the beard as it lifts the whiskers – which I've found makes removing the hair easier. It also helps prevent water from evaporating and reduces friction between your skin and the blade. Always wet the razor with warm water before shaving and shave in the direction the beard grows, pressing gently on the skin. Leave the sideburns and chin for last, since these whiskers are tougher and need more time to soften. Rinse the razor and shake off any excess water before starting. Afterwards splash cool water on the face to remove any trace of lather. You should use an after-shave lotion with little or no alcohol. Never use cologne on your face, since the high alcohol content dries your face out and makes you look older. One should use an alcohol-free antibacterial toner with a water-moistened cotton ball to normalize the skin. Applying a moisturizer is the final step. Splash on water before applying an emollient lotion to soften the skin and seal in the moisture. Next apply Gel Appaisant, also made by Pour Hommes, which is an excellent, soothing skin lotion. If the face seems dry and flaky – which makes it look dull and older – use a clarifying lotion that removes flakes and uncovers fine skin (it can also make your tan look darker). Then apply an anti-aging eye balm (Baume Des Yeux) followed by a final moisturizing 'protective' lotion. A scalp-programming lotion is used after I towel my hair dry. I also lightly blow-dry the hair to give it body and control (but without stickiness) and then add more of the lotion, shaping it with a Kent natural-bristle brush, and finally slick it back with a wide-tooth comb. I pull the Fair Isle sweater back on and reslip my feet into the polka-dot slippers, then head into the living room and put the new Talking Heads in the CD player, but it starts to digitally skip so I take it out and put in a CD laser lens cleaner. The laser lens is very sensitive, and subject to interference from dust or dirt or smoke or pollutants or moisture, and a dirty one can inaccurately read CDs, making for false starts, inaudible passages, digital skipping, speed changes and general distortion; the lens cleaner has a cleaning brush that automatically aligns with the lens then the disk spins to remove residue and particles. When I put the Talking Heads CD back in it plays smoothly. I retrieve the copy of USA *Today* that lies in front of my door in the hallway and bring it with me into the kitchen where I take two Advil, a multivitamin and a potassium tablet, washing them down with a large bottle of Evian water since the maid, an elderly Chinese woman, forgot to turn the dishwasher on when she left yesterday, and then I have to pour the grapefruit-lemon juice into a St Rémy wine glass I got from Baccarat. I check the neon clock that hangs over the refrigerator to make sure I have enough time to eat breakfast unhurriedly. Standing at the island in the kitchen I eat kiwifruit and a sliced Japanese apple-pear (they cost four dollars each at Gristede's) out of aluminum storage boxes that were designed in West Germany. I take a bran muffin, a decaffeinated herbal tea bag and a box of oat-bran cereal from one of the large glass-front cabinets that make up most of an entire wall in the kitchen; complete with stainless-steel shelves and sandblasted wire glass, it is framed in a metallic dark gray-blue. I eat half of the bran muffin after it's been microwaved and lightly covered with a small helping of apple butter. A bowl of oat-bran cereal with wheat germ and soy milk follows; another bottle of Evian water and a small cup of decaf tea after that. Next to the Panasonic bread baker and the Salton Pop-Up coffee maker is the Cremina sterling silver espresso maker (which is, oddly, still warm) that I got at Hammacher Schlemmer (the thermal-insulated stainless-steel espresso cup and the saucer and spoon are sitting by the sink, stained) and the Sharp Model R-1810A Carousel II microwave oven with revolving turntable which I use when I heat up the other half of the bran muffin. Next to the Salton Sonata toaster and the Cuisinart Little Pro food processor and the Acme Supreme Juicerator and the Cordially Yours liqueur maker stands the heavy-gauge stainless steel two-and-one-half-quart teakettle, which whistles 'Tea for Two' when the water is boiling, and with it I make another small cup of the decaffeinated apple-cinnamon tea. For what seems like a long time I stare at the Black & Decker Handy Knife that lies on the counter next to the sink, plugged into the wall: it's a slicer/peeler with several attachments, a serrated blade, a scalloped blade and a rechargeable handle. The suit I wear today is from Alan Flusser. It's an eighties drape suit, which is an updated version of the thirties style. The favored version has extended natural shoulders, a full chest and a bladed back. The soft-rolled lapels should be about four inches wide with the peak finishing three quarters of the way across the shoulders. Properly used on double-breasted suits, peaked lapels are considered more elegant than notched ones. Low-slung pockets have a flapped double-besom design – above the flap there's a slit trimmed on either side with a flat narrow strip of cloth. Four buttons form a low-slung square; above it, about where the lapels cross, there are two more buttons. The trousers are deeply pleated and cut full in order to continue the flow of the wide jacket. An extended waist is cut slightly higher in the front. Tabs make the suspenders fit well at the center back. The tie is a dotted silk design by Valentino Couture. The shoes are crocodile loafers by A Testoni. While I'm dressing the TV is kept on to *The Patty Winters Show*. Today's guests are women with multiple personalities. A nondescript overweight older woman is on the screen and Patty's voice is heard asking, 'Well, is it schizophrenia or what's the deal? *Tell us.*'

'No, oh no. Multiple personalities are *not* schizophrenics,' the woman says, shaking her head. 'We are *not* dangerous.'

'Well', Patty starts, standing in the middle of the audience, microphone in hand. 'Who were you last month?'

'Last month it seemed to be mostly Polly,' the woman says.

A cut to the audience – a housewife's worried face; before she notices herself on the monitor, it cuts back to the multiple-personality woman.

'Well,' Patty continues, '*now* who are you?'

'Well . . .,' the woman begins tiredly, as if she was sick of being asked this question, as if she had answered it over and over again and still no one believed it. 'Well, this month I'm . . . Lambchop. Mostly . . . Lambchop.'

A long pause. The camera cuts to a close-up of a stunned housewife shaking her head, another housewife whispering something to her.

The shoes I'm wearing are crocodile loafers by A Testoni.

Grabbing my raincoat out of the closet in the entranceway I find a Burberry scarf and matching coat with a whale embroidered on it (something a little kid might wear) and it's covered with what looks like dried chocolate syrup crisscrossed over the front, darkening the lapels. I take the elevator downstairs to the lobby, rewinding my Rolex by gently shaking my wrist. I say good morning to the doorman, step outside and hail a cab, heading downtown toward Wall Street.

(Easton Ellis 1991: 24–30)

That Bateman takes his obsession to murderous conclusions is almost irrelevant. What might appear extraordinary about him is in fact ordinary. Bateman is a symptom and not a cause. The vast majority of consumers in contemporary culture do not pursue their fetishistic obsessions to deathly goals. That they do this does not detract from the fact that the majority of people in industrial or post-industrial societies burn down significant amounts of their time in the active pusuit of consumption, happily stalking the shopping malls which Theodor Adorno presciently characterised as cathedrals of consumption.

Along with Max Horkheimer and Herbert Marcuse, Adorno was a member of a group of intellectuals who were known as the Frankfurt School. Working in pre-Second World War Germany many of the Frankfurt school scholars escaped to the USA before war broke out. Whilst the Frankfurt School are renowned for their bringing the study of popular culture into the academy they remained profoundly pessimistic about it. Mica Nava succinctly summarised their position in 2002: 'They argued that mass culture – which included cinema, fiction, popular music and modern commerce – was not only without aesthetic and social value, it was also part of a strategy by the culture industry to engineer political acquiescence' (p.21). In this way it is easy to trace a line of development which begins with Marx's critique of commodification (see Extracts 62 and 63 below), then moves to Marcuse's characterisation of 1960s American culture ('The people recognise themselves in their commodities; they find their soul in their automobile, hi-fi, split-level home, kitchen equipment'(1986: 9)), then moves to *American Psycho* with its commodity-obsessed Patrick Bateman, and which then culminates in the opening sequence of David Fincher's 1999 film of Chuck Palahniuk's 1996 novel *Fight Club* where the Edward Norton Narrator characterises his situation: 'Like so many others I had become a slave to the Ikea nesting instinct'. As the Narrator walks through furniture catalogues, price tags and all, the film looks for all the world like *American Psycho* come to life, animated on the screen.

WHAT'S NEXT?

➤ What are the specific signs that something is amiss in this passage? (Despite the fact that we have given away the novel's secret, that Bateman is a savage, psychopathic killer, in what ways does the text tell you that all is not well with him?)

➤ Do you think that we all have significant props, items that help define us as individuals? If so, what are yours?

➤ Read the Introduction to Martyn Lee's *The Consumer Society Reader* (2000), Oxford: Blackwell.

▼   18 **WHAT'S THE TOPIC? Self-esteem and gender WHAT'S THE TEXT? Mary Ragan 'Women and self-esteem'**

Analysing, interpreting and even coming better to understand the self may be a target of all good communication students but the key to a contented life may lie more simply in that elusive substance, self esteem. Mary Ragan advocates 'a healthy self-esteem' as the basis of the ability to 'cope, rebound and transcend'. Ragan is particularly concerned to explore the 'problems that women face in this culture, a culture that is both sexist and patriarchal'.

Her approach is both scholarly and pragmatic. She defines her terms, summarises significant research and then pursues its findings in the direction of gender as a context. Here is an energised discussion about the implications of an abstract concept. Ragan is keen to define but much keener to apply. Her essay is introduced by a backhanded application as she quotes the words of Vita Sackville-West:

> I worshipped dead men for their strength,
> Forgetting I was strong.

Here is her theme – the need, particularly for women, to recognise their strength, by valuing themselves, to acquire what Nathaniel Brandon (1995) has called the 'immune system of consciousness'. In the face of such poetry the *Oxford English Dictionary*'s definition of self-esteem as a 'favourable appreciation or opinion of oneself' seems somewhat flat. It is not surprising then that it is Brandon's definition which takes the piece forward.

A description of self-esteem put forth by Brandon (1995) consists of two dimensions: 1) confidence in our ability to think, confidence in our ability to cope with the basic challenges of life, and 2) confidence in our right to be successful and happy, the feeling of being worthy, deserving, entitled to assert our needs and wants, achieve our values, and enjoy the fruits of our efforts (p. 4). Brandon's description I think, becomes particularly problematic for women since our socialization has not been in the direction of asserting our needs, feeling 'entitled' to the pursuit of happiness, and feeling confident in our ability to cope. In fact, much of female socialization has been around the concept of 'waiting,' i.e. a girl waits to become a woman and the woman waits to be chosen by the man who will give her a life and make her feel important and valued because she is married to him. Admittedly, this notion of what it means to be a woman is slowly breaking down, but since these formative powers of socialization are so strong and deeply imbedded, I think much conscious attention must be given to the issue of female self-esteem. Carol Gilligan and her colleagues have been doing this for many years now in their research on latency age girls and the ways in which they lose their 'voice' once they enter puberty. This work and research like it provides a hopeful sign of better things to come for girls and women.

The importance of self-esteem cannot be under-estimated. It has profound consequences for every aspect of our existence: how we operate in the workplace, how we deal with people, how high we are likely to rise, how much we are likely to achieve. And in a more personal realm, the level of self-esteem influences our choice of the one with whom we fall in love, how we interact with our partner, children, and friends, and what level of personal happiness we attain.

Recent research on self-esteem shows a positive correlation between healthy self-esteem and the following qualities: realism, intuitiveness, creativity, independence, flexibility, ability to manage change, willingness to admit mistakes, benevolence, and cooperativeness. Poor self-esteem correlates with: blindness to reality, rigidity, fear of the new and unfamiliar, inappropriate conformity or inappropriate rebelliousness, defensiveness, over-controlling behavior, hostility towards others (Brandon, 1995, p. 5).

The question arises, then, whether dealing with men or with women: How is healthy self-esteem nurtured and developed? Brandon (1995), citing Stanley Coopersmith's important study *The Antecedents of Self-Esteem*, reminds us that there is no significant correlation between positive self-esteem and such factors as family wealth, education, geographic living area, social class, father's occupation, or always having mother at home. What Coopersmith did find to be significant was the quality of the relationship between the child and the important adults in his/her life (p. 172). More specifically, Coopersmith found five correlations associated with high self-esteem in children:

1   the child experiences total acceptance of thoughts, feelings and the value of his/her person;
2   the child operates in a context of clearly defined limits that are fair, non-oppressive and negotiable;
3   the child experiences respect for his/her dignity as a human person. The parents do not use violence or humiliation to ridicule or control or manipulate. The parents are willing to negotiate family rules within limits;
4   the parents uphold high expectations in terms of behavior and performance; the child is challenged to be the best he or she can be;
5   the parents themselves tend to enjoy a high level of self-esteem. They model self-efficacy and self-respect.

One quality characteristic of those with high self-esteem is appropriate risk-taking. This quality of risk-taking, and how it informs self-esteem, is especially important in women's development since female socialization often does not reward risk. Cantor and Bernay (1992) in their study of *Women in Power: The Secrets of Leadership* speak of risk as involving a search for opportunities that will bring a greater sense of purpose as well as more joy, zest, and love into our lives (p. 165). This sense of internal liveliness enables us to accomplish tasks more easily and in the process to feel more satisfied, more competent, more confident, and have greater self-esteem.

James Masterson (1985), in his work on the 'real self,' puts the same idea this way: 'The real self emerges and develops under a combination of nature/nurture forces: a combination of constitutional endowment, genetic biological pressure, and the mother's and father's capacity to acknowledge, respond and give emotional support to the unique characteristics of the emerging self during those important first three years of life (p. 29).'

It is this mirroring process which is vital to the development of the real self. Psychotherapy, at its best, provides both women and men an opportunity to regain access to the 'real self' in the context of a therapeutic relationship which is both genuine and authentic. Healthy self-esteem means honoring, not suppressing, one's true self.

<http://www.mindspirit.org>

WHAT'S NEXT?

➤ To what extent are Coopersmith's five correlations true for self-esteem in adults?

➤ What amendments would you need to make to make them viable?

▼ 19 WHAT'S THE TOPIC? Freud and theories of personality
WHAT'S THE TEXT? Mick Underwood Cultsock website

There are many theories and explanations of the self and personality but none perhaps as influential as those of Sigmund Freud. He is often dubbed 'the father of psychoanalysis' as he launched a new way of looking at the self and human behaviour, which proposed that behaviour could be traced back to inner motivations. Freud's model for the self was of an inner struggle between three elements: id, ego and super-ego, a three-way opposition.

Freud's theories are attractively intellectual; they give the curiously intelligent the hope that even the mind itself can be worked out. The approach has much in common with semiotic approaches to communication. Psychoanalysis looks to anchor symptomatic behaviour (signifiers) to inner truths (signifieds). Of course much of Freud's anchoring had a famously sexual basis and was founded in the experiences of early childhood wherein we were both free and without shame or guilt, subject only to what he called 'the pleasure principle'. Growing up then is about moving away from this ideal and facing up to its antithesis 'the reality principle' whereby we must conform to the wishes of others.

Mick Underwood's excellent Communication Studies website clarifies these ground rules before going on to ask significant questions about Freud and psychoanalysis.

PSYCHOANALYTIC THEORIES

Freud

Freud compared the human mind to an iceberg: we only see a little bit of it (the conscious) peeking out above the vast depths of the *unconscious*. Freud endeavoured to explore the unconscious by means of *free association* – a method which involves allowing the subject to talk about whatever comes into their conscious mind, however silly or trivial it may appear. Through the analysis of free associations, dreams and early childhood memories, Freud tried to figure out the basic elements of personality.

He considered personality to be composed of three parts: the *id*, the *ego* and the *superego*.

The id

The id consists of all the inherited components of personality, including sex drives and aggression. The id seeks immediate gratification of primitive impulses. It operates on the **pleasure principle**, seeking to avoid pain and maximise gratification.

If tangible gratification of the primitive impulses are unavailable, then the id may form a mental image or hallucination to reduce the tension of ungratified desire – for example, a starving man may form a mental image of a delicious meal. That is an example of what Freud termed **wish fulfilment**.

The ego

The starving man might form an image of a meal, but that won't satisfy his needs. The ego emerges out of the id because we need to deal with the real world. Thus, the ego can be said to obey the **reality principle**, for example controlling the sex drive until conditions are right in the real world for its gratification. You can think of the ego as being the id's controller. Freud likens the ego to a man on the horseback of the id. The horse is stronger than the rider, but the rider controls it. Inevitably, however, the horse's strength will predominate and the rider will sometimes lose control or will sometimes have to content himself with guiding the horse to where it wants to go.

The superego

The superego incorporates the values and morals of society which are learnt from one's parents and others. It develops as a result of rewards and punishments as one grows up. The superego's function is to control the id's impulses, especially those which society forbids, such as sex and aggression. It also has the function of persuading the ego to turn to moralistic goals rather than simply realistic ones and to strive for perfection.

The superego consists of **conscience** – all those actions the child is reproved for doing – and the **ego-ideal** – all those things the child is praised for doing. The conscience makes the individual feel guilty and the ego-ideal makes the individual feel proud, thus directing the striving for perfection.

. . .

CRITICISMS OF PSYCHOANALYSIS

When considering psychoanalytic personality theories, it is worth bearing in mind that Freud and psychoanalysis generally normally seem to be treated with great respect in cultural and communication studies, in part no doubt because of the recent influence of the French psychoanalyst Jacques Lacan, and, for some reason, being French and incomprehensible is the height of cool in cultural studies. Nevertheless, you should be aware that there has in recent years been increasingly hostile criticism of Freud and Freudian psychoanalysis, generally from outside the field of cultural studies, as far as I am aware.

As the author of a website on communication and cultural studies, I suppose I ought to feel obligated to research Freud, but my first contact with his theories many years ago led me to decide fairly rapidly that I had better things to do with my time. The little I know of Freud is therefore largely through other, more interesting (and possibly saner) people he has influenced. That, as Steven Pinker puts it, 'the idea that boys want to sleep with their mothers strikes most men as the silliest thing they have ever heard' (1998: 460), that they might envy me my penis seems to strike most women as utterly absurd, that the claim that my dreams reveal something about my psyche, intriguing though it may be, seems no more convincing than that they might be the word of God, a glimpse of the future or simply (as I am inclined to believe until someone comes along with a better account) mere random noise – none of these, I suppose, is much of an argument for rejection of one of the most influential thinkers of the century. From a Freudian point of view, of course, my rejection is no doubt itself worthy of analysis, my hostility doubtless a symptom of my repressed desire to have sex with my mother (oh, yes – and kill my father, of course). As Peter Medawar says, 'psychoanalysis has now achieved a complete intellectual closure: it explains even why some people disbelieve in it' (Medawar 1996: 127). To *other psychoanalysts*, of course, it explains that, to me it explains nothing. The irritating 'Olympian glibness' that Medawar complains of in psychoanalysis claims to be able to explain everything: 'A lava flow of *ad hoc* explanation pours over and around all difficulties, leaving only a few smoothly rounded prominences to mark where they might have lain' (Medawar 1996: 126)

If Freud had actually cured one of his patients, I might be inclined to be more interested in his theories, but there is little evidence that any were ever cured and quite convincing evidence that many of the cures he claimed were not cures at all. We now know a great deal more about the brain than Freud, who did not have the benefit of brain scans, and we therefore can explain many of his patients' symptoms in terms of organic causes, such as brain tumours, strokes, blows to the head and so on; we know now, as Freud did not, about hormones, Mendel's laws of inheritance, chromosomes. The lack of such knowledge in Freud's day may excuse him, but I don't see how it excuses us for treating such egregious nonsense with respect. Indeed, I'm not even convinced that it excuses him, since he seems to have claimed scientific status for ideas he probably made up off the top of his head and to have claimed cures where none were effected. What is interesting about Freud is his enormous influence on intellectuals and that they continue to take him seriously today despite the fact that

> Freud made no substantial intellectual discoveries. He was the creator of a complex pseudo-science which should be recognized as one of the great follies of Western civilization. In creating his particular pseudo-science, Freud developed an autocratic, anti-empirical intellectual style which has contributed immeasurably to the intellectual ills of our own era.

> (Webster 1995: 438)

Or again Medawar

> . . . considered in its entirety, psychoanalysis won't do. It is an end-product, moreover, like a dinosaur or a zeppelin; no better theory can be erected on its ruins, which will remain for ever one of the saddest and strangest of all landmarks in the history of twentieth-century thought.

> (1996: 130)

So much for psychoanalyis, then, at least as far as I'm concerned. As for Freud's personality theory, well that's up to you.

> <http://www.cultsock.ndirect.co.uk/Milhome/cshtml/psy/person2.html>

WHAT'S NEXT?

➤ Summarise Underwood's problems with Freud.

20 WHAT'S THE TOPIC? Applying Freudian analysis
WHAT'S THE TEXT? Sigmund Freud *The Psychopathology of Everyday Life*

The work of groundbreaking theorists is often subject to misinterpretation by well-meaning followers. Karl Marx, when presented with the work of some self-styled Marxists, famously remarked that if this was Marxism then he was no Marxist. This is at least equally the case with Sigmund Freud: any number of self-styled Freudians would not be recognised as such by Freud himself. He has been endlessly represented in any number of popular cultural media, not the least of which is the movies. The image of both Freud specifically and of the psychoanalyst generally as a kind of psychic detective probably owes as much to Alfred Hitchcock's 1945 film *Spellbound* which features Michael Chekhov as a Freud lookalike (complete with Freud-like glasses and beard, and a faux Viennese accent) guiding Gregory Peck through Salvador Dali designed dream sets. So let's have a look at a piece of Freud's own writing from early on in his career. In 'The forgetting of foreign words' he analyses an aspect of human behaviour which features largely in his early writings – what we reveal about ourselves when we get words wrong.

The current vocabulary of our own language, when it is confined to the range of normal usage, seems to be protected against being forgotten. With the vocabulary of a foreign language it is notoriously otherwise. The disposition to forget it extends to all parts of speech, and an early stage in functional disturbance is revealed by the fluctuations in the control we have over our stock of foreign words – according to the general condition of our health and to the degree of our tiredness. In a number of cases this kind of forgetting exhibits the same mechanism disclosed to us by the *Signorelli* example. In proof of this I shall give only a single analysis, one which is distinguished, however, by some useful characteristics: it concerns the forgetting of a non-substantival word in a Latin quotation. Perhaps I may be allowed to present a full and clear account of this small incident.

Last summer – it was once again on a holiday trip – I renewed my acquaintance with a certain young man of academic background. I soon found that he was familiar with some of my psychological publications. We had fallen into conversation – how I have now forgotten – about the social status of the race to which we both belonged; and ambitious feelings prompted him to give vent to a regret that his generation was doomed (as he expressed it) to atrophy, and could not develop its talents or satisfy its needs. He ended a speech of impassioned fervour with the well-known line of Virgil's in which the unhappy Dido commits to posterity her vengeance on Aeneas: '*Exoriare* . . .' Or rather, he *wanted* to end it in this way, for he could not get hold of the quotation and tried to conceal an obvious gap in what he remembered by changing the order of the words: '*Exoriar(e) ex nostris ossibus ultor.*' At last he said irritably: 'Please don't look so scornful: you seem as if you were gloating over my embarrassment. Why not help me? There's something missing in the line; how does the whole thing really go?'

'I'll help you with pleasure,' I replied, and gave the quotation in its correct form: '*Exoriar(e) ALIQUIS nostris ex ossibus ultor.*'

'How stupid to forget a word like that! By the way, you claim that one never forgets a thing without some reason. I should be very curious to learn how I came to forget the indefinite pronoun "aliquis" in this case.'

I took up this challenge most readily, for I was hoping for a contribution to my collection. So I said: 'That should not take us long. I must only ask you to tell me, *candidly* and *uncritically*, whatever comes into your mind if you direct your attention to the forgotten word without any definite aim.'

'Good. There springs to my mind, then, the ridiculous notion of dividing up the word like this: *a* and *liquis*.'

'What does that mean?' 'I don't know.' 'And what occurs to you next?' 'What comes next is *Reliquien* (relics), *liquefying*, *fluidity*, *fluid*. Have you discovered anything so far?'

'No. Not by any means yet. But go on.'

'I am thinking' he went on with a scornful laugh, 'of *Simon of Trent*, whose relics I saw two years ago in a church at Trent. I am thinking of the accusation of ritual blood-sacrifice which is being brought against the Jews again just now, and of *Kleinpaul's* book [1892] in which he regards all these supposed victims as incarnations, one might say new editions, of the Saviour.'

'The notion is not entirely unrelated to the subject we were discussing before the Latin word slipped your memory.'

'True, my next thoughts are about an article that I read lately in an Italian newspaper. Its title, I think, was "What St *Augustine* says about Women". What do you make of that?'

'I am waiting'.

'And now comes something that is quite clearly unconnected with our subject.'

'Please refrain from any criticism and –'

'Yes, I understand. I am thinking of a fine old gentleman I met on my travels last week. He was a real *original*, with all the appearance of a huge bird of prey. His name was *Benedict*, if it's of interest to you.'

'Anyhow, here are a row of saints and Fathers of the Church: St *Simon*, St *Augustine*, St *Benedict*. There was, I think, a Church Father called *Origen*. Moreover, three of these names are also first names, like *Paul* in *Kleinpaul*.'

'Now it's St *Januarius* and the miracle of his blood that comes into my mind – my thoughts seem to me to be running on mechanically.'

'Just a moment: St *Januarius* and St *Augustine* both have to do with the calendar. But won't you remind me about the miracle of his blood?'

'Surely you must have heard of that? They keep the blood of St Januarius in a phial inside a church at Naples, and on a particular holy day it miraculously *liquefies*. The people attach great importance to this miracle and get very excited if it's delayed, as happened once at a time when the French were occupying the town. So the general in command – or have I got it wrong? was it Garibaldi? – took the reverend gentleman aside and gave him to understand, with an unmistakable gesture towards the soldiers posted outside, that he *hoped* the miracle would take place very soon. And in fact it did take place . . .'

'Well, go on. Why do you pause?'

'Well, something *has* come into my mind . . . but it's too intimate to pass on . . . Besides, I don't see any connection, or any necessity for saying it.'

'You can leave the connection to me. Of course I can't force you to talk about something that you find distasteful; but then you mustn't insist on learning from me how you came to forget your *aliquis*.'

'Really? Is that what you think? Well then, I've suddenly thought of a lady from whom I might easily hear a piece of news that would be very awkward for both of us.'

'That her periods have stopped?'

'How could you guess that?'

'That's not difficult any longer; you've prepared the way sufficiently. Think of *the calendar saints, the blood that starts to flow on a particular day, the disturbance when the event fails to take place, the open threats that the miracle must be vouchsafed, or else* . . . In fact you've made use of the miracle of St Januarius to manufacture a brilliant allusion to women's periods.'

'Without being aware of it. And you really mean to say that it was this anxious expectation that made me unable to produce an unimportant word like *aliquis*?'

'It seems to me undeniable. You need only recall the division you made into *a-liquis*, and your associations: *relics, liquefying, fluid*. St Simon was *sacrificed as a child* – shall I go on and show how he comes in? You were led on to him by the subject of relics.'

'No, I'd much rather you didn't. I hope you don't take these thoughts of mine too seriously, if indeed I really had them. In return I will confess to you that the lady is Italian and that I went to Naples with her. But mayn't all this just be a matter of chance?'

'I must leave it to your own judgement to decide whether you can explain all these connections by the assumption that they are matters of chance. I can however tell you that every case like this that you care to analyse will lead you to "matters of chance" that are just as striking.'

I have several reasons for valuing this brief analysis; and my thanks are due to my former travelling-companion who presented me with it. In the first place, this is because I was in this instance allowed to draw on a source that is ordinarily denied to me. For the examples collected here of disturbances of a psychical function in daily life I have to fall back mainly on self-observation. I am anxious to steer clear of the much richer material provided by my neurotic patients, since it might otherwise be objected that the phenomena in question are merely consequences and manifestations of neurosis. My purpose is therefore particularly well served when a person other than myself, not suffering from nervous illness, offers himself as the object of such an investigation. This analysis is significant in a further respect: it throws light on the case of a word being forgotten without a substitute for it appearing in the memory. It thus confirms my earlier assertion that the appearance or non-appearance in the memory of incorrect substitutes cannot be made the basis for any radical distinction.

The chief importance however of the *aliquis* example lies in another of the ways in which it differs from the *Signorelli* specimen. In the latter, the reproducing of a name was disturbed by the after-effect of a train of thought begun just before and then broken off, whose content, however, had no clear connection with the new topic containing the name of Signorelli. Contiguity in time furnished the only relation between the repressed topic and the topic of the forgotten name; but this was enough to enable the two topics to find a connection in an external association. Nothing on the other hand can be seen in the *aliquis* example of an independent repressed topic of this sort, which had engaged conscious thinking directly before and then left its echoes in a disturbance. The disturbance in reproduction occurred in this instance from the very nature of the topic hit upon in the quotation, since opposition unconsciously arose to the wishful idea expressed in it. The circumstances must be construed as follows. The speaker had been deploring the fact that the present generation of his people was deprived of its full rights; a new generation, he prophesied like Dido, would inflict vengeance on the oppressors. He had in this way expressed his wish for descendants. At this moment a contrary thought intruded. 'Have you really so keen a wish for descendants? That is not so. How embarrassed you would be if you were to get news just now that you were to expect descendants from the quarter you know of. No: no descendants – however much we need them for vengeance.' This contradiction then asserts itself by exactly the same means as in the *Signorelli* example – by setting up an external association between one of its ideational elements and an element in the wish that has been repudiated; this time, indeed, it does so in a most arbitrary fashion by making use of a roundabout associative path which has every appearance of artificiality. A second essential in which the present case agrees with the *Signorelli* instance is that the contradiction has its roots in repressed sources and derives from thoughts that would lead to a diversion of attention.

So much for the dissimilarity and the inner affinity between these two typical specimens of the forgetting of words. We have got to know a second mechanism of forgetting – the disturbance of a thought by an internal contradiction which arises from the repressed. Of the two processes this is, I think, the easier to understand; and we shall repeatedly come across it again in the course of this discussion.

(Freud 1974: 45–52)

After *Spellbound*'s opening credits have finished two legends run up the screen. The first is a quotation from Shakespeare:

The fault is . . . not in the stars, but in ourselves.

The second would appear to sum up the image of psychoanalysis and psychoanalysts in the popular imagination as reproduced in popular cultural media such as film:

Out story deals with psychoanalysis, the method by which modern science treats the emotional problems of the sane.

The analyst seeks only to induce the patient to talk about his hidden problems, to open the locked doors of his mind.

Once the complexes that have been disturbing the patient are uncovered and interpreted, the illness and confusion disappear . . . and the devils of unreason are driven from the human soul.

One might add – as if by magic. When well thought of the psychoanalyst is burdened with performing not only the role of psychic detective but also magical healer. This was never Freud's intention: he offers us case histories and stories (narratives we can live by). He never sought to turn us to make new journeys but to better understand the journeys we were already on. George Boeree offers an excellent contemporary assessment of Freud:

Some of Freud's ideas are clearly tied to his culture and era. Other ideas are not easily testable. Some may even be a matter of Freud's own personality and experiences. But Freud was an excellent observer of the human condition, and enough of what he said has relevance today that he will be a part of personality textbooks for years to come. Even when theorists come up with dramatically different ideas about how we work, they compare their ideas with Freud's.

<http://www.ship.edu/~coboeree/freud.html>

WHAT'S NEXT?

> ➤ Ever since they became widely available Freud's ideas have been used by film-makers and film analysts. A good exercise to set yourself is the viewing of a sequence of films to see how film-makers have used Freud's ideas as the foundations of their film's narratives. We suggest you begin by watching Robert Benton's *Still of the Night* (1982); then move on to Alfred Hitchcock's *Spellbound* (1945) and then his *Vertigo* (1958) and his *Marnie* (1964); then move to David Fincher's *Fight Club* (1999); and conclude with David Cronenberg's *Spider* (2002).

▼ ## 21 WHAT'S THE TOPIC? Freud and psychoanalysis
WHAT'S THE TEXT? Harold Ramis, Peter Tolan and Kenneth Lonergan *Analyze This*

Whilst we introduced the previous extract with the notion that there is no substitute for the original writing of key theorists it's still worth looking at the way in which a writer's work is represented and reproduced in popular cultural forms. Even when the purpose of using a theorist's work in, say, a film, is humorous essential features of the theorist's work still leak through. Furthermore, even if those ideas are misrepresented the fact that they are still tells us a lot about those ideas. And what does it tell us about ourselves that we want to enjoy film-makers making fun of Freud's ideas?

The extract below, which is taken from the 1999 film *Analyze This*, evidences some of the points that have been made in Mick Underwood's attack on Freud, including Steven Pinker's characterisation that 'the idea that boys want to sleep with their mothers strikes most men as the silliest thing they have ever heard'. Here classical Freudian psychoanalysis (as represented by Billy Crystal's character Ben Sobol) is subjected to the greatest test of all: common sense and actual experience represented by Robert De Niro's mobster character of Paul Vitti.

Here, as a series of gags, is the dramatisation of the relationship between theory and practice. Moreover, within the development of this short sequence is a potential satire on the character of theoretical authority which might serve as a warning every bit as useful as Peter Barry's. Ben Sobol's demolition in the scene occurs in three stages: he offers an analysis of behaviour which is challenged; he then defensively dresses it up in the terminology of instinctual developmental drive; and finally he resorts to the naked appeal to authority by citing Freud's illustrious name.

Paul Vitti has been experiencing anxiety attacks and has forcefully engaged the services of psychiatrist Ben Sobol. In his first significant analysis Paul is clearly in denial about the violent character of his father's death (at this stage he simply says he died from a heart attack). We join the movie where Ben tries to probe Paul about this.

BEN   I'm just speculating, Paul, maybe that in some way you may have wanted him [your father] to die.

PAUL   Why would I want my father to die?

BEN   Well you said that you were fighting, he slapped you around, because you were rebelling against his authority. There may have been some unresolved Oedipal conflict . . .

PAUL   [interrupts impatiently] English, English . . .

BEN   Oedipus was a Greek king who killed his father and married his mother.

PAUL   Pssht! Fuckin' Greeks.

BEN   It's an instinctual developmental drive: the young boy wants to replace his father so that he can totally possess his mother.

PAUL   So what you saying, that I wanted to fuck my mother?

BEN   No no – it's a primal fantasy.

PAUL   You ever seen my mother?

BEN   Paul . . .

PAUL   Are you outta your fuckin' mind?

BEN   It's Freud.

PAUL   Well then Freud's a sick fucker and you are too for bringin' it up.

Memory theorists have argued that a sound way to remember something is by emphasising comic or exaggerated aspects of what you want to remember. So, if you want to remember key aspects of Freudian theory you could use the first two stanzas from Philip Larkin's poem 'This be the verse' as a kind of Freudian mnemonic:

They fuck you up, your mum and dad.
They may not mean to, but they do.
They fill you with the faults they had
And add some extra, just for you.

But they were fucked up in their turn
By fools in old-style hats and coats,
Who half the time were soppy-stern
And half at one another's throats.

(Larkin 2003: 142)

WHAT'S NEXT?

➤ What is your response to Freud's psychoanalytic theories?
➤ Is Paul Vitti's response an intelligent one?
➤ What benefits might you derive from examining your current or past relationships?

▼ 22 WHAT'S THE TOPIC? Nature versus nurture WHAT'S THE TEXT? Stephen Pinker *The Language Instinct*

In the discussions which we've presented so far about the self, adult behaviour (and the adult personality and mind) is assumed to be the product of a social learning environment. This is what Pinker calls the Standard Social Science Model, which crudely suggests that we are, all of us, products of our experiences. The Freudian analysis which preceded this piece is a good example, where our experiences as children are used to explain our behaviour and demeanour as adults.

Pinker is determined to offer us an alternative, or rather to inform us that there is an alternative, which he (and its advocates) labels the Causal Model. The basis of this approach is the massively greater understanding we now have about the genome (or gene-map, the template or blueprint which determines biological qualities and dispositions such as eye colour or susceptibility to certain diseases or disorders). This is Evolutionary Psychology, the study of how evolution caused the emergence of our brains and thus potentially of all the processes therein. Here Pinker offers us a pithy bullet point summary as a way of initiating a debate:

The lessons of language have not been lost on the sciences of the rest of the mind. An alternative to the Standard Social Science Model has emerged, with roots in Darwin and William James and with inspiration from the research on language by Chomsky and the psychologists and linguists in his wake. It has been applied to visual perception by the computational neuroscientist David Marr and the psychologist Roger Shepard, and has been elaborated by the anthropologists Dan Sperber, Donald Symons, and John Tooby, the linguist Ray Jackendoff, the neuroscientist Michael Gazzangia, and the psychologists Leda Cosmides, Randy Gallistel, Frank Keil, and Paul Rozin. Tooby and Cosmides, in their important recent [1992] essay 'The Psychological Foundations of Culture', call it the Integrated Causal Model, because it seeks to explain how evolution caused the emergence of a brain, which causes psychological processes like knowing and learning, which cause the acquisition of the values and knowledge that make up a person's culture. It thus integrates psychology and anthropology into the rest of the natural sciences, especially neuroscience and evolutionary biology. Because of this last connection, they also call it Evolutionary Psychology.

Evolutionary Psychology takes many of the lessons of human language and applies them to the rest of the psyche:

- Just as language is an improbable feat requiring intricate mental software, the other accomplishments of mental life that we take for granted, like perceiving, reasoning, and acting, require their own well-engineered mental software. Just as there is a universal design to the computations of grammar, there is a universal design to the rest of the human mind – an assumption that is not just a hopeful wish for human unity and brotherhood, but an actual discovery about the human species that is well motivated by evolutionary biology and genetics.
- Evolutionary psychology does not disrespect learning but seeks to explain it. In Molière's play La Malade imaginaire, the learned doctor is asked to explain how opium puts people to sleep and cites its 'sleep-producing power'. Leibniz similarly ridiculed thinkers who invoke

    Expressly occult qualities or faculties which they imagined to be like little demons or goblins capable of producing unceremoniously that which is demanded, just as if watches marked the hours by a certain horodeictic faculty without having the need of wheels, or as if mills crushed grains by a fractive faculty without needing anything resembling millstones.

In the Standard Social Science Model, 'learning' has been invoked in just these ways; in evolutionary psychology, there is no learning without some innate mechanism that makes the learning happen.

- Learning mechanisms for different spheres of human experience – language, morals, food, social relations, the physical world, and so on – are often found to work at cross-purposes. A mechanism designed to learn the right thing in one of these domains learns exactly the wrong thing in the others. This suggests that learning is accomplished not by some single general-purpose device but by different modules, each keyed to the peculiar logic and laws of one domain. People are flexible, not because the environment pounds or sculpts their minds into arbitrary shapes, but because their minds contain so many different modules, each with provisions to learn in its own way.

■ Since biological systems with signs of complex engineering are unlikely to have arisen from accidents or coincidences, their organization must come from natural selection, and hence should have functions useful for survival and reproduction in the environments in which humans evolved. (This does not mean, however, that all aspects of mind are adaptations, or that the mind's adaptations are necessarily beneficial in evolutionarily novel environments like twentieth-century cities.)

■ Finally, culture is given its due, but not as some disembodied ghostly process or fundamental force of nature. 'Culture' refers to the process whereby particular kinds of learning contagiously spread from person to person in a community and minds become co-ordinated into shared patterns, just as 'a language' or 'a dialect' refers to the process whereby the different speakers in a community acquire highly similar mental grammars.

(Pinker 1994: 453–5)

This is strong stuff. Taking a lead from those writers extracted at the beginning of Part 1 of this book we are aware that no reading is ever neutral. For an alternative view of Evolutionary Psychology hear what Clifford Geertz has to say about it. Interviewed in 2002 by Simon Philips the anthropologist observed: 'So-called evolutionary psychology is as much a social movement as a perspective. Its proponents are militant, polemical, highly organised and intent on getting their own way' (Philips 2002: 4).

WHAT'S NEXT?

➤ To what extent do you believe that our behaviour is 'susceptible' to genetic influences?

➤ What differences does this theory make to our understanding of human behaviour?

▼ **23 WHAT'S THE TOPIC? The dramaturgical model of self-presentation**
WHAT'S THE TEXT? Erving Goffman *The Presentation of Self in Everyday Life*

Erving Goffman offered a useful and insightful model of self-presentation in his influential book *The Presentation of Self in Everyday Life*. Goffman proposed that our attempts to show ourselves in the world were not unlike the attempts actors make to present characters on stage. For this reason his model is sometimes referred to as a dramaturgical model (this is a slightly off-putting word which merely makes explicit the theatrical analogy: in the original German a *dramaturg* is a member of a theatre company who selects which plays will be produced and may assist in their actual production).

Goffman suggested that our performances could be broken down and analysed according to certain characteristics:

- persona: the versions of the self that we all possess
- roles: the parts we have to play (brother, student etc.)
- teams: who we act with
- staging: where we do this
- personal style: our own particular way of doing things.

It's interesting to note that, while Goffman uses the above as analytical terms they are very close to the prescriptive terms that the Disney organisation uses when referring to key aspects of its working practices. Here are some examples of everyday language and their Disney counterparts:

Everyday term	Disney term
employee/staff	host/hostess or cast member
public areas	onstage
restricted areas	backstage
hiring for a job	casting
job interviews	auditions
crowd	audience
uniform	costume

In the extract below, Goffman is adding performance to the list and clarifying the distinction between sincere and honest on the one hand and cynical and false on the other. Partly this clarification is ironic given what he is actually saying is that the difference between the two is not as straightforward as it first seems. This is partly to do with our ability to determine what is honest or even real and partly to do with our ability to 'do' sincerity. After all, in Goffman's terms, we are always competing in a sense with the fact that 'life itself is a dramatically enacted thing'.

REALITY AND CONTRIVANCE

In our own Anglo-American culture there seem to be two commonsense models according to which we formulate our conceptions of behaviour: the real, sincere, or honest performance; and the false one that thorough fabricators assemble for us, whether meant to be taken unseriously, as in the work of stage actors, or seriously, as in the work of confidence men. We tend to see real performances as something not purposely put together at all, being an unintentional product of the individual's unselfconscious response to the facts in his situation. And contrived performances we tend to see as something painstakingly pasted together, one false item on another, since there is no reality to which the items of behaviour could be a direct response. It will be necessary to see now that these dichotomous conceptions are by way of being the ideology of honest performers, providing strength to the show they put on, but a poor analysis of it.

First, let it be said that there are many individuals who sincerely believe that the definition of the situation they habitually project is the real reality. In this report I do not mean to question their proportion in the population but rather the structural relation of their sincerity to the performances they offer. If a performance is to come off, the witnesses by and large must be able to believe that the performers are sincere. This is the structural place of sincerity in the drama of events. Performers may be sincere – or be insincere but sincerely convinced of their own sincerity – but this kind of affection for one's part is not necessary for its convincing performance. There are not many French cooks who are really Russian spies, and perhaps there are not many women who play the part of wife to one man and mistress to another; but these duplicities do occur, often being sustained successfully for long periods of time. This suggests that while persons usually are what they appear to be, such appearances could still have been managed. There is, then, a statistical relation between appearances and reality, not an intrinsic or necessary one. In fact, given the unanticipated threats that play upon a performance, and given the need (later to be discussed) to maintain solidarity with one's fellow performers and some distance from the witnesses, we find that a rigid incapacity to depart from one's inward view of reality may at times endanger one's performance. Some performances are carried off successfully with complete dishonesty, others with complete honesty; but for performances in general neither of these extremes is essential and neither, perhaps, is dramaturgically advisable.

The implication here is that an honest, sincere, serious performance is less firmly connected with the solid world than one might first assume. And this implication will be strengthened if we look again at the distance usually placed between quite honest performances and quite contrived ones. In this connection, take, for example, the remarkable phenomenon of stage acting. It does take deep skill, long training, and psychological capacity to become a good stage actor. But this fact should not blind us to another one: that almost anyone can quickly learn a script well enough to give a charitable audience some sense of realness in what is being contrived before them. And it seems this is so because ordinary social intercourse is itself put together as a scene is put together, by the exchange of dramatically inflated actions, counteractions, and terminating replies. Scripts even in the hands of unpractised players can come to life because life itself is a dramatically enacted thing. All the world is not, of course, a stage, but the crucial ways in which it isn't are not easy to specify.

(Goffman 1959: 76–8)

WHAT'S NEXT?

➤ Make a list of situations in which your performance is likely to tend towards the cynical.

▼ **24 WHAT'S THE TOPIC? Social interaction
WHAT'S THE TEXT? Richard Dimbleby and
Graeme Burton *Between Ourselves***

If Colin Cherry (Extract 85 in this book) is right and 'communication is a social affair' then it will be as well to look at in some detail interpersonal interactions between individuals in a social context. Richard Dimbleby and Graeme Burton provide an excellent starting point for this enterprise in the section headed 'What is Social Interaction?' from their standard Communication Studies text *Between Ourselves*.

They begin with a definition from Erving Goffman who sets the ball rolling with this beautifully active statement: 'The ultimate behavioural materials are the glances, gestures, positionings and verbal statements'. This is beautiful because it both clarifies the study of interpersonal communication and implicitly delivers the atmosphere of an investigation. This is just one of many statements offered within these covers and throughout the writing of this discipline that argues for the centrality of the study of Communication to the business of education. We are back here once again to a study of everyday life – its forms, its functions, and its meanings.

Dimbleby and Burton are literate compilers of information and opinion. What follows is both compact and yet logical and informative.

WHAT IS SOCIAL INTERACTION?

Quite simply, it is everyday encounters with other people.

Erving Goffman (1967), whose work we shall be looking at more closely in the next chapter, suggests Social Interaction is

> That class of events which occurs during co-presence and by virtue of co-presence. The ultimate behavioural materials are the glances, gestures, positionings and verbal statements that people feed into the situation, whether intended or not.

There are several elements here that we wish to highlight. Firstly, that social interaction consists of 'events', a sequence of happenings between two or more people when they meet face to face. Secondly, that it consists of physical behaviour, we make sounds and visual signs to express our meaning to other people. Thirdly, that these signs may or may not have been 'intended'. We may deliberately formulate our verbal statements to elicit a required response, but we may not be so conscious of our non-verbal statements which are picked up by the other person. As we shall see later in this chapter, social skills training is concerned with making our verbal and non-verbal behaviour more conscious, and with developing patterns of behaviour which in turn become unconscious. A parallel has often been made with driving a car: when we learn to drive we are conscious of all the behavioural sequences we employ, but when we are experienced drivers we perform these behaviours unconsciously.

Goffman (1963) draws a distinction between social interaction as 'co-presence' (for example, a group of people in a bus or in a waiting-room are aware of each other, but not necessarily involved with each other); and on the other hand 'focused interaction', in which two or more people are actually giving full attention to each other and developing a relationship built on verbal and non-verbal exchanges.

It is useful at this point to introduce the concept of a 'transaction', which indicates that an interaction is more than just an awareness of each other and becomes a main focus of exchange and negotiation. At its simplest this can be built on a model of stimulus and response and we shall see how these notions are employed in the later chapter on Transactional Analysis.

Myers and Myers (1985) suggest that there are three components of a transaction: a transaction can be defined as 'two or more people who mutually and simultaneously

1   take one another into account;
2   figure out their roles; and
3   conduct their interaction by a set of rules'.

There are, of course, an infinite number of possible occasions for private and public social interactions and transactions. During one day we, your authors, find ourselves in encounters with other people such as at home with wife, son and daughter; in the car, bus or train with neighbours, acquaintances and strangers; at work with colleagues, both managers and peers; in the classroom with colleagues and students; at lunch with friends; at a meeting with industrialists or other employers; at a public function with groups of people, and so on. You might like to review your typical day's interactions with other people.

The concept of social interaction has been so frequently studied and discussed that it has developed complex layers of meanings and associations. O'Sullivan, Hartley, Saunders and Fiske (1983), in their *Key Concepts in Communication* define it more fully: *'The exchange and negotiation of meaning between two or more participants located within social context.'*

We wish to investigate briefly the four main components of this definition:

1   At the heart of the notion of interaction is exchange or negotiation, that is, two or more people must be engaged together, aware of each other and giving and receiving messages that are decoded. Interaction presupposes two or more people to interact.

2   The participants have separate existences before and after any particular moment of interaction and meet in a specific social context which influences the nature of their interaction, whether they meet at an informal party, a street demo or a job interview. The personality and temperaments of the participants also influence the interaction, but recent research suggests that the situation has more effect than the individual personalities. Patterns of behaviour are a result of the interaction between a particular social situation and the personalities of the participants. Also, the participants will relate to each other according to how they perceive themselves (self-concept), how they wish to present themselves and what roles they adopt in relation to each other (e.g. submissive–dominant, friendly–hostile, formal–informal, etc.). These roles may be determined by the social context and its cultural expectations, for example if the participants are father/daughter in a family, or teacher/pupil in a school, or doctor/patient in a surgery.

3   Additionally, this definition stresses a location in a social context – interaction can not take place in a social vacuum. Inevitably an interaction exists in a particular situation which may be familiar or unfamiliar. The situation may have clear, culturally prescribed expectations – e.g. a church service or a school class – or it may be informal and open – e.g. a party amongst friends. In any case, the participants are free to some degree to define the situation for themselves: an atmosphere can be created to fulfil their needs, e.g. a coffee morning can suggest certain expectations of appropriate clothing and behaviour, but participants can redefine it as more or less informal, more or less personal, and so on.

4   The fourth element in this definition is meaning. This is the element we shall be particularly concerned with since the creation and generation of

meaning from the exchange of verbal and non-verbal behaviours dictates the outcome of all interactions. The message of an interaction is what the participants perceive to have happened between them. If communication has been effective then each participant will have closely similar perceptions of what took place.

(Dimbleby and Burton 1988: 80–2)

➤ Apply the four main components to a formal situation like a job interview. What is missed out?

▼ 25 WHAT'S THE TOPIC? Non-verbal codes
WHAT'S THE TEXT? Andrew Ellis and Geoffrey Beattie *The Psychology of Language and Communication*

Of all the behavioural material that a supreme non-material being or the genome has furnished us with, surely none is as significant or communicative as the human face. Not only is it a flexible mechanism for expressing a range of emotions but it is also the primary focus of who we are. For it to be damaged (for example by disease or accident) is thus a double blow, impairing our outward expressive abilities but also undermining what it is we can express (given the self is our primary message). Or it compels us as producers and consumers of communication to think differently about how we communicate.

As Ellis and Beattie state in their discussion of this primary 'kinesic channel of human communication' (or movable and moving means of communication): 'The face is perhaps the prime source of human non-verbal communication'.

They then pursue their discussions across debates about whether expressions are universal or individual. There is also some useful commentary on the abilities or otherwise of men and women as readers of facial expressions. Finally, they make stimulating observations about social and cultural variables with reference to smiling: is it an involuntary expression of emotion or is it a culturally learned behaviour of politeness?

KINESIC CHANNELS OF HUMAN COMMUNICATION

Facial movement

The face is perhaps the prime source of human nonverbal communication. In most forms of social interaction the face, and especially the eyes, is the region we concentrate on. It is a region with enormous 'sending capacity'. The concept of sending capacity was developed by Paul Ekman and Wallace Friesen in 1969. They suggested that the sending capacity of any part of the body can be assessed by looking at three factors: the average transmission time of any message from that part, the number of discernible stimulus patterns which can be emitted from it, and its visibility. Clearly, in terms of all of these factors, the face is an excellent source of communication. The average transmission time of even a 'micro' facial expression is very brief – even those expressions that can be easily identified and labelled in terms of emotion often last only for half a second or less. Some 'micro' facial expressions are even briefer. The complex musculature of the human face allows for a great number of discernible stimulus patterns. Ray Birdwhistell (1970), for example, has suggested that over 20,000 different facial expressions are possible. And the face of course also has maximum visibility. In some cultures there are socially-prescribed rules about the covering of the face (as in some Arab cultures), but in Western cultures the best we can do to make it less visible is to wear spectacles or sunglasses. As Ekman and Friesen point out:

> It is difficult to hide the face without being obvious about concealment, there are no inhibition manoeuvres for the face equivalent to putting the hands in the pocket or sitting upon them. A frozen, immobile poker face is more noticeable than are interlocked fingers or tensely-held feet. (1969)

Because it is such an excellent source of communication, and because our fellow human beings do tend to concentrate on it, it is a form of communication which most people learn to control to some extent. There are two sorts of messages that can be emitted through the face, first spontaneous messages – facial expressions which are emitted unintentionally and occur even when people do not know they are in a communicative situation – and secondly, intentional facial expressions which occur when people are consciously trying to communicate particular messages via the face. Buck, Savin, Miller and Caul (1972) investigated the spontaneous display of emotion in a rather ingenious paradigm. They told subjects that they were interested in galvanic skin responses to certain types of stimuli and subjects were wired up appropriately for measurement. But what Buck et al were really interested in was the spontaneous display of emotion via facial expression; the emotion being manipulated by the types of stimuli presented to the subjects. Buck video-recorded the facial expressions of his subjects as they watched the stimuli and then showed the video recordings to a second set of subjects who had to attempt to identify what class of stimuli the transmitters were being exposed to. Buck discovered that when men were used in this experiment (as encoders and decoders), they could not identify the emotional state of the encoder at more than chance level. Women, in contrast, were well above chance, being twice as accurate as the men. There are two possible explanations for this – either women are more expressive than men and therefore easier to 'read' correctly (perhaps because in Western cultures men are socialised to control their emotional expression) or perhaps women are better at interpreting facial expression than men.

In the original study males only acted as decoders for male encoders, and females for female encoders, so there was no way of deciding between these two alternatives. In a follow-up study which employed a similar procedure but had men viewing women's faces and vice versa, Buck, Miller and Caul (1974) obtained support for the first interpretation, namely that women are more expressive than men. No sex difference in decoding ability was observed. It does, nevertheless, seem that intentional communication via facial expression is more accurate than is spontaneous facial expression. This was demonstrated in a study by Zuckerman and his colleagues (1979). The superiority of deliberate over spontaneous expression in the encoding of emotion was most pronounced for pleasant emotions, and less pronounced for intense emotions.

Over the years there has been a good deal of speculation about whether facial expressions are learnt or inherited. Charles Darwin in his 1872 book *The Expression of the Emotions in Man and Animals* said 'Many of our most important expressions have not been learnt', but went on to qualify this by saying 'but it is remarkable that some which are certainly innate, require practice in the individual before they are performed in a full and perfect manner: for instance weeping and laughing' (p. 350). Darwin believed strongly in the innate basis of human facial expression, arguing that:

> The inheritance of most of our expressive actions explains the fact that those born blind display them, as I hear from the Rev R H Blair, equally well with those gifted with eyesight. We can thus also understand the fact that the young and the old of widely different races, both with man and animals, express the same state of mind by the same movements. (1872, p. 35)

Darwin's conclusions do however need to be modified in the light of the psychological research of the past century. Ekman, Friesen and Ellsworth (1972) tested Darwin's hypothesis a century later, on a pre-literature culture in the South-East highlands of New Guinea. Their subjects, who had little contact with Western culture, were shown three photographs of Caucasian faces each expressing a different emotion and were presented with three different emotional stories (e.g. 'A person's mother died'). Their task was to match the photograph of the facial expression with the emotion conveyed in the story. Both children and adults matched the expressions and the emotions correctly except in the case of 'fear' which the New Guineans often confused with surprise.

Ekman et al. also demonstrated cross-cultural similarities in the encoding of emotions. The New Guinean subjects were asked to show the emotional expression their face would have if they were the person described in the story. These videotapes were accurately decoded by American students – at least for happiness, anger and sadness. But again the Americans, like the New Guineans, had difficulty recognizing fear or surprise. Ekman's research does suggest that a number of basic emotions are conveyed by the same facial expressions, but other research has indicated important cultural differences in emotional *display*. Klineberg (1935), for example, made the following points:

> It is quite possible, however, that a smile or a laugh may have a different meaning for groups other than our own. Lafcadio Hearn has remarked that the Japanese smile is not necessarily a spontaneous expression of amusement, but a law of etiquette elaborated and cultivated from early times. It is a silent language, often seemingly inexplicable to Europeans, and it may arouse violent anger in them as a consequence. The Japanese child is taught to smile as a social duty, just as he is taught to bow or prostrate himself; he must always show an appearance of happiness to avoid inflicting his sorrow upon his friends. The story is told of a woman servant who smilingly asked her mistress if she might go to her husband's funeral. Later she returned with his ashes in a vase and said, actually laughing, 'Here is my husband'. Her white mistress regarded her as a cynical creature. Hearn suggests that this may have been pure heroism (Hearn, 1894).

Ekman (1978) concludes that Darwin was essentially correct – there are universal facial expressions of emotion – but in addition:

> Facial expressions do vary across cultures in at least two respects. What elicits or calls forth an emotion usually differs . . . Also, cultures differ in the conventions people follow about attempting to control or manage the appearance of their face in given social situations. People in two different cultures may feel sadness at the death of a loved one, but one culture may prescribe that the chief mourners must mask their facial expression with a mildly happy countenance. (p. 106)

(Ellis and Beattie 1993: 32–5)

WHAT'S NEXT?

➤ If there are universal facial expressions of emotion which emotions do you think are displayed by them?

26 WHAT'S THE TOPIC? The functions of non-verbal communication
WHAT'S THE TEXT? Michael Argyle *The Psychology of Interpersonal Behaviour*

Another source of detailed information about verbal and non-verbal communication is Michael Argyle's classic text *The Psychology of Interpersonal Behaviour*. Argyle maps in detail the codes of interpersonal behaviour in what amounts to a checklist of behavioural material. The list bears repetition:

- bodily contact
- physical proximity
- orientation
- body posture
- gestures
- head nods
- facial expression
- eye movements
- appearance
- non-linguistic aspects of speech (paralanguage)
- speech.

He then goes on in the extract below to address the functions or roles of non-verbal communication. These are threefold and examined by Argyle with clarity and detail.

THREE ROLES OF NON-VERBAL COMMUNICATION

Non-verbal communication (NVC) functions in three rather different ways (Argyle, 1972).

1. *Communicating interpersonal attitudes and emotions.* Animals conduct their entire social life by means of NVC – they make friends, find mates, rear children, establish dominance hierarchies, and cooperate in groups, by means of facial expression, postures, gestures, grunting and barking noises, etc. It looks as if much the same is true of humans too. Argyle et al. (1970) carried out an experiment in which superior, equal and inferior verbal messages were delivered in superior, equal and inferior non-verbal styles, nine combinations in all, by speakers recorded on video-tapes. Two of the verbal messages were as follows:

    (a) It is probably quite a good thing for you subjects to come along to help in these experiments because it gives you a small glimpse of what psychological research is about. In fact the whole process is far more complex than you would be able to appreciate without a considerable training in research methods, paralinguistics, kinesic analysis, and so on.

(b) These experiments must seem rather silly to you and I'm afraid they are not really concerned with anything very interesting and important. We'd be very glad if you could spare us a few moments afterwards to tell us how we could improve the experiment. We feel that we are not making a very good job of it, and feel rather guilty about wasting the time of busy people like yourself.

. . .

It can be seen that the non-verbal style had more effect than the verbal contents, in fact about five times as much; when the verbal and non-verbal messages were in conflict, the verbal contents were virtually disregarded. Much the same results were obtained in another experiment on the friendly–hostile dimension.

The explanation of these results is probably that there is an innate biological basis to these NV signals, which evoke an immediate and powerful emotional response – as in animals. In human social behaviour it looks as if the NV channel is used for negotiating interpersonal attitudes, while the verbal channel is used primarily for conveying information.

2.   *Supporting verbal communication.* Linguists recognize that timing, pitch and stress are integral to the meaning of utterances, e.g. by providing punctuation. A few linguists recognize that NVC plays a more extensive part – 'We speak with our vocal organs, but we converse with our whole body' (Abercrombie, 1968).

Completing the meaning of utterances. In addition to the *vocal* signals of timing, pitch and stress, *gestural* signals also add to meaning – by illustrating, pointing, displaying structure, etc. Frame-by-frame analysis of conversations has shown that there is a linkage between gesture and speech down to the level of the word, and that there is a hierarchical structure of gesture, where the larger movements correspond to larger verbal units, like paragraphs (Kendon, 1972). These fine movements are unintended, often unseen, and idiosyncratic, so that their full explanation is not known.

Controlling synchronizing. When two or more people are conversing they must take it in turns to speak, and usually achieve a fairly smooth pattern of synchronizing. This is done by the use of non-verbal signals such as shifts of gaze, head-nods and grunts.

Obtaining feedback. When a person is speaking he needs feedback on how the others are responding, so that he can modify his remarks accordingly. He needs to know whether his listeners understand, believe him, are surprised or bored, agree or disagree, are pleased or annoyed. This information could be provided by *sotto voce* muttering, but is in fact obtained from careful study of the other's face, especially his eyebrows and mouth.

Signalling attentiveness. For an encounter to be sustained, those involved must provide intermittent evidence that they are still attending to the others. They should not fall asleep, look out of the window, or read the paper; they should be at the right distance, in the right orientation, look up frequently, nod their heads, adopt an alert, congruent position, and react to the speaker's bodily movements.

3. *Replacing speech.* When speech is impossible, gesture languages develop. This happens in noisy factories, the army, racecourses, and underwater swimming. Some of these languages are complex and enable elaborate messages to be sent, though rather slowly, as in deaf-and-dumb language, and the sign language used by some Australian aboriginals.

It has been suggested by some psychiatrists that the symptoms of certain mental patients are a kind of NVC used when speech has failed – in pursuit of attention or love.

(Argyle 1972: 36–8)

WHAT'S NEXT?

➤   Take Argyle's list of categories and rank them according to their importance to interpersonal communication.

▼   **27 WHAT'S THE TOPIC? A vocabulary of non-verbal behaviour**
WHAT'S THE TEXT? Desmond Morris *Body Talk: A World Guide to Gestures*

Desmond Morris's approach is a little more practical and a little more populist, in the sense that some of his work is consciously aimed at a non-specialist audience. In *Body Talk* Morris is interested in cataloguing the vocabulary of gestures and then providing a multilingual, multicultural dictionary of definitions. Two things are apparent from this: first, the enormous number of gestures we give out and receive; and second, the significant differences that are applied by the user-culture in terms of meanings.

Surveying his handbook of gestures, certain themes or tendencies emerge, as do certain understandings. It is certainly possible to equate universal or widespread gestures with their character as signs. They are largely iconic enactments of human activities, such as the forefinger and middle finger 'smoke'. This is logical in the same way that it was logical for the Pioneer 10 space probe to include a pictorial representation of itself on its plaque as a genuine point of reference (see Extract 38). In the same way those gestures that are obscure in origin logically function in a symbolic fashion (using Peirce's trichotomy of signs).

The polysemic character of all communications (particularly from the point of view of the reader of communication systems) clearly emerges when examining non-verbal communication. (Polysemy is the term we use to characterise a text which is open to two or more interpretations. In other words it is many (poly) signed (semy).) Gestures lack the precision that articulated spoken or written language can achieve. But with non-verbal communication there is an additional polysemic dimension: difference of interpretation or meaning frequently emerges when the global is contrasted with the local. Thus there is no communication problem generated by the way in which a sign has stability of meaning in one region, one community, or one context, but there is frequently one where that sign is exported to another region, or community, or context. Given that polysemy can emerge in both the production and consumption of signs seeking a kind of precision of non-verbal communication in a global sense could be seen as a futile project. Where non-verbal communication achieves stability is in the local.

FOREFINGER-AND-MIDDLE-FINGER CROSS

Meaning: I swear.

Action: The first two fingers from each hand are crossed over one another.

Background: Forming the Christian cross is a commonly observed way of making an oath binding. This is sometimes done by kissing crossed forefingers, but in this instance the hands are held in front of the body.

Locality: Southern Italy.

FOREFINGER-AND-MIDDLE-FINGER POINT

Meaning: Bang, you're dead.

Action: The hand mimes the shape of a pistol and pretends to fire at the companion.

Background: This mock shooting of a friend is employed in a friendly way when he has done something foolish. It should not be confused with the following gesture.

Locality: Widespread.

FOREFINGER-AND-MIDDLE-FINGER RAISE

Meaning: Blessing.

Action: The hand is held up, palm showing, with the thumb and the first two fingers erect and the other fingers bent.

Background: This is an ancient hand position with a long history, known as the 'Mano Pantea'. It is still employed today by the Catholic Church when bestowing a blessing. According to one theory it owes its origin to the idea that the thumb and the first two fingers together symbolise the Holy Trinity. According to another it is a gesture that displays 'non-action' because the fingers are in a position that immobilizes the hand, making it impossible for it either to grip or to push. It is claimed that this gives the gesture an air of serenity and benign peacefulness.

Locality: Catholic countries.

FOREFINGER-AND-MIDDLE-FINGER SHOW

Meaning: Friendship.

Action: The first two fingers are shown to the companion held stiffly pressed together.

Background: The two fingers represent the two friends and the closeness of the fingers symbolises the tight bond that exists between the two individuals. The gesture is usually made without pointing the fingers directly at the companion, in order to avoid confusion with the previous gesture.

Locality: Saudi Arabia.

FOREFINGER-AND-MIDDLE-FINGER 'SMOKE'

Meaning: Do you have a cigarette?

Action: The first two fingers are raised near the mouth, while the lips mime the action of pulling on a cigarette.

Background: Because it is a simple mime, this gesture is understood almost everywhere in the world. In some countries it may be confused with the V-for victory signal or, more unfortunately, with the British insult-V.

Locality: Worldwide except for non-smoking cultures.

CONTINUED

FOREFINGER-AND-MIDDLE-FINGER STAB

Meaning: Threat.

Action: The separated forefinger and the middle finger are stabbed towards the companion's eyes.

Background: This gesture says 'I will poke your eyes out' and is used both as a serious threat and also as a mild, almost joking insult during an argument.

Locality: Widespread.

(Morris 1994: 90–1)

WHAT'S NEXT?

➤ Try to identify gestures which are particularly common to your locality and produce definitions of their commonly understood meanings.

▼ 28 **WHAT'S THE TOPIC? The social determinants of interpersonal communication**
WHAT'S THE TEXT? Peter Hartley
Interpersonal Communication

To conform to the logic of Communication Studies these behavioural materials can only be fully understood in their contexts, in their particular sites of interaction. In his book *Interpersonal Communication* Peter Hartley provides a vigorous and useful analysis of specific context by providing a set of questions and some prompts for how to start finding answers.

He begins by exposing the ways in which your understanding of the role of social context betrays your attitude towards meaning in communication. He conceives of two versions of society as a context:

■ 'society as the backdrop' against which humans choose to act

and

■ 'society' which 'creates or determines the ways in which we act'.

He then moves quickly to attempt a more systematic definition of the social context by setting us three significant questions:

■ What are the relevant components?
■ What are the specific factors which affect us?
■ How do they operate?

This is the starting point for a significant discussion. To set us off on the right road Hartley offers us a useful distinction between environment (the setting or background) and social structure (the ways it is organised).

WHAT IS THE SOCIAL CONTEXT AND HOW DOES IT AFFECT COMMUNICATION?

If you read any number of recent texts about human communication, you will probably find a strong emphasis on the social aspects of communication. Authors are very insistent that communication is a 'social process' and that communication always takes place within a given society at a given time. But what does this actually mean when we come to try to analyse communication?

One reason why modern authors place a strong emphasis on the social context is simply because early authors tended to neglect it. For example, there is little concern for the social context in early models of communication which simply concentrated on encoder–channel–decoder propositions. There is also something of a battle which is carried on within the social sciences between those who regard society as the backdrop against which humans choose to act and those who feel that society creates or determines the ways in which we act. If you follow the first viewpoint then you are likely to believe that there are features of human experience which are universal or common to all races and cultures. If you follow the latter viewpoint then you are likely to believe that all human action is relative to the society in which it occurs, i.e. that there are no universal features of human nature or experience.

These arguments may seem very abstract or remote but you will find that they do have very concrete practical implications. For example, communication between different cultures depends on the different cultures being able to develop a common understanding. If all experience is relative to your own culture then this communication could be impossible.

I have oversimplified this argument simply because I do not have the space to explore it fully. If you want to put me on the spot for an opinion then I will argue that there are some aspects of human experience which are virtually universal. If this was not the case then communication would be impossible. On the other hand I also maintain that you cannot fully understand any process of human communication without understanding the social context in which it occurs. But if I simply say that communication is affected by the social context then that does not take us very far. What we need is a more systematic definition of the social context:

- What are the relevant components?
- What are the specific factors which affect us?
- How do they operate?

Unfortunately many authors have been at great pains to emphasise the importance of the social context but have been rather less painstaking at saying what that means! Thus, my definition reflects a collection of rather disparate areas of research which have yielded important results.

ENVIRONMENT AND SOCIAL STRUCTURE

Firstly I shall make a distinction between environment and the social structure.

Environment

The environment is the setting or background and has both physical and social elements. For example, one research study found that experimental subjects saw the experimenter as more 'status-ful' if the laboratory was untidy. Another study showed that people judged faces differently depending on whether they were in a 'beautiful' or 'ugly' room.

Social structure

By social structure, I mean the ways in which the particular event we are looking at is organised. For example, if you attend a British wedding you will notice that people behave in fairly predictable ways as if they were following particular rules or codes of behaviour. You will notice that some people are behaving in very specific ways – for example, the best man – as they are fulfilling specific roles. If their performance goes wrong in some way then chaos and embarrassment is likely to follow. Consider the best man at a very formal wedding who tried to relax the groom as they were standing at the altar by whispering 'This is your last chance to escape. I'll cover if you want to make a run for it!' This comment was not so well received when the bride's parents proudly played back the tape of the ceremony at the reception. The best man had been standing almost next to the microphone so the comment came out loud and clear.

There is also a very definite sequence of events, e.g. the order of speeches at the reception. All these facts will vary depending on the location and status of the participant: for instance, compare a high-society upper-class wedding with a typical church wedding or with a registry office wedding. In a different culture you will notice even more dramatic differences. But the important point I want to make here is that the participants recognise the invisible 'rules of the game', i.e. they know what is required of them and act out their parts. People can feel very uncomfortable if they are unsure of the proceedings, and a lot of humour is based upon careful observation of the idiosyncrasies or ironies of some of our more formal occasions, e.g. as in the British film *Four Weddings And A Funeral* or the American film by Robert Altman, *A Wedding*.

(Hartley 1999: 78–81)

WHAT'S NEXT?

➤ Take a social event (like a wedding or a birthday party) and try and clarify the particular rules or codes of behaviour.

▼ **29 WHAT'S THE TOPIC? Transactional analysis WHAT'S THE TEXT? Eric Berne 'Last speech (to the Golden Gate Group Psychotherapy Association)'**

To some extent the explanation and understanding of interpersonal communication offered by Eric Berne was essentially a context-driven approach, though in this case the contexts are specifically emotional and psychological. In *Games People Play* Berne launched Transactional Analysis, a system for understanding what is really going on when people communicate which is part therapy, part critique.

We are, according to Berne, prey to the needs and intentions of our 'ego-states' (inner selves) which he offered in three varieties: parent, child, and adult. Successful communication feeds them, offering what Berne labelled strokes which (in proper 1960s style) promise both bodily and spiritual wellbeing. We communicate ('engage in transactions') to exchange strokes, or more selfishly to get them. This is the character and function of transactions (i.e. of human communication), the business of communication.

Berne was interested in practical action; his work was intended for the clinic not the classroom. What you have below is part of the text of his last public speech given in 1970 at the Golden Gate Group Psychotherapy Association's yearly conference just before his untimely death. Here he is characteristically pragmatic and defiant, clarifying once again:

- 'the place of theory': 'the more thousands of patients you see the better your theory is going to be';
- 'the advantage of the term "transaction" over the vaguer "interaction"': 'the value of the term transaction is that you're committed to something, you're saying that something is exchanged'; and
- 'the fundamental question in social psychology': 'Why do people talk to each other?'

About theory; a theory is one of two things. It's either a bright idea, like – I don't mind being specific – the kind of thing they do in psychology at the Rand Corporation where somebody sits down with a little computer or a very sophisticated adding machine and makes a theory of human behavior without ever having looked a human being in the eye, possibly. Or it's a real theory which is an abstract from experience. The more thousands of patients you see, the better your theory is going to be, or the more hours you spend with one patient and the less time you spend with the adding machine the better your theory is going to be.

Then the word impact is very fashionable. Everybody wants to make an impact. Now an impact, to me, is not a dull thud. Bang! Bang! That's what you should be doing with your patients, not making dull thuds. The phrase 'interpersonal interaction' to me is usually the mark of a jerk. I just don't see any point in that expression at all – just the opposite: an impersonal interaction, an interpersonal superaction, or infraction. Actually this is sort of a chicken phrase because it means: 'if I use a lot of big words I don't really have to find out what's happening, and it sounds good'. Of course, my tendency is to propose the term transaction. The value of the term transaction is that you're committed to something, you're saying that something is exchanged. Whereas if you use interaction you're saying, 'I don't know, I'm only going toward it.' Transaction means: 'At least I got to the first stage. I know that when people talk to each other they are exchanging something, and that is why people talk to each other.'

The fundamental question in social psychology is: Why do people talk to each other? Interaction essentially means no action, in most cases. People who are really going to do something do not use words like interaction. That reminds me of an old joke of mine about the way that patients are diagnosed in the average clinic; the person who has less initiative than the psychotherapist is called passive dependent. The person who has more initiative than the psychotherapist is called a sociopath.

Non-verbal, of course, is very fashionable. The thing that bothers me personally about non-verbal is using it as a kind of shibboleth. There are lots of things people do with their faces and their bodies, but as soon as you call it non-verbal it makes it sound a little phony. Also, people don't understand the verbal. There's still plenty of work to be done in the field of verbal activity so don't be discouraged if you are not going along with the nonverbal crowd.

<http://www.indigo.ie/~liztai/index.html?/~liztai/ta/berndale.html>

WHAT'S NEXT?

➤ Identify the transactions in this extract from Berne's speech and deduce the ego-state in each case.

▼ ## 30 WHAT'S THE TOPIC? Gender and interpersonal communication
WHAT'S THE TEXT? Deborah Tannen *That's Not What I Meant: How Conversational Style Makes or Breaks a Relationship*

Deborah Tannen's work has often centred on the implications of issues of gender for inter-personal communication with particular emphasis on spoken language. As such her work bridges the gap between verbal and non-verbal communication and the slightly more formal work on language while at the same time pointing up the artificiality of these kinds of divisions. Tannen herself works in the formal academic context of a university linguistics department and seems a little bemused at those of her students who have given her course on cross-cultural communication credit for saving their marriages. She frames the obvious question 'What can linguistics have to do with saving marriages?' and then goes on to tell us.

At first glance a course on cross-cultural communication might appear quite specialist. On closer examination it turns out to be most general. This is because, as Tannen points out, 'all communication is more or less cross cultural'. She elaborates by underlining some of the cultures that communication crosses:

■ regional cultures
■ ethnic cultures

- religious cultures
- class cultures
- gender cultures.

To which we might add: all of these. Tannen says that these factors 'all result in different ways of talking', not just public talking but also private talking, which is Tannen's focus. She hopes and believes that 'understanding these processes restores a sense of control over our lives, making it possible to improve communication and relationships'. Let us hope that this is true. Read on.

PREFACE

A student who took the course on cross-cultural communication that I teach in the Linguistics Department at Georgetown University commented that the course saved her marriage. At scholarly meetings, my fellow linguists stop me in the hall to tell me that they showed one of my articles to friends or relatives, and it saved their marriages.

What can linguistics have to do with saving marriages? Linguistics is the academic discipline devoted to understanding how language works. Relationships are made, maintained, and broken through talk, so linguistics provides a concrete way of understanding how relationships are made, maintained, and broken. There are branches of linguistics that are concerned mainly with the history or the grammar or the symbolic representation of language. But there are also branches of the field – sociolinguistics, discourse analysis, and anthropological linguistics – that are concerned with understanding how people use language in their everyday lives, and how people from different cultures use language in different ways. This book grows out of these branches of linguistics.

But the student who said my course saved her marriage and her husband are both American. What does cross-cultural communication have to do with them? It has to do with everyone, because all communication is more or less cross-cultural. We learn to use language as we grow up, and growing up in different parts of the country, having different ethnic, religious, or class backgrounds, even just being male or female – all result in different ways of talking, which I call conversational style. And subtle differences in conversational style result in individually minor but cumulatively overwhelming misunderstandings and disappointments.

As the novelist E. M. Forster put it in A *Passage to India*, 'a pause in the wrong place, an intonation misunderstood, and a whole conversation went awry.' When conversations go awry, we look for causes, and usually find them by blaming others or ourselves. The most generous-minded among us blame the relationship. This book shows how much of this blame is misplaced. Bad feelings are often the result of misunderstandings that arise from differences in conversational style.

A talk-show host once introduced me by saying that in his long career he had read many books about speaking, but they were all about public speaking. Yet most of the talk we engage in during our lives is not public but private speaking: talk between two or among a few people. This book is about private speaking: how it works, why it goes well sometimes and badly at other times. It explains the invisible processes of conversational style that shape relationships. Understanding these processes restores a sense of control over our lives, making it possible to improve communication and relationships in all the settings in which people talk to each other: at work, in interviews, in public affairs, and most important of all, at home.

. . .

THE WORKINGS OF CONVERSATIONAL STYLE

The meaning is the metamessage

You're sitting at a bar – or in a coffee shop or at a party – and suddenly you feel lonely. You wonder, 'What do all these people find to talk about that's so important?' Usually the answer is, Nothing. Nothing that's so important. But people don't wait until they have something important to say in order to talk.

Very little of what is said is important for the information expressed in the words. But that doesn't mean that the talk isn't important. It's crucially important, as a way of showing that we are involved with each other, and how we feel about being involved. Our talk is saying something about our relationship.

Information conveyed by the meanings of words is the message. What is communicated about relationships – attitudes toward each other, the occasion, and what we are saying – is the metamessage. And it's metamessages that we react to most strongly. If someone says, 'I'm not angry,' and his jaw is set hard and his words seem to be squeezed out in a hiss, you won't believe the message that he's not angry; you'll believe the metamessage conveyed by the way he said it – that he is. Comments like 'It's not what you said but the way that you said it' or 'Why did you say it like that?' or 'Obviously it's not nothing; something's wrong' are responses to metamessages of talk.

Many of us dismiss talk that does not convey important information as worthless – meaningless small talk if it's a social setting or 'empty rhetoric' if it's public. Such admonitions as 'Skip the small talk,' 'Get to the point,' or 'Why don't you say what you mean?' may seem to be reasonable. But they are reasonable only if information is all that counts. This attitude toward talk ignores the fact that people are emotionally involved with each other and that talking is the major way we establish, maintain, monitor, and adjust our relationships.

Whereas words convey information, how we speak those words – how loud, how fast, with what intonation and emphasis – communicates what we think we're doing when we speak: teasing, flirting, explaining, or chastising; whether we're feeling friendly, angry, or quizzical; whether we want to get close or back off. In other words, how we say what we say communicates social meanings.

Although we continually respond to social meaning in conversation, we have a hard time talking about it because it does not reside in the dictionary definitions of words, and most of us have unwavering faith in the gospel according to the dictionary. It is always difficult to talk about – even to see or think about – forces and processes for which we have no names, even if we feel their impact. Linguistics provides terms that describe the processes of communication and therefore make it possible to see, talk, and think about them.

This chapter introduces some of the linguistic terms that give names to concepts that are crucial for understanding communication – and therefore relationships. In addition to the concept of metamessages – underlying it, in a sense – there are universal human needs that motivate communication: the needs to be connected to others and to be left alone. Trying to honour these conflicting needs puts us in a double bind. The linguistic concept of politeness accounts for the way we serve these needs and react to the double bind – through metamessages in our talk.

Involvement and independence

The philosopher Schopenhauer gave an often-quoted example of porcupines trying to get through a cold winter. They huddle together for warmth, but their sharp quills prick each other, so they pull away. But then they get cold. They have to keep adjusting their closeness and distance to keep from freezing and from getting pricked by their fellow porcupines – the source of both comfort and pain.

We need to get close to each other to have a sense of community, to feel we're not alone in the world. But we need to keep our distance from each other to preserve our independence, so others don't impose on or engulf us. This duality reflects the human condition. We are individual and social creatures. We need other people to survive, but we want to survive as individuals.

Another way to look at this duality is that we are all the same – and all different. There is comfort in being understood and pain in the impossibility of being understood completely. But there is also comfort in being different – special and unique – and pain in being the same as everyone else, just another cog in the wheel.

. . .

Who's reacting?

Communication is a system. Everything that is said is simultaneously an instigation and a reaction, a reaction and an instigation. Most of us tend to focus on
the first part of that process while ignoring or downplaying the second. We see
ourselves as reacting to what others say and do, without realising that their
actions or words are in part reactions to ours, and that our reactions to them
won't be the end of the process but rather will trigger more reactions, in a continuous stream. When problems arise, we sincerely try to solve them, but we're
thinking of intentions, not style. So when styles differ, trying harder to make
things better often means doing more of the same – and making things worse.

The paradox of love and marriage

Why is it so common to find stylistic differences among partners in close relationships? I suspect it is a paradox built into our system of self-arranged
marriage. We often choose our partners on the basis of romantic attraction,
which is sparked by cultural difference. But as we settle in for the long haul, we
expect friendly companionship. And that is most often found in cultural similarity. So the seeds of disappointment are sown in the same field as those of
love.

Yet persistent struggles of the sort described are common among partners from
the same country, the same town – even the same block. This is because many
of our closest and more precious relationships are between men and women,
and men and women are guaranteed to have differences in style. Male–female
conversation is always cross-cultural.

(Tannen 1986: 15–17, 124)

WHAT'S NEXT?

> ➤ List the significant differences the cultures of region, ethnicity, religion, class
>   and gender might have on the way we talk.
> ➤ What are likely to be the major differences between public talking and private
>   talking?

31 WHAT'S THE TOPIC? 'Male' and 'female' talk
WHAT'S THE TEXT? Liz Lochhead 'Men Talk (Rap)'

The poet Liz Lochhead addresses Deborah Tannen's issues in a different mode, with satire and amusement. *Men Talk (Rap)* is a sharply barbed dramatisation of popular prejudices of male and female conversational styles along the lines of the old adage 'Men Talk. Women Gossip'.

Rather than debate or dispute it Lochhead demonstrates her argument by exposing implicitly the irony and hypocrisy at work in it. It is conceived as a rap to give it energy and life but also to suggest that one woman's gossip is another man's credible form of street expression. Crudely the 'mouthpiece' of the poem is a man underlining his own shortcomings by protesting too much about the 'Verbal Diarrhoea' of women.

This man, who likes to think he is a Real Good Listener, actually only wants an audience. He begins:

> Women
>
> Rabbit rabbit rabbit women

He then proceeds to 'rabbit', and so it goes on. Finally he returns to his title, his chorus, his theme:

> Men Talk.
>
> Men
> Think First, Speak Later
> Men Talk.

The key is that by this point no one can believe it because in a simple sense it simply isn't true.

> Women
> Rabbit rabbit rabbit women
> Tattle and titter
> Women prattle
> Women waffle and witter
>
> Men Talk. Men Talk.
>
> Women into Girl Talk
> About Women's Trouble

Trivia 'n' Small Talk
They yap and they babble

Men Talk. Men Talk.

Women yatter
Women chatter
Women chew the fat, women spill the beans
Women aint been takin'
The oh-so good advice in them
Women's Magazines.

A Man Likes A Good Listener.

Oh yeah
I like A Woman
Who likes me enough
Not to nitpick
Not to nag and
Not to interrupt 'cause I call that treason
A woman with the Good Grace
To be struck dumb
By me Sweet Reason. Yes –

A Man Likes a Good Listener

A Real
Man
Likes a Real Good Listener

Women yap yap yap
Verbal Diarrhoea is a Female Disease
Woman she spread she rumours round she
Like Philadelphia Cream Cheese.

Oh
Bossy Women Gossip
Girlish Women Giggle
Women natter, women nag
Women niggle niggle niggle

Men Talk.

Men
Think First, Speak Later
Men Talk.

(Lockhead 1984: 75–6)

➤ What is the difference between the ways in which males and females use language (according to Lochhead's character)?

➤ Compile a list of gendered words. Characterise them as positive or negative. (In *Man Made Language* Dale Spender famously remarked that 'language is not neutral' (Spender 1990: 139).) From whose perspectives are these words positive or negative?

▼ **32 WHAT'S THE TOPIC? Language**
WHAT'S THE TEXT? Stephen Pinker *The Language Instinct*

As a promoter of Evolutionary Psychology Steven Pinker (see Extract 22) is concerned to promote the belief that genetics (the study of the way in which the genome (gene map) informs our appearance and behaviour) holds the key to understanding the ways we behave physically, mentally, and verbally. In his book *The Language Instinct* he brings this approach to bear upon language which 'most educated people', he quips, 'know . . . is man's most important cultural invention'. In fact Pinker lists the knowns about language with great fluency:

■ It is 'the quintessential example of his [man's] capacity to use symbols';
■ It is 'a biologically unprecedented event irrevocably separating him (sic.) from other animals';
■ 'language pervades thought';
■ different languages cause their speakers to 'construe reality in different ways';
■ 'children learn to talk from role models and caregivers';
■ 'English is a zany, logic-defying tongue'; and
■ 'English spelling takes such wackiness to even greater heights'.

Having lulled us into a false sense of security as we mentally tick off these 'truths' about language Pinker makes his play: 'In the pages that follow I will try to convince you that every one of these common opinions is wrong'. Be warned: this is an avowedly hostile, scientific response to those who would argue that language is a human construction. As such his argument has much in common with those of Richard Dawkins who has argued that the human brain continues to evolve beyond its simple Darwinian origins. Interviewed by crime novelist Ian Rankin in 2002 (for his series of television programmes *Ian Rankin's Evil Thoughts*) Dawkins asserted that people are 'machines for survival – one of the things Natural Selection has equipped us with is a very big brain, and that very big brain has in a sense taken off and gone away from its Darwinian roots and now provides us with motivations and desires and strivings which although they ultimately owe their origin to Darwinian Natural Selection are not now directly understandable in those terms'.

In the pages that follow, I will try to convince you that every one of these common opinions is wrong! And they are all wrong for a single reason. Language is not a cultural artifact that we learn the way we learn to tell time or how the federal government works. Instead, it is a distinct piece of the biological makeup of our brains. Language is a complex, specialized skill, which develops in the child spontaneously, without conscious effort or formal instruction, is deployed without awareness of its underlying logic, is qualitatively the same in every individual, and is distinct from more general abilities to process information or behave intelligently. For these reasons some cognitive scientists have described language as a psychological faculty, a mental organ, a neural system, and a computational module. But I prefer the admittedly quaint term 'instinct'. It conveys the idea that people know how to talk in more or less the sense that spiders know how to spin webs. Web-spinning was not invented by some unsung spider genius and does not depend on having had the right education or on having an aptitude for architecture or the construction trades. Rather, spiders spin spider webs because they have spider brains, which give them the urge to spin and the competence to succeed. Although there are differences between webs and words, I will encourage you to see language in this way, for it helps to make sense of the phenomena we will explore.

Thinking of language as an instinct inverts the popular wisdom, especially as it has been passed down in the canon of the humanities and social sciences. Language is no more a cultural invention than is upright posture. It is not a manifestation of a general capacity to use symbols: a three-year old, we shall see, is a grammatical genius, but is quite incompetent at the visual arts, religious iconography, traffic signs, and the other staples of the semiotics curriculum. Though language is a magnificent ability unique to *Homo sapiens* among living species, it does not call for sequestering the study of humans from the domain of biology, for a magnificent ability unique to a particular living species is far from unique in the animal kingdom. Some kinds of bats home in on flying insects using Doppler sonar. Some kinds of migratory birds navigate thousands of miles by calibrating the positions of the constellations against the time of day and year. In nature's talent show we are simply a species of primate with our own act, a knack for communicating information about who did what to whom by modulating the sounds we make when we exhale.

Once you begin to look at language not as the ineffable essence of human uniqueness but as a biological adaptation to communicate information, it is no longer as tempting to see language as an insidious shaper of thought, and, we shall see, it is not. Moreover, seeing language as one of nature's engineering marvels – an organ with 'that perfection of structure and co-adaptation which justly excites our admiration', in Darwin's words – gives us a new respect for your ordinary Joe and the much-maligned English language (or any language). The complexity of language, from the scientist's point of view, is part of our biological birthright; it is not something that parents teach their children or something that must be elaborated in school – as Oscar Wilde said, 'Education is an admirable thing, but it is well to remember from time to time that nothing that is worth knowing can be taught'. A preschooler's tacit knowledge of grammar is more sophisticated than the thickest style manual or the most state-of-the-art computer language system, and the same applies to all healthy human beings, even the notorious syntax-fracturing professional athlete and the, you know, like, inarticulate teenage skateboarder. Finally, since language is the product of a well-engineered biological instinct, we shall see that it is not the nutty barrel of monkeys that entertainer-columnists make it out to be. I will try to restore some dignity to the English vernacular, and will even have some nice things to say about its spelling system.

(Pinker 1994: 4–6)

WHAT'S NEXT?

➤ Pinker's basic argument is that 'language is no more a cultural invention than is upright posture'. What is the influence of culture on language, then?
➤ Read David Crystal *The English Language* (2002) London: Penguin.

▼ **33 WHAT'S THE TOPIC? Narrative and language**
   WHAT'S THE TEXT? Paul Auster *New York*
   Trilogy

What Pinker says about language throws interesting light on famous cases of isolation in history and myth. The central question in all of these is 'would a child brought up in complete isolation from other humans develop language?' The answer you give to this question reveals a lot about your theory of what language is. Presumably nurturists would argue that the child, bereft of the examples of role models and caregivers, would lack the capacity to use language. On the other hand if language is, as Pinker believes, an instinct then some sort of language development will be likely, possibly inevitable.

The novelist Paul Auster reviews some of these cases in 'City of Glass', the first part of his *New York Trilogy*, as part of a sequence that deals with such a child – Peter Stillman.

The investigator Quinn, who is looking into the Stillman case, is also, through Auster, demonstrating a primary function of language: the facility it gives for expressing the imagination; for storytelling; for lying, if you like (after all the artist Pablo Picasso claimed that 'Art is a Lie that makes us realise Truth').

Here is a digression, a discussion, but also a narrative of sorts which without language we would be able to neither experience nor describe.

Quinn had heard of cases like Peter Stillman before. Back in the days of his other life, not long after his own son was born, he had written a review of a book about the wild boy of Aveyron, and at the time he had done some research on the subject. As far as he could remember, the earliest account of such an experiment appeared in the writings of Herodotus: the Egyptian pharaoh Psamtik isolated two infants in the seventeenth century BC and commanded the servant in charge of them never to utter a word in their presence. According to Herodotus, a notoriously unreliable chronicler, the children learned to speak – their first word being the Phrygian word for bread. In the Middle Ages, the Holy Roman Emperor Frederick II repeated the experiment, hoping to discover man's true 'natural language' using similar methods, but the children died before they ever spoke any words. Finally, in what was undoubtedly a hoax, the early sixteenth-century King of Scotland, James IV, claimed that Scottish children isolated in the same manner wound up speaking 'very good Hebrew'.

Cranks and idealogues, however, were not the only ones interested in the subject. Even so sane and sceptical a man as Montaigne considered the question carefully, and in his most important essay, the *Apology for Raymond Sebond*, he wrote: 'I believe that a child who had been brought up in complete solitude, remote from all association (which would be a hard experiment to make), would have some sort of speech to express his ideas. And it is not credible that Nature has denied us this resource that she has given to many other animals. But it is yet to be known what language this child would speak; and what has been said about it by conjecture has not much appearance of truth.'

Beyond the cases of such experiments, there were also the cases of accidental isolation – children lost in the woods, sailors marooned on islands, children brought up by wolves – as well as the cases of cruel and sadistic parents who locked up their children, chained them to beds, beat them in closets, tortured them for no other reason than the compulsion of their own madness – and Quinn had read through the extensive literature devoted to these stories. There was the Scottish sailor Alexander Selkirk (thought by some to be the model for Robinson Crusoe) who had lived for four years alone on an island off the coast of Chile and who, according to the ship captain who rescued him in 1708, 'had so much forgot his own language for want of use, that we could scarce understand him'. 'less than twenty years later, Peter of Hanover, a wild child of about fourteen, who had been discovered mute and naked in a forest outside the

German town of Hamelin, was brought to the English court under the special protection of George I. Both Swift and Defoe were given a chance to see him, and the experience led to Defoe's 1726 pamphlet, *Mere Nature Delineated*. Peter never learned to speak, however, and several months later was sent to the country, where he lived to the age of seventy, with no interest in sex, money, or other worldly matters. Then there was the case of Victor, the wild boy of Aveyron, who was found in 1800. Under the patient and meticulous care of Dr Itard, Victor learned some of the rudiments of speech, but he never progressed beyond the level of a small child. Even better known than Victor was Kaspar Hauser, who appeared one afternoon in Nuremberg in 1828, dressed in an outlandish costume and barely able to utter an intelligible sound. He was able to write his name, but in all other respects he behaved like an infant. Adopted by the small town and entrusted to the care of a local teacher, he spent his days sitting on the floor playing with toy horses, eating only bread and water. Kaspar nevertheless developed. He became an excellent horseman, became obsessively neat, had a passion for the colours red and white, and by all account displayed extraordinary memory, especially for names and faces. Still, he preferred to remain indoors, shunned bright light and, like Peter of Hanover, never showed any interest in sex or money. As the memory of his past gradually came back to him, he was able to recall how he had spent many years on the floor of a darkened room, fed by a man who never spoke to him or let himself be seen. Not long after these disclosures, Kaspar was murdered by an unknown man with a dagger in a public park.

It had been years now since Quinn had allowed himself to think of these stories. The subject of children was too painful for him, especially children who had suffered, had been mistreated, had died before they could grow up. If Stillman was the man with the dagger, come back to avenge himself on the boy whose life he had destroyed, Quinn wanted to be there to stop him. He knew he could not bring his own son back to life, but at least he could prevent another from dying. It had suddenly become possible for him to do this, and standing there on the street now, the idea of what lay before him loomed up like a terrible dream. He had thought of the little coffin that held his son's body and how he had seen it on the day of the funeral being lowered into the ground. That was silence. It did not help, perhaps, that his son's name had also been Peter.

(Auster 1987: 33–5)

WHAT'S NEXT?

➤ What has this passage to tell us about language and narratives (stories)?
➤ Watch François Truffaut's 1969 film *L'Enfant sauvage*.
➤ Watch Werner Herzog's 1975 film *The Enigma of Kaspar Hauser*.
➤ Read Michael Newton *Savage Girls and Wild Boys* (2002) London: Faber.

COMMUNICATION STUDIES: THE ESSENTIAL RESOURCE

34 WHAT'S THE TOPIC? Language change I
WHAT'S THE TEXT? Mark Jones 'The lost art of coining a phrase'

One of the primary characteristics of language is its flexibility and mutability. Language is constantly in the process of change but we mustn't for a moment imagine that this is a neutral process. Language is clearly a system of representation, which interestingly is exactly what Louis Althusser suggested that ideology is. That language is ideology or at least ideological is implicit in Mark Jones's article 'The lost art of coining a phrase' which concerns, and is concerned about, the ways in which the English language is being extended.

Jones is not so much concerned about what is being included in the new online edition of the *Oxford English Dictionary* but rather where these neologisms (new words) are being, in his word, forged. (The English verb 'to forge' can, fascinatingly, mean either 'to make' or 'to make falsely' or 'to counterfeit for purposes of fraud'.) 'New words are being minted', he suggests, 'at a rate not seen since Shakespeare's time'. The issue for Jones though is elsewhere: 'The only group of people who don't seem to be extending the world domination of English are the English'. Put simply: 'Our linguistic balance of payments is at crisis point. We import everything and export nothing'.

Homer Simpson has joined Dr Johnson. The yellow dad from the Simpsons and the dead English thinker in the white wig are now partners in lexicographical history. Dr Johnson gave us the first Dictionary of the English Language. Homer (a good literary name, that) has given us 'doh'.

Doh has a proud place in the new online edition of the *Oxford English Dictionary*. I hope it stays there too, because doh is one of those genuinely useful new words for an experience that has thus far been unnamed. Doh means the penny has dropped: it's used at that moment when I or someone equally stupid works out something blindingly obvious.

The literate Bostonians have a poetic synonym for the same thing: light dawns over marblehead (try saying it in a Loyd Grossman voice). Doh, I think we will agree, is much neater.

But doh is very unlikely to outlive Homer any more than wakey-wakey outlived Billy Cotton. (What? Who?) There are too many new words pushing for attention and too many big companies pushing new words at us. Lexicography has become big business. Two years ago, Microsoft linked up with the publishers Bloomsbury to produce Encarta, a multi-million dollar project claiming to be the first true dictionary of 'world English'. Not that the likes of the OED and

CONTINUED

Longman's are shrinking into dusty non-competitiveness. The doh story is only the latest in a long line of new-word press releases pushed out to a compliant media. We have discovered a rich new seam of *Zeitgeist*, and the publishers are neologising all the way to the bank.

New English words are being minted – forged? – at a rate not seen since Shakespeare's time. The bewildering fecundity of Elizabethan language was an extraordinary phenomenon produced by an extraordinary society. It was that teeming, straggling heap of a language that Dr Johnson's dictionary was designed to tame. Some writers, such as Jonathan Swift, wanted us to follow the French example and create an academy to regulate and limit the flow of new and made-up words. Johnson would have none of it: he scorned the lexicographer who deluded himself that he could 'embalm his language, and secure it from corruption and decay?' The patriotic Johnson won his historic battle with the French as surely as a Wellington or a Nelson. The nationalised French language has been dwindling in relative size and global reach ever since. (Apropos which, when was the last time you heard a chic new Frenchism? Once, you would not have been considered a civilised *boulevardier* without a scattering of *mots justes*, *je ne sais quois* and BCBGs). English, wrenched and stretched and pummelled by a tireless gabble of journos, admen, sports commentators, rappers, surfers, druggies, cops, criminals, geeks and gurus, carries on growing and dominating the global tongue.

The only group of people who don't seem to be extending the world domination of English are the English. Johnson's language is now being minted elsewhere. There are huge factories churning out the stuff in Silicon Valley, San Fernando Valley, New York, Sydney, Hong Kong and Kingston. In comparison, we have a cottage industry occasionally putting out some crafted piece of retro-slang for the niche American audience: Austin Healeys for car enthusiasts, Austin Powers for connoisseurs of dated London hip-speak.

Our linguistic balance of payments is at crisis point. We import everything and export precious little. Think of the major slang expressions of the past couple of decades that have entered the language and stayed. Yuppies, wired, cool, go for it, fashion victims, rubberneck, emote, double whammy, synergy, cyberspace – mostly made in the USA, all adopted enthusiastically by us. We couldn't even find an expression to denote our growing unease with the Hollywood habit of pouring lurid troubles in public ears. 'Too much information' had to come from America too.

In the customised spelling dictionary on my computer, I find words like aspirational, chocoholic, dotcom, morph, prequel and thirtysomething. We probably don't even recognise such coinages as Americanisms any longer, any more than we recall how American imports such as calculate, lengthy and presidential antagonised the Victorians (as, indeed, did 'antagonise').

The Victorians would be in deep trouble today, as black American street culture teaches us to redefine wicked and bad. The language of public affairs is not our own.

White American spin doctors made us ask 'Where's the beef?' and parrot 'It's the economy, stupid'. I don't think we can expect any buzzwords from the British election to storm the US linguistic charts.

We haven't lost the ability to coin vivid and vigorous expressions. The fine Anglo-Saxon tradition of gutsy little slang words for love, sex and money is still going strong. The Americans and Australians, with their incessant –y endings (scary, freaky), have nothing like snog and dosh, shag and sprog.

Only a British charity (Comic Relief) would use 'stonking' and 'pants' in its publicity material. Only an English TV chef would resurrect an old Anglo-Indian word like 'pukka'. Our TV writers are just as prolific as their American counterparts. Years after Dad's Army, we still don't panic and they still don't like it up 'em. 'Suits you' and 'loadsamoney' may well stand the test of dictionary time. New British creatures appear from the research surveys and style pages all the time: white van man, ladettes, Essex girls etc.

We've just lost the knack of getting our fellow English-speakers to pick up our phrases when we've finished with them. As an export phenomenon, British coinage is about as successful as British beef. It wasn't ever thus. Within a couple of years of the Beatles first appearing, we had the whole world sounding fab, groovy and gear. When the next biggest pop phenomenon came along, the Spice Girls had to put up websites to help their young fans understand what they were saying.

Perhaps Tony's Cronies or the Portillistas can do something to boost our flagging word economy. You can't help feeling, though, that those purely local verbal phenomena may soon be on the endangered list too.

(Jones 2001: 13)

WHAT'S NEXT?

➤ Make a list of currently popular slang expressions. Where do these come from? (Film? Television? Music?)
➤ Which of these is most likely to last reach the dictionary?

The *Daily Mail* takes a more descriptive approach to language's ingenuity, reporting the advent of text message abbreviations in the formal context of the *Concise Oxford English Dictionary*. 'To the linguistic purist', they argue, 'they may well be an abomination', but, 'in a world demanding instant communication they are here to stay'. What the *OED*, another significant abbreviation, confers is legitimacy: this is the proof that texting has arrived.

Slang, it has been said, is always the poetry of its age and perhaps that is the other reading of 'the inventiveness of the mobile messengers'. It is also fair to say that for some of these inventive PPL legitimacy is not what texting is all about. The fact that sending phone text messages is 'a second language to millions of youngsters' might also suggest that sub-cultural identity rather than an outing in the *OED* might be the more significant issue. Texting is perhaps more about outlook and lifestyle than any dictionary can contain or convey.

> ### DICTIONARY EXPANDS INTO MOBILE AGE
>
> To the linguistic purist, they may well be an abomination. But in a world demanding instant communication, they are here to stay.
>
> Text message abbreviations, which have evolved into a new language alongside the mobile phone boom, have found their way into the Oxford English Dictionary.
>
> SMS, or short messaging service, has been given its entry. It features dozens of examples of the shorthand, developed to save space and time when sending phone text messages and now a second language to millions of youngsters.
>
> Academics have raised fears of the effect on children's literacy. But the OED is clearly anxious not to be left behind. Examples which have found a place in the dictionary are HAND (Have A Nice Day), THKQ (thankyou) and PPL (people).
>
> Others are WKND for weekend PCM for please call me, and SIT for stay in touch.
>
> The inventiveness of the mobile messagers stretches further than words, however, and the dictionary dons have not ignored that fact. They have also included so-called emoticons, defined by the OED as 'representations of facial expressions which can be formed with keyboard or keypad characters'.

Most common among these are :-) and :-(which, viewed sideways show smiling or glum faces and are used to mean happy or sad.

Judy Pearsall, publishing manager for English Dictionaries said: 'We have been monitoring the phenomenal growth of text messaging with great attention.

'Its influence is now such that we felt it was time to treat it as a legitimate part of English.'

The latest version of the dictionary also includes several new words which have become commonly used in the 21st century. *Ladette*, the kind of hard-living, pint swilling girl best characterised by Zoe Ball, makes an entry, as does *hottie*, a U.S. word for attractive woman.

Number One, as in very short haircut, makes it as well as *fusion*, in its latest incarnation as a type of cooking incorporating eastern and western influences. R&B, or Rhythm and Blues, which once defined the Rolling Stones and their like, has now been adopted by the music business to refer to modern soul such as that produced by Destiny's Child.

'We are continually monitoring changes to the language,' said Miss Pearsall. 'New words are constantly being introduced and existing ones take on new meanings.'

WHAT'S NEXT?

➤ What do you think about the new additions to the *Oxford English Dictionary*? Which would you not admit?

▼ ### 36 WHAT'S THE TOPIC? Power in groups
WHAT'S THE TEXT? Peter Hartley *Group Communication*

Power is exercised by people in all manner of different ways: on a one-to-one basis, within groups, remotely, across distance, via broadcast media. Within groups power frequently resides in role. Who does what, what are their roles, in what structure do they function, are all important features of behaviour in groups. Before we move to look at the exercise of power and leadership within more formal work groups it is instructive to take a look at Peter Hartley's account of how power is exercised in less formal groups. The groups might be less formal but there is no doubting the very real character of the power being exercised.

POWER, STATUS AND AUTHORITY

One of the most challenging exercises which is sometimes used in group training is to ask the members of the group to line themselves up in a way which represents their relative power or status in the group. Imagine doing this exercise with a group which you are a member of: what would be the result? How would members react?

This exercise *cannot* be recommended as a 'fun game' to while away some idle group time. The fact is that it will almost inevitably stir up very strong emotions and reactions in group members and this reinforces one main point of this chapter: groups do develop status hierarchies, and these hierarchies can be very important and sometimes very destructive.

Different power structures

One line of research has been to identify different types of power which we can exert over one another. The typical list distinguishes five types:

- reward, whereby I have power over you because I can give you certain rewards.
- coercive, whereby I have power over you because I can punish you or threaten you in certain ways.
- legitimate, whereby I have power over you because you recognise that this is fair or legitimate. This is really the notion of authority which we discuss separately alter on.
- referent, whereby I have power over you because you identify with me or wish to be like me in certain ways. Fan worship or adulation is a common example of referent power.
- expert, whereby I have power over you because you recognise that I am an expert in specific areas.

These different types have very different implications. For example, if I obey you because of coercive power then I will be unlikely to continue to obey you if you do not keep me under fairly strict surveillance. If I obey you because of expert power, then you will not need to monitor me as I accept that what you say is right. These two examples also highlight the importance of perceptions. I must recognise the power that you have in order to respond to it, and there must be enough inducement to make me give up other alternatives. If you are trying to coerce me to change my beliefs then you may not succeed if these beliefs are very fundamental.

Another related issue is the tactics which people can use to realise these power bases and the effects that they have. Tactics can vary in terms of a number of dimensions:

- strength: tactics can be strong, as in a direct threat, or weak, as in dropping hints.
- rationality: for example, tactics can rely on rationality as in logical persuasion or can rely on emotional demands.
- laterality: tactics can be unilateral and have no concern for the other party or be more reciprocal as in discussion.

These dimensions are important both in terms of the effectiveness of the tactic and the way that the person using it is seen by other members of the group. For example, Falbo observed people in discussion groups who had been primed to use different tactics. Members who used weak/rational tactics were seen much more positively than members who used strong/non-rational tactics.

How power and status are demonstrated

Some of the most interesting examples of the realities of power and status in everyday groups were published by W.F. Whyte over half a century ago. He risked life and limb (or at least limb) by joining a street corner gang as a participant observer. He interviewed all the gang members and made extensive notes on interaction and communication. One specific event which highlighted the importance of the status hierarchy was the bowling match where Doc, the gang leader, showed an uncharacteristic loss of form. His score was overtaken by Alec, who had very low status. After some barracking from the other members, it came as no surprise that Alec's accuracy went on a downward spiral and Doc came through as winner.

Whyte observed another illustration of status pressures in his restaurant study where there was a conflict between the formal and informal systems. The cooks, who regarded themselves as high status, resented taking orders direct from the waitresses, who were regarded as low status. The solution to this was the invention of the spike, which became a standard feature of the fast food restaurant. The waitress wrote the customers' orders and then placed them on the metal spike by the cooking area. The cooks took the orders from the spike and dealt with them in the appropriate order. This re-established the cooks' sense of autonomy and high status as they did not have to react directly to instructions from waitresses. Having to develop this intermediate step may seem trivial or even insulating from an outsider's viewpoint but many issues of status are based around symbolic features of the situation.

(Hartley 1997: 112–14)

➤ Undertake Hartley's activity on paper for yourself. Mark members of your group according to their status and influence.

➤ Identify the forms that power takes in the groups that you are familiar with.

▼ 37 WHAT'S THE TOPIC? Leadership and groups
WHAT'S THE TEXT? Gerald Cole *Management: Theory and Practice*

Of course much communication theory is practically inclined, none more so than that pertaining to group communication. Here much of the research has a business bias and is directed in a serious way to maximising output (that is, productivity). In businesses of various kinds the dynamics of group work is more than an abstract idea, it often determines the difference between success and failure. 'Leadership' in these contexts often reads as 'management' and is concerned with strategies of motivation and coercion: persuading by coaxing or pressurising.

It is in this vein that Gerald Cole offers his useful review of leadership theory: he is at pains throughout to stress the relationship of the theory to practice in the work situation. His starting point is that leadership is a function of groups and their behaviour, that leadership is a term that describes some important thing that groups do. This leads him to leadership styles and ultimately theories. He stresses also the human element involved when he points out that leadership 'is essentially a human process at work in organisations'.

The crux of every management job lies in the job-holder's capacity to obtain the commitment of people to the objectives of the organization, which is another way of saying 'to exercise appropriate leadership'. Leadership is a concept which has fascinated Man for centuries, but only in recent years has any kind of *theory* of leadership emerged. . . .

LEADERSHIP: THEORY AND PRACTICE

Introduction

1. This chapter describes and comments on a number of the theoretical and practical aspects of leadership in the work situation. A review of the main theories of leadership is followed by a discussion of the alternative styles of leadership available, in practice, to a person in a management or supervisory position.

2. Before attempting a working definition of 'leadership', it would be appropriate to reflect briefly on the various types of leader which have been identified, and to consider some of the practical difficulties arising from these. The most important types of leader are as follows:

a. the **Charismatic** leader, whose influence springs mainly from personality e.g. Napoleon, Hitler, Churchill, Billy Graham and others. The difficulty with charismatic leadership is that few people possess the exceptional qualities required to transform all around them into willing followers! Another issue is that personal qualities, or traits, of leadership cannot be acquired by training, they can only be modified by it.

b. the **Traditional** leader, whose position is assured by birth e.g. kings, queens and tribal chieftains. This is another category to which few people can aspire. Except in the small family business, there are few opportunities for traditional leadership at work.

c. the **Situational** leader, whose influence can only be effective by being in the right place at the right time e.g. the butler in J.M. Barrie's 'The Admirable Crichton'. This kind of leadership is too temporary in nature to be of much value in a business. What is looked for is someone who is capable of assuming a leadership role in a variety of situations over a period of time.

d. the **Appointed** leader, whose influence arises directly out of his position e.g. most managers and supervisors. This is the bureaucratic type of leadership, where legitimate power springs from the nature and scope of the position within the hierarchy. The problem here is that, although the powers of the *position* may be defined, the job-holder may not be able to implement them because of weak personality, lack of adequate training or other factors.

e. the **Functional** leader, who secures his leadership position by what he does, rather than by what he is. In other words, a functional leader adapts his behaviour to meet the competing needs of his situation. This particular type will be looked at more closely later on in the chapter.

3. Leadership, then is something more than just personality or accident or appointment. It is intimately linked with *behaviour*. It is essentially a human process at work in organizations. As a working definition, leadership can be described as 'a dynamic process in a group whereby one individual influences

the others to contribute voluntarily to the achievement of group tasks in a given situation.' There are several points which can be made about this definition. *Firstly*, leadership is a dynamic process, not a static one. This implies that a range of leadership styles is preferable to any one 'best style'. *Secondly*, the role of the leader is to direct the group towards group goals. In an informal, or unofficial, group these roles will have been agreed by the group itself; in a formal group, the goals will have been set mainly, if not exclusively, by senior managers outside the group. *Thirdly*, the style of leadership and the reactions of the group will be determined considerably by the situation concerned (the task, external pressures etc).

4. The basic elements of the above definition of leadership are four in number as illustrated.

LEADER • skills • knowledge • personality	TASKS/GOALS
SUBORDINATES • skills • motivation	ENVIRONMENT/ SITUATION

The key leadership variables

The key variables are: (1) the leader, (2) tasks/goals, (3) the group members (subordinates), and (4) the environment/situation. Taken together these variables form the total leadership situation, and the art of leadership is to find the best balance between them in the light of the total situation.

Theories of leadership

5. Ideas about leadership in management range from the 'ideal' approaches to the Scientific Managers and the Human Relations School to the pragmatic, or adaptive, approaches of the Contingency theorists. The theories which have been put forward are generally classified under 'Trait theories', 'Style theories' and 'Contingency theories'. These will be looked at in turn.

6. **Trait Theories**. As we saw earlier in the Manual, in the discussion of classical management ideas, the debate was usually led by practising managers who were strong characters in their own right. Part of their success was undoubtedly due to personal qualities, and it is perhaps not surprising that the earliest studies that were undertaken into leadership focussed their attention on the *qualities* required for effective leaders. Handy (*Understanding Organizations*, 1976) mentions that by 1950 over 100 studies of this kind had been undertaken, but that the

number of common traits or characteristics identified by the researchers was only 5% of the total! It has proved an impossible task to identify the particular traits or characteristics that separate leaders from non-leaders. Of those traits which do appear more frequently, intelligence, energy and resourcefulness are perhaps the most representative.

7. **Style Theories**. The interest in the human factor at work which was stimulated by the researchers of Human Relations, and taken up by the social psychologists who followed them, led logically to an interest in leadership as an aspect of *behaviour* at work, rather than of personal characteristics. Since the 1950's in particular, several theories about leadership, or management, style have been put forward. These have tended to be expressed in terms of authoritarian versus democratic styles, or people-orientation versus task orientation. In some cases, despite acknowledged inconsistencies in the theories themselves, style theories have led to quite useful devices for improving training for leadership. A selection of the best-known style theories is discussed below.

8. **Authoritarian–Democratic**. Three examples of this approach to management style are as follows:

a.   D. McGregor's Theory X manager – tough, autocratic and supporting tight controls with punishment-reward systems – the authoritarian. The contrasting style is that of the Theory Y manager – benevolent, participative and believing in self-controls – the democrat. These styles flow from the assumptions about people that are the original basis of Theory X and Theory Y . . .

b.   Rensis Likert's four management systems:

System 1 – the exploitive-authoritative system, which is the epitome of the authoritarian style.

System 2 – the benevolent-authoritative system, which is basically a paternalistic style.

System 3 – the consultative system, which moves towards greater democracy and teamwork.

System 4 – the participative-group system, which is the ultimate democratic style.

. . .

c.   Tannenbaum and Schmidt's model of a continuum of leadership styles, ranging from authoritarian behaviour at one end to democratic behaviour at the other, as illustrated . . . below:

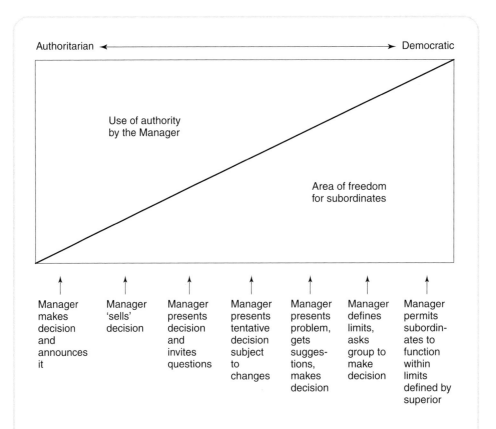

Authoritarian ←————————————————————————→ Democratic

Use of authority
by the Manager

Area of freedom
for subordinates

| Manager makes decision and announces it | Manager 'sells' decision | Manager presents decision and invites questions | Manager presents tentative decision subject to changes | Manager presents problem, gets sugges- tions, makes decision | Manager defines limits, asks group to make decision | Manager permits subordin- ates to function within limits defined by superior |

A continuum of leadership styles (adapted from Tannenbaum and Schmidt, Harvard Business Review, 1957)

9. The implication behind the three approaches is that managers have a basic choice between being either authoritarian or democratic, and that the best style – the ideal – is a democratic one. In practice, the either/or choice proposed by the theorists may be somewhat artificial. Much will depend on the other elements of the leadership situation, as in the figure above. In some circumstances an authoritarian style could be more effective than a democratic style, and vice versa. The suggestion that a democratic style is generally preferable to an authoritarian one has been criticised on the grounds that whilst this may apply to current trends in Western industrialised nations, it need not apply at all in other cultures. The main weakness of these approaches is that they place too much emphasis on the *leader's* behaviour to the exclusion of the other elements or variables of leadership.

(Cole 1984: 202–7)

➤ Find your own examples of the types of leader described earlier in the extract.

➤ Cole suggests 'in some circumstances an authoritarian style could be more effective than a democratic style, and vice versa'. Suggest circumstances in which each of these styles might be effective and circumstances in which each of these styles might be ineffective.

PART 3: COMMUNICATION PRACTICE

'Please do not understand me too quickly.'

André Gide

Part 3 of this book addresses a number of questions:

- What is effective communication?
- What are some of the factors that should be taken into account when designing communication research?
- How should communication research be undertaken?
- In what ways can the results of research be written up and presented?
- In what ways can writing be made more effective, more impressive, more original?
- What are some of the problems that affect communicating orally?
- What is rhetoric – and are there any problems with its use?

So this part of the book is about communication practice, and about communication in practice. It begins with a consideration of some of the key problems facing anyone attempting purposeful communication. It then moves to three key phases of communication research: before, during and after. In other words, it examines features of the design of communication research, it rehearses some of the ethical aspects to be borne in mind when designing research, it looks at some more contemporary influences on communication research, it looks at the internet as an increasingly used research tool in Communication Studies, and then moves to some considerations of effective communication practice in writing.

▼ 38 WHAT'S THE TOPIC? Effective communication practice
WHAT'S THE TEXT? Carl Sagan and Frank Drake 'The Pioneer 10 plaque'

Any part of a book which assumes to advise its readers about effective communication must begin with a singular message: be sensitive at all times to the needs of your audience. Of course being specific about precisely what we mean by this can be a little more

COMMUNICATION PRACTICE **121**

difficult. However, it is important to realise that a fundamental weakness in communicating with other people can be our failure to empathise or to put ourselves into the position of the recipient(s) of our message. If we endeavour to make this imaginative leap then we are much more likely to communicate effectively than if we simply assume the recipient will understand.

Let us start with a difficult communication problem. How do we go about communicating with an audience we have never met and about whom we know almost nothing. This was the challenge confronting the creator of a message attached to the Pioneer 10 space probe launched in 1972 and destined for the deepest space. It was hoped that if there were intelligent life forms out there in the universe able to read the message it would tell them something about the earth and its population. Here is the message in the form of a plaque together with an explanation of the problems posed in creating the message.

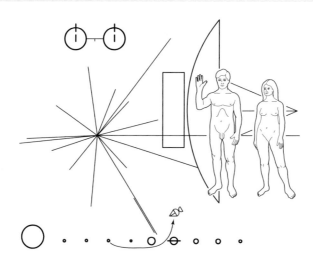

As you read these words, this picture is on its way to infinity. It is part of Pioneer 10, a space probe launched last spring. Late in 1973, Pioneer 10 will pass close to Jupiter and radio back man's first close up pictures of the giant planet. Then Jupiter's powerful gravity will act as a slingshot to hurl the spacecraft out of our solar system and into the Milky Way galaxy. With it will go man's first airmail letter into space.

The message is there because astronomers saw a chance that was too good to pass up. They persuaded NASA to attach a plaque, with the picture, to Pioneer's antenna supports. The plaque is made of aluminium but has been anodized with erosion-resistant gold to help its preservation. On the tiny chance that Pioneer will be spotted by some life-form in the galaxy, the plaque contains important information about earth and its people. What is more its message is meant to have meaning even for beings unfamiliar with human logical processes.

The two designers, Carl Sagan and Frank Drake, are from Cornell University. The artist is Linda Sagan, wife of Carl. They put a lot of thought into their message and tried to communicate a variety of things, including:

■ representative earthlings, one with his hand upraised in a gesture of greeting
■ a sideways, scaled view of Pioneer 10
■ a starburst pattern representing 14 specific stars in our galaxy
■ a representation of our solar system, showing that Pioneer 10 left from the third planet from the sun

As you think about it, the message seems to carry a lot of information in a small space. All very ingenious.

But as you think about it you are thinking with human brains. You are using information that got stored in your mind without consciously knowing it. You look at the picture from a human point of view.

Now try to free your mind from those built-in assumptions and earthling points of view. Try to see the message as though you were a creature in space with no knowledge at all of human culture. Now a whole new world of confusion arises:

■ Suppose your sense organs do not respond to the same band of electro-magnetic waves as do human eyes. Then you will never 'see' the message in the first place.
■ Let's suppose you can see the plaque. Your problems are far from over. You have never seen a human figure so you have no way of knowing that the two figures represent living creatures. You might see them as wire constructions with loose bits and pieces floating weightlessly in between. You might even decide that the creatures who sent the plaque are repre-sented by the hydrogen atoms. 'Creatures from this planet,' you tell yourself, 'have two round bodies connected by a long, straight tube.'
■ Maybe you guess that the two things are living creatures. But your culture associates 'up' with the bottom of the picture, not the top. So you say to yourself, 'These creatures have two heads, and their feet consist of a rounded object that they probably bounce around on.'

Perhaps your culture does not understand perspective and foreshortening. A *human* looking at the female figure subconsciously assumes that three of her fin-gers are not shown. But you, as a spaceling, decide that the right hand only has two parts.

Let's say that you do understand foreshortening so you get the business about the right hand. But then you assume that if the spacecraft is shown behind the

human figures, it would be much larger than the human *if placed next to them.* So the whole message of the size relationship is lost.

The man has his right hand raised in greeting. But there are cultures even on earth – among them the Chinese and the Indian – in which the raised hand is not considered a gesture of friendly greeting. Then how would you, as a space being, ever get this idea?

Now your eye wanders along the bottom line. You see a curving line with a point at one end. If you were a human you would understand the symbolism of a directional arrow. But you are not a human, Your ancestors never had the equivalent of bows and arrows. So the symbol means nothing to you, and you completely miss its message.

Because of your sensory equipment you do not see planets as circles but only as vague blobs of light. Therefore, the significance of the circles on the plaque escapes you completely.

This list of confusions could go on, but by now the message should be clear: People can recognize only what they know. Moreover, when you use language, you must keep the other person in mind. What is his background? Are you assuming that he knows things that he really doesn't know? Are you giving him all the information he needs?

Always keep this in mind: You know what you mean. But does the other person?

(Image: Carl Sagan and Frank Drake, NASA, 1973; author of text unknown)

WHAT'S NEXT?

➤ Much of this extract has been about the problems created by polysemy.
➤ Collect some more examples of polysemic texts.
➤ Identify those factors which could diminish the polysemic dimensions of a text.

Now that we have looked at some of the problems generated by communication texts (although we will return to these later in this part) let's start to look at how we can research communication. In our examination of ways in which data can be collected, analysed and presented, always remember that effective communication research is effective communication practice.

Drawing on the methods of social science Communication Studies finds a rich field in the observation of human behaviour. It is very likely that at some point in your studies of Communication you will be required to undertake research in a practical way into the field of human communication. This could well involve observation. For most of the population 'people watching' is an important and pleasurable element of their social lives. For the academic researcher, however, it is important that any observation and recording of human behaviour is set up according to sound principles. One of the chief qualities of a properly formulated research project is that the methodology, or way of carrying it out, is absolutely clear. The reason for this is that it allows other researchers in the same field to validate this research, if necessary by repeating the study using exactly the same methodology.

Before starting on any study it is clearly important that you spend some time deciding on the specifics of your methodology. It is also important that once you have decided how to carry out your study, you stick faithfully to the methodology you have chosen.

In research, there are two different approaches to collecting data. The first is called quantitative. Basically this means, as the name implies, collecting large quantities of data and analysing it. The United Kingdom census is an example of a quantitative survey. It carries out a survey which amasses a large amount of data about the population of the United Kingdom.

Perhaps more important to Communication Studies is qualitative research. Rather than seeking to amass large amounts of information, this type of research tries to get high quality information by focusing in detail on a small sample. An example of this is the ethnographic research undertaken by David Morley in the 1970s, in what is called the *Nationwide* studies, to find out information about the uses to which audiences put media such as television. This research consisted of such activities as in-depth interviews and the observation of people in their own homes. Initially published in 1980 Morley's *The Nationwide Audience* succeeded in 'looking at how one text could be decoded in different ways by different groups of social subjects' (Ang 1996: 38).

In his book *Introduction to Social Research*, Keith Punch looks at a range of methodologies for observational research. As its name implies, this is the type of research that relies on 'people watching' by observing human behaviour and recording it. Clearly this approach is likely to be particularly appropriate to a Communication Studies research project which seeks, for example, to explore turn taking in conversation.

He begins by outlining the different approaches to observation. He then talks about 'structured' and 'unstructured' approaches. For Punch these terms are a variation on the concepts of qualitative and quantitative. Unstructured approaches allow the researcher to work in a more open-ended way. For example rather then predetermining categories into which the data collected will fit, the observer is free to decide and organise the categories according to what the research throws up. This approach is closer to a qualitative methodology rather than the number crunching approach of quantitative analysis where categories clearly have to be predetermined if useful data is to be obtained.

As Punch remarks 'observation has a long tradition in the social sciences'. So you won't be surprised to find other researchers extracted in this book namechecked here. Here you will find references to other writers featured in this book: this extract both looks forward to Georg Simmel (Extract 75) and back to Erving Goffman (Extract 23).

OBSERVATION

. . .

Formal sociology traces back to Simmel, who studied the forms, structures and patterns in social interaction, based on his own direct observation: 'If society is conceived as interaction among individuals, the description of the forms of this interaction is the task of the science of society' (1950: 21-2). Contemporary practitioners of formal sociology often incorporate symbolic interactionist principles, and prefer to use full videotaped recordings of observations, often in such contrived situations as laboratories.

Dramaturgical sociology became popular with Goffman, who described his method as 'unsystematic naturalistic observation' in order to study how people interact, form relationships, accomplish meaning in their lives, and, especially, how they construct their self-presentations and carry them off in front of others. Researchers in the dramaturgical tradition have been more attentive to the observational method than Goffman, but have still relied mainly on unstructured, naturalistic recording techniques, whether working individually or in teams. The method has obvious similarities with participant observation.

Studies of the public realm extend the dramaturgical approach, and have developed into a research area in their own right. They address a wide range of issues, cover a wide range of public places, and use observational strategies which vary in researcher involvement, researcher openness, the use of teams and gender issues.

In *auto-observation*, sociologists study themselves and their companions. The use of self as a research tool goes back to the origins of sociology, and can be seen in the writings of Dilthey and Weber. Existential sociology has developed from this line of thinking. This observational approach offers great depth, yielding insights about core meanings and experiences, while raising questions about the role of the observer-researcher.

In *ethnomethodology*, the focus is on how everyday life is constructed. Since much of the interest is in processes below the surface of conscious awareness, at the taken-for-granted level, many ethnomethodologists favour observational techniques over interview and self-report data. Observation includes listening as well as looking, and everyday face-to-face interaction depends heavily on both verbal and visual behaviour. Therefore, alongside observation, some contemporary ethnomethodolgists have directed much of their attention to conversation analysis, since they see language as the fundamental base of communication and social order. Using audio- and videotaping, they gather data that can be analysed later, and repeatedly, in minute detail, and the techniques of conversation analysis have been extended to interaction analysis (Heath and Luff, 1996). Compared with observations made from the interpretive perspective (as in participant observation), ethnomethodological observation is more structural and objective, and less mediated by the subjective perspective of the researcher. . . .

Structured and unstructured approaches to observation

In naturalistic observation, observers neither manipulate nor stimulate the behaviour of those whom they are observing, in contrast to some other data gathering techniques. The situation being observed is not contrived for research purposes. This is pure or direct or non-participant observation, in contrast with participant observation . . .

In the literature on observation as a data collection technique, the terms 'quantitative' and 'qualitative' are frequently used. The terms 'structured' and 'unstructured' are preferred in this book, because observational data can be highly structured without necessarily being turned into numbers. The issue is how much structure will be brought to the observations.

Quantitative approaches tend to be highly structured, and to require predeveloped observation schedules, usually very detailed. If this approach is chosen, decisions will be required from the researcher as to whether already existing observational schedules will be used, or whether an observation schedule will be specially developed. . . .

Qualitative approaches to observation are much more unstructured. In this case, the researcher does not use predetermined categories and classifications, but makes observations in a more natural open-ended way. Whatever the recording technique, the behaviour is observed as the stream of actions and events as they naturally unfold. The logic here is that categories and concepts for describing and analysing the observational data will emerge later in the research, during the analysis, rather than be brought to the research, or imposed on the data, from the start.

When the observational strategy is unstructured, the process of observation typically evolves through a series of different activities. It begins with selecting a setting and gaining access to it, then starting the observing and recording. As the study progresses, the nature of the observation changes, typically sharpening in focus, leading to ever clearer research questions which require more selected observations. The observational data gathering continues until theoretical saturation is reached (Adler and Adler, 1994). Silverman (1993) suggests five stages in organizing an initially unstructured observation study: beginning the research (where a set of very general questions is proposed), writing field notes (usually beginning with broad descriptive categories, but later developing more focused codes and categories), looking as well as listening, testing hypotheses, and making broader links.

Both in observational data collection and generally, where focus and structure emerge during the field work, the analogy of the funnel is useful (Spradley, 1980; Silverman, 1993):

> Ethnographic research should have a characteristic 'funnel' structure, being progressively focused over its course. Over time the research problem needs to be developed or transformed and eventually its scope is clarified and delimited and its internal structure explored. In this sense, it is frequently well into the process of inquiry that one discovers what the research is really 'about', and not uncommonly it turns out to be about something rather different from the initial foreshadowed problems. (Hammersley and Atkinson, 1995: 206)

The theme of structure which is imposed or structure which emerges is familiar. . . . Structured observation, based on predetermined categories, breaks behaviour up into small parts. Unstructured observation, by contrast, can focus on the larger patterns of behaviour, more holistically and more macroscopically. There are advantages and disadvantages in both approaches. With smaller units of behaviour, we can lose the larger picture, but recording and analysing are easier and more standardized. The more holistic approach keeps the larger picture in view, but the logistics of recording and, especially, of analysing the data will be more demanding. As with other issues, this does not need to be an either-or matter. Combinations of the two approaches are possible, depending on the research purposes and context.

Practical issues in observation

There are two main practical issues in planning the collection of observational data: approaching observation, and recording.

Approaching observation (Foster, 1996b) means establishing the focus of the observations, selecting the cases for observation and, as appropriate, selecting within cases for observation. In other words, the researcher has to decide what will be observed, and why. These are sampling decisions, and they need to be made with reference to the research questions. The issue of structure applies here too. At the highly structured end, approaching the observation in terms of focus and cases is organized ahead of data collection. In unstructured observation, focus and cases may only become clear as observations are made. Gaining access is also part of the practical business of approaching observation. In some settings, this will involve negotiation with gatekeepers, and different types of research may well require different types of negotiation and access.

The general possibilities for recording observational data range from the use of video and audio-visual equipment to the use of field notes. There may be advantages to combining these different methods. The choice here is influenced by the extent to which the data are structured or unstructured – although increasingly, with today's sophisticated recording equipment, there is value in recording everything and, even if structured observation schedules are involved, using those in the analysis stage. These different recording methods each have their strengths and their limitations (Foster, 1996, a and b). The observational researcher's task is the usual one of analysing these in relation to the purposes and context of the research, and to choose accordingly. . . .

Before leaving observation . . . we should note the importance of observation in ethnography. 'The requirement for direct, prolonged on-the-spot observation cannot be avoided or reduced. It is the guts of the ethnographic approach. This does not always mean participant observation' (Spindler and Spindler, 1992: 63). And again: 'Above all else is the requirement that the ethnographer observe directly. No matter what instruments, coding devices, recording devices or techniques are used, the primary obligation is for the ethnographer to be there when the action takes place, and to change that action as little as possible by his or her presence' (1992: 64). Thus direct observation, as well as participant observation, is important in ethnography.

At the same time, ethnographic observation, as distinct from direct observation, has a special flavour, the flavour of ethnography itself. As Wolcott puts it:

> We are ethnographic observers when we are attending to the cultural context of the behaviour we are engaging in or observing, and when we are looking for those mutually understood sets of expectations and explanations that enable us to interpret what is occurring and what meanings are probably being attributed by others present. (1988: 193)

Data collection techniques in ethnography need to be aligned with this viewpoint. This means that it is not only the behaviour, or situation, itself which is of interest in ethnography. It is also, and centrally, the meaning of that behaviour or situation as seen by the people we are studying which is the focus.

(Punch 1998: 184–8)

➤ Here are some possible areas of study that you might wish to explore as part of research into human communication. For each one consider what you think might be an appropriate methodology to adopt. Explain the reasons for your choice.

■ an exploration of the skills required to make a person an effective listener
■ non-verbal behaviour in job interviews
■ non verbal communication during telephone calls

➤ Read Chapters 8 and 14 of Alan Bryman *Social Research Methods* (2001) Oxford: Oxford University Press.

▼ **40 WHAT'S THE TOPIC? Feminist research WHAT'S THE TEXT? Liesbet van Zoonen** *Feminist Media Studies*

One of the qualities that many commentators stress as being important in undertaking research is that of objectivity. Ironically, however, it is not unusual for a researcher to be quite passionate about the area they have chosen to explore. Indeed it is their concern for it that is likely to have motivated the exploration in the first place. One factor that has to be considered is the notion that as a researcher you are coming from a specific ideological viewpoint and are undertaking research in order to explore a particular issue that is pertinent to your viewpoint. In other words, no research is ever going to be value-free, it will always be ideologically determined. A key problem here is that there is a history within academic studies that certain clearly ideological positions are objective, value-free, truthful and that other positions are quite the opposite. A good example of this is research from a feminist perspective. When feminist perspectives were first introduced into social science research they provoked many adverse and opposed reactions. And, of course, those commentators who were most opposed to feminist perspectives invariably wrote and spoke as if their quite clearly sexist, patriarchal positions were objective, honest and value-free.

Whilst we would reject the simplistic notion that specific and unique characteristics may be routinely ascribed to one of two distinct and opposed genders historically the impact of feminism on research methods is traditionally associated with a move away from the hard, unforgiving scientism of men's researches to the more fluid, subtle and complex humanism of women's researches.

In the extract that follows Liesbet van Zoonen looks at the issue of feminist research methodology. She highlights the fact that someone approaching research from such an ideological perspective may do so with a 'conscientious partisanship' rather than 'value-freeness, neutrality and indifference'. In other words, the surfacing of the position the feminist researcher adopts is immeasurably more honest than the attempts of anti-feminist writers to disguise the ideological positioning of their researches and their findings.

Feminist scholarship is not a unified practice, but inevitably contains dilemmas and controversies, . . . As concerns particular methods for doing research, feminists have engaged in developing appropriate 'tools' for doing feminist research since the mid-1970s. One of the early participants in this project is the German scholar Maria Mies (1978), whose work has inspired many feminist scholars on the European continent to rethink the premises of their research. According to Mies, a feminist science should take issue with the following questions: the relation between the women's movement and women's studies (politics and science); the aims of science; research methodologies; the relation between activism and research, the relation between researcher and researched. Mies herself takes up a radical position by arguing that feminist scholarship should be an integral part of the women's movement. This implies, according to Mies, not only that the traditional requirements of value-freeness, neutrality and indifference towards research objects should be replaced by conscientious partisanship, but also that the contemplative, detached style of research should be substituted by the integration of research in emancipatory activities and that the choice of research themes should be determined by the strategic and tactical requirements of the women's movement. Whereas Mies' radical view on feminist scholarship as directly integrated in the women's movement is not widely supported, the relation between politics and science, the issue of how research should contribute to women's liberation, is central to the debate on feminist scholarship and evidently is handled in different ways.

Brenda Dervin claims that the political value of feminist scholarship lies in its desire to give women a voice in a world that defines them as voiceless: 'It is transformative in that it is concerned with helping the silent speak and is involved in consciousness raising (1987: 109). Much of the work . . . on gender and reception is concerned with precisely that, demonstrating the invisible experiences of women with popular culture. However . . . 'helping the silent speak' is not as unproblematic as it seems for it may easily lead to a celebratory and uncritical account of popular culture and pleasure (cf. Modleski, 1991). Within communication and cultural studies, this is an element of the specific form that the debate about the political and feminist relevance of research has taken. . . .

Nina Gregg emphasises another element of the question about the relevance of research for women's liberation in pointing to the availability and intelligibility of research results to women outside the academic world. She quotes Michelle Russell: 'As teachers, scholars, and students, how available will you make your

CONTINUED

knowledge to others as tools of their own liberation?' (Gregg, 1987: 14). It is interesting to note that 'making available' is a quite different requirement for Mies' postulate that feminist research is by definition available and intelligible to the women's movement.

Another central element in the debate about feminist research concerns the politics of doing research itself, the power relations a researcher herself is immersed in while conducting the research. Mies (1978) claims that feminist researchers should integrate a 'double consciousness' into the research process, that is, a consciousness of their own oppression as women and their privileged position as researchers. As a result new inequalities and exploitations would be prevented, namely those between the authoritative, well-paid, academic expert and the research subjects, women who often do not have much to gain from being the subject of research and who are positioned as merely delivering information and experiences for the professional benefit of others. A double consciousness would also permit a partial identification of the researcher with the research subject, in the sense that they both can recognise their *Betroffenheit* (a German term without adequate English translation), that is, their position as victims, their outrage, analysis, criticism and motivation for acting. Mies' identification – if not her solution – of an unequal power relation between researchers and researched is similar to the problems analysed by ethnographers recognising that the interaction between an 'informant' and a researcher is a profoundly unequal one (Radway, 1989). Especially for feminist scholars, concerned with evening out the inequalities between women, this is a disturbing feature of any kind of research methodology: 'To the extent that part of the ideology of feminism is to transform the competitive and exploitative relations among women into bonds of solidarity and mutuality, we expect assistance and reciprocated understanding to be part of the research/subject relation' (Reinharz, 1992: 265).

Feminist researchers have found ways around the inequalities involved in the research encounters, for instance by studying their own direct experiences, preferences and surroundings. In her study of the American soap opera *Dallas*, for instance, Ien Ang (1985: 10) placed a small advertisement in a Dutch women's magazine to find her informants. The ad reads as follows: 'I like watching the TV serial *Dallas*, but often get odd reactions to it. Would anyone like to write and tell me why you like watching it too, or dislike it? I should like to assimilate these reactions in my university thesis. Please write to . . . ' Others have studied their own communities or peer groups. Partly, of course, the inherent tension between the researcher and the researched is then transformed into an internal conflict of the researcher, between, in Ien Ang's case, being a fan and being an academic analyst, and more in general between being both an insider and an outsider at the same time. Other researchers have tried to 'pay their debts' to their informants by giving them help and assistance when needed. For instance, Lilian Rubin, a researcher and a psycho-therapist, made herself available for free counselling when her respondents felt a need to talk further about the issues she had raised (Zaat, 1982).

The inequalities between the feminist researcher and her research subjects are not only particularly acute in the actual observations of and encounters with the women participating in the research, but also in the phase of conjuring up and writing down their experiences into a story about the research results. Notwithstanding the precautions and services offered in return, the relation between researcher and researched will remain a problematic one in feminist research, also because in the end the authority and responsibility for writing down the story lies with the researcher. Inevitably and inherently at odds with feminist assumptions and aims, she must speak for other women, telling their stories in her voice. For some researchers, the burden of authorship, as Morley (1991) has called it, weighs so heavily that they tend to get stuck in contemplation and reflexivity rather than actually doing research (Ang, 1989).

Feminist research then, is characterised by a radical politicisation of the research process, internally as well as externally. Internally, by interrogating the power relations inherent in doing research, externally by aiming at producing results that are relevant to the feminist endeavour. This is the backdrop against which to understand the specific epistemological and methodological requirements of feminist research vis-à-vis the respective elements of the research cycle: concepts, design and operationalisation, data gathering and analysis, quality control and reporting.

(van Zoonen 1994: 128–30)

WHAT'S NEXT?

➤ Read Elizabeth Gross 'What is Feminist Theory?'(1992) in Helen Crowley and Susan Himmelweit (eds) *Knowing Women: Feminism and Knowledge,* Cambridge: The Open University.

▼ 41 WHAT'S THE TOPIC? Undertaking research ethically
WHAT'S THE TEXT? British Psychological Society research guidelines

As we have seen, a Communication Studies student is likely to need to carry out research that may involve a detailed examination of some aspect of human communication. This may take the form either of observing and recording or setting up a scenario through which to observe the behaviour of participants as part of a research exercise. Whilst, as we have stressed, this must be done with much consideration for the hypothesis being tested and the outcome that is anticipated it may not take into account to the same degree the wellbeing of the participants in the research. This, however, needs to be an important consideration for any student who intends to undertake such research.

Psychologists are one of many groups who use human participants in their research. In consequence the British Psychological Society (BPS) has produced a set of ethical principles to guide its members about the behaviour they should observe when conducting such research. These principles should also serve as a useful guideline to a Communication Studies student who intends to undertake research. Many research projects, for example for AQA Communication Studies Unit 1, will use observational research.

Before undertaking research, however, it is important to consider the issue of permission and to be clear what you understand by the statement 'where those observed would expect to be observed by strangers'. It may also help you to think if the reverse might be true. Remember that it is very easy to invade someone's privacy in one's exuberance to complete research.

What follows is a useful set of practices that you should observe in undertaking your research project. The guidelines have been heavily edited to remove a number of features which relate only to psychology research or which relate to the way in which the BPS regulates its members' research activities.

The BPS begins its guidelines by reminding psychology researchers that 'In the forefront of its considerations was the recognition that psychologists owe a debt to those who agree to take part in their studies and that people who are willing to give up their time, even for remuneration, should be able to expect to be treated with the highest standards of consideration and respect. This is reflected in the change from the term "subjects" to "participants".' Any researcher, whether working within Psychology or Communication Studies, would do well to act upon this.

2. GENERAL

2.1 In all circumstances investigators must consider the ethical implications and psychological consequences for the participants in their research. The essential principle is that the investigation should be considered from the standpoint of all participants; foreseeable threats to their psychological well-being, health, values or dignity should be eliminated. Investigators should recognise that, in our multi-cultural and multi-ethnic society and where investigations involve individuals of different ages, gender, and social background, the investigators may not have sufficient knowledge of the implications of any investigation for the participants. It should be borne in mind that the best judge of whether an investigation will cause offence may be members of the population from which the participants in the research are to be drawn.

3. CONSENT

3.1 Whenever possible, the investigator should inform all participants of the objectives of the investigation. The investigator should inform the participants of all aspects of the research or intervention that might reasonably be expected to influence willingness to participate. The investigator should, normally, explain all other aspects of the research or intervention about which the participants enquire. Failure to make full disclosure prior to obtaining informed consent requires additional safeguards to protect the welfare and dignity of participants.

3.2 Research with children or with participants who have impairments that will limit understanding and/or communication such that they are unable to give their real consent requires special safeguarding procedures.

3.3 Where possible, the real consent of children and of adults with impairments in understanding or communication should be obtained. In addition, where research involves any persons under 16 years of age, consent should be obtained from parents or from those in loco parentis.

. . .

The term in loco parentis means 'in the place of a parent' and covers any person whose work involves them becoming, to all intents and purposes, the parent of the children they are working with. All teachers work, in effect, in loco parentis.

3.4 Where real consent cannot be obtained from adults with impairments in understanding or communication, wherever possible the investigator should consult a person well-placed to appreciate the participant's reaction, such as a member of the person's family, and must obtain the disinterested approval of the research from independent advisors.

3.5 When research is being conducted with detained persons, particular care should be taken over informed consent, paying attention to the special circumstances which may affect the person's ability to give free informed consent.

3.6 Investigators should realise that they are often in a position of authority or influence over participants who may be their students, employees or clients. This relationship must not be allowed to pressurise the participants to take part in, or remain in, an investigation.

3.7 The payment of participants must not be used to induce them to risk harm beyond that which they risk without payment in their normal lifestyle.

3.8 If harm, unusual discomfort, or other negative consequences for the individual's future life might occur, the investigator must obtain the disinterested approval of independent advisors, inform the participants, and obtain informed, real consent from each of them.

3.9 In longitudinal research, consent may need to be obtained on more than one occasion.

Longitudinal research is research that takes place over a significant period of time and is designed to, amongst other things, measure changes that occur over a period of time. This is opposed to research which is designed to generate a significant picture of how things are at one particular moment, a kind of moment frozen in time – like a snapshot.

4. DECEPTION

4.1 The withholding of information or the misleading of participants is unacceptable if the participants are typically likely to object or show unease once debriefed. Where this is in any doubt, appropriate consultation must precede the investigation. Consultation is best carried out with individuals who share the social and cultural background of the participants in the research, but the advice of ethics committees or experienced and disinterested colleagues may be sufficient.

4.2 Intentional deception of the participants over the purpose and general nature of the investigation should be avoided whenever possible. Participants should never be deliberately misled without extremely strong scientific or medical justification. Even then there should be strict controls and the disinterested approval of independent advisors. . . .

5. DEBRIEFING

5.1 In studies where the participants are aware that they have taken part in an investigation, when the data have been collected, the investigator should provide the participants with any necessary information to complete their understanding of the nature of the research. The investigator should discuss with the participants their experience of the research in order to monitor any unforeseen negative effects or misconceptions.

5.2 Debriefing does not provide justification for unethical aspects of any investigation.

5.3 Some effects which may be produced by an experiment will not be negated by a verbal description following the research. Investigators have a responsibility to ensure that participants receive any necessary debriefing in the form of active intervention before they leave the research setting.

6. WITHDRAWAL FROM THE INVESTIGATION

6.1 At the onset of the investigation investigators should make plain to participants their right to withdraw from the research at any time, irrespective of whether or not payment or other inducement has been offered. It is reconised that this may be difficult in certain observational or organisational settings, but nevertheless the investigator must attempt to ensure the participants (including children) know of their right to withdraw. . . .

6.2 In the light of experience of the investigation, or as a result of debriefing, the participant has the right to withdraw retrospectively any consent given, and to require that their own data, including recordings, be destroyed.

7. CONFIDENTIALITY

7.1 Subject to the requirements of legislation, including the Data Protection Act, information obtained about a participant during an investigation is confidential unless otherwise agreed in advance. Investigators who are put under pressure to disclose confidential information should draw this point to the attention of those exerting such pressure. Participants in psychological research have a right to expect that information they provide will be treated confidentially and, if published, will not be identifiable as theirs. In the event that confidentiality and/or anonymity cannot be guaranteed, the participant must be warned of this in advance of agreeing to participate.

8. PROTECTION OF PARTICIPANTS

8.1 Investigators have a primary responsibility to protect participants from physical and mental harm during the investigation. Normally, the risk of harm must be no greater than in ordinary life, i.e. participants should not be exposed to risks greater than or additional to those encountered in their normal lifestyles.

. . .

8.3 Where research may involve behaviour or experiences that participants may regard as personal and private the participants must be protected from stress by all appropriate measures, including the assurance that answers to personal questions need not be given. There should be no concealment or deception when seeking information that might encroach on privacy.

8.4 In research involving children, great caution should be exercised when discussing the results with parents, teachers or others acting in *loco parentis*, since evaluative statements may carry unintended weight.

9. OBSERVATIONAL RESEARCH

9.1 Studies based upon observation must respect the privacy and psychological well being of the individuals studied. Unless those observed give their consent to being observed, observational research is only acceptable in situations where those observed would expect to be observed by strangers. Additionally, particular account should be taken of local cultural values and of the possibility of intruding upon the privacy of individuals who, even while in a normally public space, may believe they are unobserved.

10. GIVING ADVICE

10.1 During research, an investigator may obtain evidence of psychological or physical problems of which a participant, is, apparently, unaware. In such a case, the investigator has a responsibility to inform the participant if the investigator believes that by not doing so the participant's future well-being may be endangered.

. . .

11. COLLEAGUES

11.1 Investigators share responsibility for the ethical treatment of research participants with their collaborators, assistants, students and employees. A psychologist who believes that another psychologist or investigator may be conducting research that is not in accordance with the principles above should encourage that investigator to re-evaluate the research.

(British Psychological Society 2000: 8–11)

➤ Produce your own checklist for the ethical conducting of research. See if you can succinctly compress our extract from the BPS's guidelines into no more than one side of A4.

▼ **42 WHAT'S THE TOPIC? Internet research
WHAT'S THE TEXT? Angus Kennedy *The Rough Guide to the Internet***

Undertaking research using the Internet is both a complex and rewarding activity. For many students the Internet has replaced searching the shelves of libraries as the prime source of information.

However, the Internet is only as good at providing information as is the researcher who is using it. To get meaningful detail from the Internet it is essential to learn how to use search engines judiciously and effectively.

The following extract from *The Rough Guide to the Internet* identifies the main search tools on the Internet and suggests the means of getting the best from them.

FINDING IT

Once you're installed, setup, online, and the whole thing's purring along to perfection, you'll face yet another dilemma. How on earth do you find anything? Relax, it's not too hard once you've learned a few tricks. Before you can proceed to search for something, you'll need to take into account what it is, how new it is, where it might be stored, and who's likely to know about it. In this chapter, we show you the first places to look, and as you gain experience the rest will fall into place. We also show you how to fix Web addresses that won't work. Assuming you have Web access, the only program you'll definitely need is a browser. You already have one? Fantastic. Well, here's how to wind it out to its full potential.

Become an instant know-it-all

The art of finding something pinned up on the world's biggest scrapboard is, without doubt, the most valuable skill you can glean from your time online. If you know how to use the Net to find an answer to almost anything quickly and comprehensively, you'd have to consider yourself not only useful, but pretty saleable too. As it stands, most people simply bumble their way around, and that includes a fair share of Net veterans. Yet it's a remarkably basic skill to master once you've been pointed in the right direction. So read this chapter, then get online and start investigating. Within an hour or two you'll be milking the Net for what it's worth. It might turn out to be the best investment you'll ever make!

How it works

The Net is massive. Just the Web alone houses some 500 million pages of text, and millions more are added daily. So if you need to find something – particularly if you want to research it in depth – you're going to need some serious help. Thankfully, there's a wide selection of search tools to make the task relatively painless. The job usually entails keying your search terms into a form on a Web page and waiting a few seconds for the results.

We'll introduce you to search tools that can locate almost anything on the Web, that is linked to from the Web or archived into an online Web database, such as email addresses, phone numbers, program locations, newsgroup articles, and news clippings. Of course, first it has to be put online, and granted public access. So just because you can access US government servers doesn't mean you'll find a file on DEA Operative Presley's whereabouts.

Let's start by examining the main search tools. You'll find even more listed in the 'Search Tools and Directories' section of our Web guide. . . .

THE MAIN SEARCH TOOLS

There are three basic types of Web search tools: search engines, search agents, and hand-built directories. Apart from the odd newspaper archive, they're almost always free. Because they're so useful and popular, most are tacking other services onto the side and building themselves into so-called portals, communities, and hubs. These expressions are close to meaningless, really only stating a desire on the site's behalf to attract repeat visitors by making themselves useful. The intention is to get you to choose them as your browser home page. The next few pages discuss each category in detail, and show you how to torture them for answers.

Read me!

As with just about everything on the Net, the easiest way to learn is to dive straight into the search engines and explore how they work. But before you do, it's worth pausing to read the instructions first. Every search engine and directory has a page of Read Me tips on how to use them to their full potential. A few minutes' study will make your searching more effective.

Search engines

Use a search engine when you're looking for specific mention of something on a Web page. Examples: HotBot, AltaVista and Northern Light.

Search engines provide a way to search the contents of millions of Web pages simultaneously. All you have to do is go to the search engine's Web page and submit keywords, or search terms, into a simple form. It runs these terms past its database and, almost instantly, returns a list of results of 'hits'. For example, if you were to search on the expression 'Rough Guide to the Internet', here's what might come up on top:

1. Welcome to the Rough Guide to the Internet
The Rough Guide to the Internet is the ultimate guide to the Web, complete with a 1500+ site directory.
99% 2/24/99 http://www2/roughguides.com/net/index.html.

In this case the top line tells us the name of the page or site. The second is a description excerpted from the page, a relevancy score, retrieval date, and the page's address. If it suits, click on the link to visit the site.

Tip: Don't click on a result, and then hit the Back button if it's no good. Instead, run down the list and open the most promising candidates in new browser windows. It will save you tons of time.

It's important to know you're not searching the Web live. You're merely searching a database of Web pages located on the search engine's server. This database is compiled by a program that crawls around the Web looking for new sites, as well as changes to the ones it already knows. How much text is retrieved from each site varies between search engines. The better ones scavenge almost everything.

Alta Vista (http://www.av.com)
Excite (http://www.excite.com)
Google (http://www.google.com)
Goto (http://www.goto.com)
HotBot (http://www.hotbot.com)
InfoSeek (http://www.infoseek.com)
Lycos (http://www.lycos.com)
Northern Light (http://www.nlsearch.com)
Snap (http://www.snap.com)
Webcrawler (http://www.webcrawler.com)

Choosing a search engine

Not all search engines are equal, though some are very similar because they share technologies. Hotbot, Snap, Goto and MSN, for example, currently use the Inktomi system, which means their results won't differ greatly, but that may change over time. What will definitely differ is the way their search forms are presented.

Because the various engines source, store, and retrieve data differently, shop around to see which you prefer. You'll want the biggest, freshest, database. You'll want to be able to fine-tune your search with extra commands. And you'll want the most hits you can get on one page with the most relevant results on top.

Currently, AltaVista, Northern Light and HotBot appear to have the biggest databases. Of these three, AltaVista seems the biggest, fastest, and freshest, but HotBot is our pick, as it's by far the easiest to tune, and can return ten times as many hits per page. Although Northern Light has a bigger database and a unique system of filing returns under subject folders, it's not quite as user-friendly.

Google is a highly promising newcomer, with a large database, an intelligent system of ranking hits by relevancy (popularity), and local cache access to pages that have disappeared since it's crawl or are otherwise unavailable. Check it out, as it looks set to become a future champ.

InfoSeek has a similar-sized database, and can also give quick, accurate results especially if you're after a single URL, but there are enough other options that you're rarely likely to need it. Most of the rest, such as Lycos, Excite and Webcrawler, and those based around their respective technologies, such as AOL Netfind, really aren't worth your time.

If you need more results, rather than visit several engines in turn, query them simultaneously using an agent such as Copernic. . . . You can tell how each engine ranks from the results. For more detailed analysis see Search Engine Watch (http://www.searchenginewatch.com) which keeps tabs on all the finer details such as who owns what and how they tick.

Limitations

Search engines aren't the be all and end all of what's on the Web. They're only as good as their most recent findings, which might be just a small proportion of what's actually there and, possibly, months old. So just because you can't find it through a Web search doesn't mean it's not there. If you're after something brand new, they may not be much use. You might be better off searching Usenet or a news service.

How to word your search terms

Now here's the art. Get this right and you'll find anything. The trick is to think up a search term that's unique enough to get rid of junk results, but broad enough not to miss anything useful. It will depend entirely on the subject, so be prepared to think laterally!

Each search engine has its own quirks which you'll need to learn – otherwise you'll waste a lot of time weeding through poor results. You should try all the main search engines and study their instructions. The main things to glean are how to create a phrase, how to search on multiple phrases, and how to exclude certain words. Let's start with a complex example. Suppose we want to search for something on the esteemed author, Angus Kennedy. Let's see how you'd do it in AltaVista. If you were to enter:

> angus kennedy

it would return all pages that contain 'angus' or 'kennedy' or both. That means there'd be lots of pages about Angus cattle and JFK. We don't want to sift through those so let's make sure the pages contain both words. In AltaVista, and most other search engines, you can use a plus sign (+) to state that the page must contain a word. So let's try:

> +angus+kennedy

That's better. All the pages now contain both words. Unfortunately, though, there's no guarantee that they'll be next to each other. What we really want is to treat them as a phrase. A simple way to do this is to enclose the words within quotes, like this:

> 'angus kennedy'

Now we've captured all instances of Angus Kennedy as a phrase, but since it's a person's name, we should look for Kennedy, Angus as well. So let's try:

> 'angus kennedy' 'kennedy, angus'

As with the first example we now catch pages with either or both phrases. Now suppose we want to narrow it down further and exclude some irrelevant results, for example, others with the same name. Our target writes books about French literature, so let's start by getting rid of that pesky Rough Guide author. To exclude a term, place a minus sign (–) in front. So let's ditch him:

> 'angus kennedy' 'kennedy, angus' –'rough guide'

That's about all you need to know in most instances. These rules should work in most (but not all) engines, as well as the search forms on individual sites. Of course, you don't have to know any of this to use HotBot, as it has handy drop-down menus. However, it's good to know if you want to search for two phrases. In this case, choose 'any of the words' or 'all the words' (whichever's relevant) from the HotBot menu, and enter the phrases within quotes. Alternatively, click on 'More Search Options' and fill in the boxes.

For more complex searches in other search engines, look for an advanced search link, or refer to the Help file. Observe how they interpret capitals, dashes between words, brackets, and the Boolean operators such as AND, OR, NEAR, and NOT.

But, there's at least one product that can do all this for you, without you ever having to look at a search engine. Read on.

Search agents

Use a search agent to scan the contents of a limited number of sites. For example, to find new information, to compare prices or stock, or combine the results from several search engines. Examples: Shopper.com, Copernic and Apple's Sherlock.

Search agents, or searchbots, gather information live from other sites. For example: metasearch agents such as Copernic (http://www.copernic.com), Dogpile (http://www.dogpile.com), and MetaCrawler (http://www.metacrawler.com) can query multiple search engines and directories simultaneously; bargain finder agents, like Shopper.com (http://www.shopper.com), can look for the best deal across several online shops; and Web agents, like NetAttaché (http://www.tympani.com), can scan specific instances of an expression. Though many are accessible through a Web interface, the better ones are generally standalone clients.

If you're a serious researcher, once you've tried Copernic you'll never want to use an individual search engine again. It's a standalone program that can query several search engines, directories, Usenet archives and email databases, at once. It filters out the duplicates, displays the results on a single page in your browser and even retrieves them automatically for offline browsing. If you're running Windows 95/98/NT, don't pause for thought, download it now!

Unfortunately, the Web equivalents aren't as useful. Sure, they can query multiple search resources, but even the best, MetaCrawler, will return only up to 30 hits per site. The whole point of searching multiple engines is to get more hits, so you'd be better off starting with HotBot.

You might find the same goes for the bewildering layers of search aids built into IE5.0x and Windows 98.

(Kennedy 2003: 168–76, 179–80)

➤ Bearing in mind some of the warnings that you have been offered about designing effective communication research think about some of the comparatively new and different problems raised by using the internet for research.

➤ Having done this now prepare a parallel checklist of the advantages and disadvantages of using the internet for research. Hint: you might notice that some ideas appear in both columns.

▼ **43 WHAT'S THE TOPIC? Effective writing WHAT'S THE TEXT? Winford Hicks, Sally Adams, Harriett Gilbert *Writing for Journalists***

Now we have looked at some features involved in the designing and undertaking of communication research we can move to considerations about writing. We haven't taken the obvious route here and extracted from any number of books which offer solid gold guidelines for writing up research or handbooks on effective report writing. (Although if you do want to read a succinct overview of the whole research process read 'Working Practices' by Michael Green which is Chapter 10 of Jim McGuigan (1997) *Cultural Methodologies*, London: Sage.) Rather we're here concerned with communication in practice, with specific audiences, for specific purposes, to achieve specific effects. And for that reason we're drawing on journalistic and novelistic communication practices.

There are many books that purport to help you become a better writer. Some do so with the cynical implication that they can also make you very rich. Unfortunately the truth is that for most of us there is no quick-fix solution to becoming a better writer. As the authors of *Writing for Journalists* point out in answer to the question 'Can writing be learned':

Of course it can, providing you have at least some talent and – what is more important – that you have a lot of determination and are prepared to work hard.

One common piece of advice that you will encounter is to 'read a lot'. Basically this means finding good examples of effective writing and learning from them. So clearly if you want to improve your writing you need to think about your reading habits. You also need to sharpen your critical faculties and make some evaluation of how the style of different writers is appropriate to what they are saying.

In this extract we will look at some of the advice offered to help improve writing skills and then we will consider examples of what can be called effective writing.

In *Writing for Journalists,* Winford Hicks and his co-authors offer some particularly useful advice about how to get started on a writing assignment. For many people this can be a real stumbling block. You may know what you want to say but finding the words to start saying it can be elusive. Although the advice of Hicks, Adams and Gilbert is aimed at would-be journalists, what they have to say holds true for writing in almost any context.

CAN WRITING BE TAUGHT?

This is the wrong question – unless you're a prospective teacher of journalism. The question, if you're a would-be journalist (or indeed any kind of writer), is: can writing be learnt?

And the answer is: of course it can, providing that you have at least some talent and – what is more important – that you have a lot of determination and are prepared to work hard.

If you want to succeed as a writer, you must be prepared to read a lot, finding good models and learning from them; you must be prepared to think imaginatively about readers and how they think and feel rather than luxuriate inside your own comfortable world; you must be prepared to take time practising, experimenting, revising.

You must be prepared to listen to criticism and take it into account while not letting it get on top of you. You must develop confidence in your own ability but not let it become arrogance.

This book makes all sorts of recommendations about how to improve your writing but it cannot tell you how much progress you are likely to make. It tries to be helpful and encouraging but it does not pretend to be diagnostic. And – unlike those gimmicky writing courses advertised to trap the vain, the naïve and the unwary – it cannot honestly 'guarantee success or your money back'.

GETTING DOWN TO WRITING

Make a plan before you start

Making a plan before you start to write is an excellent idea, even if you keep it in your head. And the longer and more complex the piece, the more there is to be gained from setting the plan down on paper – or on the keyboard.

Of course you may well revise the plan as you go, particularly if you start writing before your research is completed. But that is not a reason for doing without a plan.

Write straight on to the keyboard

Unless you want to spend your whole life writing, which won't give you much time to find and research stories – never mind going to the pub or practising the cello – don't bother with a handwritten draft. Why introduce an unnecessary stage into the writing process?

Don't use the excuse that your typing is slow and inaccurate. First, obviously, learn to touch-type, so you can write straight on to the keyboard at the speed at which you think. For most people this will be about 25 words a minute – a speed far slower than that of a professional copy typist.

. . .

Even if you don't type very well, you should avoid the handwritten draft stage. After all, the piece is going to end up typed – presumably by you. So get down to it straightaway, however few fingers you use.

Write notes to get started

Some people find the act of writing difficult. They feel inhibited from starting to write, as though they were on the high diving board or the top of a ski run.

Reporters don't often suffer from this kind of writer's block because, assuming that they have found a story in the first place, the task of writing an intro for it is usually a relatively simple one. Note: not easy but simple, meaning that reporters have a limited range of options; they are not conventionally expected to invent, to be 'creative'.

One reason why journalists should start as reporters is that it's a great way to get into the habit of writing.

However, if you've not yet acquired the habit and tend to freeze at the keyboard, don't just sit there agonising. Having written your basic plan, add further headings; enumerate, list, illustrate. Don't sweat over the first paragraph: begin somewhere in the middle; begin with something you know you're going to include – an anecdote, a quote – knowing you can reposition it later. Get started, knowing that on the word processor you're not committed to your first draft.

Revise, revise

Always leave yourself time to revise what you have written. Even if you're writing news to a tight deadline, try to spend a minute or two looking over your story. And if you're a feature writer or reviewer, revision is an essential part of the writing process.

If you're lucky, a competent sub-editor will check your copy before it goes to press, but that is no reason to pretend to yourself that you are not responsible

CONTINUED

for what you write. As well as looking for the obvious – errors of fact, names wrong, spelling and grammar mistakes, confusion caused by bad punctuation – try to read your story from the reader's point of view, Does it make sense in their terms? Does it really hit the target?

Master the basics

You can't start to write well without having a grasp of the basics of English usage such as grammar, spelling and punctuation. To develop a journalistic style you will need to learn how to use quotes, to handle reported speech, to choose the right word from a variety of different ones. When should you use foreign words and phrases, slang, jargon – and what about clichés? What is 'house style'? and so on.

(Hicks, Adams and Gilbert 2000: 4–7)

WHAT'S NEXT?

➤ This advice is aimed primarily at newspaper reporters. How do you think it might be relevant to someone writing up a Communication Studies research project?

▼ 44 WHAT'S THE TOPIC? Clarity in writing I WHAT'S THE TEXT? George Orwell 'Politics and the English language'

George Orwell was one of the most important writers of the twentieth century. In addition to such novels as *1984*, he was also a prolific essayist and writer of social commentary. Despite his privileged background Orwell was a champion of the working classes and wrote extensively of working-class life in such places as the Lancashire coalfields.

He believed that there was a clear link between the character of our thoughts and the character of our language. He believed that the 'slovenliness of our language makes it easier for us to have foolish thoughts'. In an important essay, 'Politics and the English language', Orwell called for a 'fight against bad English'. He offered examples of the ways in which he felt that language had declined. (His conclusion is especially useful given that it lists six 'rules' to help writers achieve clarity.)

COMMUNICATION STUDIES: THE ESSENTIAL RESOURCE

. . . I list below, with notes and examples, various of the tricks by means of which the work of prose construction is habitually dodged:

DYING METAPHORS. A newly invented metaphor assists thought by evoking a visual image, while on the other hand a metaphor which is technically 'dead' (e.g. *iron resolution*) has in effect reverted to being an ordinary word and can generally be used without loss of vividness. But in between these two classes there is a huge dump of worn-out metaphors which have lost all evocative power and are merely used because they save people the trouble of inventing phrases for themselves. Examples are: *Ring the changes on, take up the cudgels for, toe the line, ride roughshod over, stand shoulder to shoulder with, play into the hands of, no axe to grind, grist to the mill, fishing in troubled waters, on the order of the day, Achilles' heel, swan song, hotbed.* Many of these are used without knowledge of their meaning (what is a 'rift,' for instance?), and incompatible metaphors are frequently mixed, a sure sign that the writer is not interested in what he is saying. Some metaphors now current have been twisted out of their original meaning without those who use them even being aware of the fact. For example, *toe the line* is sometimes written as *tow the line.* Another example is *the hammer and the anvil,* now always used with the implication that the anvil gets the worst of it. In real life it is always the anvil that breaks the hammer, never the other way about: a writer who stopped to think what he was saying would avoid perverting the original phrase.

OPERATORS OR VERBAL FALSE LIMBS. These save the trouble of picking out appropriate verbs and nouns, and at the same time pad each sentence with extra syllables which give it an appearance of symmetry. Characteristic phrases are *render inoperative, militate against, make contact with, be subjected to, give rise to, give grounds for, have the effect of, play a leading part (role) in, make itself felt, take effect, exhibit a tendency to, serve the purpose of,* etc., etc. The keynote is the elimination of simple verbs. Instead of being a single word, such as *break, stop, spoil, mend, kill,* a verb becomes a *phrase,* made up of a noun or adjective tacked on to some general-purposes verb such as *prove, serve, form, play, render.* In addition, the passive voice is wherever possible used in preference to the active, and noun constructions are used instead of gerunds (*by examination of* instead of *by examining*). The range of verbs is further cut down by means of the *-ize* and *de-* formations, and the banal statements are given an appearance of profundity by means of the *not un-* formation. Simple conjunctions and prepositions are replaced by such phrases as *with respect to, having regard to, the fact that, by dint of, in view of, in the interests of, on the hypothesis that;* and the ends of sentences are saved from anticlimax by such resounding common-places as *greatly to be desired, cannot be left out of account, a development to be expected in the near future, deserving of serious consideration,* brought to a satisfactory conclusion, and so on and so forth.

PRETENTIOUS DICTION. Words like *phenomenon, element, individual (as noun), objective, categorical, effective, virtual, basic, primary, promote, constitute, exhibit, exploit, utilize, eliminate, liquidate,* are used to dress up a simple statement and give an air of scientific impartiality to biased judgements. Adjectives like *epoch-making, epic, historic, unforgettable, triumphant, age-old, inevitable, inexorable, veritable,* are used to dignify the sordid process of international politics, while writing that aims at glorifying war usually takes on an archaic colour, its characteristic words being: *realm, throne, chariot, mailed fist, trident, sword, shield, buckler, banner, jackboot, clarion.* Foreign words and expressions such as *cul de sac, ancien régime, deus ex machina, mutatis mutandis, status quo, gleichschaltung, weltanschauung,* are used to give an air of culture and elegance. Except for the useful abbreviations *i.e., e.g.,* and *etc.,* there is no real need for any of the hundreds of foreign phrases now current in English. Bad writers, and especially scientific, political, and sociological writers, are nearly always haunted by the notion that Latin or Greek words are grander than Saxon ones, and unnecessary words like *expedite, ameliorate, predict, extraneous, deracinated, clandestine, subaqueous,* and hundreds of others constantly gain ground from their Anglo-Saxon opposite numbers. . . .

MEANINGLESS WORDS. In certain kinds of writing, particularly in art criticism and literary criticism, it is normal to come across long passages which are almost completely lacking in meaning. Words like *romantic, plastic, values, human, dead, sentimental, natural, vitality,* as used in art criticism, are strictly meaningless, in the sense that they not only do not point to any discoverable object, but are hardly ever expected to do so by the reader. When one critic writes, 'The outstanding feature of Mr X's work is its living quality', while another writes, 'The immediately striking thing about Mr X's work is its peculiar deadness', the reader accepts this as a simple difference of opinion. If words like *black* and *white* were involved, instead of the jargon words *dead* and *living,* he would see at once that language was being used in an improper way. Many political words are similarly abused. The word *Fascism* has now no meaning except in so far as it signifies 'something not desirable'. The words *democracy, socialism, freedom, patriotic, realistic, justice* have each of them several different meanings which cannot be reconciled with one another. In the case of a word like *democracy,* not only is there no agreed definition, but the attempt to make one is resisted from all sides. It is almost universally felt that when we call a country democratic we are praising it: consequently the defenders of every kind of régime claim that it is a democracy, and fear that they might have to stop using that word if it were tied down to any one meaning. Words of this kind are often used in a consciously dishonest way. That is, the person who uses them has his own private definition, but allows his hearer to think he means something quite different. Statements like *Marshal Petain was a true patriot, The Soviet press is the freest in the world, The Catholic Church is opposed to persecution,* are almost always made with intent to deceive. Other words used in variable meanings, in most cases more or less dishonestly, are: *class, totalitarian, science, progressive, reactionary, bourgeois, equality.* . . .

As I have tried to show, modern writing at its worst does not consist in picking out words for the sake of their meaning and inventing images in order to make the meaning clearer. It consists in gumming together long strips of words which have already been set in order by someone else, and making the results presentable by sheer humbug. The attraction of this way of writing is that it is easy. It is easier – even quicker, once you have the habit – to say *In my opinion it is not an unjustifiable assumption that* than to say *I think*. If you use ready-made phrases, you not only don't have to hunt about for words; you also don't have to bother with the rhythms of your sentences, since these phrases are generally so arranged as to be more or less euphonious. When you are composing in a hurry . . . it is natural to fall into a pretentious, Latinized style. Tags like a *consideration which we should do well to bear in mind* or *a conclusion to which all of us would readily assent* will save many a sentence from coming down with a bump. By using stale metaphors, similes, and idioms, you save much mental effort, at the cost of leaving your meaning vague, not only for your reader but for yourself. This is the significance of mixed metaphors. The sole aim of a metaphor is to call up a visual image. When these images clash — as in *The Fascist octopus has sung its swan song, the jackboot is thrown into the melting pot* — it can be taken as certain that the writer is not seeing a mental image of the objects he is naming; in other words he is not really thinking. Look again at the examples I gave at the beginning of this essay. . . .

What is above all needed is to let the meaning choose the word, and not the other way about. In prose, the worst thing one can do with words is surrender to them. When you think of a concrete object, you think wordlessly, and then, if you want to describe the thing you have been visualizing you probably hunt about till you find the exact words that seem to fit it. When you think of something abstract you are more inclined to use words from the start, and unless you make a conscious effort to prevent it, the existing dialect will come rushing in and do the job for you, at the expense of blurring or even changing your meaning. Probably it is better to put off using words as long as possible and get one's meaning as clear as one can through pictures and sensations. Afterward one can choose — not simply *accept* — the phrases that will best cover the meaning, and then switch round and decide what impressions one's words are likely to make on another person. This last effort of the mind cuts out all stale or mixed images, all prefabricated phrases, needless repetitions, and humbug and vagueness generally. But one can often be in doubt about the effect of a word or a phrase, and one needs rules that one can rely on when instinct fails. I think the following rules will cover most cases:

(i)   Never use a metaphor, simile, or other figure of speech which you are used to seeing in print.
(ii)   Never us a long word where a short one will do.
(iii) If it is possible to cut a word out, always cut it out.
(iv)   Never use the passive where you can use the active.
(v)   Never use a foreign phrase, a scientific word or a jargon word if you can think of an everyday English equivalent.
(vi)   Break any of these rules sooner than say anything outright barbarous.

These rules sound elementary, and so they are, but they demand a deep change of attitude in anyone who has grown used to writing in the style now fashionable.

(Orwell 2000: 348–60)

WHAT'S NEXT?

➤ Try to find a couple of examples of passages of confused and poorly written English. Official letters and notices are always a good starting point. Now make your own 'translation' using Orwell's guidelines to help you.
➤ Now find an example of something you wrote before you read this extract. Look at it carefully and ask yourself how many of Orwell's 'rules' it breaks.
➤ Now try to re-write the passage in light of Orwell's advice.
➤ Has it made any improvement?
➤ Extract 43 closed with a number of questions about writing – 'When should you use foreign words and phrases, slang, jargon – and what about clichés?'. How does Orwell answer those questions posed by Hicks, Adams and Gilbert?

▼ **45 WHAT'S THE TOPIC? Clarity in writing II
WHAT'S THE TEXT? Plain English Campaign
website**

Orwell first published his essay in 1946, so one possibility is that his advice may have been heeded and things may have changed. A visit to the Plain English Campaign's website reveals that this is not so. The campaign showcases some examples of clear, unambiguous writing which Orwell would no doubt approve. There are, however, many examples on the site of confused and ineffective writing. Here are some examples. Each has a 'before', the original poorly written contorted prose and an 'after', a clear and direct translation.

Your self-development activity here is to first cover up the 'after', then read the 'before', and then see if you can translate the phrase into simple, readily understandable English, and then look to see what is the Plain English Campaign's suggestion.

BEFORE

High-quality learning environments are a necessary precondition for facilitation and enhancement of the ongoing learning process.

AFTER

Children need good schools if they are to learn properly.

(Although the 'before' paragraph does not mention it, the situation does involve schoolchildren.)

BEFORE

If there are any points on which you require explanation or further particulars we shall be glad to furnish such additional details as may be required by telephone.

AFTER

If you have any questions, please ring.

BEFORE

It is important that you shall read the notes, advice and information detailed opposite then complete the form overleaf (all sections) prior to its immediate return to the Council by way of the envelope provided.

AFTER

Please read the notes opposite before you fill in the form. Then send it back to us as soon as possible in the envelope provided.

BEFORE

Your enquiry about the use of the entrance area at the library for the purpose of displaying posters and leaflets about Welfare and Supplementary Benefit rights, gives rise to the question of the provenance and authoritativeness of the material to be displayed. Posters and leaflets issued by the Central Office of Information, the Department of Health and Social Security and other authoritative bodies are usually displayed in libraries, but items of a disputatious or polemic kind, whilst not necessarily excluded, are considered individually.

AFTER

Thank you for your letter asking permission to put up posters in the entrance area of the library. Before we can give you an answer we will need to see a copy of the posters to make sure they won't offend anyone.

<http://www.plainenglish.co.uk/translations/html>

▼ **46 WHAT'S THE TOPIC? Original writing
WHAT'S THE TEXT? Alain de Botton *How
Proust Can Change Your Life***

As we have seen, Orwell argues that one of the greatest enemies of effective writing is the use of clichés. These are worn out phrases that have lost their impact through being used too often.

In his book *How Proust Can Change Your Life* Alain de Botton explains why this great author had a problem with people using clichés. Proust had been sent a novel by an aspiring writer. When he read it he found it to be full of clichés. Proust is famous for the freshness and clarity of his writing and felt that clichés were something a writer should avoid at all costs. As explained by de Botton his reaction serves as a useful illustration of the importance of trying to avoid using clichés.

Proust had a friend called Gabriel de la Rochefoucauld. He was an aristocratic young man whose ancestor had written a famous short book in the seventeenth century, and who liked to spend time in glamorous Paris nightspots, so much time that he had been labelled by some of his more sarcastic contemporaries, 'de la Rochefoucauld de chez Maxim's'. But in 1904, Gabriel forsook the night life in order to try his hand at literature. The result was a novel, *The Lover and the Doctor*, which Gabriel sent to Proust in manuscript form as soon as it was finished, with a request for comments and advice.

'Bear in mind that you have written a fine and powerful novel, a superb, tragic work of complex and consummate craftsmanship,' Proust reported back to his friend, who might have formed a slightly different impression after reading the lengthy letter which had preceded this eulogy. It seems that the superb and tragic work had a few problems, not least because it was filled with clichés:

'There are some fine big landscapes in your novel,' explained Proust, treading delicately, 'but at times one would like them to be painted with more originality. It's quite true that the sky is on fire at sunset, but it's been said too often, and the moon that shines discreetly is a trifle dull.'

We may ask why Proust objected to phrases that had been used too often. After all, doesn't the moon shine discreetly? Don't sunsets look as if they were on fire? Aren't clichés just good ideas that have proved rightly popular?

The problem with clichés is not that they contain false ideas, but rather that they are superficial articulations of very good ones. The sun is often on fire at sunset and the moon discreet, but if we keep saying this every time we encounter a sun or a moon, we will end believing that this is the last rather than the first word to be said on the subject. Clichés are detrimental in so far as they inspire us to believe that they adequately describe a situation while merely grazing its surface. And if this matters, it is because the way we speak is ultimately linked to the way we feel, because how we *describe* the world must at some level reflect how we first *experience* it.

The moon Gabriel mentioned might of course have been discreet, but it was liable to have been a lot more besides. When the first volume of Proust's novel was published eight years after The *Lover and the Doctor*, one wonders whether Gabriel (if he wasn't back ordering Dom Perignon at Maxim's) took time to notice that Proust had also included a moon, but that he had skirted two thousand years of ready-made moon talk, and uncovered an unusual metaphor better to capture the reality of the lunar experience.

> Sometimes in the afternoon sky a white moon would creep up like a little cloud, furtive, without display, suggesting an actress who does not have to 'come on' for a while, and so goes 'in front' in her ordinary clothes to watch the rest of the company for a moment, but keeps in the background, not wishing to attract attention to herself.

Even if we recognize the virtues of Proust's simile, it is not necessarily one we could easily come up with by ourselves. It may lie closer to a genuine impression of the moon, but if we observe the moon and are asked to say something about it, we are more likely to hit upon a tired rather than an inspired image. We may be well aware that our description of a moon is not up to the task, without knowing how to better it. To take licence with his response, this would perhaps have bothered Proust less than an unapologetic use of clichés by people who believed that it was always right to follow verbal conventions ('golden orb', 'heavenly body'), and who felt that a priority when talking was not to be original but to sound like someone else.

(de Botton 1997: 96–9)

➤ Take a phrase that you have heard many times before and try to find a fresh way of expressing the idea it contains.

➤ Do you think disciplines like Communication Studies are responsible for creating their own clichés?

▼ 47 **WHAT'S THE TOPIC? Writing style**
WHAT'S THE TEXT? Ernest Hemingway *By-Line*

The American writer Ernest Hemingway produced many pieces of journalism in addition to the novels, such as *A Farewell to Arms,* for which he is famous. One of the hallmarks of Hemingway's style was his use of short sentences. By using short sentences, Hemingway sought to create an impact by writing with great simplicity and great clarity. He would argue that a sentence should not be asked to do too much work. If we load it with too much information it becomes overcomplicated and the reader has to do too much work.

Here is an extract from one of Hemingway's articles, a description of a bull fight.

Read the extract carefully and consider what is the impact of using short sentences.

Out in the arena the picadors had galloped their decrepit horses around the ring, sitting straight and stiff in their rocking chair saddles. Now all but three had ridden out of the ring. These three were huddled against the red painted fence of the barrera. Their horses backed against the fence, one eye bandaged, their lances at rest.

In rode two of the marshals in the velvet jackets and white ruffs. They galloped up to the president's box, swerved and saluted, doffing their hats and bowing low. From the box an object came hurtling down. One of the marshals caught it in his plumed hat.

'The key to the bull pen,' said the Gin Bottle King.

The two horsemen whirled and rode across the arena. One of them tossed the key to a man in torero costume, they both saluted with a wave of their plumed hats, and had gone from the ring. The big gate was shut and bolted. There was no more entrance. The ring was complete.

The crowd had been shouting and yelling. Now it was dead silent. The man with the key stepped toward an iron barred, low, red door and unlocked the great sliding bar. He lifted it and stepped back. The door swung open. The man hid behind it. Inside it was dark.

Then, ducking his head as he came up out of the dark pen, a bull came into the arena. He came out all in a rush, big, black and white, weighing over a ton and moving with a soft gallop. Just as he came out the sun seemed to dazzle him for an instant. He stood as though he were frozen, his great crest of muscle up, firmly planted, his eyes looking around, his horns pointed forward, black and white and sharp as porcupine quills. Then he charged. And as he charged I suddenly saw what bull fighting is all about.

For the bull was absolutely unbelievable. He seemed like some great prehistoric animal, absolutely deadly and absolutely vicious. And he was silent. He charged silently and with a soft galloping rush. When he turned he turned on his four feet like a cat. When he charged the first thing that caught his eye was a picador on one of the wretched horses. The picador dug his spurs into the horse and they galloped away. The bull came on in his rush, refused to be shaken off, and in full gallop crashed into the animal from the side, ignored the horse, drove one of his horns high into the thigh of the picador, and tore him saddle and all, off the horse's back.

The bull went on without pausing to worry the picador lying on the ground. The next picador was sitting on his horse braced to receive the shock of the charge, his lance ready. The bull hit him sideways on, and horse and rider went high up in the air in a kicking mass and fell across the bull's back. As they came down the bull charged into them. The dough-faced kid, Chicuelo, vaulted over the fence, ran toward the bull and flopped his cape into the bull's face. The bull charged the cape and Chicuelo dodged backwards and had the bull clear in the arena.

Without an instant's hesitation the bull charged Chicuelo. The kid stood his ground, simply swung back on his heels and floated his cape like a ballet dancer's skirt into the bull's face as he passed.

'Ole!' – pronounced Oh-Lay! – roared the crowd.

The bull whirled and charged again. Without moving Chicuelo repeated the performance. His legs rigid, just withdrawing his body from the rush of the bull's horns and floating the cape out with that beautiful swing.

Again the crowd roared. The Kid did this seven times. Each time the bull missed him by inches. Each time he gave the bull a free shot at him. Each time the crowd roared. Then he flopped the cape once at the bull at the finish of a pass, swung it around behind him and walked away from the bull to the barrera.

'He's the boy with the cape all right,' said the Gin Bottle King. 'That swing he did with the cape's called a Veronica.'

(Hemingway 1967: 114–15)

> ➤ In addition to short sentences, what other stylistic devices do you think Hemingway employs? Look at the words he uses and how he constructs his sentences.
>
> ➤ What do you think Orwell would think of Hemingway's prose? Do you think it would satisfy his six rules of writing?

▼ **48 WHAT'S THE TOPIC? Making effective oral presentations**
WHAT'S THE TEXT? Newcastle University Classics Department 'Departmental guidelines on oral presentations'

Before we present our next extract we want you to first reflect on some aspects of your own communication practice.

Note your responses to the questions that follow.

Think about the last time you were asked to speak formally to a group of people. Which of these situations was it:

■ in class?
■ at a meeting?
■ at a social gathering?
■ somewhere else?

How did you prepare for your presentation?

How confident did you feel?

How effective was your presentation? Did your perception of it fit with what people in the audience felt?

How might you have improved it?

When you have jotted down your responses to these questions, look at the guidance notes from the University of Newcastle's Classics Department.

It is likely you will be asked to give a presentation on many occasions throughout your life, both as a student and later on as part of when you are working in your chosen career. Seminar presentations, group presentations, solo presentations are just a few examples of popular methods of assessment on most undergraduate courses, as they have the advantage of enabling students to share their learning experiences. At work, meetings and conferences are an increasingly common means of exchanging and disseminating information through the workforce. Being able to give a clear and effective presentation which captures and retains the interest and attention of colleagues is a much prized skill in the workplace. Students taking the AQA Communication Studies AS course are also called upon to give a ten-minute presentation which forms a key part of their assessment.

The web page that follows offers some invaluable advice on both preparing for and giving a presentation. Although the context is the university seminar, the advice on such issues as structure, handouts and visual aids is relevant to most contexts where a presentation may be called for.

STRUCTURE

Structure is often a lot less clear when material is presented verbally than when it is presented in writing, so you should be lot more rigorous about how you structure your presentation, and remember to give your audience lots of pointers on what you are going to say, when you are changing topics etc.

Preparation is at the heart of any presentation. The planning of your talk starts with a structure, which acts as a frame to support and guide your presentation. Then build on your framework by adding your details. Use titles and headings and keep your sentences brief. Bullet points – either on a handout or on an OHP – are useful to get across your ideas and remind the audience of the structure of your paper and how your detailed points fit together.

Two possible useful structures are:

- **Introduction** – tell your audience what you intend to cover, and what the main points are.
  Core – the detail. Go through each of the points in turn, making sure you give the audience cues as to when you are moving from one to the other, and how they fit together.
  Summary – now summarise what you have just said and draw your conclusions.
- **Situation** – introduce the issue at the heart of your topic.
  Complication – describe the factors affecting any presentation, the planning of this, and how it can be tackled in different ways.
  Resolution – explain your solution and its consequences.

It is sometimes useful to explain as part of your introductory section the significance of the topics you have chosen, what methodologies you are using to tackle particular issues, and why.

HANDOUTS AND VISUAL AIDS

. . .

. . . do not overload the audience. . . .

1. **Handouts:** These should be kept to a reasonable length – preferably no more than one side of A4 and two sides maximum. They should always be headed with the title of your presentation, your name and (for seminars and conference papers elsewhere) which university you are from.

   . . .

   You can also use a handout to reinforce the structure of your talk, either by explicitly providing a list of your main points or by grouping your references, bibliography and other sources and supporting material under appropriate sub-headings.

2. **Overheads:** Allow approximately 2 minutes per overhead, if you are using them for bullet points. If you are using them to show maps or plans, you might want to show them for longer. Use big drawings and text (you should be able to read them at 2m). Colour can be useful if you are trying to present complex charts and diagrams.

   Visual aids should be visual! OHPs are useful to present maps, charts, diagrams, site-plans etc., but not all material can be presented in this way. Try to avoid long extracts of text – if you need to present text, a handout is more manageable.

   Use them as prompts and ensure they help you make the point to the audience. They should support your presentation, without taking over. Too many OHPS will confuse and distract your audience.

   . . .

General points: Don't try to juggle too many kinds of media in a short talk and make sure you are happy with the operation of your equipment – focusing and switching to the spare bulb. If you are using flipcharts make sure your are familiar with the room format so they are positioned correctly.

Tie in your handouts and visual aids with what you are saying. If you have finished with an overhead before you need the next one, turn the projector off or at least remove it. Don't confuse your audience with mixed information.

Talk to your audience, not your visual aids and try not to obscure the screen by pointing to part of it – instead point to the OHP.

DELIVERING THE PRESENTATION

Talk it through aloud, referring to your overheads. It is frequently only by doing this that you will find out whether the structure works and whether your visual aids fit into the talk properly. Run through the whole talk a few times with an honest friend and get feedback on the content, style and length. Getting some feedback after the event is also useful – good presentations take practice and you will improve over time.

If you are nervous, write out the whole speech to have as insurance in case you freeze on the day. Try to keep sentences short and avoid complexities of structure. It is difficult to deliver long and complex sentences effectively in a verbal presentation and they are a lot less clear than they are in writing. It sometimes helps to put the main headings on small cards to act as prompts.

COMMUNICATION

. . .

Look at your audience . . . They will feel more involved and you will find it easier to judge the reaction and understanding of your presentation.

Movement – Many people fidget when they are nervous. When you practise you may have been made aware of this. If you jiggle with keys in your pockets, or pace up and down then make a point of holding on to the desk or lectern. You are unlikely to be aware of nervous movements, so ask friends to point them out when you practise. Try to gesture normally, as you would when speaking one-to-one.

<http://www.nd.ac.uk/classics/teaching/info/presentations.html>

WHAT'S NEXT?

➤ Now revisit the notes you made before reading this extract. Do these suggestions help? Make positive notes to yourself to guide you when planning and delivering future oral presentations.

▼ **49 WHAT'S THE TOPIC? Impressive communication**
WHAT'S THE TEXT? Dale Carnegie *The Quick and Easy Way to Effective Speaking*

For more specific advice on the skill of public speaking we turn to Dale Carnegie. From the mid-1960s the source to which countless people turned in search of self-improvement was the author of several books designed to help the ambitious succeed in business. His most famous endeavour is delightfully entitled *How to Win Friends and Influence People*.

The exuberant tone of much of Carnegie's writing can be a little off-putting, but there is at the heart of his work some sound and useful advice on such issues as public speaking and making presentations.

The following extract is taken from *The Quick and Easy Way to Effective Speaking* first published in 1962. Despite its somewhat chummy and anecdotal character, Carnegie does identify the key points that can help you make an effective delivery. For him, careful and detailed preparation is the key to becoming confident which is in itself the key to making an impressive presentation.

Assemble and arrange your ideas beforehand

What, then is the proper method of preparing a talk? Simply this: search your background for significant experiences that have taught you something about life, and assemble *your* thoughts, *your* ideas, *your* convictions, that have welled up from these experiences. True preparation means brooding over your topics. As Dr. Charles Reynold Brown said some years ago in a memorable series of lectures at Yale University: 'Brood over your topic until it becomes mellow and expansive . . . then put all these ideas down in writing, just a few words, enough to fix the idea . . . put them down on scraps of paper – you will find it easier to arrange and organize these loose bits when you come to set your material in order.' This doesn't sound like such a difficult program, does it? It isn't. It just requires a little concentration and thinking to a purpose.

Rehearse your talk with your friends

Should you rehearse your talk after you have it in some kind of order? By all means. Here is a sure-fire method that is easy and effective. Use the ideas you have selected for your talk in everyday conversation with your friends and business associates. Instead of going over the ball scores, just lean across the luncheon table and say something like this: 'You know, Joe, I had an unusual experience one day. I'd like to tell you about it.' Joe will probably be happy to listen to your story. Watch him for his reactions. Listen to his response. He may have an interesting idea that may be valuable. He won't know that you are rehearsing your talk, and it really doesn't matter. But he probably will say that he enjoyed the conversation.

Allan Nevins, the distinguished historian, gives similar advice to writers: 'Catch a friend who is interested in the subject and talk out what you have learned at length. In this way you discover facts of interpretation that you might have missed, points of arguments that had been unrealized, and the form most suitable for the story you have to tell.'

THIRD: PREDETERMINE YOUR MIND TO SUCCESS

In the first chapter, you remember, this sentence was used in reference to building the right attitude toward public speaking training in general. The same rule applies to the specific task now facing you, that of making each opportunity to speak a successful experience. There are three ways to accomplish this:

Lose yourself in your subject

After you have selected your subject, arranged it according to plan, and rehearsed it by 'talking it out' with your friends, your preparation is not ended. You must sell yourself on the importance of your subject. You must have the attitude that has inspired all the truly great personages of history – a belief in your cause. How do you fan the fires of faith in your message? By exploring all phases of your subject, grasping its deeper meanings, and asking yourself how your talk will help the audience to be better people for having listened to you.

Keep your attention off negative stimuli that may upset you

For instance, thinking of yourself making errors of grammar or suddenly coming to an end of your talk somewhere in the middle of it, is certainly a negative projection that could cancel confidence before you started. It is especially important to keep your attention off yourself just before your turn to speak. Concentrate on what the other speakers are saying, give them your wholehearted attention and you will not be able to work up excessive stage fright.

Give yourself a pep talk

Unless he is consumed by some great cause to which he has dedicated his life, every speaker will experience moments of doubt about his subject matter. He will ask himself whether the topic is the right one for him, whether the audience will be interested in it. He will be sorely tempted to change his subject. At times like these, when negativism is most likely to tear down self-confidence completely, you should give yourself a pep talk. In clear, straightforward terms tell yourself that your talk is the right one for you, because it comes out of your experience, out of your thinking about life. Say to yourself that you are more qualified than any member of the audience to give this particular talk and, by George, you are going to do your best to put it across. Is this old-fashioned Coué teaching? It may be, but modern experimental psychologists now agree that motivation based on auto-suggestion is one of the strongest incentives to rapid learning, even when simulated. How much more powerful, then, will be the effect of a sincere pep talk based on the truth?

FOURTH: ACT CONFIDENT

The most famous psychologist that America has produced, Professor William James, wrote as follows:

'Action seems to follow feeling, but really action and feeling go together; and by regulating the action, which is under the more direct control of the will, we can indirectly regulate the feeling, which is not.

'Thus the sovereign voluntary path to cheerfulness, if our spontaneous cheerfulness be lost, is to sit up cheerfully and to act and speak as if cheerfulness were already there. If such conduct does not make you feel cheerful, nothing else on that occasion can.

'So, to feel brave, act as if we were brave, use all of our will to that end, and a courage-fit will very likely replace the fit of fear.'

Apply Professor James' advice. To develop courage when you are facing an audience, act as if you already had it. Of course, unless you are prepared, all the acting in the world will avail but little. But granted that you know what you are going to talk about, step out briskly and take a deep breath. In fact, breathe deeply for thirty seconds before you ever face your audience. The increased supply of oxygen will buoy you up and give you courage. The great tenor, Jean de Reszke, used to say that when you had your breath so you 'could sit on it' nervousness vanished.

Draw yourself up to your full height and look your audience straight in the eyes, and begin to talk as confidently as if every one of them owed you money. Imagine that they do. Imagine that they have assembled there to beg you for an extension of credit. The psychological effect on you will be beneficial.

If you doubt that this philosophy makes sense, you would change your mind after a few minutes' conversation with almost any of the class members who have preceded you in following the ideas on which this book is based. Since you can't talk to them, take the word of an American who will always be a symbol of courage. Once he was the most timorous of men; by practicing self-assurance, he became one of the boldest; he was the trust-busting, audience-swaying, Big-Stick-wielding President of the United States, Theodore Roosevelt.

'Having been a rather sickly and awkward boy,' he confesses in his autobiography, 'I was, as a young man, at the first both nervous and distrustful of my powers. I had to train myself painfully and laboriously not merely as regards my body but as regards my soul and spirit.'

Fortunately, he has disclosed how he achieved the transformation. 'When a boy,' he wrote, 'I read a passage in one of Marryat's books which always impressed me. In this passage, the captain of some small British man-of-war is explaining to the hero how to acquire the quality of fearlessness. He says that at the outset almost every man is frightened when he goes into action, but that the course to follow is for the man to keep such a grip on himself that he can act just as if he were not frightened. After this is kept up long enough, it changes from pretence to reality, and the man does in very fact become fearless by sheer dint of practicing fearlessness when he does not feel it.

'This was the theory upon which I went. There were all kinds of things of which I was afraid at first, ranging from grizzly bears to 'mean' horses and gun-fighters; but by acting as if I were not afraid I gradually ceased to be afraid. Most men can have the same experience if they choose.'

Overcoming fear of public speaking has a tremendous transfer value to everything that we do. Those who answer this challenge find that they are better persons because of it. They find that their victory over fear of talking before groups has taken them out of themselves into a richer and fuller life.

A salesman wrote: 'After a few times on my feet before the class, I felt that I could tackle anyone. One morning I walked up to the door of a particularly tough purchasing agent, and before he could say 'no', I had my samples spread out on his desk, and he gave me one of the biggest orders I have ever received.'

A housewife told one of our representatives: 'I was afraid to invite the neighbors in for fear that I wouldn't be able to keep the conversation going. After taking a few sessions and getting up on my feet, I took the plunge and held my first party. It was a great success. I had no trouble stimulating the group along interesting lines of talk.'

At a graduating class, a clerk said: 'I was afraid of the customers, I gave them a feeling that I was apologetic. After speaking to the class a few times, I found that I was speaking up with more assurance and poise, I began to answer objections with authoritativeness. My sales went up forty-five per cent the first month after I started to speak to this class.'

They discovered that it was easy to conquer other fears and anxieties and to be successful where before they may have failed. You, too, will find that speaking in public will enable you to face what each day presents with a sure touch that confidence brings. You will be able to meet the problems and conflicts of life with a new sense of mastery. What has been a series of insoluble situations can become a bright challenge to increased pleasure in living.

(Carnegie 1962: 35–43)

➤ There are many clues in this extract which enable us to determine that it is clearly of its time (mid-twentieth century). To what extent have the devices that we can employ to 'win friends and influence people' changed? Do we now use entirely different contemporary devices or are there some eternal truths about effective oral presentations?

50 WHAT'S THE TOPIC? Rhetoric
WHAT'S THE TEXT? Jacquie L'Etang 'Public relations and rhetoric'

The most commonly used term used to describe the use of eloquent language to persuade people to do or to think something is 'rhetoric'. Many years ago, in a galaxy far far away, students used to study rhetoric.

Before we start moving to draw together the advice that this part of the book has tried to offer it would be useful to take a look at some contemporary perspectives on rhetoric. After that we'll look at some of the problems generated by rhetoric (with an extract from Emmett Grogan's autobiography, pp. 169–71) and then look at a contemporary rejoinder that states quite clearly that rhetoric is an unavoidable part of communication practice (with Alan Bryman's bullet points about effective writing, p. 172).

Rhetoric has had something of an intellectual renaissance due to the influence of structuralism, poststructuralism, semiotics and postmodernist thinking, streams of thought which move away from essentialist conceptions of society and knowledge towards relativist and phenomenological approaches: society and knowledge are explained as being the result of certain intellectual structures which arise partly from cultural experience and language. Debates which spring from structuralism and poststructuralism focus on the relationship between thought and language, and between the thinking, articulate subject and the object. Structuralism and semiotics explore the sources and signs of culture, and the ways in which our experiences and knowledge are influenced and structured by these. Structuralism abandoned the idea that there was an intrinsic 'essence' or meaning in a text or that the author's intention was either obvious or of paramount importance (Hartley 1994: 302). Work in the structuralist tradition tries to identify systems of structural patterns with a text which enable the reader to generate meaning. This philosophical position led to the form of analysis known as deconstruction, in which the critic or reader tries to extract that which is missing or suppressed, or regarded as deviant in the discourse(s) or power relations present in the text under review (ibid.: 304). A 'text' in this context has a very broad meaning and can refer to not only literary works but also dramatic performances, films, television and public or cultural events. Poststructuralism emphasised the reader rather than the text as a site of enquiry and therefore focused more on psychoanalytical influences on the interpretation of meaning and on external structures, such as ethnicity and gender, that facilitate meaning processes (ibid.: 304). Postmodernism presents an epistemology based on 'multiple and fragmentary worlds . . . that overlap, compete and transform themselves continuously' (Halloran 1993: 114).

These intellectual currents imply that the relationship between thought, language, signification, dialectics and knowledge is contested, dynamic and intrinsically rhetorical. Rhetoric focuses on the sign system, the devices and strategies that operate within texts and the sense-making function of specific discourses (Hartley 1994: 266). As Bizzell and Herzberg note, 'twentieth-century theories of rhetoric, in formulating the relationships between language and knowledge and in re-examining the powers of discourse, have extended the concerns of rhetoric to include nothing less than every instance of language use' (Bizzell and Herzberg, cited in Enos and Brown 1993: viii). Hartley also suggests that the forms of the cultural produce with which we are surrounded are 'highly rhetorical' and the 'Publicity, advertising, newspapers, television, academic books, government statements and so on, all exploit rhetorical figures to tempt us to see things their way' (Hartley 1994: 266).

Rhetorical thinking is thus connected to debate, argument (intentional communication) and persuasion (instrumental communication). The views of Sophists and ancient Sceptics anticipate relativism and postmodernism in their rejection of a universal standard in favour of a range of different perspectives. This is of importance to public relations for two reasons: first, because it suggests that there is no one overall standard with regard to those interests on behalf of which public relations operates, and, second, because it also suggests that there is no one overall standard for public relations practice itself. Much of the debate about the ethics of public relations has focused on its social role and conflict between client and public interest such as the promotion of causes thought to be unjustifiable (for example products or industrial processes which either are or have the potential to be injurious to the health of consumers or production workers, e.g. tobacco products or asbestos). Some have tried to get around this problem by arguing that public relations is intrinsically ethical because it promotes democracy and good citizenship (there is a detailed discussion of these claims and their supporting arguments in Chapter 6). This move necessitates consideration of questions of power and access since these elements will influence ability to communicate as well as how a piece of communication is regarded. A discussion about the social role and ethics of public relations should at least acknowledge important linked debates about knowledge acquisition and communication ethics. The field of rhetoric is an important part of such a discussion, not only because of its historical link to public relations but also because currently it directly confronts questions of dialogue, debate and persuasion with a framework which takes account of ethics and postmodernist thought.

Contemporary developments in rhetoric have returned to explore the tension between philosophy (based on foundational and universalist principles) and rhetoric (seen as relativist) and thus to the problematic of the ethics of rhetoric. The renewed interest in the ancient concept of rhetoric began in the 1950s and the expansion and development of the field has been dubbed 'The New

Rhetorics' (Enos and Brown 1993: vii–xiii). Work in this area connects with a wide range of analytical work in discourse analysis and postmodernism, as well as with more practical application of languages and argument in Departments of English or Schools of Communication and Writing. Thus is can be seen that the twin streams of analysis and practice, present in the classical tradition, are still represented today.

Cohen (1994: 69-82) identifies a number of separate perspectives in the New Rhetorics. These include an extension of the traditional understanding of rhetoric as a methodology for the study of argument; an attempt to overcome the traditional hostility between philosophy and rhetoric by using rhetoric itself as a way of explaining dialectical principles; the use of rhetoric as an analytical tool for fictional narrative; the attraction of rhetoric for postmodernists because of its rejection of philosophical conceptions of universals such as truth and knowledge. The New Rhetorics is marked by diversity, transformation and dialogue in order to achieve a broad understanding of what 'our contending viewpoints reveal about skilled human discourse' (Bazerman, cited in Enos and Brown 1993: x). These different approaches are reflected in a variety of contemporary definitions of 'rhetoric' reflecting different aspects of the historical, political and cultural baggage that the term encompasses. Bazerman suggests that the field can be approached in a variety of ways that reflect and 'characterise our approach to dividing up and studying the symbolic domain' (Bazerman 1993: 4). So, for example, one approach might look specifically at symbolic activity which seemed primarily motivated by persuasion, whereas an alternative approach might analyse the nature and focus of organisational rhetors and rhetoric. Bazerman argues from an instrumental perspective that most rhetorical study is concerned with its practical application and that our thinking about this matters because

> symbolic action is a major dynamic of society to be wielded for public and private ends. Prescriptions for traditional rhetorics, proscriptions for traditional rhetorics, proscriptions against stigmatised rhetorics, projections of new rhetorics – all advance social visions, perceived by their advocates to improve the human condition.

> (Bazerman 1993: 4)

The relevance of rhetoric to public relations lies not only in its communicative function but also in its symbolic and structural role managing meaning within and between organisations and publics and in the claim to be contributing to a better society by assisting the flow of information.

> (L'Etang 1996: 106–23)

> ➤ Is it possible to communicate (in either speech or writing) in a way that avoids rhetorical devices?

▼ 51 WHAT'S THE TOPIC? The trouble with rhetoric
WHAT'S THE TEXT? Emmett Grogan
Ringolevio: A Life Played for Keeps

It is likely to be the case that any attempt to communicate clearly, effectively, impressively, will always be dogged by the spectre of polysemy. Perhaps all texts are polysemic, perhaps all texts are ambiguous. But there is, even with the most inept attempt at communication, a sense in which we can discern whether or not someone is telling the truth, or is putting us on. Or can we? And what exactly is the status of a text if it's written by one person and delivered by another (as is the case with most politicians). Whilst we would commend Alan Bryman's advice to you (Extract 52 below) we also feel duty bound to point out that trying to intoxicate an audience with rhetoric always ends in disappointment – or fascism. Two cars in every garage, three eyes on every fish.

The following extract is taken from Emmett Grogan's autobiography. Grogan was a member of the Diggers, a 1960s counter-cultural movement. He frequently found himself at odds with the well-meaning but naïve intellectuals of that time. Here he describes how he succeeds in putting on his audience at the Dialectics of Liberation conference held at London's Roundhouse in 1968 when the scent of revolution was very much in the air.

Early the next evening, Emmett found himself standing in front of the same microphone before about one thousand of the younger, heavier members of the same audience. This time, however, he was alone with no one else on the stage. He also felt a lot younger than the previous night, when his chippy shot of drugstore scag made him feel as old as the hills and as numb-dumb-cold-dry as a dead dog. He still couldn't figure out why he hit himself in the vein with the poison of his youth. Had it just been for old time's sake or had he been trying to impress his Beat elders with his own down hipster style? He gave up attempting to answer himself with a vow that he'd never chip again.

The rows of radicals who came to hear what he had to say were anxious but attentive, and Emmett was ready for them. He had memorized his speech the day before and had thoroughly gone over it that afternoon, blocking out its dramatic pauses and polishing up his delivery. When the moderator of the day's symposium of 'Liberation,' or whatever it was supposed to be, finished introducing Emmett as a 'Digger, a hippie, an acidhead and a living mythical legend in his own time,' he stepped forward to the applause and waited for it to subside, feeling '. . . righteously righteous and stone justly just,' as his good friend and family doctor once said in a song.

The handclapping died down, and Emmett spoke strong and clearly into the microphone like an actor delivering a soliloquy, and the finger-popping revolutionaries listened to what they wanted to hear:

'Our revolution will do more to effect a real, inner transformation than all of modern history's revolts taken together! . . . In no stage of our advance, in no stage of our fighting must we let chaos rule! . . . Nobody can doubt the fact that during the last year, a revolution of the most momentous character has been swelling like a storm among the youth of the West. Look at the strength of awareness of the young people today! Look at our inner unity of will, our unity of spirit and our growing community of thought! Who could compare us with the youth of yesterday? We are unanimously convinced that strength finds its expression not in an army, in tanks and heavy guns, but rather ultimately expresses itself in the common working of a people's will! The will that is uniting our groups with the conviction that men and women must be taught the feeling of community to safeguard against the spirit of class warfare, of class hatred and of class division! . . . We are approaching a life in common, a common life of revolution! A common life to work for the revolutionary advancement of peace, spiritual prosperity and socialism! Toward a victorious renewal of life itself! . . . Our job is to wake everyone up and do away with illusions! So that when the people are finally awakened, never again will they plunge into sleep!

'The revolution will never end! It must be allowed to develop into streams of revolutions and be guided into the channel of evolution . . . History will judge the movement not according to the number of swine we have removed or imprisoned, but according to whether the revolution has succeeded in returning the power to the people and in the bridling of that power to enforce the will of the people everywhere! . . . Power to the people!'

The entire speech lasted for over ten minutes, and Emmett was satisfied with his convincing delivery that now had the whole audience up on its feet giving him an enthusiastic, standing ovation. He stood motionless by the microphone, where seconds before he was gesticulating like mad, dramatizing every word. He stood still, not bowing, or waving, or moving his lips to say, 'Thank you! Thank you!' He just stood there and waited for the crowd to settle back down, so he could finally tell them what he *really* came there to say.

It was a couple of minutes before it was quiet enough for him to again place his mouth near the microphone and say, 'I can sincerely appreciate your enthusiasm and honestly understand your excited applause, but, to be perfectly truthful, I can accept neither. You see, I neither wrote nor was I the first person to have ever given this speech. I really don't know who wrote it. I have an idea, but I really don't know. However, I do know who was the first man to make this speech. His name was Adolf Hitler, and he made his delivery of these same words at the Reichstag in, I believe, 1937. Thank you, 'n be seein' you.'

There wasn't a sound in the huge main hall of the Roundhouse for a full thirty seconds or more. Nobody even moved. Then, all at once, it exploded with the fury of one thousand persons who thought they'd been had, been messed over, come out on the short end of a dirty deal! They directed their rage at Emmett who got his ass out of there real quick, and then they completely flipped, breaking things up, setting stuff on fire, and spilling their anger outside onto the street where they began fighting with those few who thought that Emmett Grogan had showed them just how jive rhetoric really was by putting them all on, beautifully.

(Grogan 1972: 432–4)

WHAT'S NEXT?

➤ If you had been a member of Grogan's audience would you have reacted in the same way as they did?
➤ Are there any rhetorical devices one should never use?

▼ 52 WHAT'S THE TOPIC? Summing up
WHAT'S THE TEXT? Alan Bryman *Social Research Methods*

Concluding Chapter 23 ('Writing up social research') of his *Social Research Methods* Alan Bryman offers some extremely useful points about effective written communication, about clarity in writing, about rhetoric.

- Good writing is probably just as important as good research practice. Indeed, it is probably better thought of as a good research practice.
- Clear structure and statement of your research questions are important components of writing up research.
- Be sensitive to the ways in which writers seek to persuade us of their points of view.
- The study of rhetoric and writing strategies generally teaches us that the writings of scientists and social scientists do more than simply report findings. They are designed to convince and persuade.
- The emphasis on rhetoric is not meant to imply there is no external social reality; it merely suggests that our understanding of that reality is profoundly influenced by the ways it is represented by writers.

. . .

- We need to get away from the idea that rhetoric and the desire to persuade others of the validity of our work are somehow bad things. They are not. We all want to get our points across and to persuade our readers that we have got things right. The question is – do we do it well? Do we make the best possible case? We all have to persuade others that we have got the right angle on things; the trick is to do it well. So when you write an essay or dissertation, do bear in mind the significance of your writing strategy.

(Bryman 2001: 473–4)

WHAT'S NEXT?

➤ Reflecting on the advice and the example of George Orwell, the Plain English Campaign, Alain de Botton, Ernest Hemingway, and Alan Bryman, prepare a list of statements to guide your own communication practice.

▼ 53 WHAT'S THE TOPIC? Communication problems (real and contrived)
WHAT'S THE TEXT? John Cleese and Connie Booth *Fawlty Towers*: 'Communications problems'

We opened this part of the book with a consideration of the challenge that confronts a person wishing to communicate effectively. Failure to communicate effectively can at times have dire consequences. At other times it can provide a rich source of comedy. The extract that follows is taken from an episode of the classic 1980s British television situation comedy *Fawlty Towers* entitled 'Communications Problems'. One of the communication problems in the title centres on the failure of Mrs Richards' hearing aids to operate correctly, although there is some evidence to suggest that its malfunctioning may be somewhat selective.

CAST

John Cleese	Basil Fawlty
Prunella Scales	Sybil Fawlty
Andrew Sachs	Manuel
Connie Booth	Polly
Joan Sanderson	Mrs Richards
Ballard Berekley	Major Gowen
Gilly Flower	Miss Tibbs
Renee Roberts	Miss Gatsby

Scene: Interior, hotel reception area, Fawlty Towers

MISS TIBBS and MISS GATSBY   [in unison] Good afternoon

MRS RICHARDS   [speaking to two elderly ladies as they cross the hotel reception] First they give me a room with no view and then there's no lavatory paper.

MISS GATSBY   Oh!

MISS TIBBS   Would you like some of ours?

[Mrs Richards rings counter bell furiously]

MISS GATSBY   We keep an extra supply.

MISS TIBBS   Would you like some of ours?

MRS RICHARDS   [rings bell insistently] Hello! Girl! There's no paper in my room. Why don't you check these things? That's what you're being paid for, isn't it?

POLLY   Well we don't put it in the rooms.

MRS RICHARDS   What?!!

POLLY   We keep it in the lounge.

MRS RICHARDS   In the lounge!

POLLY   I'll get you some. Do you want plain ones or ones with our address on it?

MRS RICHARDS   Address on it?

POLLY   How many sheets? [look of disbelief on Mrs Richards' face.] Well how many are you going to use?

MRS RICHARDS   [rings bells furiously] Manager!

POLLY   Well? Just enough for one?

MRS RICHARDS   Manager! Manager!

BASIL FAWLTY   [emerges from the kitchen, cupping his hands to his mouth to amplify his voice] Yes. Testing. Testing.

MRS RICHARDS   There you are! I've never met such insolence in my life. I come down here to get some lavatory paper and she starts asking me the most insulting, personal things I've ever heard in my life.

POLLY   I thought she wanted writing paper.

MRS RICHARDS   I'm talking to you, what?

BASIL FAWLTY   What?

MRS RICHARDS   Are you deaf? I said 'I'm talking to you'. I've never met such insolence in my life. She said people use it in the lounge.

BASIL FAWLTY   Yes, yes, she thought—

MRS RICHARDS   Then she started asking me the most awful—

BASIL FAWLTY   No no no, please listen. [Mrs Richards talks over him apparently oblivious to what he is saying.] No no no please I can explain. No no she thought you wanted to write.

MRS RICHARDS   Wanted a fight? I'll give her a fight all right.

BASIL FAWLTY   No no no no – wanted to write.

MRS RICHARDS   What?!!

BASIL FAWLTY   Wanted to write. On the paper [makes handwriting gesture].

MRS RICHARDS   Why should I want to write on it?

BASIL FAWLTY   [exasperated] I'll have some sent up to your room immediately. Hah. [Bangs desk bell] Manuel!

MRS RICHARDS   That doesn't work either. What were you saying then?

BASIL FAWLTY   [leans forward and shouts] Turn it on [indicates hearing aid].

MRS RICHARDS   What?

BASIL FAWLTY   [leans further forward] TURN! IT! [Grabs paper and pen] TURN. IT. ON. [Holds handwritten note up to Mrs Richards.]

MRS RICHARDS   [impatiently] I can't read that. I need my glasses. [She looks through her handbag] Where are they?

BASIL FAWLTY   They're on your head, Mrs Richards.

MRS RICHARDS   [continues to look through her bag's contents] I've lost them. They're the only pair I've got. I can't read a thing without them.

BASIL FAWLTY   Excuse me [raises left hand in air]

MRS RICHARDS   Now I had them this morning—

BASIL FAWLTY   Mrs Richards. Mrs Richards.

MRS RICHARDS   When I was buying the vase. I put them on to look at it.

POLLY   Mrs Richards [leans towards her, raising right hand in air] Hello!

MRS RICHARDS   I had them at tea time.

BASIL FAWLTY   [points to her head] Mrs Richards – your glasses are there.

MRS RICHARDS   There. Well who put them in there? [Misreads Basil's pointing finger as pointing across the hotel foyer and walks across it towards the dining room door]

BASIL FAWLTY   No no no. On your head.

MRS RICHARDS   What?

BASIL FAWLTY   ON. YOUR. [Writes furiously on notepaper] ON. YOUR. Agh! [Gives up.]

WHAT'S NEXT?

➤ Make a list of each of the communication problems encountered by the characters in this extract. Consider how each one might be resolved.

I thought of London spread out in the sun
Its postal districts packed like squares of wheat

(Philip Larkin 'The Whitsun Weddings')

Part 4 of this book is about communication in context(s), the most significant of which is culture. It organises a debate about the meanings we give to the key texts of our everyday lives within a debate about what culture is.

▼ 54 WHAT'S THE TOPIC? Definitions of culture
WHAT'S THE TEXT? Dick Hebdige *Subculture: The Meaning of Style*

Before we enter that debate then, it will be useful to find that bigger debate. Dick Hebdige, in *Subculture: The Meaning of Style*, does this pretty smartly, offering, economically, an historical dimension.

CULTURE

Culture: cultivation, tending, in Christian authors, worship; the action or practice of cultivating the soil; tillage, husbandry; the cultivation or rearing of certain animals (e.g. fish); the artificial development of microscopic organisms, organisms so produced; the cultivating or development (of the mind, faculties, manners), improvement or refinement by education and training; the condition of being trained or refined; the intellectual side of civilization; the prosecution or special attention or study of any subject or pursuit. (*Oxford English Dictionary*)

Culture is a notoriously ambiguous concept as the above definition demonstrates. Refracted through centuries of usage, the word has acquired a number of quite different, often contradictory, meanings. Even as a scientific term, it

CONTINUED

refers both to a process (artificial development of microscopic organisms) and a product (organisms so produced). More specifically, since the end of the eighteenth century, it has been used by English intellectuals and literary figures to focus critical attention on a whole range of controversial issues. The 'quality of life', the effects in human terms of mechanization, the division of labour and the creation of a mass society have all been discussed within the larger confines of what Raymond Williams has called the 'Culture and Society' debate (Williams, 1961). It was through this tradition of dissent and criticism that the dream of the 'organic society' – of society as an integrated, meaningful whole – was largely kept alive. The dream had two basic trajectories. One led back to the past and to the feudal ideal of a hierarchically ordered community. Here, culture assumed an almost sacred function. Its 'harmonious perfection' (Arnold, 1868) was posited against the Wasteland of contemporary life.

The other trajectory, less heavily supported, led towards the future, to a socialist Utopia where the distinction between labour and leisure was to be annulled. Two basic definitions of culture emerged from this tradition, though these were by no means necessarily congruent with the two trajectories outlined above. The first – the one which is probably most familiar to the reader – was essentially classical and conservative. It represented culture as a standard of aesthetic excellence: 'the best that has been thought and said in the world' (Arnold, 1868), and it derived from an appreciation of 'classic' aesthetic form (opera, ballet, drama, literature, art). The second, traced back by Williams to Herder and the eighteenth century (Williams, 1976), was rooted in anthropology. Here the term 'culture' referred to a

> . . . particular way of life which expresses certain meanings and values not only in art and learning, but also in institutions and ordinary behaviour. The analysis of culture, from such a definition, is the clarification of the meanings and values implicit and explicit in a particular way of life, a particular culture. (Williams, 1965)

This definition obviously had a much broader range. It encompassed, in T.S. Eliot's words,

> . . . all the characteristic activities and interests of a people. Derby Day, Henley Regatta, Cowes, the 12th of August, a cup final, the dog races, the pin table, the dartboard, Wensleydale cheese, boiled cabbage cut into sections, beetroot in vinegar, 19th Century Gothic churches, the music of Elgar . . . (Eliot, 1948)

As Williams noted, such a definition could only be supported if a new theoretical initiative was taken. The theory of culture now involved the 'study of relationships between elements in a whole way of life' (Williams, 1965). The emphasis shifted from immutable to historical criteria, from fixity to transformation:

. . . an emphasis (which) from studying particular meanings and values seeks not so much to compare these, as a way of establishing a scale, but by studying their modes of change to discover certain general causes or 'trends' by which social and cultural developments as a whole can be better understood. (Williams, 1965)

Williams was, then, proposing an altogether broader formulation of the relationships between culture and society, one which through the analysis of 'particular meanings and values' sought to uncover the concealed fundamentals of history; the 'general causes' and broad social 'trends' which lie behind the manifest appearances of an 'everyday life'.

In the early years, when it was being established in the Universities, Cultural Studies sat rather uncomfortably on the fence between these two conflicting definitions – culture as a standard of excellence, culture as a 'whole way of life' – unable to determine which represented the most fruitful line of enquiry. Richard Hoggart and Raymond Williams portrayed working-class culture sympathetically in wistful accounts of pre-scholarship boyhoods (Leeds for Hoggart (1958), a Welsh mining village for Williams (1960)) but their work displayed a strong bias towards literature and literacy and an equally strong moral tone. Hoggart deplored the way in which the traditional working-class community – a community of tried and tested values despite the dour landscape in which it had been set – was being undermined and replaced by a 'Candy Floss World' of thrills and cheap fiction which was somehow bland *and* sleazy. Williams tentatively endorsed the new mass communications but was concerned to establish aesthetic and moral criteria for distinguishing the worthwhile products from the 'trash'; the jazz – 'a real musical form' – and the football – 'a wonderful game' – from the 'rape novel, the Sunday strip paper and the latest Tin Pan drool' (Williams, 1965). In 1966 Hoggart laid down the basic premises upon which Cultural Studies were based:

First, without appreciating good literature, no one will really understand the nature of society, second, literary critical analysis can be applied to certain social phenomena other than 'academically respectable' literature (for example; the popular arts, mass communications) so as to illuminate their meanings for individuals and their societies. (Hoggart, 1966)

The implicit assumption that it still required a literary sensibility to 'read' society with the requisite subtlety, and that the two ideas of culture could be ultimately reconciled was also, paradoxically, to inform the early work of the French writer, Roland Barthes, though here it found validation in a method – semiotics – a way of reading signs (Hawkes, 1977 [1992]).

(Hebdige 1979: 5–8)

> ➤ TS Eliot offers a list of English cultural items which he presented in the late 1940s. Make a current list. What are the differences?
> ➤ Arnold wrote of 'the best that has been thought and said'. What would your list include?

▼ **55 WHAT'S THE TOPIC? Ideology**
  WHAT'S THE TEXT? Raymond Williams
  Keywords

Central to any debate about society and culture is the debate about ideology. Once again there are a number of significantly differing understandings which are addressed in Raymond Williams's intellectual reference book *Keywords*, a sort of extended dictionary of important ideas. In the following extract it is useful particularly to focus on the difference between:

■ Ideology as abstract and false thought – the classic Marxist definition of a world turned upside down so that 'ordinary' and 'natural' relationships are made to appear those that best serve the interests of the ruling classes. An example might be views of human nature which stress the natural selfishness or competitiveness of human beings and which therefore implicitly support a system based upon selfishness and competitiveness such as Western Capitalism.

■ Ideology as a set of ideas from a definite class or group. This is the sense in which we can talk about working-class ideology, feminist ideology or the ideology of the ruling class.

There is then some direct continuity between the pejorative sense of **ideology**, as it had been used in the C19 by conservative thinkers, and the pejorative sense popularized by Marx and Engels in *The German Ideology* (1845–7) and subsequently. Scott had distinguished ideology as theory 'resting in no respect upon the basis of self-interest', though Napoleon's alternative had actually been the (suitably vague) 'knowledge of the human heart and of the lessons of history'. Marx and Engels, in their critique of the thought of their radical German contemporaries, concentrated on its abstraction from the real processes of history. Ideas, as they said specifically of the ruling ideas of an epoch, 'are nothing more than the ideal expression of the dominant material relationships, the dominant material relationships grasped as ideas'. Failure to realize this produced **ideology**: an upside-down version of reality.

> If in all ideology men and their circumstances appear upside down as in a *camera obscura*, this phenomenon arises just as much from their historical life process as the inversion of objects on the retina does from their physical life process. (*German Ideology*, 47)

Or as Engels put it later:

> Every ideology . . . once it has arisen develops in connection with the given concept-material, and develops this material further; otherwise it would cease to be ideology, that is, occupation with thoughts as with independent entities, developing independently and subject only to their own laws. That the material life-conditions of the persons inside whose heads this thought process goes on in the last resort determine the course of this process remains of necessity unknown to these persons, for otherwise there would be an end to all ideology. (*Feuerbach*, 65–6)

Or again:

> Ideology is a process accomplished by the so-called thinker consciously indeed but with a false consciousness. The real motives impelling him remain unknown to him, otherwise it would not be an ideological process at all. Hence he imagines false or apparent motives. Because it is a process of thought he derives both its form and its content from pure thought, either his own or his predecessors'. (*Letter to Mehring*, 1893)

Ideology is then abstract and false thought, in a sense directly related to the original conservative use but with the alternative – knowledge of real material conditions and relationships – differently stated. Marx and Engels then used this idea critically. The 'thinkers' of a ruling class were 'its active conceptive ideologists, who make the perfecting of the illusion of the class about itself their chief source of livelihood' (*German Ideology*, 65). Or again: 'the official representatives of French democracy were steeped in republican ideology to such an extent that it was only some weeks later that they began to have an inkling of the significance of the June fighting' (*Class Struggles in France*, 1850). This sense of **ideology** as illusion, false consciousness, unreality, upside-down reality, is predominant in their work. Engels believed that the 'higher ideologies' – philosophy and religion – were more removed from material interests than the direct ideologies of politics and law, but the connection, though complicated, was still decisive (*Feuerbach*, 277). They were 'realms of ideology which soar still high in the air . . . various false conceptions of nature, of man's own being, of spirits, magic forces, etc . . .' (*Letter to Schmidt*, 1890). This sense has persisted.

Yet there is another, apparently more neutral sense of **ideology** in some parts of Marx's writing, notable in the well-known passage in the *Contribution to the Critique of Political Philosophy* (1859):

CONTINUED

The distinction should always be made between the material transformation of the economic conditions of production . . . and the legal, political, religious, aesthetic or philosophic – in short, ideological – forms in which men become conscious of this conflict and fight it out.

This is clearly related to part of the earlier sense: the ideological forms are expressions of (changes in) economic conditions of production. But they are seen here as the forms in which men become *conscious* of the conflict arising from conditions and changes of condition in economic production. This sense is very difficult to reconcile with the sense of **ideology** as mere illusion.

(Williams 1983: 154–6)

WHAT'S NEXT?

➤ Louis Althusser suggested that 'ideology is indeed a system of representation'. Collect a set of representations of any social group and consider how far they are affected by the ideology of our society.

▼   56 WHAT'S THE TOPIC? High culture
        WHAT'S THE TEXT? Matthew Arnold *Culture and Anarchy*

CULTURAL ABSOLUTIST

Perhaps the most famous statement, and protracted defence, of the high-culture position was that of Matthew Arnold in his aptly titled *Culture and Anarchy*. Put simply Arnold saw culture and anarchy as enemies, with the former the only really reliable protection against the latter. Arnold is concerned with a sort of social improvement such that he writes of 'canvassing' on behalf of Culture, as if it were a parliamentary candidate and that he recommends Culture as 'the great help out of our present difficulties'. He goes on to the clearest statement yet of the case for the defence of the high-culture position:

■   culture is a pursuit of our 'total perfection'
■   culture is concerned with 'the best which has been thought and said in the world' and
■   culture is 'turning a stream of fresh and free thought upon our stock notions and habits'.

He goes on in this preface to explore the reasons why England has no need for an Academy of Culture in the way that the French have the Académie française to oversee, not to say police, cultural standards. Most significantly it is the freedom and openness of English culture and the warning of the inwardness of culture which will result from its organisation that is the best reason for staying clear of an academy.

And now to pass to the matters canvassed in the following essay. The whole scope of the essay is to recommend culture as the great help out of our present difficulties; culture being a pursuit of our total perfection by means of getting to know, on all the matters which most concern us, the best which has been thought and said in the world; and through this knowledge, turning a stream of fresh and free thought upon our stock notions and habits, which we now follow staunchly but mechanically, vainly imagining that there is a virtue in following them staunchly which makes up for the mischief of following them mechanically. This, and this alone, is the scope of the following essay. And the culture we recommend is, above all, an inward operation.

But we are often supposed, when we criticise by the help of culture some imperfect doing or other, to have in our eye some well-known rival plan of doing, which we want to serve and recommend. Thus, for instance, because we have freely pointed out the dangers and inconveniences to which our literature is exposed in the absence of any centre of taste and authority like the French Academy, it is constantly said that we want to introduce here in England an institution like the French Academy. We have, indeed, expressly declared that we wanted no such thing; but let us notice how it is just our worship of machinery, and of external doing, which leads to this charge being brought; and how the inwardness of culture makes us seize, for watching and cure, the faults to which our want of an Academy inclines us, and yet prevents us from trusting to an arm of flesh, as the Puritans say, – from blindly flying to this outward machinery of an Academy, in order to help ourselves. For the very same culture and free inward play of thought which shows how the Corinthian style, or the whimsies about the One Primeval Language, are generated and strengthened in the absence of an Academy, shows us, too, how little any Academy, such as we should be likely to get, would cure them. Every one who knows the characteristics of our national life, and the tendencies so fully discussed in the following pages, knows exactly what an English Academy would be like. The very same faults – the want of sensitiveness of intellectual conscience, the disbelief in right reason, the dislike of authority – which have hindered our having an Academy and have worked injuriously in our literature, would also hinder us from making our Academy, if we established it, one which would really correct them. And culture, which shows us truly the faults to be corrected, shows us this also just as truly.

(Arnold 1869: viii–x)

➤ Arnold entitled his book *Culture and Anarchy*. What does this suggest about the function of culture?

▼   57 WHAT'S THE TOPIC? High and low culture
        WHAT'S THE TEXT? Raymond Williams
        Communications

For an intelligent and balanced view of the popular culture versus high culture debate we need look no further than Raymond Williams. Writing in the early 1960s he unearths most of the important questions and particularly these two:

■   Isn't there great danger of the tradition of high culture being overwhelmed by mass culture, which expresses the tastes and standards of the ordinary man?
■   Is the tradition of high culture simply received and used by a particular social minority, which will indeed often add to it certain works and habits of its own ?

Men differ in their capacities for excellence. Yet democracy insists that everyone has an equal right to judge. Aren't we seeing, in our own time, the results of this contradiction? Isn't there great danger of the tradition of high culture being overwhelmed by mass culture, which expresses the tastes and standards of the ordinary man? Isn't it really our first duty to defend minority culture, which in its actual works is the highest achievement of humanity?

The difficulty here is that 'minority culture' can mean two things. It can mean the work of the great artists and thinkers, and of the many lesser but still important figures who sustain them. It can mean also the work of these men as received and used by a particular social minority, which will indeed often add to it certain works and habits of its own.

The great tradition is in many ways a common inheritance, and it has been the purpose of the best of modern education to make it as widely available as possible. Certainly this extension is never as easy as some people expect. Certainly it often happens that in the attempt to make difficult work more widely available, part of the value of the work is lost. Perhaps the whole attempt is wrongly conceived, and we should concentrate instead on maintaining the high tradition in its own terms.

The question is, however, can this in any case be done. The work of the great artists and thinkers has never been confined to their own company; it has always been made available to some others. And doesn't it often happen that those to whom it has been made available identify the tradition with themselves, grafting it into their own way of life? Thus, Sophocles, Shakespeare, Ibsen, Shaw, Rattigan may be a true succession, or it may not. The latest terms are always subject to error. Not every man under the towers of Oxford or Cambridge is the fellow of Cranmer, Newman, and Arnold, and these names cannot really be used to show that he is doing more important work, belongs more to the high tradition, than a teacher in a school at Croydon or a writer on the remote island of Jura. Yet, again and again, particular minorities confuse the superiority of the tradition which has been made available to them with their own superiority, an association which the passing of time or of frontiers can make suddenly ludicrous. We must always be careful to distinguish the great works of the past from the social minority which at a particular place and time identifies itself with them.

The great tradition very often continues itself in quite unexpected ways. Much new work, in the past, has been called 'low', in terms of the 'high' standards of the day. This happened to much of our Elizabethan drama, and to the novel in the eighteenth century. Looking back, we can understand this because in each case the society was changing in fundamental ways. The minorities which assumed that they alone had the inheritance and guardianship of the great tradition in fact turned out to be wrong. This mistake can happen at any time. In our own century, there are such new forms as the film, the musical, and jazz. Each of these has been seen as 'low', a threat to 'our' standards. Yet during the period in which films have been made, there have been as many major contributions, in film, to the world's dramatic tradition, as there have been major plays. Of course most films are nowhere near this level. But from the past we have only the best work, and we can properly compare with this only our own best work. Some forms may well be better than others, in that they contain much greater possibilities for the artist, but this cannot be settled until there has been time for development. The great period of the novel came more than a century after the form had become popular and had been dismissed a 'low'. It realized possibilities which nobody could then have foreseen. The prestige of an old form is never decisive. There is no reason, today, why a science-fiction story should be thought less serious than an historical novel, or a new musical than a naturalist play. 'Low' equals 'unfamiliar' is one of the perennial cultural traps, and it is fallen into most easily by those who assume that in their own persons, in their own learned tastes and habits, they are the high tradition.

This might be agreed, but does it go to the real issue? These mistakes are made, but new minorities set them right. Still, however, they are minorities. Most people are not interested in the great tradition, old or new. Most people are not interested in art, but merely in entertainment. Actual popular taste is for such things as variety, the circus, sport, and processions. Why force art on such people, especially since you will be in danger of reducing art to that level, mixing it up with the popular and commercial worlds? Wouldn't your effort be better spent on maintaining real art for those who value it?

This distinction between art and entertainment may be much more difficult to maintain than it looks. At its extremes, of course, it is obvious. But over the whole range, is there any easy and absolute distinction? Great art can give us deep and lasting experiences, but the experience we get from many things that we rightly call art is quite often light and temporary. The excitement of the circus, the procession, the variety sketch, can be quite easily forgotten, but at the time it is often intense. Sport, in our century, has become a popular spectacle: its excitements again are intense and often temporary. There may be a difference between such things and the minor decorative arts, the passing comedies, the fashionable artistic performer, but can it really be seen as a difference between 'high' and 'low'? And even where the difference seems absolute, what follows from this? What has to be shown, to sustain the argument that 'high culture' is in danger of being overwhelmed by 'mass culture', is that there is not only difference but conflict. Most of us can test this in our own experience. For, in fact, we do not live in these neatly separated worlds. Many of us go one day to a circus, one day to a theatre; one day to the football, one day to a concert. The experiences are different, and vary widely in quality both between and within themselves. Do we in fact feel that our capacity for any one of these things is affected by our use of the others?

(Williams 1966: 109–11)

> ➤ Williams's ideas of what constitutes popular entertainment have dated. Update the list that runs 'Actual popular taste is for such things as variety, the circus, sport, and processions'. From your new list choose individual items which you consider make this 'distinction between art and entertainment . . . much more difficult to maintain'.

**58 WHAT'S THE TOPIC? The Two Cultures debate persists
WHAT'S THE TEXT? Melvyn Bragg 'They want us to choose between the Beatles and Beethoven. Why can't we have both?'**

Since Matthew Arnold published *Culture and Anarchy* the idea that there existed two groups of people in society – the cultured saviours of society and its barbarian enemies – has been endlessly reproduced. Even today the notion persists that these two groups exist and are locked into mortal combat. In more recent times, in terms of the history of Communication Studies, commentators such as Raymond Williams and his successors (cultural theorists, subcultural theorists, and popular cultural theorists) have taken up the cause of popular culture in an attempt to make whole what was once broken between the two cultures. The debate persists – if only as a context in which members of certain social classes assert or demonstrate their cultural capital by virtue of understanding the terms of engagement with the debate.

Melvyn Bragg brings this Two Cultures argument completely up to date in the newspaper article below. The occasion which prompted the writing of the article was the launch of the twenty-fourth series of the Independent Television (ITV) arts programme *The South Bank Show* in 2000. Throughout its history the programme has promoted the study of both high and popular cultural forms and personalities. Bragg is concerned to defend his television show from accusations of 'dumbing down' while at the same time extending his discussion to broader themes.

In the early part of the article he makes the interesting point that technology was in fact the key to the serious consideration of popular culture. He argues that the ability for the first time to record experience of a popular cultural kind 'put popular culture on a par with the traditional forms which had long found ways to perpetuate themselves'.

Using examples Bragg then clarifies the debate. He offers a list of cultural warriors:

- Schoenberg, an avant-garde composer
- the work of Andrew Lloyd Webber in the form of the popular musical *Phantom of the Opera*
- the work of Elvis Presley.

He asks the question 'What is stronger or better?' and then gives more questions rather than answers. Bragg asks, if Schoenberg is considered superior is this any more than obedience to hierarchies?

WHY I HAVE HAD ENOUGH OF THE ARTS SNOBS

The Two Cultures debate today seems more active and urgent inside the arts than between the arts and the sciences. 'Dumbing down' has become shorthand for a miscellany of alleged failings, but central to the arguments is the battle between the traditional arts and popular culture, between art as a pursuit fully appreciated only by a select band of initiates and culture as an expression and reflection of the talents of a very large number of people. This is more often to do with the subject than with the treatment of the subject: i.e., all symphonies worthwhile, all pop music pap. It reaches a higher lunacy when otherwise unremarkable people declare that they do not watch television (fair enough) but in terms that make it clear that they are thereby awarding themselves a first-class honours degree. Theatre good, television bad.

I am about to launch the 24th season of *The South Bank Show*, which will again include documentaries on what are often classified as high and low art, on classical and common – even vulgar – subjects. As I look through the list, I believe that the old distinctions are not only less and less relevant to what is actually going on, but increasingly the refuge of the merely snobbish – a champagne-and-canapé view of the arts.

Perhaps the root of the trouble is that popular culture was taken seriously in the twentieth century by many of its creators and by intelligent and committed commentators. What the twentieth century delivered to popular culture was a ticket to posterity. Film, records, CDs, television and tapes could preserve work that in previous centuries had been snuffed out. It put popular culture on a par with the traditional forms, which had long found ways to perpetuate themselves.

Popular culture was and is the long-overdue arrival of the masses – and that is part of the trouble. Established culture has never liked the masses, and established culture in this country became hopelessly entangled in the class system, the control system – various systems of exclusion that are sometimes only distantly related to an appreciation of the arts themselves.

To make matters worse, the twentieth century's popular culture – in films and pop music alone – threw up an enormous number of highly talented writers, performers, directors and musicians, with an innovative energy that could make traditional forms seem staid. The fact that successive generations were far more likely to be enchanted by the new popular arts, such as cinema, than the historic, such as theatre, caused and still causes anxiety. This reaches absurdity as senior citizens of our official culture take it on themselves to expel whole activities such as films and rock music from the canon of what should be considered The Arts.

I hope it goes without saying that great art continued to flow from traditional sources throughout the last century. In the long run the established forms may prove to have outshone the new. But popular culture must now be reckoned with.

One of the questions it raises is this: how are we to judge what more powerfully influences us and, hence, what is stronger or better? See Schoenberg's *Moses and Aron*, *Madam Butterfly*, *Phantom of the Opera* or Elvis Presley at Las Vegas, and how do we set about judging differences? The cultural diktat of our day still tells us that Schoenberg is superior to Presley; many people go along with that. But is this any more than obedience to hierarchies laid down before popular culture gave itself a true chance to be compared?

We hear more and more about the brain, and we were told recently that Mozart is good for you – but is it better for you than Motown? How do we decide this outside subjective experience and – much less reliable – fashion, which plays such a colossal part in appreciation of the arts? Puccini and Andrew Lloyd Webber are interesting in another way: both can appeal to mass audiences and also to those who have taken the trouble to become connoisseurs, and they can do so in the same piece of music.

Many composers have found great satisfaction in using their best skills for mass audiences – Aaron Copland is a useful example. Do we get less out of his score for the film *Of Mice and Men* than we do out of his concert music? And, returning to Presley, those early songs bear a great deal of repetition – every bit as much as Schoenberg, and to more people. So the accepted notion that art is partly that which endures and bears retelling and re-examining holds as much for Elvis as it does for Moses and Aaron.

But, the argument goes, there is an altogether different quality of experience between listening to Beethoven and listening to the Beatles. Different? Granted. Quality? That's difficult. There are times when Beethoven takes you into his music so overwhelmingly that you feel your skin will burst with the sound inside your body. Yet listening to or, better, listening and dancing to the Beatles can provoke a not dissimilar ecstasy.

One danger in this argument for the old guard is that it undermines exclusivity. If just anyone can reach peaks of musical pleasure – through pop – where does that leave the vital pecking order (vital, that is, for centuries in societies that saw and often still see high art as primarily a social badge of honour)?

There is the important argument of difficulty and complication. Surely Wagner is more difficult than Van Morrison. You need to know more to enjoy more, and from that discipline of learning flow benefits that are simply not available otherwise. There is truth in that. But is difficulty itself a virtue? *Finnegans Wake* is very complicated but it is not a patch on the simple-seeming *Dubliners*. Yeats's simplest poems are among his greatest. Self-consciously difficult pop music is very often dire. As importantly, is Van Morrison easy? Which contemporary Faber poet could write successful song lyrics?

There is a rooted assumption that popular culture is easy, especially popular music. Millions who try and fail to create it find out the hard way that it is just that – hard. A simple test is to consider the doomed attempts of our greatest living operatic tenors to sing popular tunes. Almost always they are not just poor, but terrible. They can't swing they have no rhythm. They are afraid to leave the notes on the page; that magnificent growth in the throat gets in the way all the time. Pavarotti could never sing like Presley because he has neither the talent nor the training. Nureyev, although he longed to, could never dance like Fred Astaire.

To prefer Placido Domingo to Robbie Williams or vice versa is easy, and what we all do. To try to prove that preference is likely to be very tricky. And, once again, there are figures dancing across the landscape – Leonard Bernstein is one example, David Hockney another – who cut across entrenched positions and make a mockery of them.

(Bragg 2000: 14–15)

The more you explore contested issues in culture the more frustrating it can become, not least because some people seem to want to keep alive debates that are all but dead, or to revive conflicts that many people thought were resolved. Key to postmodern thinking is the idea that the hierarchies of taste rehearsed by writers like Bragg have collapsed, along with all manner of other certainties. In the postmodern age we are used to reading popular novels that draw on classic novels' plots or characters and used to seeing popular films that make reference to classic films. In this way it is the case that either the difference between high and low culture has been eroded or that audiences have not noticed that there was a distinction to be made in the first place. An instance of the way in which this works was offered by the film critic Mark Kermode in 2002:

Everything I know about 'high' culture I learnt from 'low-brow' art. Fact. I would never have heard of Heidegger, Kant or Nietzsche if their names hadn't featured in a rude Monty Python song, which included the wonderful couplet: 'Rene Descartes was a drunken fart,/I drink therefore I am'. I would never have read TS Eliot's *The Hollow Men* if Marlon Brando hadn't started slurring his way through it in Coppola's *Apocalypse Now* (ditto Conrad's *Heart of Darkness*). And I certainly would not have made an early connection with the films of Ingmar Bergman were it not for the fact that my favourite American comedian, Woody Allen, kept littering his movies and interviews with references to the maestro.

(Kermode 2002: 12)

WHAT'S NEXT?

> In whose interest are hierarchies of taste drawn up and circulated? (You might want to look at Extract 61 to help you express your ideas using the more formal language associated with 'taste' and 'distinction'.)
> What does this extract tell you about the range of cultural reference that someone like Melvyn Bragg is able to draw on?

59 WHAT'S THE TOPIC? Popular culture and the test of time
WHAT'S THE TEXT? DJ Taylor 'It's only Mick and Keef but we like them'

In 2002 the launch of the Rolling Stones final world tour prompted DJ Taylor to reflect on some of the issues raised by Bragg in the previous extract and to refer to some significant ideas about the place and role of culture in society.

Tied to the idea that popular music is easy is the notion that pop is essentially ephemeral (in Mike Jones' words 'the faint sound of a soap bubble bursting' (2003: 147)) – here today and gone tomorrow. High culture, on the other hand, is able to pass the test of time; it is in itself proof that it has lasted. Pop and rock acts, according to popular wisdom, have their brief moments in the spotlight (Andy Warhol's fifteen minutes of fame) and then invariably fade away to be replaced by more of the same. This is all very well but what prompted Taylor's article was the suspicion that The Rolling Stones, who have been touring for forty years, and who have a collective age of 280 (and that's just the four remaining white musicians formally credited as The Rolling Stones), have not read this script. Nor it seems have their audiences.

Taylor is keen to make sense of this, to ask what it is saying about society and culture. Is it simply the case that all new art forms are immediately swallowed up by what Adorno called the Culture Industry or do some popular cultural experiences inevitably find their level in the way that Shakespeare's popular theatre easily made the transition from low to high culture?

In his article Taylor makes reference to two key views on culture. Derived from nineteenth-century British political history cultural commentators typically refer to the Tory and Whig perspectives on cultural value over time. The Tories were an anti-progressive political party who sided with the British in the American Revolution. Their view of what was to be valued in culture was that the best happened a long time ago and that things have gone rapidly downhill from there. This tended to be reflected in their perspective on politics and most every aspect of life. The best is behind us. They were cultural pessimists. Opposed to them the Whigs were progressives who opposed British rule in the American Revolution. They were cultural optimists who believed that things inevitably improved in culture. The best was what we had at the moment; but even that would get better in the future. Not only culturally progressive, Whigs tended to believe in progress in all aspects of human behaviour. After the political reforms of 1830 the term Whig tended to be replaced by the term Liberal in political circles but in the context of views of history the term remains in use. Neither term, Tory or Whig, is now used in the sense of referring to a currently existing political party although 'Tory' is routinely used as a synonym for Conservative by political commentators and activists. Nonetheless the terms remain as useful labels for views on history in general and cultural history in particular.

Twenty-five years ago this summer, a time when the scent of iconoclasm drifted on the Jubilee air, I used to enjoy listening to a record called '1977' by the Clash. A no-holds-barred, three-chord assault on the sacred cows of the Seventies music business, it contained the deathless line: 'No more Elvis, Beatles or Stones in 1977'. I remembered this brash little exercise in statue-toppling only the other day when reading the newspaper accounts of the latest Rolling Stones world tour, a lavish geriatric progress which will drag its cast (collective age 280-plus) around the planet for the next six months. Further research revealed that Elvis Presley has just scored a posthumous hit single. The Beatles, of course, are everywhere: in Sir Paul's newly-married face beaming from the tabloids; in nearly every chord progression that the Gallagher brothers ever wrote. Pronounced dead a quarter of a century ago, Mick, Keef, Presley and the Fab Four – even where deceased – are, on the contrary, very much alive.

There is more to this phenomenon than odd bits of iconography. The Beatles and the Stones are still flourishing, but so, mysteriously, are the Who (John Entwistle's death notwithstanding), David Bowie and, judging from this year's Jubilee extravaganza, most of Black Sabbath. *Top of the Pops*, on which they all first pranced into view so many years ago, is about to celebrate its 2,000th airing, and the interest, as you might imagine, is focused on past glories rather than the contemporary drivel squeaked out by boy bands and tough low-life ensembles with names like the Hip-Hop Rapping Krew. If pop music exerts any communal pull these days, it is entirely retrospective. A concert by the Bootleg Beatles (tribute bands are another manifestation of the trend) is an extraordinary knees-up, half-way between an old-style variety hall and a VE Night street party, in which the age range swings between four and 80 and everyone knows the words.

Part of this is simply a reflection of what George Melly, several decades ago, called 'the revolt into style', the route – habitually mocked by purists – whereby savage irruptions of the cultural spirit are gradually extinguished, emasculated and otherwise made safe by the restraining hand of commerce. Even my father, who once maintained that the Beatles were responsible for the decline of Western civilisation and that pop stopped when Elvis's hips began, now affects to like 'Penny Lane'. But we are also witnessing a validation of a once-derided but increasingly attractive view of how the cultural process works.

Just as there is a Whig – that is, progressive – view of history, which holds that human affairs will always move gently forward to some (presumably unattainable) pinnacle of perfection, so there is a Whig view of culture. One of its most notable exponents, at any rate in the particular field of literature, was the late Sir Malcolm Bradbury. Bradbury's take on the English novel, for example, went something like this. There were we novelists, on our creative building site, the great foundation stones (Dickens, Thackeray, Eliot) at our feet, more recent materials (Joyce, Lawrence, Kafka) piled up around us. We needed only to apply our own precious contemporary mortar to send fiction lofting another few storeys into the sky.

But there is another view of culture: the Tory view. This holds that, dear me no, rather than using the achievements of our forefathers as a base from which to progress we are merely skulking around in their collective shadow, that Thackeray, say, is a better writer than Salman Rushdie, just as Corot is a better artist than Picasso, and that's that. Art, according to this analysis, doesn't invariably get better; it can often get worse. Naturally, the Tory view of art is complicated by the range of social and historical factors that provide its backdrop. Thackeray and Corot's task, it can be argued, was made easier because they lived in a different world, one more confident about its ability to represent itself accurately on canvas or in print.

And yet most art forms, if examined in any depth, reveal a centralising pattern, in which the form, having spent a certain amount of time developing its techniques, reaches an efflorescent popular high point, after which, if only to avoid stagnation, it has to change. Invariably the change involves fragmentation and, in the end, the loss of accessibility. This is more or less what has happened to the English novel and English poetry since a Victorian heyday rapidly trailed by Modernism and Bloomsbury. It is certainly what happened to painting in the later 19th century and to jazz in the mid-20th. More to the point, it was inevitable. To look at the ultra-realistic skin tones of the pre-Raphaelites is to realise that representational painting had reached a point of precision, or mimicry, beyond which it could go no further. Thereafter the road lay downward to surrealism and abstract expressionism – tedious obfuscations, from one side of the critical easel, praiseworthy experiments from the other.

All of which brings us back to the spectacle of old rubber lips lining up for another serial work-out among the stadiums of North America and beyond. One doesn't have to like or even be interested in the Rolling Stones to recognise the extent of their appeal. Not only did they establish the basis of their art form, they are still here, 40 years later, to show their imitators how the trick is turned. Which would you prefer to read – the new Martin Amis, or a previously unknown Dickens manuscript found in a forgotten cellar at Gad's Hill?

Another quintessential pop artefact from the mid-1970s was a novel by the old International Times journalist turned New Musical Express scribe Mick Farren called The Texts of the Festival – a kind of futurist hippy fantasy in which the sacred texts are the lyrics to classic Sixties pop songs. A quarter of a century on, the modern cultural carnival has its own set of defining moments, most of them coming from a very early stage in the respective art forms' development. To put it another way, the Stones will always pull in more punters than, say, the latest lo-fi sensation from Albuquerque who won't get past their third album, and

Handel always raise bigger audiences than Schoenberg, not because the mass audience is necessarily timorous but because some elements cultural laws are silently working to corral it. All the same, watching Sir Mick gamely limbering up for perhaps his 5,000th public rendition of 'Jumping Jack Flash', one could wish that Malcolm Bradbury had been right.

(Taylor 2002: 25)

WHAT'S NEXT?

➤ Which record by a pop act do you prefer – their Greatest Hits or their most recent release ?
➤ Which pop act do you prefer – a tribute band or local hopefuls ?
➤ Which television music programme do you prefer – *Born Sloppy, CD:UK, 4Play, Later, Popworld, Top of the Pops,* or *TOTP2*? And why?
➤ Thinking back to some of the ideas explored by Melvyn Bragg (in Extract 58) does cultural choice have to be a matter of either/or? Could it not be both/and?
➤ Read Chapters 3 and 5 of Oliver Bennett *Cultural Pessimism* (2001) Edinburgh: Edinburgh University Press.

▼ **60 WHAT'S THE TOPIC? The canon
WHAT'S THE TEXT? Robert Eaglestone *Doing English***

We have seen how, in *Culture and Anarchy*, Matthew Arnold proposed that culture (with a capital C) was his solution to the problem of how humankind could be saved, the best defence against the barbarians. Arnold's work is pretty much the best, and most often quoted, case for the defence of high culture, a deliberately divisive notion of what is and is not Culture. This division between high and low culture (discussed by Raymond Williams in Extract 57 and by Melvyn Bragg in Extract 58) materialises itself in all manner of ways but one of the most obvious ways is how hierarchies of taste are constructed and reproduced. Certain painters and certain paintings, certain composers and certain compositions, certain writers and certain books, certain film-makers and certain films are taken to represent truth, beauty, strength, civilisation. These hierarchies, or top ten or top twenty lists of cultural artefacts, have been characterised as 'the canon'. Derived from religious practices the word simply means a general rule or principle and in cultural contexts has come to mean works which constitute the standard by which all other works are judged. In another useful section from *Doing English* Robert Eaglestone provides a concise history of the origins of the canon in literature and the implications of this for us all. Given that the canon is invariably built from the works of dead, white, European men and given that the world is anything but dead, white, European and male, we can see how particular, vested interests are represented and reproduced by any kind of canon in any field of cultural work. As before, whatever Eaglestone has to say about the world of English Literature is equally applicable to the world of Communication Studies.

T.S. ELIOT, THE LEAVISES AND THE CANON

. . .

What we recognise as the canon today grew up hand in hand with the discipline of English in the 1920s. It is here that the assumptions of value, authenticity and authority come clearly into focus and become ever more closely linked with nationalism. Major figures in this development were the poet and critic T.S. Eliot (1888–1965) and the critics F.R. Leavis (1895–1978) and Q.D. Leavis (1906–1981).

Although T.S. Eliot is now thought of principally as a poet, his essays of literary criticism in the 1920s were extremely influential; indeed, E.M.W. Tillyard, a critic of the time, described them as 'revolutionary'. One of his most important essays was 'Tradition and the Individual Talent', published in two parts in 1919, in which Eliot argues that each artist writes in relation to a tradition,

> not merely with his own generation in his bones, but with a feeling that the whole of the literature of Europe from Homer and within it the whole of the literature of his own country has a simultaneous existence and composes a simultaneous order.

For Eliot, a tradition isn't just the past but a living thing, organised, structured and present in the mind – or even in the bones – of a great writer (always a 'he' for Eliot). This 'living tradition' of great literature makes up what Eliot later calls an 'ideal order', which ranks the great and valuable works. This is clearly a canon. In order to write a great poem, novel or play, or to appreciate a great work of literary art fully, Eliot argues that it is necessary that 'we' have these works in their 'ideal order' in our 'bones'. If this order is in our bones, it is part of who we are, not something we have to think about. 'We' must have internalised and accepted not only the list of works that people like Palgrave decided were great but, more importantly, the criteria that guided their judgement.

Eliot's idea has two consequences. The first concerns what these authoritative texts are authoritatively telling you. An authoritative list of Classical texts tells you that certain texts are authentically ancient Greek or Roman and not forgeries or inventions; the authority of books of scripture lies in the fact that they are thought to reveal the authentic word of God. But what authenticity does an authoritative list of works of literature reveal? For Eliot and those influenced by him, what underlies a great literary work and therefore makes it 'authentic' are the values of Western European (and within that English) culture and life. The canon is the 'storehouse of Western values'. These Western European values are unquestioningly assumed to be *universal human values*, the most important values that apply to all people at all times and in all places.

This leads to the second consequence: if a text doesn't seem to demonstrate these 'universal' values or expresses different ones, it is not considered valuable, and so is excluded from the canon. Eliot's seemingly innocent metaphor of 'bones' in fact reveals a rather frightening idea. It is not enough just to study the tradition – it must be in your bones, in your body. If you don't 'genetically' share the idea of the canon and the 'universal' Western European values underlying it, you can neither properly appreciate nor write great books. In their book *The Decolonization of African Literature*, Chinweizu, Onwuchekwa Jemie and Ihechukwu Madubuike, a trio of African writers and critics, sum this up from their perspective:

> most of the objections to . . . the African novel sound like admonitions from imperialist mother hens to their wayward or outright rebellious captive chickens. They cluck: 'Be Universal!' And what they don't consider universal they denounce as anthropological, atavistic (i.e. reverting to an earlier, primitive state), autobiographical, sociological, journalistic, topical ephemera, as not literary.

Again, what doesn't reveal Western values (masquerading as universal values) simply isn't authentic literature, is not worth reading and couldn't be part of the canon.

The idea was further developed by F.R. Leavis. Following Eliot's lead, he drew up a list of 'great writers'. Then, rather than saying that these were his 'favourites', he asserted that they were quite simply the best. For example, he begins his very influential work of 1948, *The Great Tradition*, by stating that the 'great English Novelists are Jane Austen, George Eliot, Henry James and Joseph Conrad'. Although he admits that other novelists have merits, the best – the ones who most authentically reveal the values he cherishes – are these four at the heart of the canon. The reasons he chooses these four are hard to pin down exactly. He writes that 'they are significant in terms of that human awareness they promote: awareness of the possibilities of life', and that they are 'creative geniuses whose distinction is manifested in their being alive in their time'. This manages to sound both convincing and authoritative and also rather vague. Of course, it is interesting to find out which books acute and well-read critics like the Leavises think are good. But their stamp of authority establishes this not just as *a* list, but as *the* list we should all share. As discussed earlier, they rely upon a personal sensibility to make judgements they claim to be objective, again because they assume that everyone shares or should share the same English and European values. One of the reasons the Leavises fostered the study of English was to cultivate a sense of national community, and it is clear that it also lay behind the choice of books in their canon.

HOW DOES THE CANON AFFECT YOU?

The canon today

The canon is still with us today. It is deeply woven into the fabric not just of English as a subject but into all forms of culture. TV and film adaptations tend to be of 'canonical' novels; publishers print 'classics'; to count as educated you are supposed to have read a smattering of 'canonical novels'. Why is the canon such a powerful idea?

First, the canon is a reflection that English always has a social *context* and could never be done in a vacuum. The canon represents the meeting point between (1) judgements of the artistic (or *aesthetic*) value of a text, and (2) the presupposition and interests, either implicit or explicit, of those who make those judgements and have the power to enforce them. What makes the issue difficult is that, despite claims to be 'objective' or 'neutral', it is simply impossible to separate out the artistic judgement from the judgement based on position and interests. These two are absolutely interwoven.

Second, the canon is *self-perpetuating*. In English at all levels, the same canonical texts come up again and again, year after year. A person who studied English and has become a teacher often teaches the texts she or he was taught, in part because she or he was taught that these texts were the most important. As students, you expect to study texts you have heard of and assume are worthwhile. Many textbooks for English and books on literature in general assume a familiarity with the canon, which also stresses its importance. In fact, textbooks from earlier in the twentieth century were often made up literally of lists and descriptions of great books. A more recent version of this is *The Western Canon* from 1994, by the American critic Harold Bloom. This book is a long defence of the idea of the canon, and ends with a list of the thousand books (he thinks) everyone 'cultured' should have read. The canon, then, is the list of books you expect to study when you do English, and reading the canon is doing English. The subject and the canon in part define each other.

However, even those who make and publish actual lists of 'great books' admit that sometimes the lists can change, as certain books come into and out of favour. But the third reason the canon is so powerful is that it *creates the criteria by which texts are judged*. The Qualifications and Curriculum Authority says, for example, that the texts you study must be of 'sufficient substance and quality to merit serious consideration', but gives no sort of yardstick to measure this; the values that make a work 'substantial' and give it 'quality' are not revealed. New or rediscovered texts are judged by the canon's standards. This means that even when, for example, A-level exam boards choose books from a wider selection of texts than normal, they first ask if the books have 'universal significance', 'positive values' or 'human significance'. Saying that a new novel fits the canon because it 'has' these, reaffirms the idea that an older novel 'had' them too. Paradoxically, the canon is not broken up, but reaffirmed.

The fourth reason the canon remains powerful is that it is involved with the senses of *identity* to which countries and groups aspire, and with the struggle to define identities. As the history of the canon suggested, its development was tied in with the development of ideas about nationality. It is for this reason that Toni Morrison (b. 1931), the Nobel prize-winning American author, wrote in 1989 that:

> Canon building is empire building. Canon defence is national defence. Canon debate, whatever the terrain, nature and range (of criticism, of history, of the history of knowledge, of the definition of language, the universality of aesthetic principles, the sociology of art, the humanist imagination) is the clash of cultures. And *all* the interests are vested.

Because it is the texts on the canon that are taught, studied and examined (and published, sold, bought, performed, made into TV mini-series . . .), the canon plays a significant role in creating a sense of shared culture and of collective national identity. Deciding which texts are in the canon is all part of deciding who we are and how we want to see ourselves, and a threat to the canon is a threat to national identity. But does the person setting the syllabus ask how you want to see yourself? As Toni Morrison says, all the interests are vested.

(Eaglestone 2000: 53–8)

The American composer, guitarist and bandleader Frank Zappa, interviewed by Bob Marshal in 1991, had this to say about the idea of classical composers having hits: '[this was] not necessarily connected to the quality of what they wrote. It's connected to how well they pleased the patron who was paying the freight – and it's the same thing today. So, all the norms, the acceptable norms of classical music, are really the taste norms of the church, the king, or the dictator that has been paying for it through the ages. It was not the taste of the people. People never got to decide' (Marshal, Dean and Falka 1991).

WHAT'S NEXT?

➤ Go to a record store or a book store. Examine what records or books are being promoted by the store as desirable, worth buying. How do these relate to actual sales figures ? Why do you think the store is trying to promote certain records or books? Is it just about sales ? And do sales figures represent a more genuine index of taste? (Look at what Frank Zappa had to say about this.)

COMMUNICATION STUDIES: THE ESSENTIAL RESOURCE

61 WHAT'S THE TOPIC? Cultural capital, habitus, popular culture and high culture
WHAT'S THE TEXT? Paul Taylor *Investigating Culture and Identity*

The following explanations of the work of Pierre Bourdieu come from Paul Taylor's useful book *Investigating Culture and Identity*. Bourdieu coined the term 'cultural capital' to describe in a simple metaphor the relationship between culture and social class: the more cultural capital you have the better able you are to function and progress in our society. According to Taylor cultural capital consists of (for example):

- knowledge, language, tastes and lifestyle
- what you know about high culture
- the size and range of your vocabulary
- your ability to recognise a decent wine
- playing rugby (union) rather than football.

This emphasises the point that high culture is only part of the jigsaw which constitutes the habitus (class in the other sense).

PIERRE BOURDIEU: CLASS AND CULTURE

The theories of culture discussed so far in this chapter have all in different ways focused on the notion of culture as ideology. They have explored how the norms and values of the dominant class help to justify the existing system and win the consent of the subject class. The work of the French cultural theorist Pierre Bourdieu moves away from this concern and instead focuses on how the culture of the ruling class helps it to preserve its elite status and differentiates it from other social classes.

Class and taste

Bourdieu shows how people's culture tastes are influenced by class. Members of the upper class are most likely to enjoy what he calls legitimate taste or 'high-brow' art and literature, for example baroque music, intellectual films and modern art. Members of the middle class are more likely to prefer 'middle-brow' taste, for example more popular classics such as Gershwin's *Rhapsody in Blue* and more popular paintings by Constable and Van Gogh. The working class (and less intellectual members of the higher classes) will prefer popular taste, for example popular classics such as *The Blue Danube* or pop music and mainstream Hollywood films.

Cultural capital

Bourdieu not only observes that people's cultural tastes are influenced by class, he also points out the role that culture plays in reproducing class relations in society. Bourdieu argues that individuals can improve their social class position by possessing not only **economic capital** (wealth), but also what he calls **cultural capital.**

Bourdieu's concept of cultural capital refers to a set of cultural competencies and dispositions, including knowledge, language, tastes and lifestyle. While economic capital is transmitted from one generation to the next through inheritance, the transmission of cultural capital is more complex. A key concept in this process is what Bourdieu calls the **habitus** – 'a matrix of perceptions, appreciations and actions' (Bourdieu and Passeron 1977). The habitus involves a distinction between good and bad taste, between high-brow and low-brow culture and so on. Children from the dominant class learn to appreciate the culture of their class and to view the popular culture of the working class as inferior. For example, middle-class parents tend to encourage their children to read 'good' books and watch the 'right' television programmes. Middle-class children are more likely to be taken on visits to theatres, art galleries and historical sites.

Cultural capital and education

All this means that when middle-class children start school they are equipped with considerable cultural capital. Schools reflect the culture of the dominant class and children from a middle-class background are equipped with the cultural knowledge and tastes to benefit from what the education system offers. Working-class children are more likely to experience a clash of cultures between the home and the school. Their dress, manners and tastes are more likely to be defined as inferior by the school. As a result middle-class children are more likely to excel in the educational system and acquire further cultural capital in the form of educational capital or formal qualifications. In the long run these are an important passport to economic capital since those with the best qualifications tend to get the best-paid jobs.

Working-class children, by contrast, quickly get the message that they have not got the qualities required by the education system and the majority either drop out or are forced out by an examination system that favours those with cultural capital. Of course there are some individuals who succeed on economic capital alone, for example the self-made man or woman who leaves school with few qualifications and who succeeds in business. However, such individuals are often despised by other members of the dominant class as *nouveaux riches* precisely because they often still have working-class cultural tastes. Such individuals are often keen to have their own children privately educated so that they can acquire the cultural capital which their parents never possessed.

(Taylor 1997: 67–8)

In the introduction to his *Consumer Society Reader* (2000) Martyn Lee neatly summarises key features of Bourdieu's work:

> Consumption, argues Bourdieu, is motivated first and foremost by the need for social groupings or 'class-fractions' to achieve recognised status or 'distinction'. In this, goods (be they works of art, music, foodstuffs, or items of interior design) present the multiple opportunities for groups to exercise their cultural skills, competences, and knowledge of the particular field in question; that is, to demonstrate something of the stock of 'cultural capital' they possess. Through the 'art' of knowing what to consume and, more importantly, the 'correct' (most erudite) manner or mode in which to consume, groups are able to objectify their status and social standing in the eyes of others, to confirm and reconfirm the boundaries of what properly constitutes the 'tasteful' and the 'tasteless', and in so doing to situate themselves on the 'right' side of such a boundary.
>
> (Lee 2000: xv)

WHAT'S NEXT?

> ➤ Try to more specifically define what cultural capital might consist of in a contemporary context (i.e. which books, films, clothes, food, etc).
> ➤ Can you relate the idea of 'the canon' to the idea of 'cultural capital'?

▼ 62 WHAT'S THE TOPIC? From Marx to Marxism WHAT'S THE TEXT? Jonathan Hale 'Politics and architecture'

In laying his ground for a study of structuralism in relation to architecture, Jonathan Hale offers not only an exemplary comment on but also a very workable overview of Marxist theory.

Hale is interested in the ways in which art forms, in this case architecture, can expose 'the underlying structures of political control and economic power'. Partly this is implicitly making the case for buildings as readable texts of a potentially polemical (controversial) character, as what he calls 'a mode of resistance and transformation with the power to effect change'. It is also acknowledging the debt owed to the work of Karl Marx for this theoretical model.

Hale places Marx and his work in a number of contexts not least as an active and useful critical voice. He also takes time to clarify a few of Marx's key concepts. Crudely this tour of the work visits:

- Marx's relationship with Hegel's historical philosophy (which saw History as an arena wherein mankind struggled for absolute knowledge);
- the importance of consciousness (as subject to rather than determiner of material life);
- the base and superstructure model (whereby everything is subordinated to economic factors);
- class theory and the ownership of the means of production (the people, the class, who own the economic base of production own the society);
- the alienation that results from class struggle (where workers are reduced to cogs in a machine);
- ideology and the world turned upside down (the ideological means of production producing an intellectual life, a world of ideas which mirrors the unequal world); and
- the idea of false consciousness (where ordinary people believe the myths to be truth).

The school of thought that today believes in the critical capacity of the work of art – for exposing the underlying structures of political control and economic power – still for the most part draws its theoretical model from the work of Karl Marx, in addition to its various reworkings by his more recent interpreters. The key issue is the idea of architecture as a mode of 'resistance' and transformation, with the power to effect change through its direct impact on the environment. As Marx pointed out, in one of his earliest writings: 'Philosophers have only *interpreted* the world, in various ways; the point, however, is to change it.' To begin to understand the work of Marx and the reason for his significant and lasting influence, it is necessary to consider a few of his key concepts before discussing their broader impact.

In approaching Marx's philosophy it is important to understand his situation in history, as a student in Berlin in the aftermath of Hegel's dominating influence. Marx arrived in Berlin in 1836, just five years after the great philosopher had died. Hegel had been teaching in Berlin as a professor of philosophy since 1818 and had left a huge and lasting legacy which the next generation now had to deal with. For Marx and a group of colleagues who called themselves the Young Hegelians, the emphasis was on trying to locate the weak points in the great edifice of Hegel's system. We have seen in Chapter 1 how Hegel had constructed a historical philosophy which presented the whole course of history as the quest for absolute knowledge. Hegel had shown the force behind this process to be the emerging 'world-spirit', an 'idea' attempting to express itself in the physical forms of the visible world. The culmination of Hegel's history took place in the mind of the philosopher, being the ultimate manifestation of 'spirit' as it comes to its own self-understanding. This idealism has gone down in history as one of Hegel's grandest conceptions and it is this great historical principle that soon attracted Marx's attention.

Rather than tinker with the minutiae in attempting to refine Hegel's system, Marx set out to attack its foundations by questioning its most basic assumptions. He dismissed philosophical history as a dry academic abstraction, cut off from the real history of everyday conditions and experience:

The Hegelian philosophy of history is the last consequence, reduced to its 'finest expression', of all this German historiography, for which it is not a question of real, nor even of political, interests, but of pure thoughts, which consequently must appear to Saint Bruno, as a series of 'thoughts' that devour one another and are finally swallowed up in 'self-consciousness'.

(Tucker 1978: 166)

It was consciousness that became the great pivot-point for Marx, about which he tried to turn Hegel's philosophy on its head, although more accurately he described it as standing Hegel on his feet. He felt that the idealist approach had tried to build a philosophy from ideas, while he was attempting to reverse this and build an alternative from experience. Hegel had, according to Marx, simply inverted the real course of history, so to correct this Marx constructed a system more closely modelled on reality. He did borrow, however, Hegel's dialectical model, where progress is described as an interplay between consciousness and reality. Where in Hegel this process leads to a refinement of concepts, with Marx it transforms the material conditions of reality. In Marx's terms this amounted to a 'dialectical materialism', although he himself only every referred to it as the 'materialist conception of history'. As he wrote in 1859, in one of his few philosophical works to be published during his lifetime:

The mode of production of material life conditions the social, political, and intellectual life-process in general. It is not the consciousness of men that determines their being, but, on the contrary, their social being that determines their consciousness.

(Tucker 1978: 4)

Marx seemed to suggest that as individuals we are restricted in our actions due to the presence of an unseen structure that appears to limit the mind's potential for free thinking. In a model comparable to the structuralist conception of the underlying systems of language, Marx set out the means by which this deterministic process might take place:

In the social production of their life men enter into definite relations that are indispensable and independent of their will, relations of production which correspond to a definite stage of development of their material productive forces. The sum total of these relations of production constitutes the economic structure of society, the real foundation, on which rises a legal and political superstructure and to which correspond definite forms of social consciousness.

(Tucker 1978: 4)

This is the now classic description of the 'base and superstructure' model, depicting the geological conception of history that Claude Lévi-Strauss was so enamoured with. The base consists of two components, firstly the 'forces of

CONTINUED

production', being the raw materials, machinery and labour required for producing industrial goods. The second part he called the 'relations of production', referring to the ways in which the work is organised, such as in the typical pyramidal structure of the capitalist corporate hierarchy.

The superstructure which rises out of this base and which is, in Marx's terms, determined by it, consists of the social, political and legal institutions that make up the society's 'consciousness'. Quite how deterministic Marx meant this model to be is still the subject of much argument among scholars. Marx does, however, suggest a direct link between the two components of the base, when he says 'the hand-mill will give you a society with the feudal lord, the steam-engine a society with the industrial capitalist' [McLellan 1975: 40]. This presents a slightly caricatured version of Marx's thinking on the process of history which, in the case of the base and superstructure relationship, was more complex than first appears. In fact the reasoning behind Marx's call for philosophers to change the world lies with the problem caused by one section of society being exploited by another. In Marx's model the class that controls the base thereby also controls the superstructure, and under capitalism this meant the working classes being locked into their relations of production. With the institutions of the superstructure being controlled by the bourgeoisie, this meant that the workers were prevented from gaining any understanding of their exploitation. Various corollaries to this scenario soon followed in Marx's thinking, as he set out the possibilities for revolution based on his analysis of historical progress. He saw that in the civilisations of the past a particular society would tend to collapse when the 'contradictions' within the system had broken out onto the surface. As he wrote at the beginning of his famous work, *The Communist Manifesto*:

> The history of all hitherto existing societies is the history of class struggles. Freeman and slave, patrician and plebeian, lord and serf, guild-master and journeyman, in a word, oppressor and oppressed, stood in constant opposition to one another, carried on an uninterrupted, now hidden, now open fight, a fight that each time ended, either in a revolutionary re-constitution of society at large, or in the common ruin of the contending classes.

> (Marx and Engels 1998: 34–5)

Besides the continuing exploitation of one class by another, in modern society a new danger had arisen inside the system. As a consequence of the division of labour within the capitalist mode of production, the new industrialised worker had now become 'alienated' from his work. By breaking up industrial processes into a series of specialised components, capitalism had robbed ordinary workers of any meaningful connection with their work. As Marx somewhat lyrically described it, referring to a previous system of production:

> Supposing that we had produced in a human manner; each of us would in his production have doubly affirmed himself and his fellow men. I would

have objectified in my production my individuality and its peculiarity and thus both in my activity enjoyed an individual expression of my life and also in looking at the object have had the individual pleasure of realising that my personality was objective, visible to the senses and thus a power raised beyond all doubt.

(McLellan 1975: 31–2)

The real importance of this process is as part of the worker's 'self-creation', where the personality of the producer is invested in their product – this existentialist idea also anticipates the work of William Morris, the pioneer English socialist and leader of the Arts and Crafts movement. Instead, the industrial product has become a mere anonymous commodity, prized for its 'exchange-value' rather than any 'use-value' in itself, and the worker, at the same time, becomes commodified under this system, valued as a labour resource rather than a unique human being.

(Hale 1998: 172–7)

WHAT'S NEXT?

➤ Look at all the advertisements in a selected magazine or broadcast at peak time on television and consider for each commodity or service :
  ■ its use-value (what it can literally do for you)
  ■ its exchange-value (what it can symbolically do for you).
➤ Read Chapter 1 of Martyn Lee's *Consumer Society Reborn* (1993) London: Routledge.

▼ **63 WHAT'S THE TOPIC? Marxism
WHAT'S THE TEXT? Ernst Fischer *Marx In His Own Words***

Whilst reading the work of Ludwig Feuerbach in 1845 Karl Marx, the German economist and philosopher, produced his eleven *Theses on Feuerbach*. Both summarising and responding to Feuerbach's work Marx's eleventh thesis (or argument) ran 'The philosophers have only *interpreted* the world, in various ways; the point, however, is to *change* it' (Marx and Engels 1968: 30). Marx conceived of a society alienated by the influence of ideology and money (his major work is simply entitled *Das Kapital*). However he did so in German, at great length, and with considerable complexity. This partly explains the especial popularity of *The Communist Manifesto*; unlike much of Marx's works it is short and relatively sweet, was completed before his death, and was intended for popular readership.

Ernst Fischer's *Marx In His Own Words* is an attempt to distil key concepts from a vast body of work, the key ideas without sacrificing the complexity. At best Fischer saves Marx from himself by reminding us of the clarity of much of his writing and thought without the need to wade through the economic data. Here Fischer (and Marx) are addressing commodity fetishism – the process whereby everyday items like consumer goods become almost revered objects of desire and false need. This is particularly galling when we read that it is people who become commodities.

This is exactly how the Narrator of the film *Fight Club* is happy to think of himself, defined by and as commodity: 'I'd flip through catalogues and wonder "what kind of dining set defines me as a person?" I had it all, even the glass dishes with tiny bubbles and imperfections – proof that they were crafted by the honest simple hardworking indigenous people of – wherever.' Here we see not only exemplification of the notion of commodification but also a preview of globalisation and its discontents: it is vital that the Narrator has particular authentic goods from somewhere in the world but he can't be bothered to find out or to remember where in the world.

THE FETISH CHARACTER OF THE COMMODITY

The declaration of 'inalienable' human rights pre-supposes a world in which everything has been alienated: let human rights, at least, be kept outside the dirty game. Everything has become a commodity: side by side with the meat market there is the art market, side by side with the car market is the book market, the labour market, the sex market, markets for information, secret services and, of course, public opinion. Above all it is man who becomes a commodity:

> Production does not only produce man as a *commodity*, the *human commodity*, man in the form of a *commodity*; in conformity with this situation it produces him as a *mentally* and *physically* dehumanised being . . .

> The worker becomes an ever cheaper commodity the more goods he creates. The *devaluation* of the human world increases in direct relation with the increase in value of the world of things.

The Young Marx was wrong when he assumed that the worker must become 'cheaper', i.e. more wretched, with the growth of production. But the dictum that the devaluation of the human world increases with the increase in value of the world of things remains valid. We have become so accustomed to living in a world of commodities, where nature is perhaps only a poster for a holiday resort and man only an advertisement for a new product, we exist in such a turmoil of alienated objects offered cheaply for sale, that we hardly ask ourselves any longer what it is that magically transforms objects of necessity (or fashion) into commodities and what is the true nature of the witches' sabbath, ablaze with neon moons and synthetic constellations, that has become our day-to-day reality.

What, then, is a commodity?

> A commodity is in the first place an object outside us, a thing that by its properties satisfies human wants of some sort or another. The nature of such wants, whether, for instance, they spring from the stomach or from fancy, makes no difference. Neither are we here concerned to know how the object satisfies these wants, whether directly as means of subsistence or indirectly as means of production . . .
>
> The utility of a thing makes it a use-value. . . . This property of a commodity is independent of the amount of labour required to appropriate its useful qualities . . . Use-values become a reality only by use or consumption: they also constitute the substance off all wealth, whatever may be the social form of that wealth. In the form of society we are about to consider, they are, in addition, the material depositories of exchange value.

Between the use-values of objects – bread or drugs, dwelling houses or weapons – nothing is comparable; the only thing they have in common is that they are used for consumption, production or destruction. But as exchange values – as commodities – objects are reduced to something comparable, measurable, common to them all.

This common 'something' cannot be either a geological, a chemical or any other natural property of commodities. Such properties claim our attention only in so far as they affect the utility of those commodities, make them use-values. But the exchange of commodities is evidently an act characterized by a total abstraction from use-value.

As use-values, commodities are, above all, of different qualities, but as exchange-values they are merely different quantities, and consequently do not contain an atom of use-value.

(Fischer 1970: 52–4)

WHAT'S NEXT?

➤ Identify personal and everyday examples of 'commodities' in the Marxist sense.
➤ Watch the 1998 animated feature film *Antz*. The character Z is voiced by Woody Allen. Relate Z's situation and his pronouncements to classic Marxist ideas.

▼ 64 WHAT'S THE TOPIC? Using semiotics to read patriarchy
WHAT'S THE TEXT? David Lodge *Nice Work*

Classic Marxism does not confine itself to the analysis of what is commonly known as economics. Rather Marx conceives of his work offering a toolkit for the analysis of all aspects of capitalist society. He certainly thought that his analysis moved from the factory floor to the bedroom. The mean and partial ownership of the means of production and distribution of wealth alienates the worker from the object of their labour. Similarly capitalism casts a pall over social and familial relations and alienates people from each other in social and sexual relationships.

Drawing on key ideas of Marx and Freud (and simultaneously rejecting Marx and Freud as yet more examples of dead, white, European males) feminists have rightly pointed to the power of the male in all aspects of economic, political, social and sexual life.

This extract from David Lodge's 1988 novel *Nice Work* serves many functions. It offers further astute application of semiotics to analyse, in this case, advertisements for Silk Cut cigarettes. It demonstrates how patriarchal order is reproduced through the furniture, the supposedly innocuous paraphernalia, of everyday life. It shows how human beings, trapped within capitalism, can unknowingly reproduce capitalist and patriarchal orders. And it exemplifies a key feature of contemporary cultural practice: you require a fair amount of cultural capital to make sense of what's going on. But when you do, enjoy.

They were returning in his car from visiting a foundry in Derby that had been taken over by asset-strippers who were selling off an automatic core moulder Wilcox was interested in, though it had turned out to be too old-fashioned for his purpose. Every few miles, it seemed, they passed the same huge poster on roadside hoardings, a photographic depiction of a rippling expanse of purple silk in which there was a single slit, as if the material had been slashed with a razor. There were no words on the advertisement, except for the Government Health Warning about smoking. This ubiquitous image, flashing past at regular intervals, both irritated and intrigued Robyn, and she began to do her semiotic stuff on the deep structure hidden beneath its bland surface.

It was in the first instance a kind of riddle. That is to say, in order to decode it, you had to know that there was a brand of cigarettes called Silk Cut. The poster was the iconic representation of a missing name, like a rebus. But the icon was also a metaphor. The shimmering silk, with its voluptuous curves and sensuous texture obviously symbolized the female body, and the elliptical slit, foregrounded by a lighter colour showing through, was still more obviously a vagina.

208

The advert thus appealed to both sensual and sadistic impulses, the desire to mutilate as well as penetrate the female body.

Vic Wilcox spluttered with outraged derision as she expounded this interpretation. He smoked a different brand, himself, but it was as if he felt his whole philosophy of life was threatened by Robyn's analysis of the advert. 'You must have a twisted mind to see all that in a perfectly harmless bit of cloth,' he said.

'What's the point of it, then? Robyn challenged him. 'Why use cloth to advertise cigarettes?'

'Well that's the name of 'em, isn't it? Silk Cut. It's a picture of the name. Nothing more or less.'

'Suppose they'd used a picture of a roll of silk cut in half – would that do just as well?'

'I suppose so. Yes, why not?'

'Because it would look like a penis cut in half, that's why.'

He forced out a laugh to cover his embarrassment. 'Why can't you people take things at face value?'

'What people are you referring to?'

'Highbrows. Intellectuals. You're always trying to find hidden meanings in things. Why? A cigarette is a cigarette. A piece of silk is a piece of silk. Why not leave it at that?'

'When they're represented they acquire additional meanings,' said Robyn. 'Signs are never innocent. Semiotics teaches us that.'

'Semi-what?'

'Semiotics. The study of signs.'

'It teaches us to have dirty minds, if you ask me.'

'Why d'you think the wretched things were called Silk Cut in the first place?'

'I dunno. It's just a name, as good as any other.'

''Cut' has something to do with tobacco, doesn't it? The way the tobacco leaf is cut. Like 'Player's Navy Cut' – my uncle Walter used to smoke them.'

'Well, what if it does?' Vic said warily.

'But silk has nothing to do with tobacco. It's a metaphor, a metaphor that means something like, "smooth as silk". Somebody in an advertising agency dreamt up the name "Silk Cut" to suggest a cigarette that wouldn't give you a sore throat or a hacking couch or lung cancer. But after a while the public got used to the name, the word "Silk" ceased to signify, so they decided to have an advertising campaign to give the brand a high profile again. Some bright spark in the agency came up with the idea of rippling silk with a cut in it. The original metaphor is now represented literally. But new metaphorical connotations accrue – sexual ones. Whether they were consciously intended or not doesn't really matter. It's a good example of the perpetual sliding of the signifier under the signified, actually.'

Wilcox chewed on this for a while, then said, 'Why do women smoke them, then, eh?' His triumphant expression showed that he thought this was a knock-down argument. 'If smoking Silk Cut is a form of aggravated rape, as you try to make out, how come women smoke 'em too?'

'Many women are masochistic by temperament,' said Robyn. 'They've learned what's expected of them in a patriarchal society.'

'Ha!' Wilcox exclaimed, tossing back his head. 'I might have known you'd have some daft answer.'

'I don't know why you're so worked up,' said Robyn. 'It's not as if you smoke Silk Cut yourself.'

'No, I smoke Marlboros. Funnily enough, I smoke them because I like the taste.'

'They're the ones that have the lonesome cowboy ads, aren't they?'

'I suppose that makes me a repressed homosexual, does it?'

'No, it's a very straightforward metonymic message.'

'Metowhat?'

'Metonymic. One of the fundamental tools of semiotics is the distinction between metaphor and metonymy. D'you want me to explain it to you?'

'It'll pass the time,' he said.

'Metaphor is a figure of speech based on similarity, whereas metonymy is based on contiguity. In metaphor you substitute something *like* the thing you mean for the thing itself, whereas in metonymy you substitute some attribute or cause or effect for the thing itself.'

'I don't understand a word you're saying.'

'Well, take one of your moulds. The bottom bit is called the drag because it's dragged across the floor and the top bit is called the cope because it covers the bottom bit.'

'I told *you* that.'

'Yes, I know. What you didn't tell me was that "drag" is a metonymy and "cope" is a metaphor.'

Vic grunted. 'What difference does it make?'

'It's just a question of understanding how language works. I thought you were interested in how things work.'

'I don't see what it's got to do with cigarettes.'

'In the case of the Silk Cut poster, the picture signifies the female body metaphorically: the slit in the silk is like a vagina – '

Vic flinched at the word. 'So you say.'

'All holes, hollow spaces, fissures and folds represent the female genitals.'

'Prove it.'

'Freud proved it, by his successful analysis of dreams,' said Robyn. 'But the Marlboro ads don't use any metaphors. That's probably why you smoke them, actually.'

'What d'you mean?' he said suspiciously.

'You don't have any sympathy with the metaphorical way of looking at things. A cigarette is a cigarette as far as you are concerned.'

'Right.'

'The Marlboro ad doesn't disturb that naïve faith in the stability of the signified. It establishes a metonymic connection – completely spurious of course, but realistically plausible – between smoking that particular brand and the healthy, heroic life of the cowboy. Buy the cigarette and you buy the life-style, or the fantasy of living it.'

'Rubbish!' said Wilcox. 'I hate the country and the open air. I'm scared to go into a field with a cow in it.'

'Well then, maybe it's the solitariness of the cowboy in the ads that appeals to you. Self-reliant, independent, very macho.'

'I've never heard such a lot of balls in all my life,' said Vic Wilcox, which was strong language coming from him.

'Balls – now that's an interesting expression . . .' Robyn mused.

'Oh no!' he groaned.

'When you say a man "has balls", approvingly, it's a metonymy, whereas if you say something is a "lot of balls", or "a balls-up", it's a sort of metaphor. The metonymy attributes value to the testicles whereas the metaphor uses them to degrade something else.'

'I can't take any more of this,' said Vic. 'D'you mind if I smoke? Just a plain, ordinary cigarette?'

'If I can have Radio Three on,' said Robyn.

(Lodge 1988: 220–4)

WHAT'S NEXT?

➤ Take an advertisement. Examine how it works. How does it reproduce a given social or political order? (Another way of looking at this would be to examine what myths the advertisement is built on.)

▼ 65 WHAT'S THE TOPIC? Feminism
WHAT'S THE TEXT? Germaine Greer *The Female Eunuch*

Germaine Greer wrote her seminal work of feminism *The Female Eunuch* in 1970 as a warning. The title's metaphor is one of emasculation, of woman as ironically castrated, neutered. The Female Eunuch is a costume famously depicted on the book's cover – on its hanger – which is where Greer sincerely hopes it will stay.

In the Foreword to the twenty-first anniversary edition she admits that she 'thought that the book should quickly date and disappear'. She continues, 'I hoped that a new breed of women would come upon the earth', but concludes with some dismay, 'You can see the Female Eunuch the world over.'

In fact she is forced, twenty years on, to restate the feminist creed – 'The freedom I pleaded for twenty years ago' – she calls it. These freedoms fall into four groups:

■ freedom to be a person
■ freedom to know and love the earth
■ freedom to learn and teach
■ freedom from fear.

Greer is as hard and uncompromising as she is clear-sighted and intelligent. Contained below is a critique of mass culture and mass society alongside a call to arms and the statement of a political and philosophical position.

Twenty years ago I wrote in the Introduction to *The Female Eunuch* that I thought that the book should quickly date and disappear. I hoped that a new breed of woman would come upon the earth for whom my analysis of sex oppression in the developed world in the second half of the twentieth century would be utterly irrelevant.

Many new breeds of woman are upon the earth: there are female body builders whose pectorals are as hard as any man's; there are women marathon runners with musculature as stringy and tight as any man's; there are women administrators with as much power as any man; there are women paying alimony and women being paid palimony; there are up-front lesbians demanding the right to marry and have children by artificial insemination; there are men who mutilate themselves and are given passports as statutory females; there are prostitutes who have combined in highly visible professional organizations; there are armed women in the front line of the most powerful armies on earth; there are full colonels with vivid lipstick and painted nails; there are women who write books about their sexual conquests, naming names and describing positions, sizes of members and so forth. None of these female phenomena was to be observed in any numbers twenty years ago.

Women's magazines are now written for grown-ups, and discuss not only pre-marital sex, contraception and abortion, but venereal disease, incest, sexual perversion, and, even more surprising, finance high and low, politics, conservation, animal rights and consumer power. Contraception having saturated its market and severely curtailed the money to be made out of menstruation, the pharmaceutical multinationals have at last turned their attention to the menopausal and post-menopausal women who represent a new, huge, unexploited market for HRT. Geriatric sex can be seen in every television soap opera. What more could women want?

Freedom, that's what.

Freedom from being the thing looked at rather than the person looking back. Freedom from self-consciousness. Freedom from the duty of sexual stimulation of jaded male appetite, for which no breast ever bulges hard enough and no leg is ever long enough. Freedom from the uncomfortable clothes that must be worn to titillate. Freedom from shoes that make us shorten our steps and push our buttocks out. Freedom from the ever-present juvenile pulchritude on Page 3. Freedom from the humiliating insults heaped on us by the top shelf of the newsagents; freedom from rape, whether it is by being undressed verbally by the men on the building site, spied on as we go about our daily business, stopped, propositioned or followed on the street, greasily teased by our male workmates, pawed by the boss, used sadistically or against our will by the men we love, or violently terrorized and beaten by a stranger, or a gang of strangers.

Twenty years ago it was important to stress the right to sexual expression and far less important to underline a woman's right to reject male advances; now it is even more important to stress the right to reject penetration by the male member, the right to safe sex, the right to chastity, the right to defer physical intimacy until there is irrefutable evidence of commitment, because of the appearance on the earth of AIDS. The argument in *The Female Eunuch* is still valid, none the less, for it holds that a woman has the right to express her own sexuality; which is not at all the same thing as the right to capitulate to male advances. *The Female Eunuch* argues that the rejection of the concept of female libido as merely responsive is essential to female liberation. This is the proposition that was interpreted by the brain-dead hacks of Fleet Street as 'telling women to go out and do it'.

The freedom I pleaded for twenty years ago was freedom to be a person, with the dignity, integrity, nobility, passion, pride that constitute personhood. Freedom to run, shout, to talk loudly and sit with your knees apart. Freedom to know and love the earth and all that swims, lies and crawls upon it. Freedom to learn and freedom to teach. Freedom from fear, freedom from hunger, freedom of speech and freedom of belief. Most of the women in the world are still afraid, still hungry, still mute and loaded by religion with all kinds of fetters, masked, muzzled, mutilated and beaten. *The Female Eunuch* does not deal with poor women (for when I wrote it I did not know them) but with the women of the rich world, whose oppression is seen by poor women as freedom.

The sudden death of communism in 1989–90 catapulted poor women the world over into consumer society, where there is no protection for mothers, for the aged, for the disabled, no commitment to health care or education or raising the standard of living for the whole population. In those two years millions of women saw the bottom fall out of their world; though they lost their child support, their pensions, their hospital benefits, their day care, their protected jobs, and the very schools and hospitals where they worked closed down, there was no outcry. They had freedom to speak but no voice. They had freedom to buy essential services with money that they did not have, freedom to indulge in the oldest form of private enterprise, prostitution, prostitution of body, mind and soul to consumerism, or else freedom to starve, freedom to beg.

You can now see the Female Eunuch the world over; all the time we thought we were driving her out of our minds and hearts she was spreading herself wherever blue jeans and Coca-Cola may go. Wherever you see nail varnish, lipstick, brassieres and high heels, the Eunuch has set up her camp. You can find her triumphant even under the veil.

(Greer 2003: 9–12)

▼ **66 WHAT'S THE TOPIC? Post-feminism: definitions
WHAT'S THE TEXT? Yvonne Tasker 'Office politics: masculinity, feminism, and the workplace in *Disclosure*'**

We live in an age of post-s. Pick almost any key notion of the twentieth century and you will invariably find a post- variety nowadays. Some of these post-s are mere frippery, intellectual game-playing. But, equally so, many post-s signify, at the very least, the movement of time and the need to newly label a new era. Similarly, some key twentieth-century movements were designed to achieve material gains or objectives. Once key participants or activists believed those goals or objectives had been achieved it was not unreasonable to propose that the enhanced position be characterised as 'post-'. This both is and is not the case with feminism and post-feminism. The term is used with great frequency and doesn't always appear to have semantic stability (as is often the case with post- words). Yvonne Tasker published the essay from which the following is extracted in 2003. Before moving on to analyse the 1994 film *Disclosure* she seeks to clear the decks by offering succinct definitions of the varied meanings and understandings of post-feminism.

It is partly in this context that the term 'post-feminism' has acquired its significance. Since post-feminism is a controversial term, let me be clear what I mean by it here. First, post-feminism signals that certain principles of gender equality are accepted within the legal frameworks of particular Western economies, however patchily that is actually translated into opportunities. Second, post-feminism suggests how discourses of independence and self-definition for women widely inform popular culture, however compromised they might be or are perceived to be. For some writers post-feminism has a straightforward – reactionary – political meaning: it encapsulates an assumption that feminist battles for equality are either already won or no longer relevant. It is in this context that journalist Susan Faludi's 1991 best-seller *Backlash* explored a contradiction between women's continuing struggles and an equality that is

CONTINUED

not only perceived to be somehow already achieved, but actually damaging to women. In another book first published in 1991, *Feminism without Women: Culture and Criticism in a 'Postfeminist' Age*, Tania Modleski identifies a trend in both mass culture and academic thought – or at least in certain texts of both – which 'in proclaiming or assuming the advent of postfeminism, are actually engaged in negating the critiques and undermining the goals of feminism – in effect, delivering us back into a prefeminist world' (1991: 3). As my qualifications indicate, I'm also skeptical about the term. And yet negation is also a response of sorts to achievement. For me, the significance of the appearance of post-feminism at the beginning of the 1990s was not so much a term without a referent, as an indication of both how much and how little had changed. The images that I'll discuss in this chapter are not, I would argue, prefeminist in Modleski's terms, though they are certainly equivocal about feminism.

(Tasker 2003: 170)

WHAT'S NEXT?

➤ To what extent have feminist battles for equality been won?
➤ Read Sadie Plant *Zeroes + Ones: Digital Women + the New Technoculture* (1997) London: Fourth Estate.

▼ ## 67 WHAT'S THE TOPIC? Post-feminism: applications
WHAT'S THE TEXT? Camille Paglia *Sex, Art and American Culture*

Like Marxists feminists are drawn from a broad church. In *Sex, Art and American Culture* Camile Paglia argues from the libertarian end of the paradigm. In the short piece below she advances the argument that 'Madonna is the true feminist' in the face of feminist criticism of the 'Justify My Love' video. This piece is a genuine polemic: it is written to provoke controversy. However it is also a genuine call for feminism to embrace 'ideas of ambiguity, contradiction, conflict, ambivalence'.

ANIMALITY AND ARTIFICE

Madonna, don't preach.

Defending her controversial new video, 'Justify My Love,' on *Nightline* last week, Madonna stumbled, rambled, and ended up seeming far less intelligent than she really is.

Madonna, 'fess up

The video is pornographic. It's decadent. And it's fabulous. MTV was right to ban it, a corporate resolve long overdue. Parents cannot possibly control television, with its titanic omnipresence.

Prodded by correspondent Forrest Sawyer for evidence of her responsibility as an artist, Madonna hotly proclaimed her love of children, her social activism, and her condom endorsements. Wrong answer. As Baudelaire and Oscar Wilde knew, neither art nor the artist has a moral responsibility to liberal social causes.

'Justify My Love' is truly avant-garde, at a time when that word has lost its meaning in the flabby art world. It represents a sophisticated European sexuality of a kind we have not seen since the great foreign films of the 1950s and 1960s. But it does not belong on a mainstream music channel watched around the clock by children.

On *Nightline*, Madonna bizarrely called the video a 'celebration of sex'. She imagined happy educational scenes where curious children would ask their parents about the video. Oh, sure! Picture it: 'Mommy, please tell me about the tired, tied-up man in the leather harness and the mean, bare-chested lady in the Nazi cap'. Okay, dear, right after the milk and cookies.

Sawyer asked for Madonna's reaction to feminist charges that, in the neck manacle and floor-crawling of an earlier video, 'Express Yourself,' she condoned the 'degradation' and 'humiliation' of women. Madonna waffled: 'But I chained myself! I'm in charge'. Well, no. Madonna the producer may have chosen the chain, but Madonna the sexual persona in the video is alternately a cross-dressing dominatrix and a slave of male desire.

But who cares what the feminists say anyhow? They have been outrageously negative about Madonna from the start. In 1985, Ms. Magazine pointedly feted quirky, cuddle singer Cyndi Lauper as its woman of the year. Great judgement; gimmicky Lauper went nowhere, while Madonna grew, flourished, metamorphosed, and became an international star of staggering dimensions. She is also a shrewd business tycoon, a modern new woman of all-around talent.

Madonna is the true feminist. She exposes the Puritanism and suffocating ideology of American feminism, which is stuck in an adolescent whining mode. Madonna has taught young women to be fully female and sexual while still exercising control over their lives. She shows girls how to be attractive, sensual, energetic, ambitious, aggressive, and funny – all at the same time.

American feminism has a man problem. The beaming Betty Crockers, hangdog dowdies, and parochial prudes who call themselves feminists want men to be like women. They fear and despise the masculine. The academic feminists think their nerdy bookworm husbands are the ideal model of human manhood.

But Madonna loves real men. She sees the beauty of masculinity, in all its rough vigour and sweaty athletic perfection. She also admires the men who are actually like women: transsexuals and flamboyant drag queens, the heroes of the 1969 Stonewall rebellion, which started the gay liberation movement.

'Justify My Love' is an eerie, sultry tableau of jaded androgynous creatures, trapped in a decadent sexual underground. Its hypnotic images are drawn from such sadomasochistic films as Liliana Cavani's *The Night Porter* and Luchino Visconti's *The Damned*. It's the perverse and knowing world of the photographers Helmut Newton and Robert Mapplethorpe.

Contemporary American feminism, which began by rejecting Freud because of his alleged sexism, has shut itself off from his ideas of ambiguity, contradiction, conflict, ambivalence. Its simplistic psychology is illustrated by the new cliché of the date-rape furore: '"No" always means "no"'. Will we ever graduate from the Girl Scouts? 'No' has always been, and always will be, part of the dangerous, alluring courtship ritual of sex and seduction, observable even in the animal kingdom.

Madonna has a far profounder vision of sex than do the feminists. She sees both the animality and the artifice. Changing her costume style and hair colour virtually every month, Madonna embodies the eternal values of beauty and pleasure. Feminism says, 'No more masks'. Madonna says we are nothing but masks.

Through her enormous impact on young women around the world, Madonna is the future of feminism.

(Paglia 1993: 3–5)

WHAT'S NEXT?

> ➤ What reasons does Paglia give for Madonna being 'the future of feminism'?
> ➤ How do you respond to the issues of representation raised by this article? Remember that Althusser suggested that 'ideology is indeed, a system of representation'.

▼ **68 WHAT'S THE TOPIC? Lyotard and postmodernism**
WHAT'S THE TEXT? John Lechte *Fifty Key Contemporary Thinkers*

Another key contemporary post- is postmodernism. Anyone looking to pinpoint the precise moment when the modern age gave way to the postmodern age, when modernity became postmodernity, would be engaging in a fruitless task. It is more productive to use the idea of postmodernism to describe a number of features of contemporary existence. These are best thought of in terms of opposed pairs of notions. The modern age was characterised by wholeness, the postmodern age by fragmentation. The modern age focused on production, the postmodern age on consumption. The modern age believed in the One Big Idea, the postmodern age recognises many viewpoints as being equally valid.

The word 'post-modernismo' was first used in the Hispanic world in the 1930s by Federico de Onis. It makes its first appearance in the anglophone world when the historian Arnold Toynbee published the eighth volume of his *Study of History* in 1954. It is there that he labels 'the epoch that had opened with the Franco-Prussian War the "postmodern age".' But it's reasonable to propose that Toynbee didn't foresee all the inflections that would later be brought to bear on the word in its later use.

In Communication Studies we tend to be led by the groundbreaking work of Jean-François Lyotard in how we use the term. The following extract is taken from the essay on Lyotard in John Lechte's excellent *Fifty Key Contemporary Thinkers* where he explains just exactly how Lyotard came to conceive of the postmodern condition.

The Postmodern Condition, written as a report on knowledge for the Quebec government, examines knowledge, science, and technology in advanced capitalist societies. Here, the very notion of society as a form of 'unicity' (as in national identity) is judged to be losing credibility. Society as unicity – whether conceived as an organic whole (Durkheim), or as a functional system (Parsons), or again, as a fundamentally divided whole composed of two opposing classes (Marx) – is no longer credible in light of a growing 'incredulity towards' legitimating 'metanarratives'. Such metanarratives (for example: every society exists for the good of its members; the whole unites the parts; the relation between the parts is just, or unjust, depending on the situation) provide a teleology legitimating both the social bond and the role of science and knowledge in relation to it. A metanarrative, then, provides a 'credible' purpose for action, science, or society at large. At a more technical level, a science is modern if it tries to legitimate its own rules through reference to a metanarrative – that is, a narrative outside its own sphere of competence.

Two influential metanarratives are the idea that knowledge is produced for its own sake (this was typical of German idealism), and the idea that knowledge was produced for a people-subject in quest of emancipation. Postmodernity, on the other hand, implies that these goals of knowledge are now contested, and, furthermore, that no ultimate proof is available for settling disputes over these goals. In the computer age where complexity is perceived to be ever increasing, the possibility of there being a single, or even dual, rationale for knowledge or science, becomes remote. Before, faith in a narrative (e.g. religious doctrines) would have resolved the potential difficulty. Since the Second World War techniques and technologies have, as Weber anticipated, 'shifted emphasis from the ends of action to its means'. Regardless of whether the form of narrative unification is of the speculative or of the emancipatory type, the legitimation of knowledge can no longer rely on a 'grand narrative', so that science is now best understood in terms of Wittgenstein's theory of 'language game'.

A language game signifies that no concept or theory could adequately capture language in its totality, if only because the attempt to do so itself constitutes its own particular language game. Thus, again, grand narratives no longer have credulity, for they are part of a language game which is itself part of a multiplicity of language games. Lyotard has written of speculative discourse as a language game – a game with specific rules which can be analysed in terms of the way statements should be linked to each other.

Science, therefore, is a language game with the following rules:

1   Only denotative (descriptive) statements are scientific.
2   Scientific statements are quite different from those (concerned with origins) constituting the social bond.
3   Competence is only required on the part of the sender of the scientific message, not on the part of the receiver.
4   A scientific statement only exists within a series of statements which are validated by argument and by proof.
5   In light of (4), the scientific language game requires a knowledge of the existing state of scientific knowledge. Science no longer requires a narrative for its legitimation, for the rules of science are immanent in its game

For science to 'progress' (i.e. for a new axiom, or denotative statement to be accepted), the individual scientist, or group of scientists, must win the approval of all other scientists in the same field. And as scientific work becomes more complex, so do the forms of proof: the more complex the proof, the more complex the technology necessary in order to achieve generally accepted levels of validation. Technology, crucial for understanding the form of scientific knowledge in the society of the last quarter of the twentieth century, follows the principle of optimal performance: maximum output for minimum input. Lyotard calls this the principle of 'performativity', and it now dominates the scientific language game precisely because a scientific discovery requires a proof which costs money. Technology thus becomes the most efficient way of achieving scientific proof: 'an equation between wealth, efficiency, and truth is thus established'. Although 'wildcat' discoveries (where technology is very minimal) can still take place, technology tends to link science to the economy. Although inexpensive, pure research in search of truth is still possible, expensive research is becoming the norm; and this means obtaining funding assistance. To get funding, the long-term relevance of the research has to be justified; and this brings pure research under the auspices of the language game of performativity.

Once performativity dominates, truth and justice tend to be the outcome of the best-funded research (best-funded, therefore most convincing): 'by reinforcing technology, one "reinforces" reality, and one's chances of being just and right increase accordingly'. And if those who have wealth to fund research also have power (and they have power, according to Lyotard, because they profit from research), the postmodern era would be one in which power and knowledge come into contact with each other as never before.

On the other hand, performativity can remain in a hegemonic position in the scientific language game only if the issue of its legitimacy is kept out of play. This is easily done if the question of legitimation is the same as the question: What is science? Once the performativity of the question is made an issue, however, the limit of performative rationality emerges, in as far as performativity cannot justify itself except through a metanarrative.

Systems theorists such as Luhmann propose that performativity is the basis on which the (social) system maintains itself, in the wake of the disenchantment of the world brought about by science and technology. As the perfect system is deemed to be the most efficient, the goal is to eliminate all dysfunctions. For the systems theorist, human beings are part of a homogeneous, stable, theoretically knowable, and therefore, predictable system. Knowledge is the means of controlling the system. Even if perfect knowledge does not yet exist, the equation: the greater the knowledge the greater the power over the system, is, for the systems theorist, irrefutable.

By contrast, Lyotard shows that systems theory is located within a modernist epistemology. For within the very terms of the system as performativity, control through knowledge lowers its performance, since uncertainty increases rather than decreases with knowledge (cf. Heisenberg). Now, a new, postmodern paradigm is coming into being, one that emphasises unpredictability, uncertainty, catastrophe (as in René Thom's work), chaos, and, most of all, paralogy, or dissensus. Dissensus challenges the existing rules of the game. Paralogy becomes impossible when recognition is withheld and legitimacy denied for new moves in the game. Silencing – or eliminating – a player from the game is equivalent to a terrorist act. The notion of being unable to present a position that is at variance with the dominant rules of argumentation and validation, provides an appropriate point of transition to Lyotard's later work, *The Differend*.

(Lechte 1994: 246–8)

WHAT'S NEXT?

➤ Read David Harvey *The Condition of Postmodernity* (1989) Oxford: Blackwell.

➤ Identify other 'texts' that might be usefully described as postmodern.

➤ Shelley Walia has written that 'the reactionary movement of post-modernism . . . is, to an extent, a giving in to the forces of capitalism'. In a similar vein, Zygmunt Bauman has characterised postmodernism's relationship with material political realities: 'Consumer and expressive freedoms are not interfered with politically, so long as they remain politically ineffective' (Baumann 1998: 88). To what extent do you believe that the greater fluidity of definitions within postmodernism mean that certainties such as opposition to capitalism are no longer possible or meaningful?

▼ **69 WHAT'S THE TOPIC? The implications of postmodernism for writing WHAT'S THE TEXT? Alan Bryman *Social Research Methods***

What are the implications of postmodernism? Well, they are many and varied. But one key way in which postmodernism is most obviously seen is in writing. For anyone trained in writing and speaking with the certainty of the traditional hard sciences the fluidity, the porousness, the sheer slipperiness of postmodernist writing comes as a shock. But if one of the key tenets of postmodernism is that certainty is impossible then it is quite logical that this uncertainty be reflected in writing, particularly when writing about postmodern objects in postmodern landscapes. Here Alan Bryman considers some of the implications of postmodernism for writing.

Postmodernism . . . is an extremely difficult idea to pin down. In one sense, it can be seen as a form of sensitivity – a way of seeing and understanding that results in a questioning of the taken-for-granted. It questions the very notion of the dispassionate social scientist seeking to uncover a pre-given external reality. Instead, postmodernists view the social scientist's account as only one among many ways of rendering social reality to audiences. The social world itself is viewed as a context out of which many accounts can be hewn. As a result, 'knowledge' of the social world is relative; any account is just one of many possible ways of rendering social reality. As Rosenau (1992: 8) puts it, postmodernists 'offer "readings" not "observations", "interpretations" not "findings" . . .'.

One of the effects of the impact of postmodernism since the 1980s has been a growing interest in the writing of social science. For postmodernists, reporting findings in a journal article is merely one means of getting across a certain version of the social reality that was investigated. Postmodernists mistrust the knowledge claims that are frequently boldly made when findings are reported and instead they adopt an attitude of investigating the bases and forms of those knowledge claims. While the writing of all types of social science is potentially in the postmodernist's firing line, it has been the kinds of text produced by ethnographers that have been a particular focus of attention. This focus has led to a particular interest in the claims to ethnographic authority that are inscribed into ethnographic texts (Clifford 1983). The ethnographic text 'presumes a world out there (the real) that can be captured by a "knowing" author through the careful transcription and analysis of field materials (interviews, notes, etc.)' (Denzin 1994: 296). Postmodernism problematizes such accounts and their authority to represent a reality because there 'can never be a final, accurate representation of what was meant or said, only different textual representations of different experiences' (Denzin 1994: 296).

However, it would be wrong to depict the growing attention being focused on ethnographic writing as exclusively a product of postmodernism. Atkinson and Coffey (1995) have argued that there are other intellectual trends in the social sciences that have stimulated this interest. Writers in the area of theory and research known as the social studies of science have been concerned with the limitations of accepted distinctions between rhetoric and logic and between the observer and the observed (e.g. Gilbert and Mulkay 1984). The problematizing of these distinctions, along with doubts about the possibility of a neutral language through which the natural and social worlds can be revealed, opened the door for an evaluation of scientific and social scientific writing. . . . Atkinson and Coffey also point to the antipathy within feminism towards the image of the neutral 'observer-author' who assumes a privileged stance in relation to members of the social setting being studied. This stance is regarded as revealing a position of domination of the observer-author over the observed that is inconsistent with the goals of feminism . . . This concern has led to an interest in the ways in which privilege is conveyed in ethnographic texts and how voices, particularly of marginal groups, are suppressed.

The concerns within these and other traditions (including postmodernism) have led to experiments in writing ethnography (Richardson 1994). An example is the use of a 'dialogic' form of writing that seeks to raise the profile of the multiplicity of voices that can be heard in the course of fieldwork. As Lincoln and Denzin (1994: 584) put it: 'Slowly it dawns on us that there may . . . be . . . not one "voice" but polyvocality; not one story, but many tales, dramas, pieces of fiction, fables, memories, histories, autobiographies, poems, and other texts to inform our sense of lifeways, to extend our understandings of the Other . . .'

Manning (1995) cites, as an example of the postmodern preference for allowing a variety of voices to come through within an ethnographic text, the work of Stoller (1989), who conducted research in Africa. Manning (1995: 260) describes the text as 'periodically' dialogic in that it is 'shaped by interactions between informants or "the other" and the observer'. This postmodern preference for seeking out multiple voices and for turning the ethnographer into a 'bit player' reflects the mistrust among postmodernists of 'meta-narratives' – that is, positions or grand accounts that implicitly make claims about absolute truths and that therefore rule out the possibility of alternative versions of reality. On the other hand, 'mini-narratives, micro-narratives, local narratives are just stories that make no truth claims and are therefore more acceptable to postmodernists' (Rosenau 1992: pxiii).

Postmodernism has also encouraged a growing reflexivity in considerations about the conduct of social research and the growing interest in the writing of ethnography is very much a manifestation of this trend. . . . This reflexivity can be discerned in the way in which many ethnographers have turned inwards to examine the truth claims inscribed in their own classic texts. . . .

In the end, what postmodernism leaves us with is an acute sense of uncertainty. It raises the issue of how we can ever know or capture the social reality that belongs to others and in so doing it points to an unresolvable tension that will not go away . . . because, to quote Lincoln and Denzin (1994 : 582) again : 'On the one hand there is the concern for validity, or certainty in the text as a from of isomorphism and authenticity. On the other hand there is the sure and certain knowledge that all texts are socially, historically, politically, and culturally located. We, like the texts we write, can never be transcendent.' At the same time, of course, such a view renders problematic the very idea of what social scientific knowledge is or comprises.

(Bryman 2001: 469–70)

> ➤ Try taking an object and describing it first of all in a modernist writing style and then in a postmodernist writing style.

▼ **70 WHAT'S THE TOPIC? Postmodernist readings**
WHAT'S THE TEXT? Jean Baudrillard
Simulations

The passage that precedes the reading of Disneyland, which is printed below, is itself prefixed by a passage from the Bible, from the Book of Ecclesiastes:

> The simulacrum is never that which contains the truth – it is the truth that conceals that there is none.
> The simulacrum is true.

This is Baudrillard's starting point for an argument about the uncertain character of reality (these days). He speaks of a story in which the cartographers (map-makers) of the Empire make a map 'so detailed that it ends up exactly covering the territory'. The map becomes frayed as the Empire declines and Baudrillard uses this metaphor for the changing character of reality itself, as if the Empire functions in the story as a kind of meta-narrative (or grand or archetypal story).

'Abstraction today,' he says, 'is no longer that of the map.' Put simply he means that representations can no longer be assumed to depend on a reliable reality. He continues: 'It is the generation by models of a real without origin or reality: a hyper real'. Rather than continuing to abstract he then demonstrates his theory with a sharp reading of Disneyland which begins by advertising the fact that 'Disneyland is a perfect model of all the entangled orders of simulation'.

HYPERREAL AND IMAGINARY

Disneyland is a perfect model of all the entangled orders of simulation. To begin with it is a play of illusions and phantasms: Pirates, the Frontier, Future World, etc. This imaginary world is supposed to be what makes the operation successful. But what draws the crowds is undoubtedly much more the social microcosm, the miniaturised and *religious* revelling in real America, in its delights and drawbacks. You park outside, queue up inside, and are totally abandoned at the exit.

In this imaginary world the only phantasmagoria is in the inherent warmth and affection of the crowd, and in that sufficiently excessive number of gadgets used there to specifically maintain the multitudinous affect. The contrast with the absolute solitude of the parking lot – a veritable concentration camp – is total. Or rather: inside, a whole range of gadgets magnetise the crowd into direct flows – outside, solitude is directed onto a single gadget: the automobile. By an extraordinary coincidence (one that undoubtedly belongs to the peculiar enchantment of this universe), this deep-frozen infantile world happens to have been conceived and realised by a man who is himself now cryogenised: Walt Disney, who awaits his resurrection at minus 180 degrees centigrade.

The objective profile of America, then, may be traced throughout Disneyland, even down to the morphology of individuals and the crowd. All its values are exalted here, in miniature and comic strip form. Embalmed and pacified. Whence the possibility of an ideological analysis of Disneyland (L. Marin does it well in Utopies, *jeux d'espaces*): digest of the American way of life, panegyric to American values, idealised transposition of a contradictory, reality. To be sure. But this conceals something else, and that 'ideological' blanket exactly serves to cover over a *third-order simulation*: Disneyland is there to conceal the fact that it is the 'real' country, all of 'real' America, which *is* Disneyland (just as prisons are there to conceal the fact that it is the social in its entirety, in its banal omnipresence, which is carceral). Disneyland is presented as imaginary in order to make us believe that the rest is real, when in fact all of Los Angeles and the America surrounding it are no longer real, but of the order of the hyperreal and of simulation. It is no longer a question of a false representation of reality (ideology), but of concealing the fact that the real is no longer real, and thus of saving the reality principle.

The Disneyland imaginary is neither true nor false; it is a deterrence machine set up in order to rejuvenate in reverse the fiction of the real. Whence the debility, the infantile degeneration of this imaginary. It is meant to be an infantile world, in order to make us believe that the adults are elsewhere, in the 'real' world, and to conceal the fact that real childishness is everywhere, particularly amongst those adults who go there to act the child in order to foster illusions as to their real childishness.

Moreover, Disneyland is not the only one. Enchanted Village, Magic Mountain, Marine World: Los Angeles is encircled by these 'imaginary stations' which feed reality, reality-energy, to a town whose mystery is precisely that it is nothing more than a network of endless, unreal circulation – a town of fabulous proportions, but without space or dimensions. As much as electrical and nuclear power stations, as much as film studios, this town, which is nothing more than an immense script and a perpetual motion picture, needs this old imaginary made up of childhood signals and faked phantasms for its sympathetic nervous system.

(Baudrillard 1983: 204–5)

COMMUNICATION STUDIES: THE ESSENTIAL RESOURCE

> ➤ Use Baudrillard's analysis as a model for writing your own deconstruction of a local or national monument.
> ➤ Read Alan Bryman *Disney and his Worlds* (1995) London: Routledge.

▼ **71 WHAT'S THE TOPIC? Postcolonialism and Orientalism**
WHAT'S THE TEXT? Edward Said *Orientalism*

An essential development of the turn away from the search for the grand narrative has been the move away from the notion that an all-embracing interpretation of the world resides in one nation, one culture, or one people. Indeed, it's logical to argue that traditional concepts of race and nation are simply testimony to the history of imperialism (or one big idea from dead, white, European men).

European notions of east and west, and what is connoted by 'east' and 'west' are further testimony to a particularly skewed, imperialist way of looking at the world. The words 'orient' (from *oriens* meaning the sun rising) and 'occident' (from *occidens* meaning the sun setting) were coined in a European geographical context and clearly indicate the position of the observer. Were that observer to be anywhere in the world other than Europe then notions of what is the east and what is the west would be very different (if you were living in Tokyo the sun would rise in the east over Hawaii). In this way we can see that historically speaking the European notion of the east is derived from an imaginary locating of Europe at the centre of the world. As Edward Said has remarked: 'European culture gained its strength and identity by setting itself off against the Orient as a sort of surrogate and even underground self' (Sim 1999: 329). Europeans defined themselves as the still centre of a chaotic world. Further, they proposed that their sense of their identity as rational, peaceful, liberal, logical and without suspicion both created and reinforced the notion that peoples of the east (Arab-Orientals) were classified as none of these things, as the very opposite.

In a contemporary context Said's notion of Orientalism has been extended, as Stuart Sim has observed, 'as a way to understand how any cultural, ethical or racial group may be 'known' and so dominated by a more powerful bloc'.

Hear what Edward Said has to say about Orientalism.

Unlike the Americans, the French and British – less so the Germans, Russians, Spanish, Portugese, Italians, and Swiss – have had a long tradition of what I shall be calling Orientalism, a way of coming to terms with the Orient that is based on the Orient's special place in European Western Experience. The Orient is not only adjacent to Europe; it is also the place of Europe's greatest and richest and oldest colonies, the source of its civilizations and languages, its cultural contestant, and one of its deepest and most recurring images of the Other. In addition, the Orient has helped to define Europe (or the West) as its contrasting image, idea, personality, experience. Yet none of this Orient is merely imaginative. The Orient is an integral part of European material civilization and culture. Orientalism expresses and represents that part culturally and even ideologically as a mode of discourse with supporting institutions, vocabulary, scholarship, imagery, doctrines, even colonial bureaucracies and colonial styles.

It will be clear to the reader . . . that by Orientalism I mean several things, all of them, in my opinion, interdependent. The most readily accepted designation for Orientalism is an academic one, and indeed the label still serves in a number of academic institutions. Anyone who teaches, writes about, or researches the Orient – and this applies whether the person is an anthropologist, sociologist, historian, or philologist – either in its specific or its general aspects, is an Orientalist, and what he or she says or does is Orientalism. . . .

Related to this academic tradition, whose fortunes, transmigrations, specializations, and transmissions are in part the subject of this study, is a more general meaning for Orientalism. Orientalism is a style of thought based upon ontological and epistemological distinction made between 'the Orient' and (most of the time) 'the Occident.' Thus a very large mass of writers, among whom are poets, novelists, philosophers, political theorists, economists, and imperial administrators, have accepted the basic distinction between East and West as the starting point for elaborate accounts concerning the Orient, its people, customs, 'mind,' destiny, and so on. . . . the phenomenon of Orientalism as I study it here deals principally, not with a correspondence between Orientalism and Orient, but with the internal consistency of Orientalism and its ideas about the Orient . . . despite or beyond any corrsespondence, or lack thereof, with a 'real' Orient.

(Said 1978: 1–3, 5)

WHAT'S NEXT?

➤ Read Kathryn Woodward (ed.) *Identity and Difference* (1997) Milton Keynes: Open University Press/Sage.

72 WHAT'S THE TOPIC? Postcolonialist readings and imagined communities
WHAT'S THE TEXT? Anthony P Cohen *The Symbolic Construction of Community*

In 1968 Robert Stoller proposed that it was useful to distinguish between sex (biological status) and gender (social and cultural status) and it is interesting to note that the term 'ethnicity', according to van den Berghe, was also coined during that period. We say interesting in the sense that this is to emphasise the extent to which such notions as gender and ethnicity are constructed and how they are thus necessarily conceived in such contexts as time and place.

This is one of Cohen's key points in the extract that follows on constructions of ethnicity and the significance of local contexts. He sees ideas about community and ethnicity as implicitly tied up with ideology and the power relationships it contains and represents. He ties ethnic identity to specific local contexts in which social and political pressure is seen as a more persuasive catalyst than 'just a well-developed collective self-consciousness'. He cites Paine who refers to communities reaching their 'to be or not to be' point where pressure on identity will cause them to either stand or fall. This leads Cohen to offer three positions on ethnicity :

- as a debased, fetishised or abandoned culture of special items (often with religious implications);
- in van den Berghe's definition as a ploy, a contrivance – 'a strategy, based upon choice and informed by a calculus of advantage'; and
- by implication as an ideological struggle in which disadvantage and subordination produce a meaningful response to the wider society's need to define communities and cultures narrowly.

RESPONDING TO THE PRESENT: ETHNICITY AND LOCALITY

However, it is obviously the case that not all communities are so resilient, and not all make such a determined and vibrant response to change. Many become deserted, culturally and/or demographically (see for example, Brody, 1973), or are wholly transformed, losing their sense of themselves or suffering its debasement thorough the fetishization of its material objects (see, Helias, 1979, also Smith, 1981, pp. 156ff.). The question therefore arises: what produces such vehemence and assertiveness? The answer can only be given in general terms, with no suggestion that similar circumstances will invariably evoke a similar response in different communities. The answer has not often been attempted in respect of local communities. The most instructive available precedents relate to the political assertion of culture difference – a phenomenon generally described through the somewhat abused label of 'ethnicity' (see Paine, 1977, 1985).

The inclination of an 'ethnic' group to assert its cultural integrity is clearly stimulated by more than just a well-developed collective self-consciousness. Many of the examples we have encountered above show that it follows from more than mere contrast with other groups. Often, it seems to follow from a sense of disadvantage, or subordination – but then many disadvantaged and subordinated groups go under. Anthony Smith suggests that the revival of ethnicity in Europe re-activated an earlier ethnic consciousness dating back over two or more centuries (1981, pp. 20ff.). Interesting though this observation may be, it does not explain why the 'revival' occurred as and when it did. Part of the answer may lie in the suggestion that Paine makes with regard to the Kautokeino Saami, when he writes of them reaching their 'to be or not to be' (*Supra*, p.79). The implication is that when groups feel they have nothing more to lose than their sense of self, then they cast caution to the winds and confront the dominant nationalisms and statisms. But there must be more to it than this for, whilst ethnic activism may be fashionable, it is nevertheless more of a thorn in the flesh, than a stake through the heart of the great polities. Indeed, one of the most authoritative, if controversial writers on the subject is inclined to dismiss the widespread assertiveness of the 1960s and 1970s as merely 'an ethnic binge'.

> The very word 'ethnicity' was coined during that period. It became fashionable to discover, cultivate and cuddle 'ethnic identities' and 'roots' . . . All of a sudden, social scientists begin to proclaim that the melting pot had failed and had been a sham to start with, that ethnic identities were precious, that assimilationism was a sinister policy of 'ethnocide' and that the state should give full recognition to ethnic and racial sentiments and should base its policies of resource distribution on criteria of race and ethnicity (van den Berghe, 1981, p. 4)

Whilst he stresses the sociobiological basis of the 'ethny' in endogamy and extended kinship, van den Berghe also sees ethnicity as a strategy, based upon choice and informed by a calculus of advantage (1981, pp. 254ff.). But he turns the problem of ethnicity on its head by making ethnic primacy the norm, and assimilation the aberration which therefore requires analysis. For example, 'ethnicity is more primordial than class. Blood runs thicker than money' (1981, p. 243). In this regard it is the very 'irrationality' of ethnicity which makes its sentiments so powerful and so readily aroused:

> Appeals to ethnic sentiments need no justification other than common 'blood'. They are couched in terms of 'our people' versus 'them' (*ibid.*)

and are most easily mobilized if 'them' can be depicted as positing a threat to 'us'.

(Cohen 1992: 104–5)

> ➤ Survey the attitudes of your class or group to the ideas of ethnicity or
> endogamy (marrying or finding partners within your own ethnic group). What
> relationship did you find between these two ideas?

▼ 73 **WHAT'S THE TOPIC? The landscape as text
WHAT'S THE TEXT? Gunther Kress and Theo
van Leeuwen *Reading Images: The Grammar of
Visual Design***

The theoretical perspectives described or exemplified in the previous sequence of extracts
are a sound starting point for examining lived experience but they are not the only
requirement. If we are to make sense of our various worlds we need to make sense of the
ways in which we might perceive them. In their *Grammar of Visual Design* Kress and van
Leeuwen address this issue by reference to what they call the 'semiotic landscape', which
is the context in which the modes of communication are seen in their own environment.

The authors develop the notion of the landscape as text – it's simply another feature of
everyday life which can be read. Furthermore, as narratives which can be read, landscapes are stories in development: not only do they have a present but they also have a
past, a back story.

The extract below, which constitutes the continuation of this argument, serves to set the
readings of cultural experience in a meaningful context. In its careful description of the
area it prepares for the debate that might follow about the character of texts and reading.

THE SEMIOTIC LANDSCAPE

The place of visual communication in a given society can only be understood in
the context of, on the one hand, the range of forms or modes of public communication available in that society, and, on the other hand, their uses and
valuations. We refer to this as 'the semiotic landscape'. The metaphor is worth
exploring a little, as is its etymology. Just as the features of a landscape (a field,
a wood, a clump of trees, a house, a group of buildings) only make sense in the
context of their whole environment ('waste land' has meaning only in that context, as has 'field' or 'track'), so particular modes of communication should be

seen in *their* environment, in the environment of all the other modes of communication which surround them, and of their functions. The use of the visual mode is not the same now as it was even fifty years ago in Western societies; it is not the same from one society to another; and it is not the same from one social group or institution to another.

Each feature of a landscape has its history, as does the landscape as a whole, and each is subject to constant remaking. It is here that the etymology of the word *landscape* is revealing. While to the casual beholder a landscape simply *is*, and may even have a timeless appearance ('the timeless beauty of the English, or Spanish, countryside'), it is in fact a product of social action and of a social history, of human work on the land, on nature: *-scape*, with its relatives *to shape* in English and *schaffen* (both 'to work' and 'to create') in German, indicates this. And this applies also to the 'semiotic landscape". Metaphoric excursions of this kind can be stretched too far; however, we will allow ourselves one other point of comparison. Landscapes are the result, not just of human social work, but also of the characteristics of the land itself. The flat land by the river is most suitable for the grazing of cattle or the growing of wheat; the hillsides for vineyards or forestry. At the same time, the characteristic values of a culture may determine which of the potential uses of the land are realized, whether the hillsides are used for vineyards or forestry, for example. And cultural values may even induce people to go against the grain of the land, to use the steep hillside for growing rice, for example, which opposes the 'natural potential' of the land almost to the limit.

Semiotic modes, similarly, are shaped both by the intrinsic characteristics and potentialities of the medium and by the requirements, histories and values of societies and their cultures. The characteristics of the medium of air are not the same as those of the medium of stone, and the potentialities of the speech organs are not the same as those of the human hand. Nevertheless, cultural and social valuations and structures strongly affect the uses of these potentialities. It is not an accident that in Western societies written language has had the place which it has had for the last three or four millennia, and that the visual mode has in effect become subservient to language, as its mode of expression in writing. Linguistic theories have more or less naturalized the view that the use of air and the vocal organs is the natural, inevitable semiotic means of expression. But even speech is, in the end, cultural. We are not biologically predisposed to use speech as our major mode of communication. Indeed, there is some evidence that the adaptation to speech of the physical organs which developed initially to prevent humans from choking while breathing *and* eating, have begun to lead to some ineffectiveness of these organs for their original task. When the need arises, we *can* and do use other means of expression, as in the highly articulated development of gesture in sign languages, and also in theatrical mime and certain Eastern forms of ballet. And while these are at present restricted to relatively marginal domains, who is to say that this will always remain so in the future development of humankind?

The new realities of the semiotic landscape are, as we have already indicated, primarily brought about by social and cultural factors: by the intensification of linguistic and cultural diversity within the boundaries of nation states, and by the weakening of these boundaries, due to multiculturalism, electronic media of communication, technologies of transport and global economic developments. Global flows of capital and information dissolve not only cultural and political boundaries but also semiotic boundaries. This is already beginning to have the most far-reaching effects on the characteristics of English (and Englishes), globally, and even within the national boundaries of England.

(Kress and van Leeuwen 1996: 33–4)

WHAT'S NEXT?

> ➤ List some of the ways in which your experience has become more visual in the early years of the twenty-first century. What has been the impact of these changes on the way you behave – what you do and how you do it?

▼ ## 74 WHAT'S THE TOPIC? The cityscape as text
WHAT'S THE TEXT? Mike Davis *City of Quartz: Excavating the Future in Los Angeles*

If there is any sphere of human activity where we can be sure that the term postmodernism has meaning it is in architecture. Architects and urban theorists alike have long used the term to describe an unembarrassed melange of architectural styles which are our contemporary cityscapes. Postmodern architecture might take the form of one single building which draws on several eras of architectural design or a typical town or city centre where no attempt is made to harness all the buildings into one general unifying design.

But towns and cities are key sites for battle: economic, social, political, ethnic. Here we can read economic, social, political, class, and ethnic histories. Here we can see the rule of vested interests and the marginalisation of the dispossessed. Mike Davis offered an incendiary reading of postmodern Los Angeles in his 1990 book *City of Quartz: Excavating the Future in Los Angeles*. Many postmodern theorists seek to collapse traditional notions of space and place – and even time – as a response to the contemporary world. Davis responds to the challenge of a frequently daunting experience – visually, aesthetically, historically. But he is always grounded. He is a native of Southern California and doesn't offer 'travel writing' where the exotic and the quirky is sought out, held up to ridicule, and then discarded. He writes of the very material realities of contemporary Los Angeles in this extract.

The carefully manicured lawns of Los Angeles' Westside sprout forests of ominous little signs warning: 'Armed Response!' Even richer neighborhoods in the canyons and hillsides isolate themselves behind walls guarded by gun-toting private police and state-of-the-art electronic surveillance. Downtown, a publicly subsidized 'urban renaissance' has raised the nation's largest corporate citadel, segregated from the poor neighborhoods around it by a monumental architectural glacis. In Hollywood, celebrity architect Frank Gehry, renowned for his 'humanism,' apotheosizes the siege look in a library designed to resemble a foreign-legion fort. In the Westlake district and the San Fernando Valley the Los Angeles Police barricade streets and seal off poor neighborhoods as part of their 'war on drugs.' In Watts, developer Alexander Haagen demonstrates his strategy for recolonizing inner-city retail markets: a panopticon shopping mall surrounded by staked metal fences and a substation of the LAPD in a central surveillance tower. Finally, on the horizon of the next millennium, an ex-chief of police crusades for an anti-crime 'giant eye' – a geo-synchronous law enforcement satellite – while other cops discreetly tend versions of 'Garden Plot,' a hoary but still viable 1960s plan for a law-and-order armageddon.

Welcome to post-liberal Los Angeles, where the defense of luxury lifestyles is translated into a proliferation of new repressions in space and movement, undergirded by the ubiquitous 'armed response'. This obsession with physical security systems, and, collaterally, with the architectural policing of social boundaries, has become a zeitgeist of urban restructuring, a master narrative in the emerging built environment of the 1990s. Yet contemporary urban theory, whether debating the role of electronic technologies in precipitating 'postmodern space,' or discussing the dispersion of urban functions across poly-centered metropolitan 'galaxies', has been strangely silent about the militarization of city life so grimly visible at the street level. Hollywood's pop apocalypses and pulp science fiction have been more realistic, and politically perceptive, in representing the programmed hardening of the urban surface in the wake of the social polarizations of the Reagan era. Images of carceral inner cities (*Escape from New York*, *Running Man*), high-tech police death squads (*Blade Runner*), sentient buildings (*Die Hard*), urban bantustans (*They Live!*), Vietnam-like Street wars (*Colors*), and so on, only extrapolate from actually existing trends.

Such dystopian visions grasp the extent to which today's pharaonic scales of residential and commercial security supplant residual hopes for urban reform and social integration. The dire predictions of Richard Nixon's 1969 National Commission on the Causes and Prevention of Violence have been tragically fulfilled: we live in 'fortress cities' brutally divided between 'fortified cells' of affluent society and 'places of terror' where the police battle the criminalized poor. The 'Second Civil War' that began in the long hot summers of the 1960s has been institutionalized into the very structure of urban space. The old liberal paradigm of social control, attempting to balance repression with reform, has long been superseded by a rhetoric of social warfare that calculates the interests of the urban poor and the middle classes as a zero-sum game. In cities like Los Angeles, on the bad edge of post-modernity, one observes an unprecedented tendency to merge urban design, architecture and the police apparatus into a single, comprehensive security effort.

This epochal coalescence has far-reaching consequences for the social relations of the built environment. In the first place, the market provision of 'security' generates its own paranoid demand. 'Security' becomes a positional good defined by income access to private 'protective services' and membership in some hardened residential enclave or restricted suburb. As a prestige symbol – and sometimes as the decisive borderline between the merely well-off and the 'truly rich' – 'security' has less to do with personal safety than with the degree of personal insulation, in residential, work, consumption and travel environments, 'unsavory' groups and individuals, even crowds in general.

Secondly, as William Whyte has observed of social intercourse in New York, 'fear proves itself.' The social perception of threat becomes a function of the security mobilization itself, not crime rates. Where there is an actual rising arc of street violence, as in Southcentral Los Angeles or Downtown Washington D.C., most of the carnage is self-contained within ethnic or class boundaries. Yet white middle-class imagination, absent from any firsthand knowledge of inner-city conditions, magnifies the perceived threat through a demonological lens. Surveys show that Milwaukee suburbanites are just as worried about violent crime as inner-city Washingtonians, despite a twentyfold difference in relative levels of mayhem. The media, whose function in this arena is to bury and obscure the daily economic violence of the city, ceaselessly throw up spectres of criminal underclasses and psychotic stalkers. Sensationalized accounts of killer youth gangs high on crack and shrilly racist evocations of marauding Willie Hortons foment the moral panics that reinforce and justify urban apartheid.

Moreover, the neo-military syntax of contemporary architecture insinuates violence and conjures imaginary dangers. In many instances the semiotics of so-called 'defensible space' are just about as subtle as a swaggering white cop. Today's upscale, pseudo-public spaces – sumptuary malls, office centres, culture acropolises, and so on – are full of invisible signs warning off the underclass 'Other.' Although architectural critics are usually oblivious to how the built environment contributes to segregation, pariah groups – whether poor Latino families, young Black men, or elderly homeless white females – read the meaning immediately.

. . .

THE FORBIDDEN CITY

The first militarist of space in Los Angeles was General Otis of the *Times*. Declaring himself at war with labor, he infused his surroundings with an unrelentingly bellicose air:

> He called his home in Los Angeles the Bivouac. Another house was known as the Outpost. The *Times* was known as the Fortress. The staff or the paper was the Phalanx. The *Times* building itself was more fortress than newspaper plant, there were turrets, battlements, sentry boxes. Inside he stored fifty rifles.

A great, menacing bronze eagle was the *Times's* crown; a small, functional cannon was installed on the hood of Otis's touring car to intimidate onlookers. Not surprisingly, this overwrought display of aggression produced a response in kind. On 1 October 1910 the heavily fortified *Times* headquarters – citadel of the open shop on the West Coast – was destroyed in a catastrophic explosion blamed on union saboteurs.

Eighty years later, the spirit of General Otis has returned to subtly pervade Los Angeles' new 'postmodern' Downtown: the emerging Pacific Rim financial complex which cascades, in rows of skyscrapers, from Bunker Hill southward along the Figueroa corridor. Redeveloped with public tax increments under the aegis of the powerful and largely unaccountable Community Redevelopment Agency (CRA), the Downtown project is one of the largest postwar urban designs in North America. Site assemblage and clearing on a vast scale, with little mobilized opposition, have resurrected land values, upon which big developers and off-shore capital (increasingly Japanese) have planted a series of billion-dollar, block-square megastructures: Crocker Center, the Bonaventure Hotel and Shopping Mall, the World Trade Center, Broadway Plaza, Arco Center, CitiCorp Plaza, California Plaza, and so on. With historical landscapes erased, with megastructures and superblocks as primary components, and with an increasingly dense and self-contained circulation system, the new financial district is best conceived as a single, demonically self-referential hyperstructure, a Miesian skyscape raised to dementia.

Like similar megalomaniac complexes, tethered to fragmented and desolated Downtowns (for instance, the Renaissance Center in Detroit, the Peachtree and Omni Centers in Atlanta, and so on), Bunker Hill and the Figueroa corridor have provoked a storm of liberal objections against their abuse of scale and composition, their denigration of street landscape, and their confiscation of so much of the vital life activity of the center, now sequestered within subterranean concourses or privatized malls. Sam Hall Kaplan, the crusty urban critic of the *Times*, has been indefatigable in denouncing the anti-pedestrian bias of the new corporate citadel, with its fascist obliteration of street frontage. In his view the superimposition of 'hermetically sealed fortresses' and air-dropped 'pieces of suburbia' has 'dammed the rivers of life' Downtown.

Yet Kaplan's vigorous defense of pedestrian democracy remains grounded in hackneyed liberal complaints about 'bland design' and 'elitist planning practices.' Like most architectural critics, he rails against the oversights of urban design without recognizing the dimension of foresight, of explicit repressive intention, which has its roots in Los Angeles' ancient history of class and race warfare. Indeed, when Downtown's new 'Gold Coast' is viewed en bloc from the standpoint of its interactions with other social areas and landscapes in the central city, the 'fortress effect' emerges, not as an inadvertent failure of design, but as deliberate socio-spatial strategy.

The goals of this strategy may be summarized as a double repression: to raze all association with Downtown's past and to prevent any articulation with the non-Anglo urbanity of its future. Everywhere on the perimeter of redevelopment this strategy takes the form of a brutal architectural edge or glacis that defines the new Downtown as a citadel vis-à-vis the rest of the central city. Los Angeles is unusual amongst major urban renewal centers in preserving, however negligently, most of its circa 1900–30 Beaux Arts commercial core. At immense public cost, the corporate headquarters and financial district was shifted from the old Broadway–Spring corridor six blocks west to the greenfield site created by destroying the Bunker Hill residential neighborhood. To emphasize the 'security' of the new Downtown, virtually all the traditional pedestrian links to the old center, including the famous Angels' Flight funicular railroad, were removed.

The logic of this entire operation is revealing. In other cities developers might have attempted to articulate the new skyscape and the old, exploiting the latter's extraordinary inventory of theaters and historic buildings to create a gentrified history – a gaslight district, Faneuil Market or Ghirardelli Square – as a support to middle-class residential colonization. But Los Angeles' redevelopers viewed property values in the old Broadway core as irreversibly eroded by the area's very centrality to public transport, and especially by its heavy use by Black and Mexican poor. In the wake of the Watts rebellion, and the perceived Black threat to crucial nodes of white power (spelled out in lurid detail in the McCone Commission Report), resegregated spatial security became the paramount concern. The Los Angeles Police Department abetted the flight of business from Broadway to fortified redoubts of Bunker Hill by spreading scare literature typifying Black teenagers as dangerous gang members.

As a result, redevelopment massively reproduced spatial apartheid. The moat of the Harbor Freeway and the regraded palisades of Bunker Hill cut off the new financial core from poor immigrant neighborhoods that surround it on every side. Along the base of California Plaza, Hill Street became a local Berlin Wall separating the publicly subsidized luxury of Bunker Hill from the lifeworld of Broadway, now reclaimed by Latino immigrants as their primary shopping and entertainment street. Because politically connected speculators are now redeveloping the northern end of the Broadway corridor (sometimes known as 'Bunker Hill East'), the CRA is promising to restore pedestrian linkages to the

Hill in the 1990s, including the Angels' Flight incline railroad. This, of course, only dramatizes the current bias against accessibility – that is to say, against any spatial interaction between old and new, poor and rich, except in the framework of gentrification or recolonization. Although a few white-collars venture into the Grand Central Market – a popular emporium of tropical produce and fresh foods – Latino shoppers or Saturday strollers never circulate in the Gucci precincts above Hill Street. The occasional appearance of a destitute street nomad in Broadway Plaza or in front of the Museum of Contemporary Art sets off a quiet panic; video cameras turn on their mounts and security guards adjust their belts.

Photographs of the old Downtown in its prime show mixed crowds of Anglo, Black and Latino pedestrians of different ages and classes. The contemporary Downtown 'renaissance' is designed to make such heterogeneity virtually impossible. It is intended not just to 'kill the street' as Kaplan fears, but to 'kill the crowd', to eliminate that democratic admixture on the pavements and in the parks that Olmsted believed was America's antidote to European class polarizations. The Downtown hyperstructure – like some Buckminster Fuller post-Holocaust fantasy – is programmed to ensure a seamless continuum of middle-class work, consumption and recreation, without unwonted exposure to Downtown's working-class street environments. Indeed the totalitarian semiotics of ramparts and battlements, reflective glass and elevated pedways, rebukes any affinity or sympathy between different architectural or human orders. As in Otis's fortress *Times* building, this is the archisemiotics of class war.

(Davis 1990: 223–6, 228–31)

WHAT'S NEXT?

➤ Read James Donald (1997) 'This, here, now: imagining the modern city' in Sarah Westwood and John Williams (eds) *Imagining Cities: Scripts, Signs, Meanings*, London: Routledge.
➤ Watch Patrick Keiller's 1994 film *London*.
➤ Where would you go to find out the true or secret history of where you live? (Please note: Contrary to what some writers on cities would seem to think no place is special and especially capable of being read. All places are special and all places can be read.)

Afforded a cultural context the whole world becomes a text or rather becomes alive with potential meaning. The piece below is taken from *Simmel on Culture* and concerns adornment, the fancy as opposed to the ordinary dress, such as jewels 'which gather the personality's value and significance of radiation as if in a focal point'. Georg Simmel is interested in exploring the ways in which 'everything that adorns man' can potentially accentuate the personality.

The piece begins with a statement of the dynamic and essentially contradictory relationship between the desire to please and the desire to be pleased. This is situated squarely in the middle of a debate about appearance: 'this meaning is to single the personality out'. As such he is much more interested in special items like jewellery and tattoos than he is in ordinary clothes.

miscellaneous belongings.

He also offers an interesting angle on the relationship between the paraphernalia of adornment and the human body, suggesting that 'Everything that adorns man can be ordered along a scale in terms of its closeness to the physical body'. The scale that Simmel proposes goes from tattooing ('typical of primitive peoples') which is 'inexchangeable and personal' towards 'metal and stone adornments' which are entirely unindividual and can be put on with everything'. As Simmel points out, 'Between these two stands dress'.

What follows is a sophisticated reading of a cultural phenomenon which is centred on the personality and its presentation. Originally published in 1908, Simmel's writing anticipates much contemporary writing about 'dressing to impress'.

ADORNMENT

The meaning of adornment finds expression in peculiar elaborations of these motives, in which the external and internal aspects of their forms are interwoven. This meaning is to single the personality out, to emphasise it as outstanding in some sense – but not by means of power manifestations, not by anything that externally compels the other, but only through the pleasure which is engendered in him and which, therefore, still has some voluntary element in it. One adorns oneself for oneself, but can do so only by adornment for others. It is one of the strangest sociological combinations that an act, which exclusively serves the emphasis and increased significance of the actor, nevertheless attains this goal just as exclusively in the pleasure, in the visual delight it offers to others, and in their gratitude. For, even the envy of adornment only indicates the desire of the

---

envious person to win like recognition and admiration for himself; his envy proves how much he believes these values to be connected with the adornment. Adornment is the egoistic element as such: it singles out its wearer, whose self-feeling it embodies and increases at the cost of others (for, the same adornment of all would no longer adorn the individual). But, at the same time, adornment is altruistic: its pleasure is designed for the others, since its owner can enjoy it only in so far as he mirrors himself in them; he renders the adornment valuable only through the reflection of this gift of his. Everywhere, aesthetic formation reveals that life orientations, which reality juxtaposes as mutually alien, or even pits against one another as hostile, are, in fact, intimately interrelated. In the same way, the aesthetic phenomenon of adornment indicates a point within sociological interaction – the arena of man's being-for-himself and being-for-the-other – where these two opposite directions are mutually dependent as ends and means.

Adornment intensifies or enlarges the impression of the personality by operating as a sort of radiation emanating from it. For this reason, its materials have always been shining metals and precious stones. They are 'adornment' in a narrower sense than dress and coiffure, although these, too, 'adorn'. One may speak of human radioactivity in the sense that every individual is surrounded by a larger or smaller sphere of significance radiating from him; and everybody else, who deals with him, is immersed in this sphere. It is an inextricable mixture of physiological and psychic elements: the sensuously observable influences which issue from an individual in the direction of his environment also are, in some fashion, the vehicles of a spiritual fulguration. They operate as the symbols of such a fulguration even where, in actuality, they are only external, where no suggestive power or significance of the personality flows through them. The radiations of adornment, the sensuous attention it provokes, supply the personality with such an enlargement or intensification of its sphere; the personality, so to speak, *is* more when it is adorned.

Inasmuch as adornment usually is also an object of considerable value, it is a synthesis of the individual's having and being; it thus transforms mere possession into the sensuous and emphatic perceivability of the individual himself. This is not true of ordinary dress which, neither in respect of having nor of being, strikes one as an individual particularity; only the fancy dress, and above all, jewels, which gather the personality's value and significance of radiation as if in a focal point, allow the mere *having* of the person to become a visible quality of its *being*. And this is so, not *although* adornment is something 'superfluous', but precisely *because* it is. The necessary is much more closely connected with the individual; it surrounds his existence with a narrower periphery. The superfluous 'flows over', that is, it flows to points which are far removed from its origin but to which it still remains tied: around the precinct of mere necessity, it lays a vaster precinct which, in principle, is limitless. According to its very idea, the superfluous contains no measure. The free and princely character of our being increases in the measure in which we add superfluousness to our having, since no extant structure, such as is laid down by necessity, imposes any limiting norm upon it.

This very accentuation of the personality, however, is achieved by means of an impersonal trait. Everything that 'adorns' man can be ordered along a scale in terms of its closeness to the physical body. The 'closest' adornment is typical of primitive peoples: tattooing. The opposite extreme is represented by metal and stone adornments, which are entirely unindividual and can be put on by every-body. Between these two stands dress, which is not so inexchangeable and personal as tattooing, but neither so unindividual and separable as jewellery, whose very elegance lies in its impersonality. That this nature of stone and metal – solidly closed within itself, in no way alluding to any individuality; hard, unmodifiable – is yet forced to serve the person, this is its subtlest fascination. What is really elegant avoids pointing to the specifically individual; it always lays a more general, stylised, almost abstract sphere around man – which, of course, prevents no finesse from connecting the general with the personality. That new clothes are particularly elegant is due to their being still 'stiff'; they have not yet adjusted to the modifications of the individual body as fully as older clothes have, which have been worn, and are pulled and pinched by the peculiar move-ments of their wearer – thus completely revealing his particularity. This 'newness', this lack of modification by individuality, is typical in the highest measure of metal jewellery: it is always new; in untouchable coolness, it stands above the singularity and destiny of its wearer. This is not true of dress. A long-worn piece of clothing almost grows to the body; it has an intimacy that militates against the very nature of elegance, which is something for the 'others', a social notion deriving its value from general respect.

(Simmel 1997: 206–8)

WHAT'S NEXT?

Simmel's piece is provocative. So why not respond to some of those provocations? Here are some positions to debate.

➤ One adorns oneself but can do so only by adornment for others. Adornment is altruistic (its pleasure is designed for others) since their owner can enjoy it only in so far as they mirror themselves in them; they render the adornment valuable only through the reflection of this gift of theirs.
Is this true ?

➤ 'Adornment itensifies or enlarges the impression of the personality by operat-ing as a sort of radiation emanating from it.'
What do you think Simmel means by this ? What examples can you provide of this phenomenon?

➤ 'Everything that adorns man can be ordered along a scale in terms of its close-ness to the physical body. The closest adornment is typical of primitive peoples: tattooing. The opposite extreme is represented by metal and stone adorn-ments, which are entirely unindividual and can be put on by everybody.'
What might closeness to the body signify?

▼ **76 WHAT'S THE TOPIC? Reading everyday life II WHAT'S THE TEXT? Margaret Visser *The Way We Are***

Reading like a combination of Barthes (see Extract 14) and Simmel (see Extract 75), Margaret Visser's collection *The Way We Are* offers readings of contemporary objects which are focused, insightful and witty. Moreover, they serve to remind us that readings of the ordinary are just as, if not more, revealing than readings of those objects which advertise themselves as extraordinary or special. Read the signs in the street.

Here she takes a long hard look at high heels.

In Alfred Hitchcock's movie *The Lady Vanishes*, a nun is shockingly revealed to be no nun. She is sitting sedately enough, but we suddenly notice, protruding from beneath her habit, a pair of high-heeled shoes. Footwear of that shape immedi-ately signals to us that this is a woman playing the sexual game.

When clothing resembling nuns' habits was ordinary female apparel, there were no such things as heels of any sort. Heels appeared for the first time in France in the 1590s. They were quite high and worn first by men. It was soon realised that heels had their uses as stirrup-holders on riding boots. But their first pur-pose was to raise their owners, enable them to pose impressively, and stretch their legs so that their calf muscles bulged curvaceously out.

Women quickly took to wearing heels although their legs were hidden by volu-minous skirts, and when they did hemlines rose to show off their shoes. High-heeled shoes are still meant predominantly for posing in, as Miss America does in her swimsuit. She keeps her legs together, one knee gently bent. Pictures of women in bathing suits with heeled legs astride make a more up-to-date, but not necessarily a more feminist, statement.

High heels have never been made for comfort or for ease of movement. Their first wearers spoke of themselves as 'mounted' or 'propped' upon them; they were strictly court wear, and constituted proof that one intended no physical exertion, and need make none.

The Chinese had long known footwear that had the same effect, with high wooden pillars under the arch of each shoe, so that wearers required one or even two servants to help them totter along. Women had their feet deformed, by binding, into tiny almost useless fists, which were shod in embroidered bootees: men got out of the thought of these an unconscionable thrill.

The European versions of stilt-shoes were Venetian chopines, which grew in height to twenty inches and more. The shoes attached to these pedestals sloped slightly towards the toe, and this is believed to be one origin of the heel. The other was the thoroughly mundane and practical patten or wooden clog, which raised the whole foot and was slipped over shoes to protect them from mud and water in the street.

High heels seem to have derived from an attempt to lighten raised shoes, by first creating an arch, then letting the toe down to the ground. The metatarsi of the foot (the long bones that end in toes) would remain bent, and bear the weight of the downward thrust.

And immediately the comforts of left and right shoes ceased to exist. 'Straights,' or both shoes made exactly alike, arrived with heels; people had to swap their left and right shoes every day, to keep them in shape. Fitted lefts and rights returned only when fashion dispensed with heels – until the pantograph changed shoemaking technology in the nineteenth century and made heeled lefts and rights feasible.

High heels became distinctively female dress during the eighteenth century: men heartily approved. 'Heels' cause a woman's bottom to undulate twice as much as flat shoes permit; they pleasingly hobble the female and give the male a protective function, they add curve to the leg by shortening the heel cords and raising calf muscles. Sling-back shoes and curving heels help draw attention to the *back* of a woman: it is the ancient device of rewarding the turning of a male's head. Tall cones or 'stiletto' heels are aggressive yet incapacitating, like long fingernails.

There has always been a preference for tiny feet in women: even prehistoric Venuses' legs tend to taper to a point. This might be because animals, especially stream-lined ones like cats, dogs, and horses, have short feet or hooves. High heels and skimpy shoes reduce feet and lengthen legs; they emphasise the animal in woman. Also – and this is important sexually – stretched legs show that she is taut and *trying*.

Pointed toes redouble the discomfort factor, and cut feet smaller still. Points plus heels aim at lightness, emphasising the 'animal' message – but also stylising it. They give women an ethereal aspect by raising them from the earth and from common sense.

After the French Revolution the idea of using high heels to advertise status became embarrassing, and women and men went immediately into flats (very insubstantial ones if you were upper class). Men soon regained a small heel to secure the straps under their feet that held their trouser legs tight. It was at this very date that ballerinas, heelless in ordinary life, took to dancing on points.

Fashion historians tell us that women don strong shoes, low heels, and round toes whenever society feels threatened and politics uncertain. They are a sure sign that people – men as well as women – are worried, and gearing up for a fight.

(Visser 1997: 37–40)

WHAT'S NEXT?

➤ Take an everyday item of clothing and research how it came to signify as it presently does. How does it generate the meanings it does? Draw on the widest possible range of sources – including your own memory and your own history – to inform your reading.

▼ **77 WHAT'S THE TOPIC? The human figure as text I**
WHAT'S THE TEXT? David Fickling 'Lizard Man'

In contrast to the sheer sophistication of the readings of Simmel and Visser comes 'Lizard Man', a descriptive account of a work of art. Erik Sprague has taken adornment as far as it can go via forked tongue and Teflon implants. In many ways the case is an extreme manifestation of Simmel's central point that 'the meaning is to single the personality out'. With sharpened teeth and scale-like tattoos Mr Sprague's personality is very much singled out. Moreover the cost and value of the body modifications conforms to Simmel's notion that adornment is 'a synthesis of the individual's having and being'.

Mr Sprague also introduces a discussion about the construction of identity in and through communication texts. The article suggests that he 'claims to be one of the five people in the world who have tried to transform themselves altogether'.

If you imagine most PhD students as bookish, bespectacled figures with a penchant for chunky-knit cardigans, the appearance of Erik Sprague may come as something of a shock.

The 28-year-old, who likes to be known as Lizard Man, has had his tongue surgically forked and Teflon implants sewn under the skin of his forehead to give his face the knobbly appearance of a reptile.

His teeth have been filed down to sharpened points, his body is covered with scale-like tattoos and he has even sculpted his fingernails to make them look like claws.

He claims he wants to become a lizard and plans to have an artificial tail fitted if the medical expertise ever becomes available.

Mr Sprague, who describes himself as a performance artist but is also studying for a doctorate in philosophy, has spent more than 400 hours under the tattooist's needle.

To most people that might sound painful enough – but he is planning to have twice as many tattoos again to fulfil his dream of covering his entire body with ink.

He is taking time out from a course at the University of Albany in New York to go on tour with the infamous Jim Rose Circus Sideshow, where other unusual 'acts' include a man who hammers nails up his nose and another who lifts concrete blocks with rings attached to his penis.

Mr Sprague's other notable achievements include fire-breathing, piercing his cheeks with needles, swallowing swords and suspending himself from hooks through the skin of his back.

He says his decoration is not simply adornment but 'body modification' – and claims to be one of five people in the world who have tried to transform themselves altogether. The others used tattoos to turn themselves into a zebra, tiger, leopard and a jigsaw puzzle.

Asked why he does it, Mr Sprague said: 'I like reptiles, especially sea crocodiles. Although many of them don't make great house pets.'

(Fickling 2001: 3)

WHAT'S NEXT?

➤ Mr Sprague's action seems almost to take the cosmetic out of cosmetic surgery. What messages are given out and given off by the range of available cosmetic surgeries and bodily modifications?

➤ Read V Vale and Andrea Juno (eds) *Modern Primitives* (1989) San Francisco: Re/Search Publications.

▼ 78 WHAT'S THE TOPIC? The human figure as text II
WHAT'S THE TEXT? Susan Jeffords *Hard*
Bodies: Hollywood Masculinity in the Reagan Era

The kind of complete transformation that Lizard Man desired is at the centre of Susan Jeffords' critical account of the ideology and issues deriving from the film *Robocop*. Here again the human body is both a significant text and, as a result, a significant site of debate. Ronald Reagan's presidency of the USA brought in a new wave of right-wing politics during which the president took a hard-line on politics in such matters as the Cold War (the United States' antagonist relationship with the former Soviet Union).

Understandably as American politics hurtled to the right so, quickly, did American popular culture. The 1980s was, in Hollywood for example, an era of mega-buck movies whose less than subtle blend of violence and patriotism became known as 'Warnography' (a combination of 'War' and 'Pornography' which suggested the less than uplifting effects of these films). Put simply, what this extract from Susan Jeffords' book *Hard Bodies* does is to draw out the meanings of these men (and particularly their bodies) by focusing on the ultimate Hollywood hard body *Robocop*.

THE MOVIES ARE LOOKING FOR A FEW GOOD WHITE MEN

. . .

The intimate connection between the hard body and its mechanistic dark side is not simply a means to construct an anticommunist narrative but the means for constructing, in a Hegelian sense, a story of the nation as well. Reagan's pro-technology militarism – one of the three consistent features of his political agenda (along with tax cuts and decreasing government bureaucracy) – was justified exclusively in terms of a 'missile gap' that presumably existed between the Soviet Union and the United States. It is why Reagan's demonization of the Soviet Union as an 'evil empire' was not merely a revived form of an antiquated McCarthyism but a necessary component of his efforts to restructure a post-Carter America. But just as the American hard body needed the external negative body of the Soviet Union against which to define itself, it would require a domestic version in order to transcribe itself at home.

In 1987, that foreign body came home. In *Robocop*, Paul Verhoeven brought the Terminator and Rambo together in a plot that revolved around the transformation of a dying police officer's mutilated body into a fully computerized, titanium-shielded, law-enforcement officer, who has only his face and brain remaining from his human body. He is, according to his creator, Robert Morton (Miguel Ferrer), 'the best of both worlds: the fastest reflexes modern technology has to offer, an on-board computer-assisted memory, and a lifetime of law-enforcement programming.' *Robocop* (Peter Weller) is literally the hard body that Rambo represented, both personally and nationally. Neither emotions nor bullets can penetrate his titanium exterior, and he has the strength and determination that made Rambo a hero. Robocop is able to meet any kind of criminal – from the small-time robber to the rapist to the major drug dealer – and bring them all to justice. After Robocop's appearance, Morton predicts that crime will be eliminated from Detroit in forty days because 'there's a new guy in town. His name's Robocop.' This is, of course, the kind of claim that Reaganism wanted to make for its revived U.S. military – that communism could be eliminated with the appearance of the 'new guy in town.'

But there's trouble in paradise. Robocop doesn't eliminate crime, primarily because he discovers that crime doesn't exist just on the streets but in the board rooms of the largest corporation in Detroit, OCP – Omni Consumer Products. In the representational constructs of this film OCP is no ordinary corporation but one that has, in addition to taking over hospital, prison, and space-exploration markets, now taken over the police force and governance of Detroit itself. OCP controls all of the services citizens in the 1980s have come to expect government to provide. More than this, through contracts and the manufacture of weapons, OCP's CEO, Richard Jones (Ronny Cox), can boast, 'We practically *are* the military.' Unlike the Rambo films, which blamed Congress and interfering governmental bureaucracies for preventing victory over communism – a constant Reagan theme – *Robocop* portrays that governmental bureaucracy in the guise of the biggest beneficiary of Reagan economics, the conglomerate corporation. Yet this corporation, like the mechanized terminators, sees humans only as instruments of corporate interests and profits, not as individuals. As the OCP official, Johnson (Felton Perry) says of Alex Murphy, the police officer whose body is transformed into Robocop, 'He signed the release forms when he joined the force. He's legally dead. We can do pretty much what we want to.'

But it is precisely the services of OCP – health care, law enforcement, administration, and so on – that were targeted by the Reagan agenda as features of a government bureaucracy that had grown too large and had interfered in too many areas of people's lives. OCP is called a corporation, but it clearly functions in Detroit as a government. Indeed, it has displaced any elected authorities and plans to build a whole new city that it will own outright. This is certainly not the kind of corporate model that Reagan believed would enhance and strengthen the U.S. economy, nor the kind of model that he proposed as the resource for privatizing many of the very services Reagan wished government to cut. By characterizing OCP as a quasi-governmental body, one that is decidedly bureaucratic, *Robocop* holds out for its viewers the possibility of a different kind of corporation as well as a different kind of government, ones that would keep to their own arenas and not overextend their mandates for services, whether consumer or social.

Ryan and Kellner [1988] offer a clue why the hard body seemed so ambivalent in the late 1980s:

> As conservative economic values became ascendant, increasingly technical criteria of efficiency came to be dominant. In addition, conservative economic development emphasizes the displacement of excessively costly human labour by machines . . . One antinomy of conservatism is that it requires technology for its economic programme, yet it fears technological modernity on a social and cultural plane.

Thus at the international level, the hard body seemed to mobilize nationally desired strengths and abilities against communist threats, and therefore seemed appropriate when used against 'other people', but at the domestic level, the hard body veered into the threatening arenas of automation and regimentation that were antithetical to the very conservative values of individual freedom and deregulation that the Reagan administration was instituting as government policy. This was occurring not only at the level of public mythologies but at the level of daily economic production, as, on the one hand, increasing numbers of jobs were given over to computerized automation, and, on the other hand, increasing numbers of jobs were being lost to foreign competitors or oversees investment sites that offered fully automated factories or cheaper labor. As early as 1980, stories began to appear about the pending job losses from automation. In October of 1980, *Omni* magazine asked the question: 'Can you earn a living after the Robot Revolution?' Their answer was largely negative: 'If we don't change our present patterns, the inevitable and widespread use of robots will come at the cost of high unemployment, high inflation, social unrest, and violence both physical and psychological.' This is precisely the picture that *Robocop* paints.

(Jeffords 1994: 106–11)

WHAT'S NEXT?

➤ Read 'The Burden of the American Hero' in Ziauddin Sardar and Merryl Wyn Davies *Why do People Hate America?* (2002) Cambridge: Icon Books.

▼ **79 WHAT'S THE TOPIC? Gender as text
WHAT'S THE TEXT? Janice Winship 'Handling sex'**

The feminist movement of the 1960s and 1970s has profoundly influenced the way in which we all view the world and has informed the ways in which we read the texts of the world.

As we have already seen feminism challenges patriarchy, the system which invests power in men and subordinates women to a position of inferiority. The media are seen by feminists as key players in supporting patriarchies. Inevitably feminist commentators have taken issue with the way in which they feel women are exploited, subordinated and, some would argue, degraded by such forms as advertising and the tabloid press.

This extract from an essay by Janice Winship is taken from a collection of feminist essays entitled *Looking On*, edited by Rosemary Betterton, and published in 1987. In the essay she identifies advertising as a form that she considers oppressive to women and focuses on the role of hands as they are used in advertisements. She argues that women's anatomies are used much more often metonymically than are men's. This means that part of a woman's body is used to represent the whole person. She goes on to state that if we compare the use of men's and women's hands in advertising, the gender difference is crucial to the meaning we read into the image. For example, a woman's hand pouring a jug of custard represents 'home-made goodness', casting the woman in the role of home maker and carer for husband and children. On the other hand a male hand pouring custard might signify 'culinary delight', that is, some special gourmet treat created by a (male) chef.

In the extract that follows Winship offers a reading of an advertisement for a video recorder in which the action is seen from the perspective of a male whose hand is controlling the images on the screen. The advertisement's slogan reads 'Who said slow motion replays were just for "Match of the Day"?' The image on the video screen is four women performing a fan dance. The hand working the video remote control is clearly masculine. The advertisement constitutes a masculine conception of the use of the home video.

As readers of the ad we are clearly put in the position of the viewer of a the TV screen; moreover that position is occupied by a man whose hand we see controlling the screen. *If* we are men this could be our hand. The hand is marked as masculine both by a *lack* of feminine marks – no varnished nails – the caption – 'Who said slow motion replays were just for "Match of the Day"?' – and the TV image – the fanciful strip 'girls'. As if an appeal to the most popular TV programme for men were not enough, adding insult to injury, the ad relies on that other 'spectator sport' peculiarly masculine in style, that of 'bird' watching. I use the sexist term only because the 'Simulated picture' indicates too well the calculating construction of the ad: not just any old picture from the telly, but one showing women who are decoratively attired *like* extravagant birds. They are caught at some moment in a striptease act posing with what Goffman has neatly described as 'the bashful knee bend'. However his interpretation of this as representing 'a forgoing of full effort . . . the position adds a moment to any effort', and his assertion that because women are seen supporting each other in this pose the question of gender relations does not arise, seems not to be quite the point. The gesture is surely one of submission in which the woman is pausing to gaze or to be gazed at – by men. And it is this representation of women which the male hand is seen to control; at the press of a button 'you' (he) can stop and start, obliterate or bring into gaze the strip act, like the director of a film. As the ad says, 'All you need now is a canvas chair with "Director" on it.' What is being advertised is the video and the control of the image which it provides, but what seems to be at stake is a control of women's sexuality: women as fare for men's play. Further, in a reversal which gives them no power or status at all, *women work on the screen, while men play* – with them.

(Winship 1987: 32–3)

WHAT'S NEXT?

➤ Choose a print advertisement that uses some part of the male or female anatomy and consider what impact would be made by changing this (if possible) for the same part from the opposite sex.

➤ Choose two current print advertisements that use part of the male or female anatomy and provide a reading of each paying particular attention to the issues of gender representation and the relationship between men and women.

➤ This essay was written in 1987. Do you think the assertions that advertising is oppressive to women still holds true? Do you feel any advertising is oppressive to any other 'minority' group? Provide specific examples to support your argument.

80 WHAT'S THE TOPIC? Celebrity as text I
WHAT'S THE TEXT? Julie Burchill 'All the pretty songs'

I touched you at the sound check
You're just the same as I am.

So sang Morrissey in The Smith's epic study of fandom 'Paint a Vulgar Picture'. That song begins 'at the record company party' and continues 'on their hands a dead star'. The story is a recognisable modern myth, it is iconic. Pop and rock stars are obvious texts, even to the non-specialist. Exponents of the divided self they revel in the postmodern crisis of identity. They remind us of the pleasures and terrors of self-presentation and how easily the self can be reduced to image, identity to a front. They live near the edge so that we don't need to, rushing to the boundaries to remind us where they are. The cost is usually enormous in damaged hotel bedrooms and ravaged lives, but our grief is vicarious: paid by us they pay for us.

Kurt Cobain was an innovative and influential singer, guitarist and songwriter of the ultimate Seattle band, Nirvana. He was young and beautiful and talented and, like Ziggy Stardust, he made it too far. When he died at his own hands in 1994 his apparent suicide note made clear the extent to which the celebrity mask had come unattached. The image he had helped to make no longer even protected him.

This article by Julie Burchill is in fact a review of Cobain's authorised biography *Heavier than Heaven* (a significant anchor if ever there was one). In it she offers up Cobain, in reverence and respect, as a decodable text and surveys her own version of 'the evidence'.

Of course, poor Kurt Cobain, my latest belated crush, is in no position to do this, as he shot himself in the head in the greenhouse of his Seattle home in 1994. But as I last heard 'Smells Like Teen Spirit' – absolutely my favourite song ever, which is about as bold and original as saying that *Citizen Kane* is your favourite film, but never mind – only a few weeks ago, I was very glad to read this biography, the result of four years' research and 400 interviews, not to mention the sainted Kurt's police and medical records, *and* his unpublished journals. I was in hog heaven all the way through – in a caring, wistful way, of course.

I've said it before, but to some extent all biographies are murder mysteries – though whydunnits rather than whodunnits – even if no one dies. The killing of the old unloved self so that the shiny new icon can emerge intact involves just as much shame and subterfuge as your average homicide, and Kurt Cobain's reinvention as 'Kurt Cobain' was a sadder story than most, especially as he

CONTINUED

discovered too late that being famous was the last thing he wanted. Unlike the fake angst of your average crooner, this was the real thing. Troubled from adolescence by a mysterious stomach ailment which left him permanently nauseous and led to his initial self-medication through opiates, Cobain also carried what he called 'the suicide gene' – two uncles had not only killed themselves but committed a very stoic, tenacious type of suicide (they both missed first time, but stuck at it), which sent a stir of echoes into his own multiple-death experiences.

Suicide wasn't just a casual thing with him; it was his one true love.

From the moment fame hit, his life was a black, farcical round of ODs, rehab and suicide attempts, Cobain running about trying to dispose of himself with Courtney Love, his paid minders and his record company in hot pursuit to keep the cash cow alive. He first died – clinically, actually died – less than seven hours after 'Teen Spirit' was played on MTV; or, in the words of Charles Cross, at 'the very moment an entire generation fell in love with him'. He was genuinely repelled by the fame game: soon after Nirvana first made it and every sucker in showbiz wanted to be his friend, Cobain and his wife Courtney Love left a party in his honour and, after rejecting amicable advances from the likes of Keanu Reeves, retreated to their hotel room where they hung a sign on the door saying 'No famous people please, we're fucking'. But the idea that he was 'faking it' became an obsession. From his first hit – 'With the lights out it's less dangerous/Here we are now, entertain us/I feel stupid and contagious' – to his last note, 'The fact is I can't fool you. Any one of you. It simply isn't fair to you or me. The worst crime I can think of would be to rip people off by faking it and pretending I'm having fun,' he was simply the man who knew too much, certainly far too much to be a silly, shiny thing like a pop star. He signed his note 'Peace, love, empathy, Kurt Cobain', underlining the word 'empathy' twice; he had used it five times in all in his suicide letter.

True to his word, he shot himself in the greenhouse, so as to make less of a mess, and he left a pile of clean towels beside his body lest anyone discovering him should be sullied by his blood.

American downfalls always seem bigger and sadder than other types – attain instant gravitas – because we seem to hear the lonesome wind of the American dream, the settling and the savagery and the submission of all else, howling through one simple life (That's why, say, American Beauty and American Gigolo sound like such profound titles compared with Belgian Beauty and German Gigolo). But, like Marilyn Monroe, Kurt Cobain really did live a life of quite startling sadness and achievement, and it is not being too creepy to call his life a genuine American Tragedy. Here's a laugh: while reading this book in a foreign hotel room, tears streaming down my face, with BBC Choice on for comfort in the background amid a host of phlegm-clearing German channels, I was amazed to hear the opening bars of 'Smells Like Teen Spirit' – on Top Gear, of all the filthy items. Hearing St Kurt's finest three minutes being used to sell boys' toys designed to appeal to all that is dumbest, dullest and meanest in mankind made me squeal with anger. Kurt wouldn't have reacted like that, though, and that's why he was so cool. You get the impression that he – poor wise, defeated boy – never would have expected anything else anyway.

Nevermind.

(Burchill 2001: 10)

WHAT'S NEXT?

➤ In Extract 15 we looked at an active reading of a musical star of the 1970s, Shakin' Stevens. Kurt Cobain was younger and is more dead than Shakin' Stevens. What meanings does Julie Burchill want to assign to Kurt Cobain's case and what clues might this piece offer for contemporary attitudes towards death and fame?

▼ **81 WHAT'S THE TOPIC? Celebrity as text II**
WHAT'S THE TEXT? Ellis Cashmore *Beckham*

Elsewhere in his book-length meditation on David Beckham Ellis Cashmore (2002: 191) offers remarkable utterances from two people. A teenage Morrissey scrawled in his notebook: 'I'm sick of being the undiscovered genius, I want fame NOW not when I'm dead'. More recently Posh Spice announced she wanted to be 'as famous as Persil Automatic'. As with previous readings of space, place, adornment and clothing, this is a literate and informed reading which is ripped straight from the front pages of today's newspapers.

Manchester United fans often chant (to the tune of José Fernandez Diaz's *Guantanamera*): 'One David Beckham. There's only one David Beckham.' Actually, there are two: the flesh-and-blood father with a fondness for cars, decorously pale looks and fine soccer skills; and the icon, the celebrity, the commodity, the Beckham that exists independently of time and space and resides in the imaginations of countless acolytes. For women, he's *le beau idéal*, a figure on whom fantasies are spun; for men, he's a colossus standing astride all dominions of sport, commanding their admiration, affection and devotion.

He's become a global phenomenon, a towering presence, not only in football but in all of popular culture. The Beckham phenomenon is so perfectly congruent with our times, it could have been created. Actually, it was. This book is about how.

Clichés that would normally seem crass feel oddly appropriate: A-list celeb, gay icon, rich-and-famous. Somehow, they all fit. But, of course, Beckham is not just a footballer. He is the sports celebrity *par excellence*. Whichever way you hold him to the light, Beckham is an extraordinary being, a rare thing, a total one-off. He's everywhere, in newspapers, television, the internet, on countless posters that decorate young people's bedroom walls.

He attracts accolades like a magnet attracts iron filings. He's Britain's best-dressed male, according to GQ magazine, and was only edged out of the number one position as 'sexiest man' by Robbie Williams in *Heat's* poll. In the 2002 'Young rich' lists of two national newspapers, he came fifth. BBC Sports Personality of 2001, World Footballer of the Year runner-up. His fans are from all over the world, and they include the kind of passionate gay following that most athletes might find awkward. Some reckon he and his wife have wandered into the emotional territory once occupied so serenely by Princess Diana. They have certainly commanded the attention of the paparazzi in much the way Diana did.

Yet, when you think about it, what does he do? Lead armies into battle, discover cures for diseases, perform miracles? He plays football, primarily. Auxiliary activities include buying lots of extravagantly expensive cars and clothes, being a doting father, accompanying his wife to glittery premières, appearing in ads and, well, that's about it. Yet Beckham has given the sports pages, the tabloids, the internet websites and the television networks more stories than they can ever wish for. Has he disclosed his political views, his stance on any great global cause, his personal habits even? Of course not. So, why is he exalted to the point where you can almost imagine his being beatified? The answer is not because he is a good footballer. (I repeat this in case his fans mistake it for a typo.) It's because he's a product that we all consume. We're part of a generation of emotionally expressive, self-aware, brand-conscious, label-observant, New-Man attentive, gossip-hungry, celebrity worshippers. We, the fans, the television viewers, the writers, the audience, make Beckham *Beckham*. We've become an unpaid backing choir for his aria, and one that can stop singing any time we like. The moment we do, Beckham turns back into a footballer.

This book is a departure from the usual sports biography. It's neither an extravaganza, celebrating the wonderful and unique gifts of its subject, nor a piercing insight into the subject's personal life. It certainly isn't a muck-raking exercise, dishing the dirt on private secrets that have previously escaped the public's attention. But, it *is* about Beckham. It starts from the premiss that there is more than one way to understand somebody. Looking inside them, trying to disclose their inner core, their intimate character, their true personality, is only one means of discovery. Another is to look outside them. This is my approach. To understand Beckham in this way requires looking not so much at him or his unique talent, but at the culture of which he has become an important part.

. . .

The central conceit of Paul Verhoeven's film *Total Recall* – based on Philip K. Dick's short story 'We can remember it for you wholesale' – is that consumers don't actually need to visit places or do things when they can instead have embolisms planted in their memories, providing them with cheaper and safer ways of realizing all their ambitions. In the plot, Doug Quaid is a working class nobody who aspires to go to Mars, but can't afford it. Instead, he opts for the experience of visiting Mars, which is delivered straight into his memory in less time than it takes to get a tooth filled. The story is predicated on the same reasoning that takes people to Tampa's Bush Gardens rather than the Serengeti, to Alton Towers where the rides are advertised as terrifying but no one comes to harm, and on packaged adventure holidays where the risks are minimal. In other words, we want to experience rather than do. It makes us privy to a province we secretly aspire to, but have no realistic chance of reaching.

The excitement, love, glamour and intrigue proposed not by Beckham but by the narratives drawn about his life reflect more about contemporary culture than about the player himself. They tell us that we now have a generation hooked on the irrational pleasures of celebrity watching or, more accurately, celebrity fantasizing. People dream about becoming fabulously wealthy and globally famous, but they have no effective means of achieving these dreams. Their orientation, like that of all good consumers, is to carry on dreaming. This includes watching TV shows that dangle tantalizing carrots, buying lottery tickets, and following the pursuits of others who are already fabulously wealthy and globally famous. In short, consuming. This is why we're guided to celebrities, why the media produce more of them, and why the market commodifies them. Consumption is the new phoney egalitarianism in which anybody can be somebody. The danger is that the fickle and expendable hopes of consumers rest less on aspiration and ambition, more on the presence of others. These others embody the elusive, yet yearned for, properties that the consumer can never possess, but can still experience endlessly through the likes of Beckham.

This sounds a dispiriting way to end a book on one of the most attractive and glamorous celebrities to have emerged in recent times, particularly as he excites high emotions in consumers. He can make them feel good, perhaps even great. Of course, his ability to do this rests on the fact that they lack alternative ways of feeling good. This is a harsh, though not unfair, assessment of Beckham's wide constituency of fans. And that includes Us. Are we sad? Maybe. Are we powerless? Probably. Do we use our imaginations? Definitely.

Beckham has no magical powers. He can't levitate or take flight. He can't win wars, save the planet, or end famine. He can't change water into wine, heal the sick, or communicate telepathically. He plays football. Yet he seems to glide so high that it sometimes seems as if he can do anything he turns his mind to. That we can have spun such an extraordinary aura around such an ordinary person is testimony to our inventiveness. It's also testimony to a culture that values a restricted idea of the good life, one that includes the kind of romance and glamour so often set before us but rarely within our grasp. Yet, we go on chasing destinies that will forever elude us, slaloming between the real world and the parallel one where They live so exuberantly. This is the world where David Beckham looms large. here may be two worlds, but this is a single culture. It's a culture that nurtures, maintains and protects our right to be consumers.

(Cashmore 2002: 4–5, 194–5)

WHAT'S NEXT?

➤ Read Chris Rojek *Celebrity* (2001) London: Reaktion.

▼ ## 82 WHAT'S THE TOPIC? Reading the media
WHAT'S THE TEXT? John Fiske *Reading the Popular*

Just as Julie Burchill has read Kurt Cobain and Ellis Cashmore read David Beckham so in the following extract John Fiske presents a more general and academic reading of that favoured television genre the Quiz Show. *Reading the Popular* is Fiske's collection of popular cultural case studies, investigations into the meanings of cultural communication, offering such surprises (sic) as 'The beach', 'Madonna' and 'the music video'. Here, in a chapter entitled 'Everyday Quizzes, Everday Lives', Fiske turns his attentions to the implications of certain kinds of quiz show.

He begins by setting the phenomenon in both practical and academic contexts. He indicates the popularity and volume of this product, and its attractiveness to producers and advertisers and audiences. From this basis he discusses, with the help of significant theorists, the use that consumers make of media products, citing:

■ Bourdieu's productive theory of cultural capital, whereby popular culture might be seen to provide the resources through which its consumers might be able to respond to and talk about it (without rejecting it). In this way they may feel less alienated by thinking they have their own analytical tools.

- De Certeau's theories of everyday life which see ordinary social practices as 'a series of tactical evasions or resistances of the order that society tries to organise them into'.

This prepares him for a clarifying statement about the differences between shopping on quiz shows and ordinary economic shopping. These are:

- the money earned on quiz shows is earned through native wit or everyday knowledge (plus luck);
- in real shopping money is earned by selling yourself rather as the products you would like to buy are sold (in the same system); and
- therefore quiz show spending is free from the subjugation or implied guilt of earning.

Fiske offers three significant examples: *Sale of the Century, Wheel of Fortune* and *The New Price is Right* which is featured below. Here he begins to examine further who the audience is and thus the specific ways in which the experience is meaningful to them.

The differences between shopping on quiz shows such as *Wheel of Fortune* or *Sale of the Century* and ordinary economic shopping are vital. On quiz shows one 'earns' the money to spend through native wit or everyday knowledge coupled with some luck; in 'real' shopping one spends money by subjecting oneself to the same economic system that produces the commodities. It is money earned on their terms. The symbolic money of quiz shows is not bound by the economic laws that govern social difference and subordination in capitalist societies; rather, it is the product and valorization of an everyday knowledge and set of life skills, that, by it, can be transformed directly into material goods or the pleasures of a holiday. This articulates openly the ability of people to detach the pleasures and meanings of spending from the pain and subjection of earning.

Commodities can constitute popular cultural capital and, on quiz shows, their detachment from the restrictions of economic subjugation allows these tactical, vernacular meanings greater scope than in everyday life where the freedom and pleasure of spending is always, finally, held in check and contradicted by the subjugation involved in earning . . .

Popular culture works in the interstices of our governed and controlled society. It is essentially defensive, withholding itself from the control of the social order, sometimes playing along with it, yet always ready to seize an opportunity for a guerrilla strike, for a play of tactical resistance, always alert for moments of weakness that it can turn to its own advantage. De Certeau (1984) argues that we need a new way of

Thinking about everyday practices of consumers supposing from the start that they are of a tactical nature. Dwelling, moving about, speaking, reading, shopping and cooking are activities that seem to correspond to the characteristics of tactical ruses and surprises: clever tricks of the 'weak' within the order established by the 'strong', an act of putting one over on the adversary turf, hunter's tricks, maneuverable, polymorph mobilities, jubilant, poetic and warlike discoveries.

(pp. 39–40)

The 'bargain' is just such a 'trick', and 'bargain hunting' is the guerrilla strike of the shopper. The bargain, the sale-priced item, is a sign of the producer's weakness, a sign of misjudging the market, that consumers had not behaved according to the rules the producers had predicted. So, getting a bargain is exploiting a weakness in the system and turning it to ones own advantage, a perfect tactical moment.

In *Sale of the Century*, the bargains offered during the progress of the competition are excessive signs of this. Their 'real-world value' is given, then their bargain price (which is about 10 percent of the 'real' value). The bargain price is, of course, to be paid for in metaphoric money that has been won through the contestant's wit, speed of response and everyday knowledge. But even the price of 5-8 metaphoric dollars may cost the buyer his or her lead in the competition so the host will often increase the temptation by adding $100–$300 in real money to the bargain and simultaneously decreasing the metaphoric money needed to buy it. Such 'bargaining' is a dialogue between the powerful and the weak, and in the game world of the quiz shows the weak can only win: the bargain bought is an economic win; the bargain resisted maintains the contestant's lead in the competition.

Similarly when a simplified version of *Wheel of Fortune* is played in shopping malls, the metaphoric money required to play consists of receipts for goods already bought in the mall; the prizes are vouchers for more goods from the shops in the mall. Using a receipt as money is a carnivalesque inversion, a momentary freedom from the normality of economic subjection.

The New Price is Right displays bargain hunting par excellence. The contestants are nearly all women and the knowledge required is what our society treats as 'women's' knowledge, that of the prices and comparative values of commodities. The show consists of a variety of games and competitions in which the winner is the one who best knows commodity prices and values, who is, in other words, the best shopper. But if all the show does is reproduce and repeat women's role in domestic labour, why, we must ask ourselves do women find it pleasurable? If women are the shoppers for the family in 'real' life, why should they choose to fill their leisure with more of the same?

(Fiske 1989: 136–8)

Fiske's way of reading popular televison very much functions from the outside in. There are other ways of reading. In Kevin Smith's 1995 film *Mallrats* there is a early scene at the mall where TS is commenting on a new television game show called 'Truth or Date'. He characterises its genesis thus: 'Oh it's this cheesey dating game ripoff thing, it's supposed to be for college kids, it's just trying to recapture the 90s youth market with a staple of 70s television.' A more brutal, materialist reading of how television programmes and films are conceived comes from Camille Paglia in *Sex, Art and American Culture* (1994): 'In the 60s, LSD gave vision, while marijuana gave community. But coke, pricey and jealously hoarded, is the power drug, giving a rush of omnipotent self-assurance. Work done under its influence is manic, febrile, choppy, disconnected. Coke was responsible for the plot incoherence of fifteen years of TV sitcoms and glitzy "high-concept" Hollywood movies.'

WHAT'S NEXT?

> ➤ Which way of reading popular culture do you find the more convincing: the perspective of production or the perspective of consumption?

▼ 83 WHAT'S THE TOPIC? Readings of place
WHAT'S THE TEXT? JG Ballard *Running Wild*

The constructed environment as an idea works on a number of levels with respect to the following important questions:

- by whom is it constructed? (sender, receiver, medium)
- where is it constructed? (physically, intellectually)
- how is it constructed? (technically, economically, aesthetically, socially)

JG Ballard has been imagining futures by reimagining the present for over forty years. He has an eye to the potential of constructed environments and their capacity to provide information of a social, political, cultural and psychological kind. He is aware too of the functioning of narratives through such places. Ballard's fictions and his writing style were characterised by Iain Sinclair in *London Orbital* (2002) as not being 'prophetic in a way that would be recognised by HG Wells . . . The tone is matter of fact' (Sinclair 2002: 219).

In Ballard's masterpiece *Crash,* there is an eerie understanding of how strange what we call the real world is. Hence we see the thin line between creative writing and cultural studies:

We had entered an immense traffic jam. From the junction of the motorway and Western Avenue to the ascent ramp of the flyover the traffic lanes were packed with vehicles, windshields leaching out the molten colours of the sun setting above the western suburbs of London. Brake-lights flared in the evening air, glowing in the huge pool of cellulosed bodies. Vaughan sat with one arm out of the passenger window. He slapped the door impatiently, pounding the panel with his fist. To our right the high wall of a double-decker airline coach formed a cliff of faces. The passengers at the windows resembled rows of the dead looking down at us from the galleries of a columbarium. The enormous energy of the twentieth century, enough to drive the planet into a new orbit around a happier star, was being expended to maintain the immense motionless pause.

(Ballard 1995: 151)

On show here is Ballard's matter of fact writing style identified by Sinclair. Just because Ballard is writing about apocalyptic events doesn't mean his writing style has to mirror it, indeed the effect of reading about savage and brutal events written in cool and sober tones makes this all the more estranging.

In his 1988 novella *Running Wild*, he offers a nightmare of executive housing estates which becomes an actual nightmare for some of its inhabitants. Just as we gave away the secret of *American Psycho*'s plot but insisted that this wouldn't detract from our deriving serious ideas from it so too will this be the case with *Running Wild*. The nightmare hinted at in the final paragraph here is that all the adults of the housing estate have been killed. *Running Wild*, written as a police psychiatrist's report into the murders, concludes that it was the children of the estate who committed the brutal murders. As Sinclair has it: 'The child terrorists of *Running Wild* are the result of benevolent eugenic planning' (2002: 221). The gated communities of Ballard's Berkshire, just as much as those of Mike Davis's Los Angeles, are designed to keep out the terrors without; they do nothing to address the terrors within.

In *Running Wild* Ballard demonstrates that which we already know – that our encounters with the physical world, natural or contrived, are always meaningful, and are simultaneously both natural and contrived.

Having exhausted my central nervous system with the police video, I returned to my office at the Institute of Psychiatry and tried to calm myself by looking at the origins and creation of Pangbourne Village.

The small Berkshire town of Pangbourne lies five miles to the north-west of Reading and approximately thirty miles to the west of London. Despite its title, the Pangbourne Village estate was not built near the site of any former or existing village. Like the numerous executive housing estates built in the 1980s in areas of deregulated farmland between Reading and the River Thames, Pangbourne Village has no connections, social, historical or civic, with Pangbourne itself.

The chief attraction for Camelot Holdings Ltd, the architects and property developers, was the proximity of the M4 motorway, and the ready access it offers to Heathrow Airport and central London, an ease of access that might well have benefited the assassins and kidnappers. All the residents of Pangbourne Village worked either in central London or in the silicon valley of high-technology computer firms along the M4 corridor. Pangbourne Village is only the newest (completed 1985) and most expensive (the ten houses, all with swimming pools, projection theatres and optional stables, each sold for approximately £590,000) of a number of similar estates in Berkshire which house thousands of senior professionals – lawyers, stockbrokers, bankers – and their families.

Secure behind their high walls and surveillance cameras, these estates in effect constitute a chain of closed communities whose lifelines run directly along the M4 to the offices and consulting rooms, restaurants and private clinics of central London. They remain completely apart from their local communities, except for a small and carefully selected under-class of chauffeurs, housekeepers and gardeners who maintain the estates in their pristine condition. Their children mix only with each other at exclusive fee-paying schools or in the lavishly equipped sports clubs sited on the estates.

Pangbourne Village is remarkable only for having advanced these general trends towards almost total self-sufficiency. The entire estate, covering some thirty-two acres, is ringed by a steel-mesh fence fitted with electrical alarms, and until the tragic murders was regularly patrolled by guard-dogs and radio-equipped handlers. Entry to the estate was by appointment only, and the avenues and drives were swept by remote-controlled TV cameras. All police officers concerned in the investigation agree that the penetration of these defences by a large group of assassins was a remarkable and, as yet, inexplicable event.

(Ballard 1997: 11–13)

WHAT'S NEXT?

➤ Watch Jean-Luc Godard's *Alphaville* (1965). Watch Ridley Scott's *Blade Runner* (1982).
➤ Take a place with which you are familiar. Try to imagine it as the set for a science fiction or futuristic film. Write the outline for this film. If possible take photographs to illustrate your film outline.

**84 WHAT'S THE TOPIC? Society as text
WHAT'S THE TEXT? Iain Chambers *Popular
Culture: The Metropolitan Experience***

On the other side of the line Iain Chambers offers the socio-historical perspective on lived experience. The specific, and ultimately psychotic, trends that Ballard addresses in *Running Wild* are played out across the life and times of Chambers's metropolitan experience. Chambers is particularly dramatic in his opening to a section entitled 'Buildings and Food' (an allusion to Talking Heads' second album). 'The city was considered to be a conspiracy against real needs,' he says, 'it was lived as a drama, a crisis, not as an opportunity'.

Chambers details the onset and onslaught of modernism – 'that seamless web of total design that stretches from a wrist-watch to a city'. He writes of the New Brutalism which delivered 'unadorned concrete, exposed pipes, steel and glass' but also of its consequences – a backlash that 'threw the baby out with the bathwater' and embraced a naïve sentimentality for Victorian and Georgian house styles. In losing our nerve we forfeited 'the grace, imagination and vertical integration . . . the high drama or the glamour that were the great assets of American modernism'. Whereas the Americans made new cities the British preferred what Chambers calls a 'pragmatic eclecticism' which produced variety rather than intensity, a modest proposal rather than a modernist manifesto.

The following extract leads this into a discussion of diet and food.

> Both public housing and the property boom of the 1960s (symbolized by the Centre Point tower on the corner of New Oxford Street and Tottenham Court Road) changed Britain's urban skylines. But the heavy slabs of grey concrete, accentuated by their relatively low height, usually lacked the grace, imagination and vertical integration, encouraged by street-grid co-ordination, of North American skyscrapers.
>
>> Constrained by ideology as well as by economics, the British could not emulate the high drama or the glamour that were the great assets of American modernism. Indeed it is the timidity rather than the vulgarity of English 'skyscrapers' that is their most depressing feature.
>>
>> (Esher, 1983, 285)
>
> In the wake of the brave new world spirit of the 1950s and the widespread criticisms of modern, but sometimes paternalistic, sometimes insensitive, architectural solutions that at times seemed to be in sharp contrast to the daily needs and habits of those living in the abstractly conceived houses, streets and

neighbourhoods, the 1970s and 1980s have revealed a more pragmatic eclecticism. The new town of Milton Keynes, the Barbican project, the redevelopment of Covent Garden, and the realization of the TV-AM studios in Camden Town, represent four very different forms of townscapes, streetscapes, urban living and building. Yet, from Milton Keynes's million square feet of shopping centre, all at ground level with direct car access along its linear front, to the intimacy of Covent Garden's piazza, architecture seems to have refined the former ideals of modernism ('designing the city') into more modest proposals for local, working solutions and architectural decoration. In a phrase coined within architecture itself, it has gone 'post-modern'.

Changes in the city were not limited to the physical shape of buildings and public housing. They also involved the gradual making of new sensibilities and changing tastes in the home, design, shopping and food. Over the last 150 years it is not only the city that has changed much of its appearance; there has also occurred a revolution in food and eating habits, in the preparation, presentation and distribution of everyday alimentation. Our diet, even more than our homes or streets, has changed dramatically. Over a very brief period of time our bodies have been subject to a massive intake of processed foods (in particular refined carbohydrates – flour and sugar) and a corresponding reduction in raw fibre intake that has produced a new pathology: diabetes, varicose veins, obesity, coronary thrombosis, constipation. This, in turn, has induced further changes in eating habits. Along with 'real ale', integral food-stuffs – wholemeal bread, brown rice, muesli – re-enter the self-consciously 'healthy' middle-class diet; sugar is abandoned. Shops, supermarkets and restaurants increasingly support these alimentary alternatives.

So, the range available to the contemporary palate is potentially wider than ever before, stretching from international fast food (Wimpy, McDonalds, Pizza Express) to the widespread discovery of post-Empire culinary tastes (Indian and Chinese cooking) and macrobiotic diets. The resources of the world are not, however, limitless. The range and richness of diet in Britain, as in northern Europe, and the United States, frequently also represents the poverty of diet elsewhere. When third-world agricultures are turned over to the production of cash crops, often for livestock feed for Europe and North America, local malnutrition and famine can be directly connected to the hamburger on our plate and the milk in our cup. Meanwhile, British supermarkets, as marked by class distinctions as any other public institution in British life – the creamy-illuminated Sainsbury delicatessen contrasting sharply with the mountain-high stacked cans of baked beans in Tesco's – offer you the ingredients of a planetary cuisine, from oven-ready pasta to fresh mango, Danish bacon and barbecue sauce.

These rapid changes in diet and buildings are also linked to the reorganization of domestic space and labour following the large-scale introduction of such domestic consumer items as electric fires, fridges, washing machines, improved cookers, Hoovers, the private car (essential for effective supermarket shopping), food blenders, eye-level grills, microwave-ovens. In the relatively brief span of three decades (1950s–1980s), both the shape and contents of public and private space have changed sharply. And although the effects have no doubt been largely limited to the level of our subconscious, it has affected both the structure and feel of our experiences and expectations.

(Chambers 1986: 45–9)

WHAT'S NEXT?

➤ What might food, diet, or taste in food inform our notions of gender, social class, and ethnicity?

➤ What perspectives might be adopted on your answers to the above by feminists, Marxists, and postcolonialists?

PART 5: DEBATES AND CONTROVERSIES IN COMMUNICATION

Everything is divided
Nothing is complete.

(David Byrne, 'Making Flippy Floppy')

I have opinions, strong opinions, but I don't always agree with them.

(George W Bush)

Drawing together the significant threads of a programmed sequence of Communication Studies readings, one unavoidable issue tends to predominate, the debate about what communication is, and the subsidiary debate about what there is to study. In point of fact this case and issue, this debate, opened this book: *Communication Studies: The Essential Resource* began its approach to the study of Communication with what is in fact essential to the discipline – its integrity and its object (communication). It seems appropriate then, at the beginning of this book's final part to return to that debate, to the business of definition, a last set of loose ends before everything is provisionally tied up.

▼ 85 **WHAT'S THE TOPIC? Theories of communication I**
WHAT'S THE TEXT? Colin Cherry *On Human Communication*

There comes a time, perhaps, when every Communication student has their shot at the Communication Studies equivalent of the Meaning of Life question: what is communication? Colin Cherry, whose reflections are offered in the extract below, had his go in the 1950s but it still stands as an elegant description of a process approach to the study of Communication. He does engage with signs and codes in the latter part of this piece but only largely at the level of encoding and decoding messages.

Principally Cherry offers us some key words.

Communication is essentially a social affair. Man has evolved a host of different systems of communication which render his social life possible – social life not in the sense of living in packs for hunting or for making war, but in a sense unknown to animals. Most prominent among all these systems of communication is, of course, human speech and language. Human language is not to be equated with the sign systems of animals, for man is not restricted to calling his young, or suggesting mating, or shouting cries of danger; he can with his remarkable faculties of speech give utterance to almost any thought. Like animals, we too have our inborn instinctive cries of alarm, pain, etcetera: we say Oh!, Ah!; we have smiles, groans, and tears; we blush, shiver, yawn, and frown. A hen can set her chicks scurrying up to her, by clucking – communication established by a releaser mechanism – *but human language is vastly more than a complicated system of clucking.*

The development of language reflects back upon thought; for with language thoughts may become organized, new thoughts evolved. Self-awareness and the sense of social responsibility have arisen as a result of organized thoughts. Systems of ethics and law have been built up. Man has become self-conscious, responsible, a social creature.

Inasmuch as the words we use disclose the true nature of things, as truth is to each one of us, the various words relating to personal communication are most revealing. The very word 'communicate' means 'share', and inasmuch as you and I are communicating at the moment, we are one. Not so much a union as a unity. Inasmuch as we agree, we say that *we are of one mind*, or, again, that we understand *one another*. This one another is the unity. A group of people, a society, a culture, I would define as 'people in communication'. They may be thought of as 'sharing rules' of language, custom, of habit; but who wrote these rules? These have evolved out of those people themselves – rules of conformity. Inasmuch as that conformity is the greater or the less, so is the unity. The degree of communication, the sharing, the conformity, is a measure of one-mindedness. After all, what we share, we cannot each have as our own possession, and no single person in this world has ever been born and bred in utter isolation. 'No man is an island, entire of itself.'

Speech and writing are by no means our only system of communication. Social intercourse is greatly strengthened by habits of gesture – little movements of the hands and face. With nods, smiles, frowns, handshakes, kisses, fist shakes, and other gestures we can convey most subtle understanding. We also have economic systems for trafficking not in ideas but in material goods and services; the tokens of communication are coins, bonds, letters of credit, and so on. We have conventions of dress, rules of the road, social formalities, and good manners; we have rules of membership and function in businesses, institutions, and families. But life in the modern world is coming to depend more and more upon 'technical' means of communication, telephone and telegraph, radio and printing.

Without such technical aids the modern city-state could not exist one week, for it is only by means of them that trade and business can proceed; that goods and services can be distributed where needed; that railways can run on a schedule; that law and order are maintained; that education is possible. Communication renders true social life practicable, for communication means organization. Communications have enabled the social unit to grow, from the village to the town, to the modern city-state, until today we see organized systems of mutual dependence grown to cover whole hemispheres (McDougall, 1927).

The development of human language was a tremendous step in evolution; its power for organizing thoughts, and the resulting growth of social organization of all kinds, has given man, wars or no wars, street accidents or no street accidents, vastly increased potential for survival.

As a start, let us now take a few of the concepts and notions to do with communication, and discuss them briefly, not in any formal scientific sense, but in the language of the market place. A few dictionary definitions may serve as a starting point for our discursive approach here; later we shall see that such definitions are not at variance with those more restricted definitions used in scientific analysis. The following have been drawn from the *Concise Oxford English Dictionary*

> *Communication*, n. Act of imparting (esp. news); information given; intercourse; . . . (Military, Pl.) connexion between base and front.

> *Message*, n. Oral or written communication sent by one person to another.

> *Information*, n. Informing, telling; thing told, knowledge, items of knowledge, news, (on, about) . . .

> *Signal*, n., v.t. & i. Preconcerted or intelligible sign conveying information . . . at a distance. . .

> *Intelligence*, n. . . . understanding, sagacity . . . information, news.

> *News*, n. pl. Tidings, new information . . .

> *Knowledge*, n. . . . . familiarity gained by experience, person's range of information . . .

> *Belief*, n. Trust or confidence (*in*); . . . acceptance as true or existing (of any fact, statement, etc; . . .) . . .

> *Organism*, n. Organized body with connected interdependent parts sharing common life . . .; whole with interdependent parts compared to living being.

> *System*, n. Complex whole, set of connected things or parts, organized body of material or immaterial things. . . ; method, organization, considered principles of procedure, (principle of) classification; . . .

Such dictionary definitions are the 'common usages' of words; scientific usage frequently needs to be more restricted but should not violate common sense – an accusation often mistakenly levelled against scientific words by the layman.

The most frequent use of the words listed above is in connection with *human* communication, as the dictionary suggests. The word 'communication' calls to mind most readily the sending or receipt of a letter, or a conversation between two friends; some may think of newspapers issued daily from a central office to thousands of subscribers, or of radio broadcasting; others may think of telephones, linking one speaker and one listener. There are systems too which come to mind only to specialists; for instance, ornithologists and entomologists may think of flocking and swarming, or of the incredible precision with which flight manoeuvres are made by certain birds, or the homing of pigeons – problems which have been extensively studied, yet are still so imperfectly understood. Again, physiologists may consider the communicative function of the nervous system, coordinating the actions of all the parts of an integrated animal. At the other end of the scale, the anthropologist and sociologist are greatly interested in the communication between large groups of people, societies and races, by virtue of their cultures, their economic and religious systems, their laws, languages, and ethical codes. Examples of 'communication systems' are endless and varied.

When 'members' or 'elements' are in communication with one another, they are associating, cooperating, forming an 'organization', or sometimes an 'organism'. Communication is a social function. That old cliché, 'a whole is more than the sum of the parts', expresses a truth; the whole, the organization or organism, possesses a structure which is describable as a set of *rules*, and this structure, the rules, may remain unchanged as the individual members or elements are changed. By the possession of this structure the whole organization may be better adapted or better fitted for some goal-seeking activity. Communication means a *sharing* of elements of behaviour or modes of life, by the existence of sets of rules.

(Cherry 1996: 10–12)

WHAT'S NEXT?

> ➤ Cherry describes communication as 'essentially a social affair'. What functions do you think communication has?
> ➤ Read the editor's Introduction to Paul Cobley (ed.) *The Communication Theory Reader* (1996) London: Routledge.

COMMUNICATION STUDIES: THE ESSENTIAL RESOURCE

▼ 86 WHAT'S THE TOPIC? Theories of communication II
WHAT'S THE TEXT? Raymond Williams *Communications*

In 1962 Williams published what turned out for this subject to be a genuinely ground-breaking book as part of the series 'Britain in the Sixties'. He called this book simply *Communications*. Of course the roots of Communication Studies go back much further than that, some would argue as far as the most basic enquiries of the earliest philosophers. Williams is aware of this longer road but he is also particularly concerned to register the various ways in which the first half of the twentieth century had produced 'a dramatic tightening of interest in this world of communications'.

His reading of the situation is both radical and progressive, finding no coincidence in the connection between 'powerful new means of communication', 'the extension of democracy', and interestingly 'the attempts by many kinds of ruling group to control and manage democracy'. For Williams, as a Marxist, many of the implications will logically be social and economic: 'changes in the nature of work' and 'new kinds of social opportunity'. Moreover he sees 'a great expansion in the scale of ordinary society' and 'social problems which seem to be of a quite new kind'.

When he gets to define the new discipline it is as 'an important response to this new situation'. From that point on, Williams warms to his task with words every bit as inspiring now as they were when they were first written and published.

What do we mean by communication? The oldest meaning of the word, in English, can be summarized as the passing of ideas, information, and attitudes from person to person. But, later, communication came also to mean a line or channel from place to place. Since the Industrial Revolution there has been so much improvement in this kind of communication – in canals, railways, steamships, cars, aircraft – that often, when we say communications, we mean these ways of travelling and carrying. Yet there is another major line of modern improvement and invention. Steam printing, the electric telegraph, photography, wireless, film, television are new ways of passing ideas, information, and attitudes from person to person, and we call them, also, communications. So that now the word has different meanings in common use, and there is often confusion between them. I think that for describing the physical means of travelling and carrying, our other word, transport, is better than communications, but I suppose both will go on being used. In any case, in this book, I mean by communications the institutions and forms in which ideas, information, and

CONTINUED

attitudes are transmitted and received. I mean by communication the process of transmission and reception.

In our own generation, there has been a dramatic tightening of interest in this world of communications. The development of powerful new means of communication has coincided, historically, with the extension of democracy and with the attempts, by many kinds of ruling group, to control and manage democracy. The development has also coincided with important changes in the nature of work and in education, which have given many people new kinds of social opportunity. There has been a great expansion in the scale of ordinary society, both through the new communications systems and through the growth of many kinds of large-scale organization. Acting together, these developments have created social problems which seem to be of a quite new kind.

The growth of interest in communications is an important response to this new situation. It came, really, as a breakthrough in experience, cutting across our usual categories. Already some of our basic ideas of society are being changed by this new emphasis. From one familiar approach, through traditional economics, we have seen the central concerns of society as property, production, and trade. These approaches remain important, but they are now joined by a new emphasis: that society is a form of communication, through which experience is described, shared, modified, and preserved. We are used to descriptions of our whole common life in political and economic terms. The emphasis on communications asserts, as a matter of experience, that men and societies are not confined to relationships of power, property, and production. Their relationships in describing, learning, persuading, and exchanging experiences are seen as equally fundamental. This emphasis is exceptionally important in the long crisis of twentieth-century society. Many people, starting from older versions of society, have seen the growth of modern communications not as an expansion of men's powers to learn and to exchange ideas and experiences, but as a new method of government or a new opportunity for trade. All the new means of communication have been abused, for political control (as in propaganda) or for commercial profit (as in advertising). We can protest against such uses, but unless we have a clear alternative version of human society we are not likely to make our protests effective.

My own view is that we have been wrong in taking communication as secondary. Many people seem to assume as a matter of course that there is, first, reality, and then, second, communication about it. We degrade art and learning by supposing that they are always second-hand activities: that there is life, and then afterwards there are these accounts of it. Our commonest political error is the assumption that power – the capacity to govern other men – is the reality of the whole social process, and so the only context of politics. Our commonest economic error is the assumption that production and trade are our only practical activities, and that they require no other human justification or scrutiny. We need to say what many of us know in experience: that the life of man, and the business of society, cannot be confined to these ends; that the struggle to learn, to describe, to understand, to educate, is a central and necessary part of our humanity. This struggle is not begun, at second hand, after reality has occurred. It is, in itself, a major way in which reality is continually formed and changed. What we call society is not only a network of political and economic arrangements, but also a process of learning and communication.

Communication begins in the struggle to learn and to describe. To start this process in our minds, and to pass on its results to others, we depend on certain communication models, certain rules or conventions through which we can make contact. We can change these models, when they become inadequate, or we can modify and extend them. Our efforts to do so, and to use the existing models successfully, take up a large part of our living energy. The history of a language is a record of efforts of this kind, and is as central a part of the history of a people as its changing political and economic institutions. Moreover, many of our communication models become, in themselves, social institutions. Certain attitudes to others, certain forms of address, certain tones and styles, become embodied in institutions which are then very powerful in social effect. The crisis in modern communications has been caused by the speed of invention and by the difficulty of finding the right institutions in which these technical means are to be used. In modern Britain, we have a whole range of uses of printing, of photography, of television, which do not necessarily follow from the technical means themselves. Many have been shaped by changing political and economic forces. Many, also, have been shaped by what are really particular communication models: the idea that speaking or writing to many people at once is speaking or writing to 'the masses'; the idea that there are clear types of people and interest – 'Third Programme', 'Home Service', and 'Light'; 'quality' and 'popular' – that we can separate and label. These arguable assumptions are often embodied in solid practical institutions, which then teach the models from which they start. We cannot examine the process of general communication in modern society without examining the shapes of these institutions. Further, if we understand the importance of communication, in all our social activities, we find that in examining the process and the institutions we are also looking at our society – at some of our characteristic relationships – in new ways.

This book is an introduction to this field of inquiry. It begins with an outline of the history of our modern means and institutions of communication. It goes on to examine, in various ways, some of the methods and content of some of our most important institutions. It then passes to the very lively arguments and controversies which have sprung up around these institutions, and which seem to be extending and intensifying year by year, as the sense of crisis mounts. It turns finally to a series of suggestions and proposals, which can be used as a basis for a general discussion of possible developments and changes.

I have been working in this field now for many years, and I am very conscious of the difficulties involved in any short book on so complicated and controversial a subject. So far as possible, I have based the book on methods of teaching which I have used over several years in classes for members of the Workers' Educational Association and for trade unionists. The object, in such teaching, was not only to present certain facts and methods of study, but also to start a process of independent inquiry and common discussion. I hope that the book can be used in these same ways, for a kind of communication which I believe to be valuable.

I said in *Culture and Society* (1780-1950): 'I shall be glad to be answered, in whatever terms . . . When we consider how matters now stand, our continuing interest and language could hardly be too lively.' I have greatly valued the very many answers I actually received, agreeing and disagreeing. The original invitation stands.

(Williams 1966: 9–13)

WHAT'S NEXT?

➤ Williams points out that 'Many people seem to assume as a matter of course that there is, first, reality, and then, second, communication about it'. Why is this not the case?
➤ How does Williams's conception of the primacy of 'reality' and the secondary character of communication compare with the views of John Berger and William S Burroughs as evidenced in Extract 2?

▼ ## 87 WHAT'S THE TOPIC? Theories of communication III
WHAT'S THE TEXT? Judith Williamson *Consuming Passions*

The passion that Raymond Williams employs in his rationale for a new discipline is the element that Judith Williamson is pursuing in her study of consumer culture. In a sense she takes up Williams's baton for she is concerned about what we buy and see and do and only too aware of the ever new social problems that ensue. In her introduction to *Consuming Passions* the problematic is contained in the first lines: 'We are consuming passions all the time – at the shops, at the movies, in the streets, in the classroom: in the old familiar ways that no longer seem passionate because they are the shared paths of the social world, the known shapes of our waking dreams'. Like Williams, Williamson is concerned with and for the way we live now and, like Williams, is all for constructing a radical response. She turns first on the academics who she accuses of pursuing desire in a way that 'is not unrelated to the obsession with "revealing" sex on every hoarding'. She pinpoints a vital feature of any study of mass culture, or anything else for that matter, when she points out: 'People who study things aren't fuelled by different drives from anyone else'.

What she wants is an end to the pretence and the beginning of a new critical examination of the key areas. She sees passion as the key, the new fuel of engagement: 'a longing that breaks beyond the present, a drive to the future'. 'Passion,' she asserts, 'is another story.' It is a story that we must read *and* write.

We are consuming passions all the time – at the shops, at the movies, in the streets, in the classroom: in the old familiar ways that no longer seem passionate because they are the shared paths of our social world, the known shapes of our waking dreams. Passions born out of imbalance, insecurity, the longing for something *more*, find forms in the objects and relations available; so that energies fired by what might be, become the fuel for maintaining what already is. Every desire that needs to be dulled, every sharpness at the edge of consciousness that needs to be softened, every yearning that tries to tear through some well-worn weakness in the fabric of daily life, must be woven back into that surface to strengthen it against such exposure. 'Consuming passions' can mean many things: an all-embracing passion, a passion for consumerism; what I am concerned with is the way passions are themselves consumed, contained and channelled into the very social structures they might otherwise threaten.

The subject most avidly consumed in academic work over recent years has been 'desire', which has gained prestige in the theoretical world as a 'radical' topic. But in our society where sensuality is frozen, arrested in the streets of our cities, stretched out over every surface, public imagery has accustomed us to a sexuality that is served up in slices, and theory offers the cold slab of the dissecting table to further this operation. For academic interest in 'desire' is not unrelated to the obsession with 'revealing' sex on every hoarding. People who study things aren't fuelled by different drives from anyone else. Desire has become the subject of numerous books, conferences, articles, lunchtime lectures and so on; but the drive to read endless articles about it in theoretical journals has ultimately the same impetus as the drive to read endless articles about it in *Cosmopolitan* or *Over 21*; it is just that academic work satisfies both appetite and duty, and gives an important sense of control. Desire itself is channelled into this endless, obsessive theorizing about desire – harnessed in its own pursuit; and with theory, as with sex, the more elusive its object, the more interesting this pursuit is.

CONTINUED

But passion – passion is another story. It is to be written *about*, but not *with*: for the essence of all this academic work on 'desire' is to *stay cool*. In the dominant ideology of our culture, and particularly its more 'intellectual' layers, it has never been fashionable to *over-invest* in any activity. And the bourgeois etiquette whereby any violent display of feeling is automatically taboo, any raising of the voice rude no matter what the reason, merely sets out the pattern of a much wider social phenomenon, the consensus by which any form of the 'extreme' is outlawed. Passions are fine on the cinema screen or in hi-fi advertisements – but not on the demonstration or picket line. For in the peculiar but familiar customs of consumer capitalism, our emotions are directed towards objects, rather than actions.

Marx talks of the commodity as 'congealed labour', the frozen form of a past activity; to the consumer it is also congealed longing, the final form of an active wish. And the shape in which fulfilment is offered seems to become the shape of the wish itself. The need of change, the sense that there must be something else, something different from the way things are, becomes the need for a new purchase, a new hairstyle, a new coat of paint. Consuming products does give a thrill, a sense of both belonging and being different, charging normality with the excitement of the unusual; like the Christmas trips of childhood to Oxford Street, to see the lights – and the lighted windows, passions leaping through plate-glass, filling the forms of a hundred products, tracing the shapes of a hundred hopes. The power of purchase – taking home a new thing, the anticipation of unwrapping – seems to drink up the desire for something new, the restlessness and unease that must be engendered in a society where so many have so little active power, other than to withdraw the labour which produces its prizes. These objects which become the aims of our passions are also shored up to protect us from them, the bricks of a dam held together by the very force it restrains. Passion is a longing that breaks beyond the present, a drive to the future, and yet it must be satisfied in the forms of the past.

For passion has no form of its own and yet, like the wind, is only revealed in forms; not a ready-made object, it is what breathes life into objects, transforming movement into shape. It is not found in things, but in ways of doing things; and the *ways* things are done are another kind of shape, less solid to our touch than products, but equally forms in which passions are consumed. These forms, not merely of objects but of our activities, provide at once our passions' boundaries and their expression: they are a shared language, for the shapes of our consciousness run right through society, we inhabit the same spaces, use the same things, speak in the same words. The same structures are found at every 'level'; the property laws that underpin bourgeois capital also govern personal relationships, marriage, sex, parenthood; the deferred gratification of emotional investment mirrors the very forms and strategies of economic investment. And they are found on every 'side': the back-to-nature organic commune in Wales or California reveals many of the qualities and values of capitalist 'private enterprise' and distaste for urban politics; the need for constant change in 'radical' styles reflects a consumer system based on built-in obsolescence. The forms of oppression frequently provide the mould for its resistance; thus the Labour Party sets itself the task of producing a strong 'leader' to 'match' Mrs Thatcher, rather than questioning the *terms* of 'leadership' in the air at the last election. And the highly visible, individual violence focused on by the media in mining communities during the miners' strike, exists in exact proportion to the less immediately visible, social violence of the plans that have caused it – plans for closures which could ravage those communities in an ultimately much more far-reaching way.

The dominant political notion in Britain has been for decades that of a 'consensus': there are agreed limits to what is and is not acceptable, and although these are constantly shifting, they must always be seen as fixed, since they form the ground-plan of social stability. The shapes of an era are more easily found in its fashions, its furniture, its buildings – whose lines do seem to trace the 'moods' of social change – than in the equally significant outlines of its thoughts and habits, its conceptual categories, which are harder to see because they are precisely what we take for granted.

How then *can* we 'see' them? If it is in shapes and forms that passions live – as lightning lives in a conductor – it is likely to be in images – in films, photographs, television – that such conduits are most clearly visible. Our emotions are wound into these forms, only to spring back at us with an apparent life of their own. Movies seem to *contain* feelings, two-dimensional photographs seem to *contain* truths. The world itself seems filled with obviousness, full of natural meanings which these media merely reflect. But *we* invest the world with its significance. It doesn't have to be the way it is, or to mean what it does. Who doesn't know, privately, that sense that desire lives, not in ourselves, but in the form of the person desired – in the features of their face, the very lines of their limbs? The contours of our social world are equally charged, the shapes of public life equally evocative, of passions that are in fact our own. And in the most crucial areas of meaning, public and private intersect: for example, in the way that 'Woman' carries a weight of meanings and passions hived off from the social and political world and diverted into 'sexuality', a process seen at its crudest in the way Britain's highest circulation daily paper replaces news with the page 3 pin-up. The whole drive of our society is to translate social into individual forms: movements are represented by 'leaders' ('Arthur Scargill's strike'), economic problems are pictured as personal problems ('too lazy to get a job'), public values are held to be private values ('let the family take over from the Welfare State').

This transformation of social forces into individual terms is not inevitable; but we are used to the same old furnishings of our conceptual world and frightened to grope around in the dark for different ones. It is a relief when half-formed fantasies, new outlines struggling out of old arrangements, fall back into their familiar shapes, daylight certainties stripped of danger. But even in the yearning for normality, for conformity, can be found the passion for a shared world; a sense of possibility expressed in the sensation of the obvious. There is a kind of poignancy for the way things *are*, when the familiar seems to contain more than itself: in the way that a landscape can be filled with longing, a street – as in so many songs – paved with passions. ('*I get a funny feeling inside of me, just walking up and down – Maybe it's because I'm a Londoner that I love London Town'.*) There is a passion when you glimpse what could be in what already is – in a lighted bus through a winter city, on a summer's day in a public park. In the present forms of our passions it is possible to trace, not only how they are consumed, but the very different future they might ultimately produce.

(Williamson 1986: 11–15)

WHAT'S NEXT?

➤ What is it exactly that Judith Williamson has a passion for?

▼ ## 88 WHAT'S THE TOPIC? The trouble with models WHAT'S THE TEXT? Denis McQuail and Sven Windahl *Communication Models for the Study of Mass Communication*

Clearly a useful place to engage in a discussion about the character of communication is with communication models, those packed arrangements of theoretical description. From the moment we meet the model devised by the sociologist Harold Lasswell (usually referred to as the Lasswell Formula) we are engaged in two levels of response. Most straightforwardly we are testing the usefulness ('the something we can use' that Peter Barry charged us with finding in Extract 1) of the simplified description in graphic form (model) when applied to a piece of reality (real life communication situations). However we are also exercising, exploring and sometimes challenging, the perspective on communication that the specific model offers, in other words what the model has to add to the discussion 'what is communication?'

In this context Lasswell's formula becomes a classic statement of process theory in which communication is transmission, the act of sending a message from one place or participant to a receiver or destination. This is a discussion which McQuail and Windahl have at each stage of their book of communication models.

What features below is part of the introduction to the second edition of their book in which they address both the functions and failings of models.

In the first edition we commented on the relative lack of interest in communication models at that time. This no longer seems to be the case, presumably because the advantages we perceived are now more widely acknowledged. Even so, the potential advantages and drawbacks call for some further comment. For our purpose, we consider a model as a consciously simplified description in graphic form of a piece of reality. A model seeks to show the main elements of any structure of process and the relationships between these elements. Deutsch (1966) notes the following main advantages of models in the social sciences. Firstly, they have an *organising* function by ordering and relating systems to each other and by providing us with images of wholes that we might not otherwise perceive. A model gives a *general* picture of a range of different particular circumstances. Secondly, it helps in explaining, by providing in a simplified way information which would otherwise be complicated or ambiguous. This gives the model a heuristic function, since it can guide the student or researcher to key points of a process or system. Thirdly, the model may make it possible to predict outcomes or the course of events. It can at least be a basis for assigning probabilities to various alternative outcomes, and hence for formulating hypotheses in research. Some models claim only to describe the structure of a phenomenon. In this sense, a diagram of the components of a radio set could be described as 'structural'. Other models, which we call 'functional', describe systems in terms of energy, forces and their direction, the relations between parts and the influence of one part on another.

The models presented in this book fall mainly into the latter category, simply because all communication is in some degree dynamic and involves some elements of process or change. Even so, some of the models are very simple and tell us little about the forces at work which relate elements to each other. While models in general can be purely verbal, or diagrammatic, or mathematical, we have presented only those which are both verbal and diagrammatic.

It has been argued against the use of models that they tend to trap their originators and users within rather limited confines which they then become eager to defend against attack. Such a tendency can have a delaying effect on the development of a science, although this has probably not happened in the case of communication research, where old models have tended to be soon discarded or modified. A similar risk is that a model, or even a succession of models, can tend to perpetuate some initial questionable, but fundamental, assumptions about the components of a model or the processes at work. An example in the field of communication is the tendency to represent communication as a one-directional process in which a 'sender' deliberately tries to influence a 'receiver'. Such a representation tends to deny the circularity, negotiability and openness of much communication.

It should at least be remembered that there are some risks in using models, even for heuristic purposes. They are inevitably incomplete, oversimplified and involve some concealed assumptions. There is certainly no model that is suitable for all purposes and all levels of analysis and it is important to choose the correct model for the purpose one has in mind. One of the purposes of the book is to give some indication of the proper purpose and level of different models, partly by showing how they have been used in communication research. The reader should become aware of the possibilities of testing models against circumstances or cases and of adapting any given model to suit the chosen application. The models presented are not so sacred that they cannot easily be given a somewhat different shape and formulation. It should become apparent that anyone is in a position to construct their own models of a given aspect of the communication process and we hope that this book will encourage students of mass communication to adopt this process as a means of elucidation.

We view models primarily as aids to thought which are especially appropriate in the study of communication. Why they should be so appropriate is not easy to demonstrate, but it may stem from the fact that communication is a binding force in social relationships and has consequences for this structure without being readily open to observation. There is, consequently, an attraction in being able to 'draw' the 'lines' which stand for the links we know to exist but cannot see and to use other devices to show the structure, topography, strength and direction of relationships. So much of the subject of communication has to be dealt with in verbal abstractions that it is an aid and a relief to have at least something 'fixed' in graphic form, however much the element of abstraction may remain.

(McQuail and Windahl 1993: 2–4)

WHAT'S NEXT?

> ➤ Which communication models do you find most useful?
> ➤ What do these models teach you about the character of communication?

▼ 89 WHAT'S THE TOPIC? Can process and semiotic models be combined?
WHAT'S THE TEXT? John Lye 'Synopsis of Roman Jakobson's model of communication'

A model that does partly appear to pull together insights offered by both process and semiotic approaches is that of Roman Jakobson. Jakobson, as a literary critic, was interested in the modes of communication, the different kinds of relationship which are established in the act of communication between the sender, the text, and the audience. He proposed that the six essential modes of communication could be theoretically traced to the six essential components of any communication act. Unsurprisingly these components were identified as:

- addresser (sender)
- addressee (receiver)
- context
- message
- contact
- code.

Jakobson's simple but engaging thesis then is that:

- Every act of communication involves these components

and/but:

- In each individual act of communication one of these components is likely to dominate

and so:

- The mode of communication is determined by the dominant component

e.g. connative communication is communication which has a dominant receiver (comedy is connative in this sense: it needs a receiver input – a response – to exist).

context

referential

message

poetic

addresser _____ addressee

emotive   *connative*

contact

phatic

code

metalinguistic

Functions (italicized phrases)

The context or referential function is what is being spoken of, what is being referred to. In the expression 'PLEASE put the *fucking* CAT OUT NOW!' the referential burden of the message is 'I am requesting that the domesticated cat (that is in our care) be put outside the house (in which we now are) at this time (and not later)'.

The poetic function is the focus on the message (the use of the medium) for its own sake. The associations (equivalence, similarity and dissimilarity, synonymity and antonymity); the repetitions of sound values, stresses, accents; the word and phrase boundaries and relationships (e.g. elided vs end-stopped words): as these are combined in sequence. 'Just don't make a pass at every lass in the class,' said Jumpin' Jack Flash.

The emotive or expressive function of language refers to the attitude of the addresser towards that of which (or to whom) he speaks: through emphasis, intonation, loudness, pace, etc. This is a really, really IMPORTANT point.

The phatic function is the use of language to keep people in contact with each other, the maintenance of social relationships – includes 'idle chat'. Kinda interesting, eh? What do you think about being phatic together? Fun? Like your hat, get it at the Bay?

The metalinguistic function is that use of language by which people check out with each other whether they are 'on the same page', using the same codes in the same contexts. Are you with me on this one?

The connative function refers to those aspects of language which aim to create a certain response in the addressee. Learn this now!

<http://www.brocku.ca/commstudies.courses/2F50/jakobson.html>

> ➤ Apply this model to the communication likely between a television programme and its audiences on any channel and at any given time.

▼ 90 WHAT'S THE TOPIC? The age of anxiety
WHAT'S THE TEXT? Marshall McLuhan
Understanding Media: The Extensions of Man

Marshall McLuhan is a name from the early days of Communication and Media Studies, a man with a string of aphorisms at his disposal, one of the key voices which defined the discipline. Part visionary, part philosopher, part entertainer, McLuhan's purpose was to unsettle America and through this, the world. He did so in a style that is a mixture of articles, essays, jottings, and provocative illustrations as if to prove his perhaps most famous aphorism: the medium is the message.

The extract below consists of, first, the introduction to *Understanding Media* which he published in 1964 and, second, the first paragraph of the first chapter appropriately titled 'the medium is the message'. McLuhan, like Postman (see Extract 93), foresaw a crisis approaching: 'After three thousand years of explosion . . . the Western World is imploding'.

He goes on to discuss the ways in which our senses have been served by technology in the sense that they have been extended to encompass the technology. They are, in McLuhan's words, 'the extensions of man'.

After three thousand years of explosion, by means of fragmentary and mechanical technologies, the Western world is imploding. During the mechanical ages we had extended our bodies in space. Today, after more than a century of electric technology, we have extended our central nervous system itself in a global embrace, abolishing both space and time as far as our planet is concerned. Rapidly, we approach the final phase of the extensions of man – the technological simulation of consciousness, when the creative process of knowing will be collectively and corporately extended to the whole of human society, much as we have already extended our senses and our nerves by the various media. Whether the extension of consciousness, so long sought by advertisers for specific products, will be 'a good thing' is a question that admits of a wide solution. There is little possibility of answering such questions about the extensions of man without considering all of them together. Any extension, whether of skin, hand, or foot, affects the whole psychic and social complex.

Some of the principal extensions, together with some of their psychic and social consequences, are studied in this book. Just how little consideration has been given to such matters in the past can be gathered from the consternation of one of the editors of this book. He noted in dismay that 'seventy-five per cent of your material is new. A successful book cannot venture to be more than ten per cent new'. Such a risk seems quite worth taking at the present time when the stakes are very high, and the need to understand the effects of the extensions of man becomes more urgent by the hour.

In the mechanical age now receding, many actions could be taken without too much concern. Slow movement insured that the reactions were delayed for considerable periods of time. Today the action and the reaction occur almost at the same time. We actually live mythically and integrally, as it were, but we continue to think in the old, fragmented space and time patterns of the pre-electric age.

Western man acquired from the technology of literacy the power to act without reacting. The advantages of fragmenting himself in this way are seen in the case of the surgeon who would be quite helpless if he were to become humanly involved in his operation. We acquired the art of carrying out the most dangerous social operations with complete detachment. But our detachment was a posture of non-involvement. In the electric age, when our central nervous system is technologically extended to involve us in the whole of mankind and to incorporate the whole of mankind in us, we necessarily participate, in depth, in the consequences of our every action. It is no longer possible to adopt the aloof and dissociated role of the literate Westerner.

. . .

This is the Age of Anxiety for the reason of the electric implosion that compels commitment and participation, quite regardless of any 'point of view'. The partial and specialized character of the viewpoint, however noble, will not serve at all in the electric age. At the information level the same upset has occurred with the substitution of the inclusive image for the mere viewpoint. If the nineteenth century was the age of the editorial chair, ours is the century of the psychiatrist's couch. As extension of man the chair is a specialist ablation of the posterior, a sort of ablative absolute of backside, whereas the couch extends the integral being. The psychiatrist employs the couch, since it removes the temptation to express private points of view and obviates the need to rationalize events.

The aspiration of our time for wholeness, empathy and depth of awareness is a natural adjunct of electric technology. The age of mechanical industry that preceded us found vehement assertion of private outlook the natural mode of expression. Every culture and every age has its favorite model of perception and knowledge that it is inclined to prescribe for everybody and everything. The mark of our time is its revulsion against imposed patterns. We are suddenly eager to have things and people declare their beings totally. There is a deep faith to be found in this new attitude – a faith that concerns the ultimate harmony of all being. Such is the faith in which this book has been written.

(McLuhan 1987: 11–13)

WHAT'S NEXT?

➤ What are the implications (consequences) of having our senses 'enhanced'?

▼ 91 WHAT'S THE TOPIC? Globalisation WHAT'S THE TEXT? George Ritzer *The McDonaldization of Society*

When Marshall McLuhan coined the term 'the global village' it was in a spirit of hope and expectation, in the belief that technology could and would change even the great globe itself. This was about communication as contact, as mediation, as community. In 1964 Labour Prime Minister Harold Wilson tapped into the mood of the times when he launched his first term of government with a famous speech about the 'white heat of new technology'. The Beatles were among the first recording artists to demonstrate the implications of the new technology when they took over the village hall for a live world-wide satellite link-up at Christmas 1968. Their message was the message of the Sixties: 'It's easy . . . All you need is Love'. 'Village' was aptly chosen because it suggested community not competition or coercion. It was clearly going to bring us all together.

There was one Sixties text that failed to share this vision – Patrick McGoohan's acclaimed television series *The Prisoner*, which took a more sceptical not to say pessimistic view of the newly informative (because technological) society. For refusing to provide information Number 6 (the McGoohan character) is sent to (appropriately) The Village, a bizarre collection of architectural texts (actually in Portmeirion, in North Wales), where he is encouraged to become part of the community and from where he continually tries to escape. Ironically, for many contemporary critics like George Ritzer, McGoohan's village seems like a picnic for the global village has turned out to be a large slice of virtually-real estate bought up and out by transnational (worldwide) companies like Microsoft and The Walt Disney Corporation and, in this piece, McDonald's (all of which demand the obligatory™). For good or ill the news is: the global village gave way to globalisation. And as the global village becomes (metaphorically) even more like an out of town shopping centre so too do the services provided become broader and the influence more intense. When we have McDoctors in our health centres and McTeachers in our schools it will be too late.

George Ritzer ends a book-length study of the implications of the activities of the fast food chain McDonald's (the McDonaldization of the book's title) with a guide to fighting back.

INDIVIDUAL RESPONSES: SUBVERTING THE PROCESS OF MCDONALDIZATION

Beyond the work world, those who are uncomfortable with or opposed to McDonaldization have a variety of other options open to them. Before we discuss those choices, it should be pointed out that such people (those who view the rationalised cage as rubber or iron) ought to try to extract the best of what the McDonaldized world has to offer without succumbing to its dangers and excesses. This will not be easy to do, because the lure of McDonaldized institutions is great, and it is easy to find oneself becoming a devotee of, and enmeshed in, rationalized activities. Thus, those who use rationalized systems for what they have to offer need to keep the dangers of McDonaldization always in the forefront of their thinking. But, being able to get one's bank balance in the middle of the night, to avoid hospital emergency rooms by having minor problems cared for at 'McDoctors', and to lose weight quickly and safely at Nutri/System, among many others conveniences, are all attractive possibilities for most people. The secret is clearly to be able to take advantage of the best that the McDonaldized world has to offer without becoming imprisoned in that world.

How can one do this? For one thing, it would be advisable to use McDonaldized systems *only* when such use is unavoidable, when no alternatives are available, or when what they have to offer cannot be matched by nonrationalized systems. Perhaps we might think about putting warning labels on McDonaldized systems much like those found on cigarette packs. One possibility:

> Sociologists warn us that habitual use of McDonaldized systems are destructive to our physical and psychological well-being as well as to society as a whole.

Above all, people should avoid the routine and systematic use of McDonaldized systems. To avoid the iron cage, one must seek out nonrationalized niches wherever and whenever possible. Such a search for these niches is difficult and time-consuming. It is far easier to use the various aspects of our McDonaldized society than it is to find and utilize nonrationalized alternatives. Yet, it is precisely such efforts that are necessary if we are to avoid the worst effects of the iron cage. Avoiding McDonaldization requires hard work and vigilance.

The most extreme step would be to pack one's bags and leave the highly McDonaldized American society. The problem with moving to another society is that other societies are themselves likely to be well along in the rationalization process or soon likely to embark on the process. Thus, a move to another society might buy people some time, but eventually, McDonaldization would have to be confronted, this time in a less familiar context.

A less extreme step is to search out a wide range of nonrationalized niches in our McDonaldized society such as those described above in the work world. But, as we have seen, it is not enough for people to search out such niches, it is also necessary for others to have created nonrationalized enterprises in those niches or with such niches built into them. Indeed, the creation of such enterprises is not only a good in itself, but the enterprises can also be quite successful. Since there will always be people (one hopes) who rebel against McDonaldization, there is success to be had, to say nothing of the undying gratitude of the rebels in the creation of nonrational enterprises. Thus, the founding and frequenting of non-rationalised enterprises in niches throughout society are mechanisms for coping with the excesses of rationalization.

. . .

It is particularly important that steps be taken to prevent children from becoming mindless supporters of McDonaldization.

- Instead of using a 'McChild' care center, leave your child with a neighborhood parent interested in earning some extra money.
- Keep your children away from television as much as possible. It is especially important that they not be exposed to the steady barrage of commercials from rationalised institutions, especially on Saturday morning cartoon shows.
- Lead efforts to keep McDonaldization out of the school system.
- If you can afford it, send your child to a small, non-McDonaldized educational institution.
- Above all, when possible, avoid taking your children to fast-food restaurants or their clones in other areas of society. If no alternatives are present (for example, you're on a highway and the only options are various fast-food chains), blindfold your child until the ordeal is over.

There *are* steps that can be taken to cope with McDonaldization. However, I hold little hope that such actions, even if they were all to be employed by many people, would reverse the trend toward McDonaldization. Despite this seeming inevitability, I think the struggle is worthwhile. First, it will serve to mitigate the worst excesses of McDonaldized systems. Second, it will lead to the discovery, creation, and use of more niches where people who are so inclined can escape McDonaldization for at least a part of their day or even a larger portion of their lives. Finally, and perhaps most important, the struggle itself is ennobling. As a general rule, such struggles are nonrationalized, individual, and collective activities. It is in such struggles that people can express genuinely human reason in a world that in virtually all other ways has set up rationalized systems to deny people the ability to behave in such human ways.

(Ritzer 1983: 182–3, 186–7)

WHAT'S NEXT?

➤ What is it exactly that we should be struggling against?
➤ Is resistance futile?
➤ Is it too easy and too seductive to think that the world would be a better place if only McDonald's, Starbucks, the Gap, and other targets of the anti-capitalism and anti-globalisation activists were destroyed?
➤ Read Douglas Coupland *Microserfs* (1996) London: Regan Books

▼   92 WHAT'S THE TOPIC? The mediatised life
    WHAT'S THE TEXT? Raymond Williams 'Drama
    in a dramatised society'

There can be no going back for once we have experienced 'reality' via the medium of film or television things can never be the same again. An example of writing which deals with the apparent hyperreality of contemporary mass communications was delivered in lecture form by Raymond Williams. In 'Drama in a dramatised society' he explores the impact that the enormous volume of film and, particularly, television drama might have had on society. Jean Baudrillard uses the term 'mediatised' to characterise the way in which all forms of media conform to the same kind of code, to the way, ultimately, in which we cannot make meaningful distinctions between one form of media representation and another. Used, as he willingly admits, by Philip Auslander in a looser fashion, the notion of mediatisation is vital to an understanding of the way in which all that we might have traditionally characterised as television, film, live performance or even real life now conform to the same kinds of modes of representation and cannot be regarded as separate and distinct. In this way the 1970s advertising slogan for Memorex blank cassette tape 'Is it live or is it Memorex?' is meaningless. As is the question 'Is it real or is it on television?'

Drama is no longer coextensive with theatre; most dramatic performances are now in film and television studios. In the theatre itself – national theatre or street theatre – there is an exceptional variety of intention and method. New kinds of text, new kinds of notation, new media and new conventions press actively alongside the texts and conventions that we think we know, but that I find problematic just because these others are there. Dramatic time and sequence in a play of Shakespeare, the intricate rhythms and relationships of chorus and three actors in a Greek tragedy: these, I believe, become active in new ways as we look at a cutting bench or an editing machine, in a film or television studio, or as we see new relations between actor and audience in the improvised theatre of the streets and the basements.

Again, we have never as a society acted so much or watched so many others acting. Watching, of course, carries its own problems. Watching itself has become problematic. For drama was originally occasional, in a literal sense: at the Festival of Dionysus in Athens or in medieval England on the day of Corpus Christi when the wagons were pulled through the streets. The innovating commercial theatres of Elizabethan London moved beyond occasion but still in fixed localities: a capital city, then a tour of provincial cities. There was to be both expansion and contraction. In Restoration London two patent theatres – the monopoly centres of legitimate drama – could hardly be filled. The provincial theatre-building of the eighteenth century, the development of variety theatres and music-halls, the expansion of London's West End theatres in the second half of the nineteenth century: all these qualified occasion but in the light of what was to come were mainly quantitative changes. It is in our own century, in cinema, in radio and in television, that the audience for drama has gone through a qualitative change. I mean not only that *Battleship Potemkin* and *Stagecoach* have been seen by hundreds of millions of people, in many places and over a continuing period, nor only that a play by Ibsen or O'Neill is now seen simultaneously by ten to twenty million people on television. This, though the figures are enormous, is still an understandable extension. It means that for the first time a majority of the population has regular and constant access to drama, beyond occasion or season. But what is really new – so new I think that it is difficult to see its significance – is that it is not just a matter of audiences for particular plays. It is that drama, in quite new ways, is built into the rhythms of everyday life. On television alone it is normal for viewers – the substantial majority of the population – to see anything up to three hours of drama, of course drama of several different kinds, a day. And not just one day; almost every day. This is part of what I mean by a dramatised society. In earlier periods drama was important at a festival, in a season, or as a conscious journey to a theatre; from honouring Dionysus or Christ to taking in a show. What we now have is drama as habitual experience: more in a week, in many cases, than most human beings would previously have seen in a lifetime.

Can this be merely extension: a thing like eating more beef muscle or wearing out more shirts than any ancestor could have conceived as a widespread human habit? It certainly doesn't look like a straight line extension. To watch simulated action, of several recurrent kinds, not just occasionally but regularly, for longer than eating and for up to half as long as work or sleep; this, in our kind of society, as majority behaviour, is indeed a new form and pressure. It would of course be easy to excise or exorcise this remarkable fact if we could agree, as some propose, that what millions of people are so steadily watching is all or for the most part rubbish. That would be no exorcism: if it were true it would make the fact even more extraordinary. And it is in any case not true. Only dead cultures have scales that are reliable. There are discernible, important and varying proportions of significant and trivial work, but for all that, today, you can find kitsch in a national theatre and an intensely original play in a police series. The critical discriminations are at once important and unassumable in advance. What is it, we have to ask, in us and in our contemporaries, that draws us repeatedly to these hundreds and thousands of simulated actions: these plays, these representations, these dramatisations?

It depends where you ask that question from. I ask it from watching and from contributing to the extraordinary process itself. But I can hear – who can not? – Some familiar voices: the grave merchants whose apprentices and shopboys slipped away to Bankside; the heads of households whose wives, and the heads of colleges whose students, admitted to read English, would read novels and comedies in the morning. These sober men would know what to say about contemporary California, where you can watch your first movie at six-thirty in the morning and if you really try can see seven or eight more before you watch the late movie in the next recurrent small hours. Fiction; acting; idle dreaming and vicarious spectacle; the simultaneous satisfaction of sloth and appetite; distraction from distraction by distraction. It is a heavy, even a gross catalogue of our errors, but now millions of people are sending the catalogue back, unopened. Till the eyes tire, millions of us watch the shadows of shadows and find them substance; watch scenes, situations, actions, exchanges, crises. The slice of life, once a project of naturalist drama, is now a voluntary, habitual, internal rhythm; the flow of action and acting, of representation and performance, raised to a new convention, that of a basic need.

We cannot know what would have happened if there had been, for example, outside broadcasting facilities at the Globe. In some measure, at least, we must retain the hypothesis of simple extension of access. Yet I would argue that what has happened is much more than this. There are indeed discoverable factors of a probably causal kind. We are all used to saying – and it still means something – that we live in a society which is at once more mobile and more complex, and therefore, in some crucial respects, relatively more unknowable, relatively more opaque than most societies of the past, and yet which is also more insistently pressing, penetrating and even determining. What we try to resolve from the opaque and the unknowable, in one mode by statistics – which give us summaries and breakdowns, moderately accurate summaries and even more accurate breakdowns, of how we live and what we think – is offered to be resolved in another mode by one kind of dramatisation. Miner and power worker, minister and general, burglar and terrorist, schizophrenic and genius; a back-to-back home and a country house; metropolitan apartment and suburban villa; bed-sitter and hill-farm: images, types, representations: a relationship beginning, a marriage breaking down; a crisis of illness or money or dislocation or disturbance. It is not only that all these are represented. It is that much drama now sees its function in this experimental, investigative way; finding a subject, a setting, a situation; and with some emphasis on novelty, on bringing some of that kind of life into drama.

Of course all societies have had their dark and unknowable areas, some of them by agreement, some by default. But the clear public order of much traditional drama has not, for many generations, been really available to us. It was for this reason that the great naturalist dramatists, from Ibsen, left the palaces, the forums and the streets of earlier actions. They created, above all, rooms; enclosed rooms on enclosed stages; rooms in which life was centred but inside which people waited for the knock on the door, the letter or the message, the shout from the street, to know what would happen to them; what would come to intersect and to decide their own still intense and immediate lives. There is a direct cultural continuity, it seems to me, from those enclosed rooms, enclosed and lighted framed rooms, to the rooms in which we watch the framed images of television: at home, in our own lives, but needing to watch what is happening, as we say, 'out there': not out there in a particular street or a specific community but in a complex and otherwise unfocused and unfocusable national and international life, where our area of concern and apparent concern is unprecedentedly wide, and where what happens on another continent can work through to our own lives in a matter of days and weeks – in the worst image, in hours and minutes. Yet our lives are still here, still substantially here, with the people we know, in our own rooms, in the similar rooms of our friends and neighbours, and they too are watching: not only for public events, or for distraction, but from a need for images, for representations, of what living is now like, for this kind of person and that, in this situation and place and that. It is perhaps the full development of what Wordsworth saw at an early stage, when the crowd in the street (the new kind of urban crowd, who are physically very close but still absolute strangers) had lost any common and settled idea of man and so needed representations – the images on hoardings, the new kinds of sign – to simulate if not affirm a human identity: what life is and looks like beyond this intense and anxious but also this pushed and jostled private world of the head.

That is one way of putting it; the new need, the new exposure – the need and exposure in the same movement – to a flow of images, of constant representations, as distinct from less complex and less mobile cultures in which a representation of meaning, a spectacle of order, is clearly, solidly, rigidly present, at certain fixed points and is then more actively affirmed on a special occasion, a high day or a festival, the day of the play or the procession. But there is never only need and exposure: each is both made and used. In the simplest sense our society has been dramatised by the inclusion of constant dramatic representation as a daily habit and need. But the real process is more active than that.

Drama is a special kind of use of quite general processes of presentation, representation, signification. The raised place of power – the eminence of the royal platform – was built historically before the raised place of the stage. The presentation of power, in hierarchical groupings, in the moving emphases of procession, preceded the now comparable modes of a represented dramatic state. Gods were made present or made accessible by precise movements, precise words, in a known conventional form. Drama is now so often associated with what are called myth and ritual that the general point is easily made. But the relation cannot be reduced to the usual loose association. Drama is a precise separation of certain common modes for new and specific ends. It is neither ritual which discloses the God, nor myth which requires and sustains repetition. It is specific, active, interactive composition: an action not an act; an open practice that has been deliberately abstracted from temporary practical or magical ends: a complex opening of ritual to public and variable action; a moving beyond myth to dramatic *versions* of myth and of history. It was this active variable experimental drama – not the closed world of known signs and meanings – that came through in its own right and in its own power; significantly often in periods of crisis and change, when an order was known and still formally present but when experience was pressing it, testing it, conceiving breaks and alternatives; the dramatic possibility of what might be done within what was known to have been done, and each could be present, and mutually, contradictorily potent, in specific acted forms. We need to see this especially now, when myth and ritual, in their ordinary senses, have been broken up by historical development, when they are little more, in fact, than the nostalgia or the rhetoric of one kind of scholar and thinker, and yet when the basic social processes, of presentation, representation, signification have never been more important. Drama broke from fixed signs, established its permanent distance from myth and ritual and from the hierarchical figures and processions of state; broke for precise historical and cultural reasons into a more complex, more active and more questioning world. There are relativities within its subsequent history, and the break has been made many more times than once. Any system of signs, presenting and representing, can become incorporated into a passive order, and new strange images, of repressed experience, repressed people, have again to break beyond this. The drama of any period, including our own, is an intricate set of practices of which some are incorporated – the known rhythms and movements of a residual but still active system – and some are exploratory – the difficult rhythms and movements of an emergent representation, rearrangement, new identification. Under real pressures these distinct kinds are often intricately and powerfully fused; it is rarely a simple case of the old drama and the new.

But drama, which separated out, did not separate out altogether. Congruous and comparable practices exist in other parts of the society as in the drama, and these are often interactive: the more interactive as the world of fixed signs is less formal. Indeed what we often have now is a new convention of deliberate overlap. Let me give the simplest example. Actors now often move from a part in a play, which we can all specify as dramatic art, to deploy the same or similar skills in the hired but rapturous discovery of a cigar or a facecream. They may be uneasy about it but, as they say, it's better than resting. It's still acting after all; they are no more personally committed to that cigar than to the character of that bluff inspector, for which they were also hired. Somebody wrote it, somebody's directing it: you're still in the profession. Commercials in Britain have conventional signs to tell you they're coming, but the overlap of method, of skill and of actual individuals is a small and less easily-read sign of a more general process, in which the breaks are much harder to discern.

Our present society, in ways it is merely painful to reiterate, is sufficiently dramatic in one obvious sense. Actions of a kind and scale that attract dramatic comparisons are being played out in ways that leave us continually uncertain whether we are spectators or participants. The specific vocabulary of the dramatic mode – drama itself, and then tragedy, scenario, situation, actors, performances, roles, images – is continually and conventionally appropriated for these immense actions. It would moreover be easier, one can now often feel, if only actors acted, and only dramatists wrote scenarios. But we are far past that. On what is called the public stage, or in the public eye, improbable but plausible figures continually appear to represent us. Specific men are magnified to temporary universality and so active and complex is this process that we are often invited to see them rehearsing their roles, or discussing their scenarios. Walter Bagehot once distinguished between a real ruling class and a theatrical ruling show: the widow of Windsor, he argued, in his innovating style of approving and elegant cynicism, is needed to be shown, to be paraded, before a people who could never comprehend the more complex realities of power. I watched this morning the televised State opening of Parliament. It is one thing to say that it was pure theatre; it is harder to see, and to say, that beyond its residual pageantry was another more naturalised process which is also in part a cousin of theatre. Monarchs, of course, have always done something like this, or had it done for them. Those who lasted were conscious of their images even if they called them their majesties. Moreover, like many actors, people find roles growing on them: they come to fit the part, as he who would play the King. What is new, really, is not in them but in us.

It is often genuinely difficult to believe in any part of this pervasive dramatisation. If we see it in another period or in or from another place, it visibly struts and frets, its machinery starts audibly creaking. In moments of crisis, we sometimes leave this social theatre or, as easily, fall asleep in it. But these are not only roles and scenarios; they are conventions. When you can see a convention, become really conscious of it, it is probably already breaking down. Beyond what many people can see as the theatricality of our image-conscious public world, there is a more serious, more effective, more deeply rooted drama: the dramatisation of consciousness itself. 'I speak for Britain' runs the written line of that miming public figure, though since we were let in on the auditions, and saw other actors trying for the part, we may have our reservations; we may even say 'Well I'm here and you don't speak for me.' 'Exactly,' the figure replies, with an unruffled confidence in his role, for now a different consciousness, a more profound dramatisation, begins to take effect; 'you speak for yourself, but I speak for Britain'. 'Where is that?' you may think to ask, looking wonderingly around. On a good day from a high place you can see about fifty miles. But you know some places, you remember others; you have memories, definitions and a history.

Yet at some point along that continuum, usually in fact very early, you have – what? Representations; typifications; active images; active parts to play that people are playing, or sometimes refusing to play. The specific conventions of this particular dramatisation – a country, a society, a period of history, a crisis of civilisation; these conventions are not abstract. They are profoundly worked and reworked in our actual living relationships. They are our ways of seeing and knowing, which every day we put into practice, and while the conventions hold, while the relationships hold, most practice confirms them. One kind of specific autonomy – thisness, hereness – is in part free of them; but this is usually an autonomy of privacy, and the private figure – the character of the self- is already widely offered to be appropriated in one or other of these dramatised forms: producer or consumer, married or single, member or exile or vagrant. Beyond all these there is what we call the irreducible: the still unaccommodated man. But the process has reached in so far that there are now, in practice, conventions of isolation itself. The lonely individual is now a common type: that is an example of what I mean by a dramatic convention, extending from play to consciousness. Within a generation of that naturalist drama which created the closed room – the room in which people lived but had to wait for news from outside – another movement had created another centre: the isolated figure, the stranger, who in Strindberg's *Road to Damascus* was still actively looking for himself and his world, testing and discarding this role and that image, this affirming memory and that confirming situation, with each in turn breaking down until he came back, each time, to the same place. Half a century later two ultimately isolated figures, their world not gone but never created, sat down on the road waiting for what? – call it Godot – to come. Let's go, they said, but they didn't move. A decade later other more radically isolated figures were seen as buried to their necks, and all that was finally audible, within that partial and persuasive convention, was a cry, a breath. Privacy; deprivation. A lost public world; an uncreatable public world.

These images challenge and engage us, for to begin with, at least, they were images of dissent, of conscious dissent from fixed forms. But that other miming, the public dramatisation, is so continuous, so insistent, that dissent, alone, has proved quite powerless against it. Dissent, that is, like any modern tragic hero, can die but no more. And critical dissent, a public form you can carry around to lectures or even examinations: it too comes back to the place where it started, and may or may not know it for the first time. A man I knew from France, a man who had learned, none better, the modes of perception that are critical dissent, said to me once, rather happily: 'France, you know, is a bad bourgeois novel.' I could see how far he was right: the modes of drama-tisation, of fictionalisation, which are active as social and cultural conventions, as ways not only of seeing but of organising reality, are as he said: a bourgeois novel, its human types still fixed but losing some of their conviction; its human actions, its struggles for property and position, for careers and career-ing relationships, still as limited as ever but still bitterly holding the field, in an interactive public reality and public consciousness. 'Well yes,' I said politely, 'England's a bad bourgeois novel too. And New York is a bad metro-politan novel. But there's one difficulty, at least I find it a difficulty. You can't send them back to the library. You're stuck with them. You have to read them over and over.' But critically,' he said, with an engaging alertness. 'Still reading them,' I said.

I think that is where we now are. People have often asked me why, trained in lit-erature and expressly in drama, making an ordinary career in writing and teaching dramatic history and analysis, I turned – *turned* – to what they would call sociology if they were quite sure I wouldn't be offended (some were sure the other way and I'm obliquely grateful to them). I could have said, debating the point, that Ruskin didn't turn from architecture to society; he saw society in architecture – in its styles, its shaping intentions, its structure of power and of feeling, its façades and its interiors and the relations between them; he could then learn to read both architecture and society in new ways. But I would prefer to speak for myself. I learned something from analysing drama which seemed to me effective not only as a way of seeing certain aspects of society but as a way of getting through to some of the fundamental conventions which we group as society itself. These, in their turn, make some of the problems of drama quite newly active. It was by looking both ways, at a stage and a text, and at a society active, enacted, in them, that I thought I saw the significance of the enclosed room – the room on the stage, with its new metaphor of the fourth wall lifted – as at once a dramatic and a social fact.

(Williams 1989: 3–11)

➤ Using both Williams's and Goffman's ideas consider what insights can be derived by thinking about life as drama.

➤ Williams wrote his piece in 1974. What has happened to the consumption of drama between then and now?

➤ Williams asserts that 'only dead cultures have scales that are reliable'. What do you think he meant by this? Measured in this way do you inhabit a culture that is alive or dead?

▼ 93 WHAT'S THE TOPIC? Technology as culture
WHAT'S THE TEXT? Neil Postman *Technopoly: The Surrender of Culture to Technology*

The primary relationship between communication and technology has long been present in the work of technological determinists like Neil Postman. Postman has long argued that technology shapes cultural (as well as psychological and intellectual) experience. In his extreme statements this is even more apparent. Early on in his book *Technopoly* he argues that 'Tools are not integrated into the culture, they attach the culture. They bid to *become* the culture'.

The whole of *Technopoly* is a controlled but provocative assault on received wisdom, teasing out the differences between a tool-using culture and a technocracy. Here we certainly see Williamson's desire for passion exemplified. Postman is passionate and intelligent. He places the problem historically as a product of the uneasy relationship between 'the technological and the traditional' world views which is finally being resolved by the rise of Technopoly (which he later defines as 'totalitarian technocracy').

Technopoly, for Postman, redefines 'what we mean by religion, by art, by family, by politics, by history, by truth, by privacy, by intelligence'. It eliminates alternatives by making them 'invisible and therefore irrelevant'. This is partly why Postman is so insistent on the need for systems of classification (taxonomies): it is our only defence against invisibility.

I find it necessary, for the purpose of clarifying our present situation and indicating what dangers lie ahead, to create still another taxonomy. Cultures may be classed into three types: tool-using cultures, technocracies, and technopolies. At the present time, each type may be found somewhere on the planet, although the first is rapidly disappearing: we must travel to exotic places to find a tool-using culture. If we do, it is well to go armed with the knowledge that, until the seventeenth century, all cultures were tool-users. There was, of course, considerable variation from one culture to another in the tools that were available. Some had only spears and cooking utensils. Some had water mills and coal- and horsepower. But the main characteristic of all tool-using cultures is that their tools were largely invented to do two things: to solve specific and urgent problems of physical life, such as in the use of waterpower, windmills, and the heavy-wheeled plow; or to serve the symbolic world of art, politics, myth, ritual, and religion, as in the construction of castles and cathedrals and the development of the mechanical clock. In either case, tools did not attack (or, more precisely, were not intended to attack) the dignity and integrity of the culture into which they were introduced. With some exceptions, tools did not prevent people from believing in their traditions, in their God, in their politics, in their methods of education, or in the legitimacy of their social organization. . . .

And so two opposing world-views – the technological and the traditional – coexisted in uneasy tension. The technological was the stronger, of course, but the traditional was there – still functional, still exerting influence, still too much alive to ignore. This is what we find documented not only in Mark Twain but in the poetry of Walt Whitman, the speeches of Abraham Lincoln, the prose of Thoreau, the philosophy of Emerson, the novels of Hawthorne and Melville, and, most vividly of all, in Alexis de Tocqueville's monumental *Democracy in America*. In a word, two distinct thought-worlds were rubbing against each other in nineteenth-century America.

With the rise of Technopoly, one of those thought-worlds disappears. Technopoly eliminates alternatives to itself in precisely the way Aldous Huxley outlined in *Brave New World*. It does not make them illegal. It does not make them immoral. It does not even make them unpopular. It makes them invisible and therefore irrelevant. And it does so by redefining what we mean by religion, by art, by family, by politics, by history, by truth, by privacy, by intelligence, so that our definitions fit its new requirements. Technopoly, in other words, is totalitarian technocracy.

. . .

Technopoly is a state of culture. It is also a state of mind. It consists in the deificaiton of technology, which means that the culture seeks its authorization in technology, finds its satisfactions in technology, and takes its orders from technology. This requires the development of a new kind of social order, and of necessity leads to the rapid dissolution of much that is associated with traditional beliefs. Those who feel most comfortable in Technopoly are those who are convinced that technical progress is humanity's superhuman achievement and the instrument by which our most profound dilemmas may be solved. They also believe that information is an unmixed blessing, which through its continued and uncontrolled production and dissemination offers increased freedom, creativity, and peace of mind. The fact that information does none of these things – but quite the opposite – seems to change few opinions, for unwavering beliefs are an inevitable product of the structure of Technopoly. In particular, Technopoly flourishes when the defenses against information break down.

The relationship between information and the mechanisms for its control is fairly simple to describe: Technology increases the available supply of information. As the supply is increased, control mechanisms are strained. Additional control mechanisms are needed to cope with new information. When additional control mechanisms are themselves technical, they in turn further increase the supply of information. When the supply of information is no longer controllable, a general breakdown in psychic tranquillity and social purpose occurs. Without defenses, people have no way of finding meaning in their experiences, lose their capacity to remember, and have difficulty imagining reasonable futures.

One way of defining Technopoly, then, is to say it is what happens to society when the defenses against information glut have broken down. It is what happens when institutional life becomes inadequate to cope with too much information. It is what happens when a culture, overcome by information generated by technology, tries to employ technology itself as a means of providing clear direction and humane purpose. The effort is mostly doomed to failure. Though it is sometimes possible to use a disease as a cure for itself, this occurs only when we are fully aware of the processes by which disease is normally held in check. My purpose here is to describe the defenses that in principle are available and to suggest how they have become dysfunctional.

(Postman 1995: 22–4, 71–2)

WHAT'S NEXT?

➤ What evidence of a technopoly is there in your experience?

▼ **94 WHAT'S THE TOPIC? Communication through technology
WHAT'S THE TEXT? Kate Kellaway 'Deadlier than the snailmail'**

Some of the implications of New Technology are very much practical rather than theoretical, though theory informs this practice. McLuhan's war cry of 'the medium is the message' is a good place to start along with Postman's famous analogy:

> To a man with a pencil, everything looks like a list.
> To a man with a camera, everything looks like an image.
> To a man with a computer, everything looks like data.

In respect of Kate Kellaway's piece about e-mail 'Deadlier than the snailmail', one could also add the notion that meaning is as much determined by the receiver as the transmitter. (Indeed not to do so is to give in to the intentional fallacy, the error of thinking that everything that a reciever derives from a communication is what the communicator intends for them to receive.) Centrally the point is that using technology subtly alters how you see, shape and interact with the world. It also alters the ways in which your communication about these things might be viewed. Kate Kellaway is searching for a so-called Netiquette, a set of ground rules for e-mail whilst simultaneously reflecting on the need for such rules.

Largely the points Kellaway makes are about register and tone, mode of address and mode of reception. She claims, for example, that 'e-mails invite informality, speed and jocularity' which may prove a problem if we imagine that e-mail is an all-purpose format. Kellaway's piece explores these problems and offers advice, none healthier than 'e-mails beg to be deleted (save or print only if you must)'.

Email offers limitless scope for misunderstanding and embarrassment. That's why a few ground rules are required . . .

Hi! This is 4 u – love and xxx k

How should the ideal email be composed? I've often wondered whether there was a techie version of Nancy Mitford (an idea that would have made her swoon with distaste) who could supply us with the 'u and non u' of email, the 'e and non-e'? And now, incredibly, it seems that there is.

Step forward Rolf Kurth of Debrett's. He intends to come to our rescue – and evidently we need rescuing. According to recent research (for the email provider MSN Hotmail), email is promoting rampant illiteracy. Non-letter writers are said to be offending in cyberspace with amorous sign-offs (to professional emails), hasty kisses and cavalier misspellings. These people do not know how to mind their e's (or queues).

Netiquette is a touchy business. Not least of all because no one can agree on what it is. Unfortunately, Kurth, author of Debrett's *Guide to Correspondence*, proves a disappointment. He conservatively insists on preserving good writing as a form of politeness. This does not help me at all. When I write an email, I feel like a foxed beginner. If I treat an email as if it were a letter – in a style that Debrett's might pass – it seems arduous, futile, gawkily dated. I feel like the uncomfortable possessor of a tie at a picnic, or someone transfixed by nostalgia for an epistolary past (for 'snail mail'). Should I skip 'Dear X' and crack straight on with the message? Should I scrap upper case and dash ahead with lower-case panache to show myself a proper mistress of the form? What is the best tone to adopt?

One thing is for sure: literature and emails do not get on together, as last week's cautionary tale about poet laureate Andrew Motion illustrated. Laura Fish, a novelist on a one-year creative-writing course at UEA, accused Motion (her tutor) of harassment; she claimed to have received 40 'explicit' emails from him. He has returned the accusation and has also been reported saying that he does not expect his emails to appear in any collected letters. I fear for his biography. But I am sure he is right to be dismissive about his emails. They are – almost always – inferior to letters. It is like writing on water. Emails beg to be deleted (save or print only if you must).

Emails invite informality, speed and jocularity. The 'subject' line asks for a witticism (tiresome, if your message is not intended to amuse). As one of my friends observes 'for some people the title/subject seems to be the key to the whole thing'; they get thousands of emails and only bother with the enticing come-ons. For others, the come-ons are more than enticing. I have a friend who is an English philosophy professor working in the States. Let us call him Roland.

He embraced email with zealous enthusiasm before any of his English friends had any experience of it. He fell in love, via a prodigious email correspondence, with another academic whom he had met fleetingly at a conference. A 'seed was sown' which flowered on the net. Now, he remembers the time (1994) as 'heady'. There was a liberating sense that, through email, you could 'be anything you liked'. Email, he points out, is particularly good for people who can be 'quite shy and hopeless face to face'.

For the first couple of days, the emails between Roland and A (let us call her Anna) were flat – then 'suddenly this thing caught fire'. He found the speed 'really exciting. It's great when you're on a good footing – you have just had your thirteenth email, so immediately you send off a reply. Instead of waiting for the second post, you could be expectant all the time.' In a new relationship you would never write a love letter every day, let alone 13 times a day, nor would you 'phone to chat idly about breakfast or muse, "I wonder what you look like in the morning?"'

Roland says: 'You have to ask yourself, what line has been crossed here? Because, obviously a line has been crossed.' He found e-romance pleasurably clandestine (emailers typically behave as if engaged in espionage). 'I was very aware that A was out with friends and was slipping away to a terminal to send me a few comments.'

In the movie *You've Got Mail*, Tom Hanks and Meg Ryan exploit the incognito drama of email romance. They play business rivals who meet in an internet chat-room and then start a cyber affair . . . It is only after they meet that the dime drops.

Roland and Anna used to write '30,000 words' between them in a single week. But Anna's emails were, Roland sees now, full of little signs of doubt about the form. She finished one with: 'I wish you could see the way I sign my name, the way I do my A's.' In another, she wrote: 'I wonder if we'd get on so well if we were in the same room.'

Another friend, romancing on the net, revels in the flirtatious punctuation to her day and points out that emails are 'nonchalant, off the cuff. The medium lends itself to irony which helps to make things seem light'. It is not always possible to keep things light: one in 10 computer users surveyed have ended a relationship by email.

When you are in love, perhaps netiquette does not count. But Roland was warned from the outset by his university that people might not recognise nuances so that if he was cracking jokes in emails, he should always put a colon, a dash and a closed parenthesis to indicate a smiling face. There is also what he calls an 'eyebrow-raised smiley' which looks like this – ;-) – 'If you suspect that a comment may be a little off-colour, you put that at the end. It is as if acknowledging that it might be off colour were a way to cancel its objectionable nature.'

In the same way there is a symbol to try and defuse anger. It is horribly easy to reply too quickly to an email and fire off something you will later regret. This is known by some as a 'flare'. It is suggested that if you want to write something angry, you preface it with the words: 'Flame On'. I personally think this is as idiotic as waving a Bunsen burner around while having a row. As Stephen Pritchard, *The Observer*'s letters editor, crisply points out, if you need symbols, it is a sign that you are not writing clearly enough. Roland agrees but adds: 'It seems that you can't count on anyone to understand the dead stream of characters'.

Rosamund Heartgood, a financial journalist, would be surprised to hear that e-love is alive, let alone well. She believes 'the romance with email is over. The illusion that email is a new way of communicating has gone.' The more emails people get, the more they 'dread signing on. People are beginning to withdraw from email'. She goes further: 'It is a very bad way of communicating because we haven't learnt how to use it. It is a hybrid between writing and the telephone. We use it like the telephone, colloquially, but forget that people cannot hear our tone of voice.' She argues that 'friendships can easily deteriorate through email correspondence'. She warns against writing thank-you letters by email: "Thanks for lunch, we had a good time", sounds grumpy and offhand.'

Her advice: 'When in doubt, try a bit harder, lay it on a bit thicker or the emotional message may get lost.' She is contemptuous of colleagues (usually male) who use 'email as a kind of power tool, all abbreviations and capital letters, to suggest that they are too busy to press the shift key down'. She believes you should never use email to convey anything negative. 'It is cowardly and will almost certainly backfire on you.'

I remember the loud quality of the silence in the office when people first started to gossip by email. It is a hazardous business. Email encourages Freudian slips (copying to the wrong people, for example). Rosamund once wrote an email about her editor. It contained what she intended be an amusing parody of a recent conversation she had had with him. She was a little concerned when the colleague she emailed it to did not laugh.

Suddenly, she realised what she had done: she had sent it to the editor by mistake. Now she counsels: 'A good rule of thumb is that unless a message has to be instant: wait until the next day.' And her last rule is to sign off simply.

That's it. :-)

A COMPENDIUM OF NETIQUETTE

DOs
Always greet your correspondent
Think before you write
Re-read before sending
Wait a day, if possible, before answering
If you are angry, wait even longer
If you can't wait, use the FLAME ON/OFF procedure (see in text)
Be brief
Think creatively about your subject line
Use upper and lower case
Spell and punctuate properly
Sign off simply

DON'Ts
Don't start your message in the subject field
Don't overuse acronyms like BTW (by the way) or IMHO (in my humble opinion); you may not be understood
Do not forward personal email without getting author's permission first

Don't write anything you would not put on a postcard
Don't write in capital letters: it will be perceived as shouting
Don't use e-mail as a weapon or to conduct difficult conversations; that is cowardly
Don't be negative

(Kellaway 2001: 4)

➤ List the advantages and disadvantages of e-mail as a form of communication
➤ What differences do you notice between netiquette and the conventions of letter-writing?

▼ **95 WHAT'S THE TOPIC? Communication technology**
WHAT'S THE TEXT? Sam Sifton 'Speak fluent Yettie'

At first glance the article below seems to be one of those amusing albeit obsessive exercises in practical linguistics, a sort of Esperanto for the cultist (cult in this case referring to cult television programme or series or film or book). *Star Trek* fans have signed up for courses on how to speak fluent Klingon run by community colleges. JRR Tolkien made monumental attempts to bring us the rudiments of old Elvish in *The Lord of the Rings*. Yetties would clearly fit this bill as a memorable adversary of the memorable Doctor Who (for those readers over a certain age or of a certain temperament or obsession).

But no. This geekish lexicon is the dictionary of Young Entrepreneurial Technocrats (or Yetties), movers and shakers in the volatile world of computing. These people are either disciples of the Bill Gates Story or a menacing Officer class for Postman's drear Technopoly. Whichever way you look, there's plenty of evidence here of a set of issues for students of Communication. On one level this is a classic example of what Bernstein called a restricted code, in this case an almost genuinely secret language that allows some to participate and excludes others and leaves them to merely wonder.

It is also evidence of the profound influence that technology has on communication from work through lifestyle to language. What Sam Sifton shows us is more than a glossary, it is the exposure of a culture, a way of life. Here are the digerati in all their e-glory, exchanging emotions for emoticon and indulging themselves in the ultimate egosurf. Despite the dotcom crash, there's still an army of Yetties out there, and their geekish lexicon is growing fast.

AMBIMOUSETEROUS Dude, that's cool: you can use your mouse with either hand!

ASK A simply stated question, as when a programmer cuts a manager off with a brutal, 'Look, what's your ask?'

BANDWIDTH Time, in the context of your modem and your internet service provider's information-carrying capacity and speed. Can also be applied to humans, viz, 'I'd love to help you with that inordinately time-consuming project, but I simply don't have the bandwidth.' See also 'Broadband'.

BOOKMARK A web browser can 'bookmark' a website so that the user can return to it without retyping the site's address. In yettie parlance, however, the word means 'to take note of' – as in, 'I bookmarked that guy when I met him at Comdex, and then hired him three months later.'

BROADBAND Technology that offers the transfer of multiple signals via a single conduit, allowing for high-speed information exchange. Serious bandwidth is the result of broadband technology. Colloquially, 'the future', with your internet, cable TV and phone service all coming into the house through a big, fat pipe.

BROWSER A program that reads pages on the internet. In other words, 'Mum, it's the screen that comes up on the computer I bought you, when you first access the world wide web. The thing that shows you the top news of the day and lets you search for pictures of baby pandas.'

BUG A small error in design or code in hardware or software. Also, the explanation for any secondary personality defect in a co-worker.

BURGER A start-up company created in the hope that it can be sold – or 'flipped' – before its underlying problems are discovered.

COBWEB SITE Refers to a website so devoid of fresh content that it has grown virtual cobwebs.

CODE MONKEY A computer programmer capable only of grinding out primitive work and incapable of performing sophisticated operations.

CRACKER An ill-intentioned hacker. Crackers break into –'crack' – computer systems in order to access, steal, or destroy sensitive information. 'Cracker' is not a synonym for 'hacker'. Outside the yettie environment, however, it is often used as such, to the dismay of the latter group. See 'Hacker'.

CRASH Any sudden, drastic computer failure.

CUBE Alternative form of the word 'cubicle', in which workers toil over their monitors.

CUBE FARM A large, open office space filled with cubicle-bound yettie employees.

CYBERSPACE Mainstream jargon for the internet.

DEAD TREE EDITION The hard, printed-on-paper copy of any given document.

DIGERATI A slickster media term for the digital elite.

DOC Diminutive of 'document'. A yettie's frequently updated resumé, for instance.

DOMAINIST A person who judges others simply on the basis of their e-mail domain, eg, hotmail, aol, btinternet, waitrose, angelfire etc.

DOWN Not functioning. Just at the moment when mainstream culture got used to the notion of 'down' as a modern, rappy analogue of the jazzy 'with it', the yetties went and changed everything.

DOUBLEGEEKING Using two computers at once.

DOWNLOAD To transfer data from a 'host' to a 'client', ie, from a server to a PC. More colloquially, a chief executive may download on his subordinates.

E- A prefix used to indicate virtually anything with an internet root, from e-mail to e-commerce.

EGOSURF Using search engines on the web to find sites or documents that mention one's own name.

E-MALINGER To cruise around the web mindlessly looking at sites and sending e-mails, instead of doing one's job.

EMOTICON A series of typed characters that, when viewed sideways, are meant to indicate the emotional state of the writer. Thus :) is a smiley face and :(is a frowny face, and :-(is a frowny face with a nose and :-l is a straight face with a nose. It used to be that words themselves performed this task, except in the case of pre-teen girls, who have always used hearts to dot their i's.

EQUITY The amount of the company that the employee 'owns'. In the New Economy, equity is most often not worth the paper it will never be printed on.

EYEBALLS Marketing slang for the number of people looking at a particular website at any given time, for whatever reason. A site wants more eyeballs, always.

FAT CLIENT A personal computer with a huge amount of memory and a large hard drive, used to store information that might otherwise take up space on a company's server.

FILTER Settings on a browser that prevent certain websites and certain types of websites – pornographic websites, for instance – from being accessed from an employee's computer. In the yettie parlance, filters 'suck'.

FLAME To send someone an inflammatory e-mail message.

FLAME WAR A high-volume exchange of flames.

404 Not where you thought it was, so named for the '404 File Not Found' error message given by some web browsers. Car keys often go 404.

FUZZY LOGIC A type of logic that discerns more than simple true and false values. Used mostly for artificial intelligence applications and some spell-checking programs.

GEEK Formerly a carnival performer known for stunts involving biting the heads off live chickens, snakes and vermin. More currently, someone with a passion for computers and computer science, to the exclusion of other, more human interests. Context has determined the word's flavour for the past decade: in teenage speak, 'geek' is a pejorative; in yettievilles of whatever size, it's a mark of high praise.

GEEKOSPHERE Broadly, the confusing, mysterious world inhabited by geeks. More narrowly, the cubicle in which a programmer works.

HACKER Any expert programmer possessed of deep intellectual curiosity and, often, greasy hair. May spend days at a computer terminal, divining the intricacies of a system or network or program, in order to make it better, See 'Cracker'.

HARDWIRED That which cannot be altered. Just as your Macintosh is hardwired to run the Apple operating system, for example, a yettie – particularly a yettie with more equity than you – may be hardwired to be an asshole.

HIT A documented visit to a particular website. A site advertising free down-loadable video footage of a graphic sexual act involving a celebrity might record a lot of hits. Hits are an analogue of the Old Economy media term 'readers'.

INCUBATOR A company that helps develop, fund, and often-times house an internet start-up company in the hope that the investment will pay off in spades.

INTERNET For the record, the internet is a vast network of interconnected computers that use TCP/IP protocol to exchange information. See also 'World wide web', which is different.

INTERNET TIME The belief that everything on the internet happens faster than anywhere else. Everything: the growth and decline of companies; the introduction of successive new technologies; the movement of information; the acquisition of wealth; even the length of time one 'should' work for a company before leaving for another.

KILLER APP An application program that clinches the decision to purchase the system on which the application appears. The classic example is the spreadsheet program Lotus 1-2-3. which in many ways introduced the personal computer to the business world. Developing a killer app can make a yettie very, very wealthy.

↑KLUDGE Any product or program thrown together without refinement, or consideration of good design. In its adjectival form, kludgey.

(THE) MATRIX Another synonym for the internet, this one taken from the 1999 Keanu Reeves vehicle of the same name.

↓MEATSPACE The 'real world' of human interaction. For the brainier sort of yettie, meatspace has nothing on the Matrix.

METRICS Originally understood as the statistical data included in the user's manuals for software and hardware products, metrics is increasingly defined as any statistical data relating to the New Economy.

MODE Frame of mind. One could be in crunch mode, for instance, when finishing a business plan, or in party mode, when breaking out the crisps and beer.

MONITOR PET Any small stuffed animal or doll affixed to, or resting upon, a computer monitor.

MULTITASKING To perform several tasks at once. The slack tone in the voice of the yettie friend you called on the phone? He's checking his e-mail during the call. That clicking sound? He's answering his e-mail during the call.

NETIQUETTE Network etiquette, or the informal code of conduct that has evolved in cyberspace.

NEWSGROUP An online discussion group based on a specific topic, such as Afrofuturism, or the band Ben Folds.

NONLINEAR Verb meaning to erupt in uncontrollable – and often illogical – anger.

OFFLINE In private: 'Let's talk about this offline.'

PHREAKING The act of cracking a phone system, usually to make long-distance calls for free.

PRAIRIE-DOGGING A series of heads popping up from cubicles throughout a cub farm, usually in reaction to a dramatic stimulus such as a loud argument.

SERVER A computer that supplies data and applications for the use of other computers.

SHAREWARE A sluttish yettie.

STICKINESS That ineffable something that gives a website returning eyeballs and lots of hits.

TRAFFIC The load on a communications device or a system. Heavy traffic is a good thing on a website, but for the user it means slowdowns in load times, as thousands attempt to retrieve the same information over the same wires.

UNINSTALLED To be fired or laid off.

UNSTRUNG No wires! A catch-all term for wireless internet applications and technology.

UPGRADE To replace a current version of a software program with a newer or enhanced version; or, in the case of hardware, adding more memory; or in the case of a boyfriend, to move from a programmer to a chief executive.

VESTING Pejorative term in large companies, used to refer to an employee's slacking off just prior to the actual vesting of his stock options, at which point he will undoubtedly sell and retire. Thus: 'I wouldn't expect too much help from Zack; he's vesting.'

WORLD WIDE WEB A section of the internet that presents information through linked graphic pages maintained by both public and privately owned computers around the world. You ought to know that by now.

YESTERDAY In the New Economy, 'now'.

(Sifton 2001: 36–7)

WHAT'S NEXT?

➤ What does this lexicon tell you about the attitudes and values of the people who use it?
➤ Compile a short list of technical terms associated with a group of which you are a member and compare this with Yettie.

WHAT'S THE TOPIC? The technologically mediated self
WHAT'S THE TEXT? Charles Cheung 'A home on the web: presentations of self on personal homepages'

One way to guarantee a positive result from your ego surf (a search for your own name on the Web) is to have your own personal homepage. This relatively new but significantly escalating phenomenon is addressed in Charles Cheung's essay 'A home on the web: presentations of self on personal homepages'. Here we see the interpersonal implications of new media and new formats.

Cheung begins with a simple anecdote. When he was aged ten he made a comic book, which only his relative read. Now the issue of publishing is very much simpler. Self-publishing is now a matter of effort not money and less negatively regarded (though vanity publishing is a characterisation that is not without truth). However, the personal homepage, on which you might offer your creative self, is a lot more complex than your name on a published book (even if you've paid for it yourself).

Cheung examines these complexities; he's interested in the ways in which website authors present their multiple and contradictory selves. He is interested in the issues that their presentations raise for Communication students, particularly the issues of identity and self-presentation. Cheung explores two main themes: the experience of emancipation felt in a number of ways and at a number of levels by those compiling these sites; and the highly contrived character of the selves that they present. For Cheung personal websites do emancipate their compilers but largely because they are 'polished and elaborate . . . sign vehicles . . . subject to manipulation'.

> When I was young, I loved Japanese animation and comics so much that I wanted to become a comic book artist myself. When I was 10, I made a book called 'Comic Kingdom of Charles', which included a biography detailing my struggles to become a 10-year-old amateur comic producer, a two-page feature about my family, a scrapbook with photos of me and my school friends, and selected comic strips I had drawn. I wanted other kids to read my book, but I didn't have the money to publish it. I wanted to circulate it among my classmates, but I was afraid they'd laugh at my efforts. In the end, my only reader was a relative who wasn't very interested in comics. I still think it was a brilliant piece of work for a 10-year-old kid but, needless to say, it has never been published.

CONTINUED

Today, my story would have a very different ending. When I was a little boy, access to a large reading public was limited to a privileged few. Writers could compose novels and short stories, academics could publish papers, artists could produce their work, successful business people might write autobiographies, and stars could 'confess all' to magazine journalists. . . .

Lynda's homepage (www.crosswinds.net/~lyndavandenelzen/HOME.htm) illustrates this creative process. Using the different expressive resources of the personal homepage – in Lynda's case biography, links, fan activity and a newsletter, but also including music, sound effects, poetry, fiction, original artwork, graphics and desktop backgrounds – website authors present their 'multiple and contradictory, selves. As detailed below, several examples of this sort of expressive resource manipulation are evident from Lynda's homepage.

☞ The *biography* is a good place for homepage authors to present their multiple and contradictory selves in an orderly way. Lynda's section called 'Me, I, and Myself' is an example. Lynda first confesses to her readers that she falls short of the standard of being an 'exemplary student', as she doesn't study much or have long-range career plans. However, she is not particularly unhappy, as her diverse range of hobbies helps her to define herself as a 'young girl with eclectic taste'. She sets herself apart from her peers – as she says, 'I've always been different from everyone else, so why stop now?' Then she goes on to say that she is a mature 'optimist' who enjoys life, but is also a 'political cynic' and a keen 'individualist' who has some complaints about society. The multiple selves presented here are obvious.

☞ Site authors can use *Web page links* and devote a certain number of *sections* to highlighting certain aspects of their selves. In Lynda's case, we see this in the 'Links' and – you guessed it, Web fans – the 'X-Files Page'. In the 'Links' section, Lynda includes links to some websites about the writer T.S.Eliot, the SF television programme *The X-Files*, and the female singer-songwriters Tori Amos and Sarah McLachlan. In the 'X-Files' section, she includes episode transcripts (presumably 'lifted' from another site), a couple of X-Files desktop backgrounds and some pictures from the programme. The overall effect is that she presents herself as a young woman with eclectic taste who is also a fan of this popular TV series.

☞ If the *biography* is best for more organized self-presentation, the *diary newsletter* and *journal* are more suitable for making an immediate record of spontaneous thoughts, random ideas and notes about recent encounters or events. In Lynda's homepage, she uses the 'Newsletter' section to record her complicated feelings towards life in general.

Lynda's homepage is just one example of the millions of personal homepages. In fact, people from all walks of life have started to use personal homepages to present positively their self-defined 'virtual' selves: cancer patients, retired scientists, kids with disabilities, vinyl collectors, kung fu movie lovers, transsexuals, DIY enthusiasts, pornographic movie lovers – virtually anyone with any identity.

Listed in Yahoo! there are even hundreds of cats with their own homepages. The degree of creative freedom the medium of the personal homepage provides for net users to construct and present their 'selves' is enormous.

The personal homepage, as discussed above, allows ordinary people to present their 'selves' to the net public. But the emancipatory possibilities of the personal homepage are perhaps more important than the sheer size of the audience it can reach. This section will illustrate two other emancipatory characteristics of the personal homepage.

First, personal homepage production 'emancipates' the author because it allows a much more polished and elaborate delivery of impression management compared with face-to-face interaction. Goffman (1959: 34) suggests that, besides 'verbal assertions', there are many 'sign vehicles' that are widely recognized as expressions given off unintentionally by people, by which others can evaluate how successful or sincere the self-presentation is. Some sign vehicles, like sex, age and race, are extremely difficult to conceal or manipulate in face-to-face interaction. Although the rest – such as clothing, posture, speech pattern, facial expression, bodily gesture and intonation – are relatively more manipulatable, Goffman emphasizes the difficulties in exerting total control over these sign vehicles (14-18). In a nutshell, Goffman suggests that presentation of self in everyday life is a delicate enterprise, subject to moment-to-moment mishaps and unintentional misrepresentations.

Moreover, most self-presentation in everyday life is not like a formal job interview in which we can do a 3-minute self-introduction. On the contrary, most face-to-face interaction proceeds in a spontaneous manner, during which we will never have an assigned block of time to present ourselves in an orderly and systematic fashion. More often than not, we constantly have to adjust our presentation to the unexpected reactions of others: their suspicious gazes, their impatient gestures or their provocative questions. The selves we present are always much more unorganized and haphazard than we intend.

In contrast, the 'sign vehicles' used in homepage self-presentation are more subject to manipulation. For example, in real life we sometimes 'give off an impression' we regret. If we chortle when our boss is making an idiotic argument in a meeting, we cannot rewind the scene and remind ourselves not to chortle when they make the point again. On our personal homepage, however, we can manipulate all the elements until we are satisfied: we can always experiment with the background colour, choose the most presentable head shot, censor the foul language accidentally written in the biography draft, and ponder as long as we like before deciding whether to tell the readers that our partner just dumped us. . . . In other words, the personal homepage allows careful construction of our personal portrayal before its release to the audience. All the mishaps mentioned by Goffman that may affect one's self-presentation in everyday life can be avoided on the personal homepage.

Second, the personal homepage can be emancipatory because it insulates the author from direct embarrassment, rebuff and harassment. As all face-to-face interaction involves the co-presence of others, we always have the chance to experience rejection and shame. Miller argues that the personal homepage is immune to these two problems:

> On the Web you can put yourself up for interaction without being aware of a rebuff, and others can try you out without risking being involved further than they would wish. There is another liberation that can be negative too. One of the regulating and controlling forces in face-to-face interaction is embarrassment. That is less likely to work on the Web. Others may find your Web page ridiculous, but you probably won't be aware of it. Those others who might be prompted to find ways to mend your presentation to reduce their own embarrassment in a face-to-face encounter are unlikely to feel pressure to smooth over the interaction between themselves and a Web page. So, in two senses, it is easy to make a fool of yourself on the Web: there is little to stop you doing it, but doing it will cause you little pain.

> (Miller 1995)

Moreover, although much has been written on cyberstalkers, who track down Web contacts in the real world, the personal homepage is still a relatively safe environment. Homepage authors can easily maintain relative anonymity by leaving out certain bits of 'vital' personal data by which others would be able to identify their physical location. Furthermore, there is little evidence that any more than a tiny minority of homepage authors have experienced harassment from unknown audiences.

> (Cheung 2000: 34–5)

WHAT'S NEXT?

> ➤ Write two versions of a 100-word statement designed to feature as an introduction on the homepage of your personal website. Make the first as sincere as you can and use the second to present an alternative (and positive) version. Compare these statements and then use them to write your own homepage introduction.

▼ 97 WHAT'S THE TOPIC? Communication and socialisation I
WHAT'S THE TEXT? Basil Bernstein *Class, Codes and Control*

Basil Bernstein is perhaps best known for his work on restricted and elaborated codes and their relationship with social class. More significantly here, Bernstein makes some useful points about socialisation and communication, in this case, more narrowly, language – to be precise speech.

In the paragraph immediately before the extract, Bernstein has been making the case that different speech forms or codes symbolise the form of the social relationship. Put simply, he is proposing that the restricted speech codes of, for example, working class children contain within them models of limitation and disadvantage. He puts it more elegantly as '[they must] create for the speakers different orders of relevance and relation' (1971: 174). Bernstein is essentially arguing for the ideological character of language, in fact of all communication: 'The experience of the speakers is then transformed by what is made significant or relevant by the speech form' (1971: 174).

Here values in language become values in life and language becomes a significant ideological context. (This is just one of the features of language addressed by Berger (in Extract 2), by Wittgenstein (in Extract 3), by Barley (in extract 10), by Tannen (in Extract 30), by Liz Lochhead (in Extract 31), by Eaglestone (in Extract 60) and by many of the other writers extracted in this book.) Quite clearly language plays a key role in establishing social identity; in other words it functions as an agency of socialisation.

BERNSTEIN

I am required to consider the relationship between language and socialisation. It should be clear from these opening remarks that I am not concerned with language, but with speech, and concerned more specifically with the contextual constraints upon speech. Now what about socialisation? I shall take the term to refer to the process whereby a child acquires a specific cultural identity, *and* to his responses to such an identity. Socialisation refers to the process whereby the biological is transformed into a specific cultural being. It follows from this that the process of socialisation is a complex process of control, whereby a particular moral, cognitive and affective awareness is evoked in the child and given a specific form and content. Socialisation sensitises the child to the various orderings of society as these are made substantive in the various roles he is expected to play. In a sense, then, socialisation is a process for making people safe. The process acts selectively on the possibilities of man by creating through time a sense of the inevitability of a given social arrangement, and through limiting the areas of permitted change. The basic agencies of socialisation in contemporary societies are the family, the peer group, school and work. It is through these agencies, and in particular through their relationship to each other, that the various orderings of society are made manifest.

Now it is quite clear that given this view of socialisation it is necessary to limit the discussion. I shall limit our discussion to socialisation within the family, but it should be obvious that the focusing and filtering of the child's experience within the family in a large measure is a microcosm of the macroscopic orderings of society. Our question now becomes: what are the sociological factors which affect linguistic performances within the family critical to the process of socialisation?

Without a shadow of doubt the most formative influence upon the procedures of socialisation, from a sociological viewpoint, is social class. The class structure influences work and educational roles and brings families into a special relationship with each other and deeply penetrates the structure of life experiences within the family. The class system has deeply marked the distribution of knowledge within society. It has given differential access to the sense that the world is permeable. It has sealed off communities from each other and has ranked these communities on a scale of invidious worth. We have three components: knowledge, possibility and invidious insulation. It would be a little naïve to believe that differences in knowledge, differences in the sense of the possible, combined with invidious insulation, rooted in differential *material* well-being, would not affect the forms of control and innovation in the socialising procedures of different social classes. I shall go on to argue that the deep structure of communication itself is affected, but not in any final or irrevocable way.

As an approach to my argument, let me glance at the social distribution of knowledge. We can see that the class system has affected the distribution of knowledge. Historically, and now, only a tiny percentage of the population has been socialised into knowledge at the level of the meta-languages of control and innovation, whereas the mass of the population has been socialised into knowledge at the level of context-tied operations.

A tiny percentage of the population has been given access to the principles of intellectual change, whereas the rest have been denied such access. This suggests that we might be able to distinguish between two orders of meaning. One we could call universalistic, the other particularistic. Universalistic meanings are those in which principles and operations are made linguistically explicit, whereas particularistic orders of meanings in which principles and operation are relatively linguistically implicit. If orders of meaning are universalistic, then the meanings are less tied to a given context. The meta-languages of public forms of thought as these apply to objects and persons realise meanings of a universalistic type. Where meanings have this characteristic then individuals have access to the grounds of their experience and can change the grounds. Where orders of meaning are particularistic, where principles are linguistically implicit, then such meanings are less context-independent and *more* context-bound, that is, tied to a local relationship and to a local social structure. Where the meanings are universalistic, they are in principle available to all because the principles and operations have been made explicit, and so public.

(Bernstein 1971: 174–6)

WHAT'S NEXT?

➤ Bernstein suggests that socialisation makes people safe. What does it mean to be safe in the early days of the twenty-first century?

▼ 98 WHAT'S THE TOPIC? Communication and socialisation II
WHAT'S THE TEXT? Michael Moore *Stupid White Men*

Often we are socialised into a series of assumptions and prejudices embedded in the language that we are given and find. The agencies of this socialisation – family, culture, the media (Althusser's Ideological State Apparatuses) – often can seem to work together to provide a uniform vision. Althusser uses the expression 'in teeth-gritting harmony'. This is not just about what we say but also what we see.

It is partly this that Michael Moore is attacking in his richly controversial book *Stupid White Men*. He's writing out of an American context but, in the spirit of globalisation, he could be writing about any number of locations, any number of contexts. In a direct readable style he assaults the readers' perceptions by pointing out who are the villains statistically – the white people of the title. He then goes on to work through a mass of stereotypes by simply making them white. The title of the chapter from which it is extracted is 'Kill Whitey'.

I don't know what it is, but every time I see a white guy walking toward me, I tense up. My heart starts racing, and I immediately begin to look for an escape route and a means to defend myself. I kick myself for even being in this part of town after dark. Didn't I notice the suspicious gangs of white people lurking on every street corner, drinking Starbucks and wearing their gang colors of Gap Turquoise or J. Crew Mauve? What an idiot! Now the white person is coming closer, closer – and then – *whew*! He walks by without harming me, and I breathe a sigh of relief.

White people scare the crap out of me. This may be hard for you to under-stand – considering that I *am* white – but then again, my color gives me a certain insight. For instance, I find *myself* pretty scary a lot of the time, so I know what I'm talking about. You can take my word for it: if you find yourself suddenly sur-rounded by white people, you better watch out. A*nything* can happen.

As white people, we've been lulled into thinking it's safe to be around other white people. We've been taught since birth that it's the people of that *other color* we need to fear. T*hey're* the ones who'll slit your throat!

Yet as I look back on my life, a strange but unmistakable pattern seems to emerge. E*very* person who has ever harmed me in my lifetime – the boss who fired me, the teacher who flunked me, the principal who punished me, the kid who hit me in the eye with a rock, the other kid who shot me with his BB gun, the executive who didn't renew TV N*ation*, the guy who was stalking me for three years, the accountant who double-paid my taxes, the drunk who smashed into me, the burglar who stole my stereo, the contractor who overcharged me, the girlfriend who left me, the next girlfriend who left even sooner, the pilot of the plane I was on who hit a truck on the runway (he probably hadn't eaten in days), the other pilot who decided to fly through a tornado, the person in the office who stole checks from my check book and wrote them out to himself for a total of $16,000 – every one of these individuals has been a white person! Coincidence? I think not!

I have never been attacked by a black person, never been evicted by a black person, never had my security deposit ripped off by a black landlord, never *had* a black landlord, never had a meeting at a Hollywood studio with a black executive in charge, never seen a black agent at the film/TV agency that used to represent me, never had a black person deny my child the college of her choice, never been puked on by a black teenager at a Mötley Crüe concert, never been pulled over by a black cop, never been sold a lemon by a black car salesman, never *seen* a black car salesman, never had a black person deny me a bank loan, never had a black person try to bury my movie, and I've never beard a black person say, 'We're going to eliminate ten thousand jobs here – have a nice day!'

I don't think I'm the only white guy who can make these claims. Every mean word, every cruel act, every bit of pain and suffering in my life has had a Caucasian face attached to it.

So, um, why is it *exactly* that I should be afraid of black people?

I look around at the world I live in – and, folks, I hate to tell tales out of school, but it's not the African-Americans who have made this planet such a pitiful, scary place to inhabit. Recently a headline on the front page of the Science section of the *New York Times* asked the question 'Who Built the H-Bomb' The article went on to discuss a dispute that has arisen between the men who claim credit for making the first bomb. Frankly, I could have cared less – because I already know the only pertinent answer: 'IT WAS A WHITE GUY!' No black guy ever built or used a bomb designed to wipe out hordes of innocent people, whether in Oklahoma City, Columbine, or Hiroshima.

No, my friends, it's *always* the white guy. . . .

You name the problem, the disease, the human suffering, or the abject misery visited upon millions, and I'll bet you ten bucks I can put a white face on it faster than you can name the members of 'N Sync.

And yet when I turn on the news each night, what do I see again and again? B*lack* men alleged to be killing, raping, mugging, stabbing, gangbanging, looting, rioting, selling drugs, pimping, ho-ing, having too many babies, dropping babies from tenement windows, fatherless, motherless, Godless, penniless. 'The suspect is described as a black male . . . the suspect is described as a black male. . . . THE SUSPECT IS DESCRIBED AS A BLACK MALE . . .' No matter what city I'm in, the news is always the same, the suspect always the same unidentified black male. I'm in Atlanta tonight, and I swear the police sketch of the black male suspect on TV looks just like the black male suspect I saw on the news *last* night in Denver and the night before in L.A. In every sketch he's frowning, he's menacing – and he's wearing the same knit cap! Is it possible that it's the same black guy committing every crime in America!

. . .

It's odd that, despite the fact that most crimes are committed by whites, black faces are usually attached to what we think of as 'crime'. Ask any white person who they fear might break into their home or harm them on the street, and if they're honest, they'll admit that the person they have in mind doesn't look much like them. The imaginary criminal in their heads looks like Mookie or Hakim or Kareem, not little freckle-faced Jimmy.

How does the brain process a fear like this, when everything it sees says the opposite! Are white people's brains hardwired to see one thing but believe the opposite because of race! If that's the case, then do all white people suffer from some shared low-grade mental illness! If every time the sun was out it was nice and bright and clear, but your brain told you to stay inside because it definitely looked like a storm was brewing, well, we might encourage you to seek some professional help. Are white people who see black bogeymen around every corner any different!

Obviously, no matter how many times their fellow whites make it clear that the white man is the one to fear, it simply fails to register. Every time you turn on the TV to news of another school shooting, it's always a white kid who's conducting the massacre. Every time they catch a serial killer, it's a crazy white guy. Every time a terrorist blows up a federal building, or a madman gets four hundred people to drink Kool-Aid, or a Beach Boys songwriter casts a spell causing half a dozen nymphets to murder 'all the piggies' in the Hollywood Hills, you know it's a member of the white race up to his old tricks.

So why don't we run like hell when we see whitey coming towards us? Why don't we ever greet the Caucasian job applicant with, 'Gee, uh, I'm sorry, there aren't any positions available right now'? Why aren't we worried sick about our daughters marrying white guys?

And why isn't Congress trying to ban the scary and offensive lyrics of Johnny Cash ('I shot a man in Reno/just to watch him die'), the Dixie Chicks ('Earl had to die'), or Bruce Springsteen ('. . . I killed everything in my path/I can't say that I'm sorry for the things that we done'). Why all the focus on rap lyrics? Why doesn't the media print rap lyrics like these and tell the truth?

> I sold bottles of sorrow, then chose poems and novels.
>
> > – Wu-Tang Clan
>
> People use yo' brain to gain.
>
> > – Ice Cube
>
> A poor single mother on welfare . . . tell me how you did it.
>
> > – Tupac Shakur
>
> I'm trying to change my life, see I don't wanna die a sinner.
>
> > – Master P
>
> > (Moore 2002: 56–61)

WHAT'S NEXT?

- ➤ Examine the national television news coverage of crime perpetrated by white and black people. What trends do you notice?
- ➤ Moore is describing an American context. How much of what he says is particular to America? Can it be applied to any other contexts in the world?

99 WHAT'S THE TOPIC? Communication and socialisation III
WHAT'S THE TEXT? Anthony P Cohen *The Symbolic Construction of Community*

Cohen rubs down some of the key notions of language and socialisation when he focuses anthropologically on the ways in which isolated communities arrange their various staged initiations into the community. Cohen explores below the relationship between community and society, arguing that 'community . . . is where one learns to "be social". He continues, 'We could say it is where one acquires "culture"'.

In this socialisation process Cohen is keen to stress how people acquire symbols rather than rules. For him a community inheres in . . . attachment or commitment to a common body of symbols'. In Bernstein's model language provides models for our place in the scheme of things. For Cohen 'it must again be emphasised that the sharing of symbols is not necessarily the same as the sharing of meanings'. For Bernstein language might be a repository of ideology and role; for Cohen it is something separate to which we orientate.

SYMBOLISM AND MEANING

'If you live in Shinohata', wrote Ronald Dore, 'the "outside world" begins three hundred yards down the road . . .' (Dore, 1978, p. 60) We do not have to construe community just in terms of locality, but more properly, in the sense which Dore expresses so lucidly and describes with such affectionate evocation of the Japanese village he studied at intervals for twenty-five years: the sense of a primacy of belonging. Community is that entity to which one belongs, greater than kinship but more immediately than the abstraction we call 'society'. It is the arena in which people acquire their most fundamental and most substantial experience of social life outside the confines of the home. In it they learn the meaning of kinship through being able to perceive *its* boundaries – that is, by juxtaposing it to non-kinship; they learn 'friendship'; they acquire the sentiments of close social association and the capacity to express or otherwise manage these in their social relationships. Community, therefore, is where one learns and continues to practice how to 'be social'. At the risk of substituting one indefinable category for another, we could say it is where one acquires 'culture'.

Learning to be social is not like learning grammar or the Highway Code. It is not reducible to a body of rules. Of course, one can identify rule-like principles in culture. Thus, for example, we can say that the Temne of Sierra Leone reserve the right hand to upper bodily behaviour; the left, to cope with the lower body

(Littlejohn 1972). We could make a similarly generalised statement in suggesting that the Whalsay Islanders of Shetland avoid open dispute or the public assertion of opinion (Cohen 1977). These 'principles' are sufficiently observed in practice that their contravention would identify the perpetrator as outside or as deviant. They differ from more objective rules, however, in that they are not associated unambiguously, nor even obviously, with a fixed and shared rationale. The Temne might well discriminate between left-and right-handedness, but this is not to say that they all do so for the same reason, nor for any 'conscious' reason, nor that they would accept the interpretations of their behaviour offered by Littlejohn's supposedly authoritative informant. People attach their own meanings to such prescriptions and proscriptions. In this respect, they are less *rules* of society than its symbols. Thus, when we speak of people acquiring culture, or leaning to be social, we mean that they acquire the symbols which will equip them to be social.

This symbolic equipment might be compared to vocabulary. Learning words, acquiring the components of language, gives you the capacity to communicate with other people, but does not tell you *what* to communicate. Similarly with symbols: they do not tell us *what* to mean, but give us the capacity to make meaning. Culture, constituted by symbols, does not impose itself in such a way as to determine that all its adherents should make the same sense of the world. Rather, it merely gives them the capacity to make sense and, if they tend to make a similar kind of sense it is not because of any deterministic influence but because they are doing so with the same symbols. The quintessential referent of community is that its members make, or believe they make, a similar sense of things either generally or with respect to specific and significant interests, and, further, that they think that the sense may differ from one made elsewhere. The reality of community in people's experience thus inheres in their attachment or commitment to a common body of symbols. Much of the boundary-maintaining process we shall look at later is concerned with maintaining and further developing this commonality of symbol. But it must again be emphasised that the sharing of symbol is not necessarily the same as the sharing of meaning.

People's experience and understanding of their community thus resides in their orientation to its symbolism. It will be clear, then, that a crucial step for us in attempting to unravel analytically the concept of community must involve some further discussion of the relations among symbolism, culture and meaning.

In what has become one of the most celebrated statements in recent anthropological writing, Geertz proclaims, '. . . man is an animal suspended in webs of significance he himself has spun . . .' These webs constitute 'culture,' whose analysis is, '. . . not an experimental science in search of law but an interpretive one in search of meaning' (1973, p. 5). There are three interrelated and powerful principles contained within Geertz's precise and eloquent formulation. The first is that culture ('webs of significance') is created and continually re-created by people through their social interaction, rather than imposed upon them as a

Durkheimian body of social fact or as Marxist superstructure. Secondly, being continuously in process, culture has neither deterministic power nor objectively identifiable referents ('law'). Third, it is manifest, rather, in the capacity with which is endows people to perceive meaning in, or to attach meaning to social behaviour. Behaviour does not 'contain' meaning intrinsically; rather, it is found to be meaningful by an act of interpretation: we 'make sense' of what we observe. The sense we make is 'ours', and may or may not coincide with that intended by those whose behaviour it was. Thus, in so far as we 'understand' the behaviour which goes on around us and in which we participate, we make and act upon interpretations of it: we seek to attach meaning to it. Social interaction is contingent upon such interpretation; it is, essentially, the transaction of meanings.

(Cohen 1992: 15–17)

WHAT'S NEXT?

➤ What do you think Cohen means by 'the symbols which will equip them to be social'? Find examples of these symbols.
➤ Describe the community you are a part of. What are its characteristics?

▼ 100 **WHAT'S THE TOPIC? The reputation of communication professionals**
WHAT'S THE TEXT? Humbert Wolfe 'The British journalist'

For all the talk in contemporary culture about the all-pervasive character of communication it is remarkable how poor are the reputations enjoyed by communication professionals. Our final text is short and sweet and is designed to make a final statement about the quality and function of the British media.

You cannot hope
to bribe or twist,
thank God! the
British journalist.

> But, seeing what
> the man will do
> unbribed, there's
> no occasion to.
>
> <http://www.prorev.com/quotes3.htm>

Frank Zappa once offered this succinct characterisation of rock journalism: 'People who can't write doing interviews with people who can't think in order to prepare articles for people who can't read' (1989: 221). An even bleaker insider view about journalism as a whole was offered by Hunter S Thompson in his 1988 book *Generation of Swine*: 'I have spent half my life trying to get away from journalism, but I am still mired in it – a low trade and a habit worse than heroin, a strange seedy world full of misfits and drunkards and failures. A group photo of the top ten journalists in America on any given day would be a monument to human ugliness' (Thompson 1988: 10).

WHAT'S NEXT?

➤ List those issues which the media and the press do unbribed which might be a cause for concern for Wolfe and ourselves.
➤ Why is it the case that communication professionals such as journalists have such bad reputations? Is this deserved?

▼ ENDS (AND BEGINNINGS)

Communication Studies is a multifaceted discipline, concerned with the study of the production, transmission and consumption of meanings via diverse media (oral, print, broadcast, film, computer networks) in an array of contexts (interpersonal, racial, cultural, political, organisational, international). Communication is thus an interdisciplinary field that embraces a variety of approaches and methodologies from both the social sciences and the humanities. The field has historical roots in several disciplines (notably journalism, speech and drama, rhetoric and composition, psychology and sociology).

(Hoyes and Castonguay)

In my end is my beginning.

(Eliot 1936: 196)

So it's been a long journey from beginning by approaching theory to ending by reciting poetry, from beginnings to ends, from certainties to circumspections. What you are now reading is a lead-out rather than a lead-in, a showing of the door to an audience. In current publishing jargon this is an 'outro'. In some ways the word could be taken to succinctly represent the discipline of Communication Studies: simultaneously irrepressibly newfangled and old-fashioned. The 'outro' was, for example well-known to theatre audiences of the late sixteenth and early seventeenth century, where it was usually called an epilogue, or more impressively *epilogus*. This is where the writer would have a moment to review the themes and lessons of the play by having one of the actors come forward and deliver a few lines of comment. In so doing the actor would either practically or symbolically disrobe, in other words come out of character and return to the world of the audience just as the audience are returned to that world. Conventionally these plays also had an 'Induction' in which the audience were prepared for the play. For this book there is less of a need for costumes to be removed to show you that this was indeed a play. With every extract we've offered you we've given it an intro to take you into the world of the extract and then we've given you an outro where we've asked you to do some more things, to take you out of the world of the extract and back into the street, to your world of studies outside the text you've been immersed in.

In John Marston's play *The Malcontent* the *epilogus* is probably delivered by the actor playing Duke Altofronto who, having recovered his dukedom, makes a short speech of acceptance which ends with him reminding the audience that it is a play they're watching:

ALTOFRONTO: The rest of idle actors, idly part.
And as for me I here assume my right,
To which I hope all's pleased: to all, goodnight.

With the play properly over all that is left is for the moral or warning to be delivered. Intrigued, the audience waits for this. The first lines of this *epilogus* would work equally well in this book today:

Your modest silence, full of heedy stillness,
Makes me thus speak:

In other words you're reading this 'outro' in case there's a way to pull this unruly collection of texts into order. So we ought to say something. Marston's final lines would do, but they are a trifle archaic:

Receive this piece, which hope nor fear yet daunteth;
He that knows most, knows most how much he wanteth.

Marston is saying take this play that was not put off by either hope or fear (optimism or pessimism) and you will learn how the wise are those who know what they want (where want is cleverly capable of meaning both desire and yet also lack). We hope this book has taught a similar lesson, not least by the range of texts offered and the fact that we always seem to find ourselves coming back to the same issues.

For some writers (such as TS Eliot) this is a main feature of journeys. Novelist Ursula K LeGuin has suggested that 'All journeys are returns'. Certainly that was the case when the sixteen-year run of the classic British situation comedy *Only Fools and Horses* came to an end (and, despite the death of one of its three leading actors this end was only temporary as Christmas 2002 witnessed the final final episode). The writer John Sullivan chose for the last episode (the third part of a final three-part sequence) to not only conclude the long-running narrative in which Del and Rodney finally do become millionaires but also to bring the audience to a broader understanding of what was in fact finishing. He did this among other means by decisively returning that key 1980s and 1990s television icon Nelson Mandela House to its 'real' position as a set in a BBC compound, even allowing Del, Rodney and Uncle Albert to walk decisively out through gates decorated with the BBC logo into a cartoon sunset strongly reminiscent of the yellow brick road in *The Wizard of Oz*. (The house of Communication Studies is full of halls which echo with images seen, half-seen, half-remembered, and seen again, albeit in new situations.) This was an outro. And it was a truly self-reflexive, twenty-first-century, postmodern outro which reminded viewers that all along they had simply been watching a television programme. And it was doubly clever, achieving the impossible trick of eating your cake and having it, by simultaneously debunking the sentimentality of the ending of a long-running series whilst evoking a sentimental sense of loss in viewers at this very ending.

Just as we gave the game away with the narratives of *American Psycho* and *Running Wild* so we have already told you that Sullivan could not ultimately resist the pressure to resurrect the show. And so he undermined the impact of his original closure. On the other hand we are content that these our words will at least bring you far enough away from the texts to see them for what they are or perhaps for whatever you want them to be. This is strangely consistent for our journey has returned to the ultimate motivation of our first text. You may remember that Peter Barry asked 'for something we can use, not something that will use us' (2002: 8) and in doing so set an agenda for the book that was partly about how to look and was partly about realising that every text, every theorist, every theory would be setting their own agenda.

Maybe the multifaceted character of the discipline is something we should pick up at the turnstiles as we enter. In a classic study of Communication Studies itself (*Communication Theory: Epistemological Foundations*) first published in 1996 James Anderson surveyed seven communication theory textbooks and found 249 distinct theories of communication. Even more amazing than the number of theories identified was the fact that only 22 per cent of theories appeared in more than one book and only 7 per cent appeared in more than three books. So it is not surprising that our rattle bag should contain so many unruly voices, all clamouring for attention, all vying with each other to proclaim the veracity of their position.

What *our* words generally provide are various kinds of anchorage: in the introductions, in the contextualisations, and in the activities. What each individual author or text then contributes are infinite ways of understanding the whole, of understanding what communication might be in a particular set of circumstances. At the very least this endeavour is properly multidisciplinary and each discipline offers its particular take on the character and functions of communication. And these are just a starting point – just the first one hundred; there are many more voices to include.

And just to prove that John Sullivan isn't the only one to eat his cake and have it here we are adding to our hot 100.

Clifford Geertz has argued that 'man is an animal suspended in webs of significance he himself has spun'. If this is so then what you have here are a hundred such webs with room for a good many more.

Marshall McLuhan claimed that 'if we should wish to recover the older world we can do it only by an intensive study of the ways in which the media have swallowed it'. If you fancy a little 'intellectual and cultural archaeology' then that is here too.

Or as Robert De Niro says at the end of *Casino,* a film whose soundtrack fair clamours with voices and voice overs: 'And why mess up a good thing? And that's that'.

WHAT'S NEXT?

➤ Read 'The Formation of a Field', Chapter 1 of John Comer *Studying Media: Problems of Theory and Method* (1998) Edinburgh: Edinburgh University Press.

▼ GLOSSARY

absent presence where something is missing, is absent, but where that very absence is noticeable, is remarkable. In classic Western films women are frequently an absent presence. In television, representations of multi-ethnic London (*Eastenders*) and Salford (*Coronation Street*), black and Asian people are frequently an absent presence (Barthes)

bodily contact one of the key forms of non verbal communication identified in *Bodily Communication* bodily contact can tell us a lot about age, ethnicity, gender, or social status (Argyle)

body posture the way we hold our bodies, the way we address other people through the medium of our bodies (Argyle)

causal (relationships) where there is a clear and unambiguous relationship between one object's action and another object's reaction this is termed a causal relationship; the one thing has happened because the other thing happened; in the study of communication people often assume that relationships are causal when they are anything but

connotation the meanings in a text that are revealed through the receiver's own cultural experience

deconstruction the process of taking apart a text in order to analyse its parts

denotation the specific, direct or obvious meaning of a sign rather than its associated meanings; where there is societal consensus about the meaning of a sign

Dionysian literally derived from the Greek god Dionysos who was feted with orgiastic festivals of wine and food; in contemporary times taken to mean a celebration of the flesh (the opposite of Apollonian (after the Greek god Apollo), taken to mean a celebration of the cerebral)

discourse a particular type of language associated with communication within and between groups with common interests, e.g. the discourse of medicine

discourse analysis a branch of linguistics that concerns itself with the analysis of the ways in which people speak; as much about the how as the what of communication

ego the conscious self which attempts to reconcile the actions and influence of the id and the super-ego in order to maximise pleasure and minimise pain (Freud)

Eros after the Greek god of love; in Freud's use of mythological ideas as metaphors for human instincts Eros stood for positive sexual instinct, the pleasure principle; the opposite of Thanatos (Freud)

ethnography literally derived from the words for people and drawing ethnography is the study of audiences in relation to texts; it tries to draw or describe how audiences use texts

ethnomethodology the body of research methods that examine how everyday life is constructed; typical ethnomethodological techniques include detailed observation: looking, listening, transcribing every feature of everyday human behaviour however seemingly trivial

eulogy a speech or piece of writing produced in praise of somebody

Evolutionary Psychology a branch of psychology which seeks to study how evolution caused the emergence of our brains; it stands in stark contrast to more humanistic or cultural forms of explanation of why people do the things they do (Pinker)

feedback the response received by the sender of a message

gestures a form of non verbal communication in Argyle's taxonomy; he divides gestures into emblems (movements which easily translate into speech), illustrators (gestures which support or reinforce speech) and self-touching (gestures which provide information about, for example, the emotional state of the speaker when speaking) (Argyle)

hyperbole an exaggerated rhetorical device, a bizarre or extravagant image

icon a sign that works by its similarity to the object it stands for (Peirce)

id represents instincts and innate needs (Freud)

ideology literally a system of ideas but within the social sciences more commonly taken to mean the underpinning ideas within a society, those ideas which often pose as commonsensical or obvious or natural

index a sign that works by reminding us of the existence of something else; for example, smoke is an index of fire (Peirce)

interaction a reciprocal action and communication between two individuals

irony a rhetorical strategy in which meaning is conveyed by using those words opposite in meaning to the intended communication

jargon vocabulary specific to a particular group

kinesics the study of the way meanings are generated by bodily movement (Argyle)

langue the shared system which all users of a language share (de Saussure, Barthes)

Laswell Formula devised by sociologist Harold Laswell a structured way of identifying the elements present in any communication for the purposes of analysis; it is often presented in the form of five key questions: who? says what? through which channel? to whom? with what effect?

lexicography a writing system

linguistics the scientific study of language

Marxism derived from the writings of Karl Marx; Marxist analyses are founded on a conflict model of social structuring: the class whose interests are best served by social, economic and political structure are the smallest; the class whose interests are worst served by social structure are the largest; the dominant minority class succeeds in covering up this inequality by dressing up appeals to their interest in the language of commonsense or by appeals to a nonmaterial being who cannot be contradicted (for example, 'as Jesus said, the poor are always with us')

metalinguistic function the function of actually identifying the communication code being used (Jakobson)

metaphor a figure of speech in which something is described in terms of something which it resembles

metonymy a rhetorical device where one thing is transported in to stand for another related thing, for example, people refer to 'the bottle' when they mean 'drink', they refer to 'the crown' when they mean 'the institution of monarchy'

netiquette conventions to be observed when using email; derived from a contraction of 'network' and 'etiquette'

neurosis a state of mental confusion characterised by unconscious conflict

Oedipus Complex the urge of men to want to sexually possess their mothers; while ever this urge is unresolved or unrecognised mental equilibrium is impossible (Freud)

orientation the way in which people orient their whole bodies to others (Argyle)

oxymoron a figure of speech in which two contradictory items are combined; sometimes this is an unconscious production of confusing communication, at other times it is a deliberate attempt to wrap up a difficult idea in a stylish phrase

paradigm a collection of signs from which a choice can be made

paralanguage communication that is in the form of utterances other than the words themselves that run alongside articulated speech which can support, emphasize, reinforce, or contradict the words themselves, e.g. volume, pitch, stress

parole the everyday use of language as opposed to the system of language and the conventions that govern it (de Saussure, Barthes)

participant observation a form of social research in which the observer does not stand apart from the objects of their study but rather inserts themselves into the context being researched and becomes a participant; in this way the analysis of the researcher's own behaviour yields useful data about the object of study which would not be available were the researcher to adopt an objective, distanced or remote position

patriarchy social organisations in which men occupy the key positions of power

persona an adopted form of identity

personification literally to give personality to something which isn't a person

phatic communication aspects of language that serve to reinforce social relationships rather than communicate information, e.g. saying 'Have a nice day' when meeting someone

pleasure principle what the ego tries to achieve (Freud)

polysemy the capacity of a text to have more than one meaning or to be open to a range of different readings; some commentators argue that all texts are essentially polysemic

poststructuralism builds on and out of critique of structuralist thinkers (Althusser, Bourdieu, Jakobson, and Lévi-Strauss, for example); poststructuralist thinkers such as Deleuze, Derrida, and Foucault) focus on issues such as difference, subjectivity, culture, and otherness

presupposition where something is assumed, is taken for granted

process (school of communication) a school of thought in which communication is conceived of as a process through which information is transmitted

proposition literally the act of proposing; more commonly taken to mean a statement, a judgement, or premise

proximity (physical proximity) the form of non verbal behaviour which derives meaning from the degrees of closeness people achieve with each other; as with other forms of non verbal behav-

iour this is often assumed to vary according to age, ethnicity, or gender; some commentators believe that proximity can be precisely charted such that certain ratios around people take on the status of particularly signifying zones (Argyle)

psychoanalysis first described by Freud as physical analysis psychoanalysis is the process whereby psychoanalysts concentrate on what patients say, or fail to say, whilst free associating without constraint (Freud)

representation the act of presenting the world again

role a part we play

Romance language the name used to group together those languages which developed out of popular Latin – French, Italian, Portuguese, Provençal, and Spanish

sarcasm a contemptuous or scornful form of humour

script describes the way in which people structure time in the long term; a life plan (Berne)

self-esteem what we think of ourselves

self-image how we see ourselves

semantics the study of the relationships between signs and meanings

semiotics / semiology the study of signs and how they communicate; a school of thought which conceives of communication as the generation and sharing of meaning (de Saussure, Peirce)

sexism the placing of unnecessary importance on sex – or gender – as a determinant of social interaction

sign the smallest unit of communication; anything which stands for or represents an object, idea or mental concept

signification the process of signifying; signs going about their business

signified one of the two components of the sign (in Saussure) – the mental concept of the sign

signifier one of two components of the sign (in Saussure) – the physical aspect of the sign, whether written or spoken

simile a form of metaphor where one item is explicitly linked to another to evoke an image in the mind of the receiver, frequently using words such as 'like' or 'as' for example, My love is like a red red rose

soap opera initially named after the daytime American serials which were sponsored by soap powder manufacturers the term is now used to more generally describe any continuing television melodrama

social identity the form of ourselves which we project in social contexts

socialisation the process whereby people are inducted into the club of society, through which constructs such as morals, civilised behaviour, normal behaviour are instilled in people

staging in the performative conception of social interaction this describes the way in which people manipulate their physical environment to achieve particular goals; extending the metaphor of the theatrical stage notions such as front stage and backstage are used to describe those areas in which people, respectively, behave in a more restrained and controlled manner and in a less guarded fashion (Goffman)

stroke the acknowledging of another person's presence by, for example, saying hello to them when you meet them; to say hello to a person is to provide a positive stroke, to ignore that person is to give a negative stroke (Berne)

structuralism structuralist thinkers such as Althusser, Bourdieu, Jakobson, and Lévi-Strauss built on the work of de Saussure to focus on the material analysis of relations between, for example, culture and society, always motivated by the idea that structures are differential and relational

superego manifests itself in guilt, shame or conscience; it prolongs the influence of parents and significant others (Freud)

symbol a sign which works by virtue of an arbitrary relationship between sign and object; it only works when users agree to associate the same meanings to the same sign (Peirce)

symbolic interactionism system of ideas most closely associated with Herbert Blumer; symbolic interactionism proposes that meanings are generated as a result of interactions between people and are always subject to revision and amendment as those interactions continue

synecdoche a rhetorical device where a part stands for the whole, for example, 'Behold I see a fleet of sail' where the sail (a part) stands in for the ship (the whole)

text any form of communication which can be read or interpreted

Thanatos taken directly from *thanatos*, the Greek word for death, this is taken, in Freud's mythology, to mean the unconscious but active pursuit of death; the opposite of Eros (Freud)

transaction a two person interaction (Berne)

Transactional Analysis theory in which interpersonal communication can be studied in relation to different ego states adopted by people (Berne)

▼ REFERENCES

ARTICLES AND CHAPTERS IN BOOKS

Abercrombie, K (1968) 'Paralanguage', in *British Journal of Diseases of Communication*, 3: 55–9.

Adler, PA and Adler, P (1984) 'Observational techniques', in NK Denzin and YS Lincoln (eds), *Handbook of Qualitative Research*, Thousand Oaks, Calif.: Sage.

Adorno, T and Horkheimer, M (1972) 'The culture industry: enlightenment as mass deception', in *Dialectic of Enlightenment*, New York: The Seabury Press.

Ang, I (1989) 'Wanted audiences. On the politics of empirical research', in E Seiter, H Borchers, G Kreutzner and E Worth (eds) *Remote Control: Television, Audiences and Cultural Power*, London: Routledge.

Ang, I and Hermes, J (1991) 'Gender and/in media consumption', in James Curan and Michael Gurevitch (eds) *Mass Media and Society*, London: Edward Arnold.

Argyle, M, Salter, V, Nicholson, H, Williams, M, and Burgess, P (1970) 'The communication of inferior and superior attitudes by verbal and nonverbal signals', *British Journal of Social and Clinical Psychology*, 9: 222–31.

Atkinson, P and Coffey, A (1995) 'Realism and its discontents: on the crisis of cultural representation in ethnographic texts', in B Adam and S Allan (eds) *Theorizing Culture: An Interdisciplinary Critique after Postmodernism*, London: UCL Press.

Barley, S (1983) 'Semiotics and the Study of Occupational and Organisational Cultures', *Administrative Science Quarterly*, Issue No. 28, 393–413.

Barthes, R (1973) 'Myth today' in *Mythologies*, London: Paladin.

Bazerman, C (1993) 'A contention over rhetoric', in T Enos and SC Brown (eds) *Defining the New Rhetorics*, London: Sage.

Bragg, M (2000) 'They want us to choose between the Beatles and Beethoven. Why can't we have both?', *Guardian*, 12 September.

Buck, RW, Savin, VJ, Miller, RE and Caul, WF (1972) 'Communication of affect through facial expressions in humans', *Journal of Personality and Social Psychology*, 23: 362–71.

Buck, RW, Miller, RE and Caul, WF (1974) 'Sex, personality and physiological variables in the communication of affect via facial expression', in *Journal of Personality and Social Psychology*, 30: 587–96.

Burroughs, WS (1979) 'The Book of Breeething', in William S Burroughs *Ah Pook Is Here and Other Texts*, London: John Calder.

Burchill, J (2001) 'All the Pretty Songs', *Guardian*, 22 September.

Cheung, C. (2000) 'A home on the web: presentations of self on personal homepages' in *Web Studies*, London: Arnold.

Clifford, J (1983) 'On ethnographic authority', *Representations*, 1: 118–46.

Cohen, D (1994) 'Classical rhetoric and modern theories of discourse', in I Worthington (ed) *Persusasion: Greek Rhetoric in Action*, London: Routledge.

Conklin, HC (1955) 'Haunoo Color Categories', *Southwestern Journal of Anthropology*, 11: 339–44.

Denzin, NK (1994) 'Evaluating qualitative research in the poststructural moment: the lessons James Joyce teaches us', *International Journal of Qualitative Studies in Education*, 7: 295–308.

Dervin, B (1987) 'The potential contribution of feminist scholarship to the field of communication', *Journal of Communication*, 37: 107–20.

Donald, J (1997) 'This, here, now: imagining the modern city', in Sarah Westwood and John Williams (eds) *Imagining Cities: Scripts, Signs, Meanings*, London: Routledge.

Ekman, P (1978) 'Facial expression', in AW Siegman and S Feldstein (eds) *Nonverbal Behaviour and Communication*, Hillsdale, Mich.: Lawrence Erlbaum.

Ekman, P and Friesen, W (1969) 'Nonverbal leakage and cues to deception', *Psychiatry*, 32: 88–106.

L'Etang, J (1996) 'Public relations and rhetoric', in J L'Etang and M Pieczka (eds) *Critical Perspectives in Public Relations*, London: Thomson Business Press.

Falbo, T (1977) 'The multi-dimensional scaling of power strategies', *Journal of Personality and Social Psychology*, 35: 537–48.

Fickling, D. (2001) 'Lizard man', *Metro*, 15 May.

Foster, P (1996) 'Observational research', in R Sapsford and V Jupp (eds) *Data Collection and Analysis*, London: Sage.

Frake (1961) 'The diagnosis of disease among the Subanum of Mindanao', *American Anthropologist*, 63: 113–32.

Gee, JP, Michaels, S and O'Connor, MC (1992) 'Discourse analysis', in MD LeCompte, WL Millroy and J Preissle (eds) *The Handbook of Qualitative Research in Education*, San Diego, Calif.: Academic Press.

Goodenough, WH (1956) 'Componential analysis and the study of meaning', *Language*, 32: 195–216.

Green, M (1997) 'Working practices', in Jim McGuigan (ed.) *Cultural Methodologies*, London: Sage.

Gregg, N (1987) 'Reflections on the feminist critique of objectivity', *Journal of Communication Inquiry*, 11 (1): 8–18.

Gross, E (1992) 'What is Feminist Theory?' in Helen Crowley and Susan Himmelweit (eds) *Knowing Women: Feminism and Knowledge*, Milton Keynes: The Open University.

Hackett, H (2002) 'Response to AQA "A" level Communication Studies question paper CMS 2', Stourbridge: Assessment and Qualifications Alliance.

Halloran, SM (1993) 'Further thoughts on the death of rhetoric', in T Enos and SC Brown (eds) *Defining the New Rhetorics*, London: Sage.

Hartley, P (1994) 'Rhetoric' and 'Structuralism', in T O'Sullivan, D Saunders, M Montgomery and J Fiske *Key Concepts in Communication and Cultural Studies*, New York: Routledge.

Heath, C and Luff, P (1996) 'Explicating face-to-face interaction', in N Gilbert (ed.) *Researching Social Life*, London: Sage.

Hoyes, J and Castonguay, J (2001) 'Communication Studies', in Victor E Taylor and Charles E Winquist (eds) *Encyclopedia of Postmodernism*, London: Routledge.

Johnson, FC and Klare, GR (1961) 'General models of communication research: a survey of a decade', *Journal of Communication*, 11: 13–26.

Jones, M (2001) 'The lost art of coining a phrase', *Evening Standard*, Friday 15 June.

—— (2003) 'The music industry as workplace', in Andrew Beck (ed.) *Cultural Work*, London: Routledge.

Jupp, V (1996) 'Documents and research', in R Sapsford and V Jupp (eds) *Data Collection and Analysis*, London: Sage.

Kellaway, K (2001) 'Deadlier than the snailmail', *Observer*, 8 April.

Kendon, A (1972) 'Some relationships between body motion and speech: an analysis of an example', in A Siegman and B Pope (eds) *Studies in Dyadic Communication*, Elmsford: Pergamon.

Kermode, M (2002) 'When Woody met Ingmar', *Independent Review*, 27 December, 12.

Lincoln, YS and Denzin, NK (1994) 'The fifth moment', in NK Denzin and YS Lincoln (eds) *Handbook of Qualitative Research*, Thousand Oaks, Calif.: Sage.

Lodge, D (1986) 'Shakin' Steven Superstar', in David Lodge *Write On*, London: Martin Secker & Warburg.

Lounsbury, FC (1956) 'A semantic analysis of Pawnee kinship usage', *Language*, 32: 158–94.

—— (1969) 'The structural analysis of kinship semantics', in S Tyler (ed.) *Cognitive Anthropology*, New York: Holt Rinehart & Winston.

McRobbie, A (1978) 'Jackie: an ideology of adolescent femininity', University of Birmingham Centre for Contemporary Cultural Studies stenciled paper.

Macdonald, K and Tipton, C (1996) 'Using documents', in N Gilbert (ed.) *Researching Social Life*, London: Sage.

Manning, PK (1995) 'The challenge of postmodernism', in J Van Maanen (ed.) *Representation in Ethnography*, Thousand Oaks, Calif.: Sage.

Manning, PK and Callum-Swan, B (1994) 'Narrative, content, and semiotic analysis', in NK Denzin and YS Lincoln (eds) *Handbook of Quantitative Research*, Thousand Oaks, Calif.: Sage.

Marshal, B, Dean, C and Fialka, G (1991) 'Statistical density', in *T'Mershi Duween*, 18 April.

Mies, M (1978) 'Women's research or feminist research? The debate surrounding feminist science and methodology', in MM Fonow and JA Cook (eds) *Beyond Methodology: Feminist Scholarship as Lived Experience*, Bloomington, Ind.: Indiana University Press.

Modleski, T (1991) 'Cinema and the dark continent: race and gender in popular film', in Linda S Kauffman (ed.) *American Feminist Thought at Century's End: A Reader*, Oxford: Blackwell.

Morley, D (1980) 'Texts, readers, subjects', in Hall, S, Hobson, D, Lowe, A, and Willis, P (eds) *Culture, Media, Language*, London: Routledge.

Morley, D and Silverstone, R (1991) 'Domestic communications: technologies and meanings', *Media, Culture and Society*, 12 (1): 31–55.

Morrison, T (1989) 'Unspeakable things unspoken: the African-American presence in American literature', *Michigan Quarterly Review*, 27, 1, 1–34.

Nava, M (2002) 'Consumption's potent political purchase', *Times Higher Education Supplement*, 20/27 December, 21.

Philips, S (2002) 'Critical eye over facts in the field', *Times Higher Education Supplement*, MLA Convention supplement, 20/27 December, 4.

Potter, J and Wetherell, M (1994) 'Analysing discourse', in A Bryman and RG Burgess (eds) *Analysing Qualitative Data*, London: Routledge.

Radway J (1989) 'Ethnography among elites; comparing discourses of power', *Journal of Communication Inquiry*, 13(2), 3–12.

Richardson, L (1994) 'Writing: a method of inquiry', in NK Denzin and YS Lincoln (eds) *Handbook of Qualitative Research*, Thousand Oaks, Calif.: Sage.

Sapsford, R and Abbott, P (1996) 'Ethics, politics and research', in R Sapsford and V Jupp (eds) *Data Collection and Analysis*, London: Sage.

Shannon, CE and Weaver, W (1948) 'The mathematical theory of communication', *Bell System Technical Journal*, 27: 379–623.

Sifton, S (2001) 'Speak fluent yettie', *Independent Magazine*, 3 November.

Sim, S (1999) 'Orientalism' in Stuart Sim (ed.) *The Routledge Critical Dictionary of Postmodern Thought*, London: Routledge.

Spindler, G and Spindler, L (1972) 'Cultural process and ethnography: an anthropological perspective', in MD LeCompte, WL Millroy and J Preissle (eds) *The Handbook of Qualitative Research in Education*, San Diego, Calif.: Academic Press.

Tannenbaum, R and Schmidt, WH (1973) 'How to choose a leadership pattern: should a manager be democratic or autocratic – or something in between!', *Harvard Business Review*, May/June: 162–8.

Tasker, Y (2003) 'Office politics: masculinity, feminism and the workplace in *Disclosure*', in Andrew Beck (ed.) *Cultural Work*, London: Routledge.

Taylor, DJ (2002) 'It's only Mick and Keef but we like them', *Independent on Sunday*, 8 September.

Tooby, J and Cosmides, L (1992) 'The Psychological Foundations of Culture', in JH Barkow, L Cosmides and J Tooby (eds), *The Adapted Mind: Evolutionary Psychology and the Generation of Culture,* Oxford: Oxford University Press.

Tuchman, G (1978) 'Introduction: the symbolic annihilation of women', in G Tuchman, A Daniels and J Benet (eds) *Hearth and Home: Images of Women in the Mass Media*, New York: Oxford University Press.

—— (1991) 'Qualitative methods in the study of news', in KB Jensen and N Jankowski (eds) *A Handbook of Qualitative Methods for Mass Communication Research*, London: Routledge.

Williams, R. (1989) 'Drama in a dramatised society', in Alan O'Conor (ed.) *On Television*, London: Routledge.

Winship, J (1987) 'Handling Sex', in Rosemary Betterton (ed.) *Looking On: Images of Femininity in the Visual Arts and Media*, London: Pandora.

Wolcott, HF (1988) 'Ethnographic research in education', in RM Jaegar (ed.) *Complementary Methods for Research in Education*, Washington DC: American Educational Research Association.

Wooffitt, R (1996) 'Analysing accounts', in N Gilbert (ed.) *Researching Social Life*, London: Sage.

Zaat, M (1982) 'De door Lilian Rubin gerolgde methode van onderzoek' [Lilian Rubin's method], *Tijdschrift voor Vrouwenstudies*, 3(1), 74–91

Zuckerman, M, Larrance, DT, Hall, JA, De Frank, RS and Rosenthal, R (1979) 'Posed and spontaneous communication of emotion via facial and vocal cues', *Journal of Personality*, 47: 712–33.

BOOKS

Adorno, T (1991) *The Culture Industry: Selected Essays on Mass Culture*, London: Routledge.

Althusser, L (1971) *Lenin and Philosophy and Other Essays*, London: New Left Books.

Anderson, J (1996) *Communication Theory: Epistemological Foundations*, London: Guilford Books.

Ang, I (1985) *Watching Dallas*, London: Methuen.

—— (1991) *Desperately Seeking the Audience*, London: Routledge.

—— (1996) *Living Room Wars: Rethinking Media Audiences for a Postmodern World*, London: Routledge.

Argyle, M (1972) *The Psychology of Interpersonal Behaviour*, Harmondsworth: Penguin.

—— (1987) *Bodily Communication*, London: Methuen.

Arnold, M (1869) *Culture and Anarchy*, London: John Murray.

Auslander, P (1999) *Liveness: Performance in a Mediatized Culture*, London: Routledge.

Auster, P (1987) *New York Trilogy*, Harmondsworth: Penguin.

Austin, JL (1962) *How to do Things with Words*, Oxford: Oxford University Press.

Ballard, JG (1995) *Crash*, London: Flamingo.

—— (1997) *Running Wild*, London: Flamingo.

Barry, P (2002) *Beginning Theory*, Manchester: Manchester University Press.

Barthes, R (1967) *Elements of Semiology*, London: Cape.

—— (1973) *Mythologies*, London: Paladin.

Baudrillard, J (1983) *Simulations*, Los Angeles, Calif.: Semiotext(e).

Bauman, Z (1988) *Freedom*, Milton Keynes: Open University Press.

Beck, A, Bennett, P, and Wall, P (2002) *Communication Studies: The Essential Introduction*, London: Routledge.

Beckett, S (1965) *Waiting for Godot*, London: Faber.

Bennett, O (2001) *Cultural Pessimism*, Edinburgh: Edinburgh University Press.

Berelson, B (1952) *Content Analysis in Communication Research*, New York: Hafner.

Berger, J (1972) *Ways of Seeing*, London: BBC/Penguin.

Berne, E (1996) *Games People Play: The Psychology of Human Relationships*, New York: Ballantine.

Bernstein, B (1971) *Class, Codes and Control*, London: Routledge.

Birdwhistell, RL (1970) *Kinesics and Context: Essays in Body-motion Communication*, Harmondsworth: Penguin.

Bloom, H (1995) *The Western Canon*, London: Macmillan.

Blumer, H (1969) *Symbolic Interactionism: Perspective and Method*, Englewood Cliffs, NJ: Prentice-Hall.

Bourdieu, P and Passerson, J-C (1977) *Reproduction in Education, Society and Culture*, Beverly Hills, Calif.: Sage.

Brandon, N (1995) *The Six Pillars of Self Esteem*, New York: Bantam Doubleday Dell.

British Psychological Society (2000) *Code of Conduct, Ethical Principles & Guidelines*, Leicester: BPS.

Bryman, A (1995) *Disney and his Worlds*, London: Routledge.

—— (2001) *Social Research Methods*, Oxford: Oxford University Press.

Burchill, J (1986) *Girls on Film*, New York: Pantheon.

Cantor, DW, Bernay, T and Feinstein D (1992) *Women In Power: The Secrets of Leadership*, Boston, Mass.: Houghton–Mifflin.

Cantor, MG and Cantor, JM (1992) *Prime-Time Television Content and Control*, London: Sage.

Carnegie, D (1936) *How to Win Friends and Influence People*, Kingswood: World's Work Ltd.

Carnegie, D and Carnegie, D (1962) *The Quick and Easy Way to Effective Speaking,* Garden City, NJ: Dale Carnegie & Associates, Inc.

Carter, R, Goddard, A, Reah, D, Sanger, K, and Bowring, M (2001) *Working With Texts*, second edition, London: Routledge.

Cashmore, E (2002) *Beckham*, London: Polity.

de Certeau, M (1984) *The Practice of Everyday Life*, Berkeley, Calif.: University of California Press.

Chambers, I (1986) *Popular Culture: The Metropolitan Experience*, London: Routledge.

Cherry, C (1996) *On Human Communication*, Cambridge, Mass.: MIT Press.

Chinweizu, Jemie, O and Madubuike, I (1983) *The Decolonization of African Literature*, Washington, DC: Howard University Press.

Cobley, P (ed.) (1996) *The Communication Theory Reader*, London: Routledge.

Cohen, AP (1992) *The Symbolic Construction of Community*, London: Routledge.

Cole, G (1984) *Management: Theory and Practice*, Eastleigh: DP Publications.

Comer, J (1998) *Studying Media: Problems of Theory and Method*, Edinburgh: Edinburgh University Press.

Conrad, J (1994) *Heart of Darkness*, Harmondsworth: Penguin.

Coopersmith, S (1967) *The Antecedents of Self Esteem*, Los Angeles, Calif.: Freeman & Co.

Cope, W (ed.) (1998) *The Funny Side*, London: Faber.

Coulthard, M (1985) *An Introduction to Discourse Analysis*, London: Longman.

Coupland, D (1996) *Microserfs*, London: Regan Books.

Crouse, T (1972) *The Boys on the Bus*, New York: Ballatine.

Crystal, D (2002) *The English Language*, Harmondsworth: Penguin.

Darwin, C (1872) *The Expression of Emotion in Man and Animal*, New York: GP Putnam & Sons.

Davis, M (1990) *City of Quartz: Excavating the Future in Los Angeles*, London: Verso.

de Botton, A (1997) *How Proust Can Change Your Life*, London: Picador.

Defoe, D (1726) *Mere Nature Delineated*, reprinted in Andrew Wear (ed.) (2002) *Writings on Travel, Discovery and History by Daniel Defoe*, London: Pickering & Chatto.

Denzin, NK (1989) *The Research Act: A Theoretical Introduction to Sociological Methods*, New York: McGraw-Hill.

Deutsch, K (1966) *The Nerves of Government*, New York: Free Press.

Dickens, C (1971) *Our Mutual Friend*, Harmondsworth: Penguin.

Dimbleby, R and Burton, G (1988) *Between Ourselves*, London: Arnold.

Dore, R (1978) *Shinohata: A Portrait of a Japanese Village*, New York: Pantheon Books.

Eaglestone, R (2000) *Doing English*, London: Routledge.

Eagleton, T (1983) *Literary Theory: An Introduction*, Oxford: Basil Blackwell.

Easton Ellis, B (1991) *American Psycho*, New York: Vintage Books.

Eco, U (1976) *A Theory of Semiotics*, Bloomington, Ind.: Indiana University Press.

—— (1981) *The Role of the Reader: Explorations in the Semiotics of Texts*, London: Hutchinson.

Ekman, P, Friesen, W and Ellsworth, PC (1972) *Emotion in the Human Face: Guidelines for Research and an Integration of Findings*, New York: Pergamon Press.

Eliot, TS (1936) *Collected Poems 1909–1962*, London: Faber.

—— (1975) *Selected Prose*, London: Faber.

Ellis, A and Beattie, G (1993) *The Psychology of Language and Communication*, Hillsdale, Mich.: Lawrence Erlbaum Associates.

Enos, T and Brown, SC (eds) (1993) *Defining the New Rhetorics*, London: Sage.

Esher, L (1983) *A Broken Wave: The Rebuilding of England 1940–1980*, Harmondsworth: Penguin.

L'Etang, J and Pieczka, M (eds) (1996) *Critical Perspectives in Public Relations*, London: Thomson Business Press.

Faludi, S (1992) *Backlash*, New York: Vintage.

Farren, M (1973) *The Texts of the Festival*, London: Mayflower Books.

Feldman, M (1995) *Strategies for Interpreting Qualitative Data*, Thousand Oaks, Calif.: Sage.

Fischer, E (1970) *Marx In His Own Words*, Harmondsworth: Penguin.

Fiske, J (1982) *Introduction to Communication Studies*, London: Routledge.

—— (1989) *Reading the Popular*, London: Routledge.

Forster, EM (1979) *A Passage to India*, Harmondsworth: Penguin.

Foster, PC (1996) *Observing Schools: A Methodological Guide*, London: Paul Chapman.

Freud, S (1974) *The Psychopathology of Everyday Life*, Harmondsworth: Penguin.

Garfinkle, H (1967) *Studies in Ethnomethodology*, Englewood Cliffs, NJ: Prentice-Hall.

Geertz, C (1973) *The Interpretation of Cultures*, New York: Basic Books.

Gilbert, GN and Mulkay, MJ (1984) *Opening Pandora's Box: A Sociological Analysis of Scientists' Discourse*, Cambridge: Cambridge University Press.

Gilgan, C et al. (1988) *Mapping the Moral Domain*, Cambridge, Mass.: Harvard University Press.

Gitlin, T (1980) *The Whole World's Watching*, Berkeley, Calif.: University of California Press.

Glaser, BG and Strauss, AL (1967) *The Discovery of Grounded Theory: Strategies for Qualitative Research*, Chicago, Ill.: Aldine.

Goffman, E (1959) *The Presentation of Self in Everyday Life*, Harmondsworth: Penguin.

—— (1963) *Behaviour in Public Places*, New York: Free Press.

—— (1967) *Interaction Ritual*, New York: Anchor Press.

—— (1974) *Frame Analysis*, New York: Harper & Row.

—— (1979) *Gender Advertisements*, London: Macmillan.

—— (1981) *Forms of Talk*, Philadelphia, Pa.: University of Pennsylvania Press.

Gray, A (1992) *Video Playtime: The Genealogy of a Leisure Technology*, London: Routledge.

Greer, G (2003) *The Female Eunuch*, London: Flamingo.

Grogan, E (1972) *Ringolevio: A Life Played For Keeps*, London: Heinemann.

Guiraud, P (1975) *Semiotics*, London: Routledge & Kegan Paul.

Hale, J (1998) *Building Ideas: An Introduction to Architectural Theory*, Cambridge, Mass: MIT Press.

Hammersley, M and Atkinson, P (1995) *Ethnography: Principles in Practice*, London: Routledge.

Handy, C (1976) *Understanding Organizations*, Harmondsworth: Penguin.

Hartley, P (1997) *Group Communication*, London: Routledge.

—— (1999) *Interpersonal Communication*, London: Routledge.

Hartshorne, C, Weiss, P, and Burks, AW (eds) (1997) *Collected Papers of Charles Sanders Peirce*, Cambridge, Mass.: Harvard University Press.

Harvey, D (1989) *The Condition of Postmodernity: An Enquiry into the Origins of Social Change*, Cambridge: Blackwell.

Hawkes, T (1992) *Structuralism and Semiotics*, London: Routledge.

Hebdige, D (1979) *Subculture: The Meaning of Style*, London: Routledge.

Hearn, L (1894) *Glimpses of Unfamiliar Japan*, Boston, Mass.: Houghton, Mifflin.

Hemingway, E (1967) *By-Line*, Harmondsworth: Penguin.

Herder, JG (1966) *Outlines of a Philosophy of the History of Man*, New York: Bergman.

Heritage, J (1984) *Garfinkel and Ethnomethodology*, Cambridge: Polity.

Hicks, W, Adams, S and Gilbert, H (2002) *Writing For Journalists*, London: Routledge.

Hoggart, R (1958) *The Uses of Literacy*, Harmondsworth: Penguin.

Huxley, A (1994) *Brave New World*, London: Flamingo.

Jacobson, R and Halle, M (1956) *The Fundamentals of Language*, The Hague: Mouton.

Jeffords, S (1994) *Hard Bodies: Hollywood Masculinity in the Reagan Era*, Piscataway, NJ: Rutgers University Press.

Kennedy, A (1999) *The Rough Guide to the Internet*, Harmondsworth: Penguin.

Klineberg, O (1935) *Race Differences*, New York: Henry Holt.

Korzybski, A (1995) *Science and Sanity: An Introduction to Non-Aristotelian Systems and General Semantics*, New York: Institute of General Semantics.

Kress, G and van Leeuwen, T (1996) *Reading Images: The Grammar of Visual Design*, London: Routledge.

Lacan, J (1977) *Ecrits: A Selection*, London: Tavistock.

Larkin, P (2003) *Collected Poems*, London: Marvell Press and Faber.

Leach, ER (1976) *Culture and Communication*, Cambridge: Cambridge University Press.

Lechte, J (1994) *Fifty Key Contemporary Thinkers*, London: Routledge.

Leavis, FR (1987) *The Great Tradition*, Harmondsworth: Penguin.

Lee, M (1993) *Consumer Society Reborn: the Cultural Politics of Consumption*, London: Routledge.

—— (ed.) (2000) *The Consumer Society Reader*, Oxford: Blackwell.

Lévi-Strauss, C (1969) *The Raw and the Cooked (Volume 1 of Mythologies)*, Chicago, Ill.: University of Chicago Press.

Lochhead, L (1984) *Dreaming Frankenstein and Collected Poems*, Edinburgh: Polygon.

Lodge, D (1988) *Nice Work*, Harmondsworth: Penguin.

Lyotard, JF (1984) *The Postmodern Condition*, Manchester: Manchester University Press.

McCarthy, M (1991) *Discourse Analysis for Language Teachers*, Cambridge: Cambridge University Press.

McDougall, W (1927) *The Group Mind*, London: Cambridge University Press.

McLellan, D (1975) *Karl Marx*, New York: Penguin.

McGregor, D (1960) *The Human Side of Enterprise*, New York: McGraw-Hill.

McLuhan, M (1987) *Understanding Media: The Extensions of Man*, London: Routledge.

McQuail, D and Windahl, S (1993) *Communication Models for the Study of Mass Communication*, London: Longman.

McRobbie, A (1991) *Feminism and Youth Culture: From 'Jackie' to 'Just Seventeen'*, Basingstoke: Macmillan.

Marcuse, H (1986) *One Dimensional Man: Studies in the Ideology of Advanced Industrial Society*, London: Ark.

Marx, K and Engels, F (1968) *Selected Works*, London: Lawrence & Wishart.

—— (1998) *The Communist Manifesto*, ed. E Hobsbawm, London: Verso.

Masterson, J (1985) *The Real Self: A Developmental and Object Relations Approach*, New York: Brunner Mazel.

Miles, MB and Huberman, AM (1984) *Qualitative Data Analysis*, Thousand Oaks, Calif.: Sage.

Miller, D (1995) *Acknowledging Consumption: A Review of New Studies*, London: Routledge.

Modleski, T (1991) *Feminism Without Women: Culture and Criticism in a 'Postfeminist' Age*, London: Routledge.

Molière (1989) *Le Malade imaginaire*, in *Five Plays*, London: Methuen.

Moore, M (2002) *Stupid White Men*, Harmondsworth: Penguin.

Montaigne, M de (1988) *An Apology for Raymond Sebond*, Harmondsworth: Penguin.

Morgan, J and Welton, P (1992) *See What I Mean?* London: Arnold.

Morley, D (1980) *The Nationwide Audience: Structure and Decoding*, London: BFI.

Morris, D (1994) *Body Talk: A World Guide to Gestures*, London: Jonathan Cape.

Myers, GE and Myers, MT (1985) *Dynamics of Human Communication*, New York: McGraw-Hill.

Newton, M (2002) *Savage Girls and Wild Boys*, London: Faber.

Orwell, G (2000) *Essays*, Harmondsworth: Penguin.

O'Sullivan, T, Hartley, J, Saunders, D, and Fiske, J (1983) *Key Concepts in Communication Studies*, London: Routledge.

O'Sullivan, T, Hartley, J, Saunders, D, Montgomery, M, and Fiske, J (1994) *Key Concepts in Communication and Cultural Studies*, London: Routledge.

Paglia, C (1993) *Sex, Art and American Culture*, New York: Viking.

Palahniuk, C (1996) *Fight Club*, London: Vintage.

Parker, MH (1949) *Language and Reality: A Course in Contemporary Criticism*, London: Frederick Muller.

Patton, MQ (1980) *Qualitative Evaluation Methods*, Newbury Park, Calif.: Sage.

Peirce, CS (1958) *Collected Papers of Charles Sanders Peirce*, Cambridge, Mass.: Harvard University Press.

Pinker, S (1994) *The Language Instinct*, Harmondsworth: Penguin.

—— (1998) *How the Mind Works*, New York: Penguin.

Plant, Sadie (1997) *Zeroes + Ones: Digital Women + The New Technoculture*, London: Fourth Estate.

Postman, N (1995) *Technopoly: The Surrender of Culture to Technology*, New York: Vintage.

Propp, V (1958) *Morphology of the Folktale*, Austin, Tex.: University of Texas Press.

Punch, K (1998) *Introduction to Social Research*, London: Sage.

Radway, J (1984) *Reading the Romance: Women Patriarchy and Popular Literature*, Chapel Hill, NC: University of North Carolina Press.

Reinharz, S (1992) *Feminist Methods in Social Research*, New York: Oxford University Press.

Ritzer, G (1983) *The McDonaldization of Society*, London: Sage.

Rojek, C (2001) *Celebrity*, London: Reaktion.

Rosenau, PM (1992) *Post-Modernism and the Social Sciences: Insights, Inroads, and Intrusions*, Princeton, NJ: Princeton University Press.

Ryan, M and Kellner, D (1988) *Camera Politica: The Politics and Ideology of Contemporary Hollywood Film*, Bloomington, Ind.: Indiana University Press.

Said, E (1978) *Orientalism*, London: Routledge.

Sardar, Z and Davies, MW (2002) *Why do People Hate America?* Cambridge: Icon.

Saussure, F de (1966) *Course in General Linguistics*, New York: McGraw-Hill.

Shannon, CE and Weaver, W (1949) *The Mathematical Theory of Communication*, Urbana, Ill.: University of Illinois Press.

Shelley, M (1994) *Frankenstein*, Harmondsworth: Penguin.

Silverman, D (1993) *Interpreting Qualitative Data: Methods for Analysing Talk, Text and Interaction*, London: Sage.

Sim, S (ed.) (1999) *The Routledge Critical Dictionary of Postmodern Thought*, London: Routledge.

Simmel, G (1950) *The Sociology of Georg Simmel*, Glencoe, Ill.: Free Press.

—— (1997) *Simmel on Culture,* London: Sage.

Sinclair, I (2002) *London Orbital*, London: Granta.

Spender, D (1998) *Man Made Language*, London: Pandora.

Spradley, JP (1980) *Participant Observation*, New York: Holt, Reinhart and Winston.

Stanislavsky, K (1980) *An Actor Prepares*, London: Methuen.

Staniszewski, MA (1995) *Seeing Is Believing: Creating the Culture of Art*, London and New York: Penguin.

Stoller, P (1989) *The Taste of Ethnographic Things*, Philadelphia, Pa.: University of Pennsylvania Press.

Strauss, A and Corbin, J (1990) *Basics of Qualitative Research: Grounded Theory Procedures and Techniques*, Newbury Park, Calif.: Sage.

Strindberg, A (1991) *Road to Damascus*, in *Plays: Three*, translated and introduced by Michael Meyer, London: Methuen.

Tannen, D (1986) *That's Not What I Meant! How Conversational Style Makes or Breaks Relationships,* New York: Ballantine.

Tannen, D (1990) *You Just Don't Understand: Men and Women in Conversation*, London: Virago.

Taylor, P (1997) *Investigating Culture and Identity*, London: Collins.

Thompson, HS (1988) *Generation of Swine*, London: Picador.

Tocqueville, A de (2000) *Democracy in America*, Chicago, Ill.: University of Chicago Press.

Tolkien, JRR (1966) *The Lord of the Rings*, London: Allen & Unwin.

Toynbee, A (1954) *Study of History*, London: Oxford University Press.

Tylor, EB (1871) *Primitive Culture*, New York: Brentano's.

Tucker, RC (ed.) (1978) *The Marx–Engels Reader*, New York: Norton and Co.

Vale, V and Juno, A (eds) (1989) *Modern Primitives*, San Francisco, Calif.: Re/Search Publications.

van Zoonen, L (1994) *Feminist Media Studies*, London: Sage.

Visser, M (1997) *The Way We Are*, Harmondsworth: Penguin.

Webster, F (1995) *Theories of the Information Society*, London: Routledge.

Whyte, WF (1955) *Street Corner Society: The Social Structure of an Italian Slum*, Chicago, Ill.: University of Chicago Press.

Williams, R (1958) *Culture and Society 1780–1950*, London: Chatto & Windus.

—— (1966) *Communications*, Harmondsworth: Penguin.

—— (1983) *Keywords*, London: Fontana.

—— (1989) *On Television*, ed. Alan O'Conor, London: Routledge.

Williamson, J (1986) *Consuming Passions*, London: Marion Boyars.

Wittgenstein, L (1969) *Philosophical Grammar*, Oxford: Blackwell.

Wollen, P (1969) *Signs and Meaning in the Cinema*, London: Secker & Warburg/BFI.

Woodward, K (ed.) (1997) *Identity and Difference*, Milton Keynes: Open University Press.

Zappa, F (with Peter Occhiogross) (1989) *The Real Frank Zappa Book*, London: Picador.

FILMS

Altman, R (1978) *A Wedding*, TCF/Lion's Gate.

Ashby, H (1979) *Being There*, Lorimar/North Star/CIP.

Benton, R (1982) *Still of the Night*, MGM/UA.

Carpenter, J (1981) *Escape From New York*, Avco Embassy/International Film Investors/ Goldcrest.

—— (1988) *They Live!,* Guild/Alive Films.

Coppola, F (1979) *Apocalypse Now*, Omni/Zoetrope.

Cronenberg, D (2002) *Spider*, Capitol Films.

Darnell, E and Johnson, T (1998) *Antz*, PDI/Dreamworks.

Eisenstein, S (1925) *The Battleship Potemkin*, Goskino.

Ephron, N (1998) *You've Got Mail*, Warner Brothers.

Fincher, D (1999) *Fight Club*, Twentieth Century Fox.

Ford, J (1939) *Stagecoach*, UA.

Glaser, PM (1987) *The Running Man*, Rank/Braveworld.

Godard, J-L (1965) *Alphaville*, Chaumiane/Filmstudio.

Herzog, W (1974) *The Enigma of Kasper Hauser*, Contemporary/Zud Deutscher Rudfunk/Werner Herzog.

Hitchcock, A (1938) *The Lady Vanishes*, Gaumont British/Gainsborough.

—— (1945) *Spellbound*, David O Selznick.

—— (1958) *Vertigo,* Paramount.

—— (1964) *Marnie,* Universal/Geoffrey Stanley Inc.

Hopper, D (1988) *Colors*, Rank/Orion.

Keiller, P (1994) *London*, BFI/Channel 4.

McTiernan, J (1988) *Die Hard*, Fox/Gordon Company/Silver Pictures.

Mankievitch, JL (1953) *Julius Caesar*, MGM.

Newell, M (1994) *Four Weddings and a Funeral*, Rank/Polygram/Channel 4/Working Title.

Ramis, H (1999) *Analyze This,* Warner Brothers/Village Roadshow Pictures/NPV Entertainment.

Schrader, P (1980) *American Gigolo*, Paramount/Pierre Associates.

Scott, R (1982) *Blade Runner*, Warner/Ladd/Blade Runner Partnership.

Smith, K (1995) *Mallrats*, Gramercy/Alphaville/View Askew.

Smith, M (1997) *Bean: the Ultimate Disaster Movie,* Polygram.

Truffaut, F (1970) *L'Enfant Sauvage*, UA/Films de Carrosse.

Verhoeven, P (1987) *Robocop*, Rank/Orion.

—— (1990) *Total Recall*, Guild/Carolco.

RECORDS

The Clash (1977) '1977', CBS single S-CBS 5058, available on *Clash On Broadway* (2000), Epic 497453 2

Nirvana (1991) 'Smells Like Teen Spirit', *Nevermind*, DGC 24425.

Vernon Reid (1996) 'St Cobain', *Mistaken Identity*, Sony 483921 2.

The Smiths (1987) 'Paint A Vulgar Picture', *Strangeways Here We Come*, Rough Trade, WEA 4509–9 1899–2.

Talking Heads (1978) *More Songs About Buildings and Food*, Sire, WEA 7599–27425–2.

—— (1983) 'Making Flippy Floppy', *Speaking in Tongues*, Sire, WEA 7599–23883–2.

TELEVISION PROGRAMMES AND SERIES

Buffy the Vampire Slayer (1997–2003) Mutant Enemy Inc/Kuzui/Sandollar/Twentieth Century
    Fox Television.
Dad's Army (1968–77) BBC.
Fawlty Towers (1975 and 1979) BBC.
Friends (1994–2003) Bright/Kauffman/Crane Production in association with Warner Bros.
    Television.
Only Fools and Horses (1981–2000) BBC.
The Prisoner (1967–8) ITV
Ian Rankin's Evil Thoughts (2002) RDF Television/Channel 4.
Star Trek (1969–71) NBC
T.V. Nation (1994–5) NBC [1994]; Fox [1995]
The X-Files (1994–2003) Ten Thirteen Productions/Twentieth Century Fox Television .

WEBSITES

Eric Berne's last speech: <http://indigo.ie/~liztai/index.html?/~liztai/ta/berndate.htm>.
Goerge Boeree on Sigmund Freud: <http://www.ship.edu/~cgboeree/freud.html>.
John Lye on Roman Jakobson: <http://www.brocku.ca/commstudies.courses/2F50/jakobson.html>.
George Orwell's essay 'Politics and the English Language': <http://www.resort.com/~prime8/
    Orwell/patee.html>; <http://www.mtholyoke.edu/acad/intrel/orwell46.htm> <http://www.k-
    1.com/Orwell/index.cgi/work/essays/language.html>.
Pioneer 10's plaque: <http://www.space.com/php/multimedia/imagedisplay/img_display.php?pic=
    h_pioneer_update_02,0.gif&cap=Pioneer%2010's%20plaque%3Cbr%3E%3C/br%3Eclick
    %20to%20enlarge>
Plain English Campaign homepage: <http://www.plainenglish.co.uk/>.
Mary Ragan women and self esteem: <www.mindspirit.org>.
Mick Underwood's homepage: <http://www.cultsock.ndirect.co.uk/MUHome>/
Shelley Walia's review of Perry Anderson's *The Origins of Postmodernity* <http://www.biblio-
    india.com/articles/mj99_arl1.asp?mp=MJ99>.

▼ INDEX

Abercrombie, K 85
Adams, Sally 145–8
adornment 239–42
Adorno, Theodor 57–8, 191
advertising 249–50; *see also* commercials
alienation 202, 204, 206, 207, 208
Allen, Woody 190, 207
Alphaville 261
AltaVista 141, 142, 143
Althusser, Louis 107, 182, 218, 313, 326, 328
Altman, Robert 93
American Beauty 252
American Gigolo 252
American Psycho (Ellis) 53–8, 260, 322
Amis, Kingsley 21
Amis, Martin 193
Anderson, James 323
Ang, Ien 125, 132
anthropology: communication systems 268; cultural 42; culture definitions 178, 318; signs 32; structural 2
Antz 207
Apocalypse Now 190
architecture: Marxist theory 201, 202; modernism 262–3; Ruskin 293; urban space 233, 234, 235, 236–7
Argyle, Michael 84–6, 324, 325, 326, 327
Arnold, Matthew 42, 178, 180, 182–4, 187, 194
art: bourgeois 45; culture definitions 42, 178; high/low culture 185–6, 188, 189; Marxism 201, 202; second-hand nature of 270; Sprague 244–5; tool-using cultures 295; Tory view of culture 193; ways of seeing 9, 10, 12; *see also* literature; music
Astaire, Fred 7, 190

Atkinson, P 128, 223
attentiveness 86
audience 159, 160, 161, 163, 164
Auslander, Philip 48, 286
Austen, Jane 196
Austin, J L 15
authoritarian leadership styles 117–18, 119
auto-observation 126–7
auto-suggestion 163

Bagehot, Walter 291
Ball, Zoe 111
Ballard, J G 259–61, 262
bargain hunting 258
Barley, Stephen 18, 31–5
Barrie, J M 115
Barry, Peter 7–8, 31, 71, 276, 322
Barthes, Roland 18, 35, 46, 52, 242, 324; culture 179; *langue/parole* 29–30, 325, 326; semiotic reading of *Julius Caesar* 43–5
base/superstructure model 202, 203–4
Battleship Potemkin 287
Baudrillard, Jean 225–7, 286
The Beatles 109, 189, 192, 283
Beckham, David 253–6
Beethoven, Ludwig van 189
Being There (Kosinski) 9
Bennett, Oliver 194
Benton, Robert 70
Berger, John 9–12, 15, 272
Bergman, Ingmar 190
Berne, T 60
Berne, Eric 93–5, 327, 328
Bernstein, Basil 301, 311–13, 317
bias 19, 20
Bill Haley and the Comets 47
biography 308

community: and ethnicity 229–30; symbolic construction of 317–19
confidence 59, 163, 164–5; *see also* self-esteem
confidentiality 137
connative communication 279, 280
connotation 52, 324
connotative codes 34–5
Conrad, Joseph 190, 196
conscience 63
consent of research participants 135
conservatism 191, 248
consumer culture 57, 214, 255, 256, 272–4; *see also* mass culture
consumption 57, 201, 207, 219, 255; *see also* shopping
context: cultural 41; interpretation of text 17; particularistic meaning 313; referential communication 280; semantic 33–4; semiotics 29, 41; social 77, 79, 90–3, 197, 266
conventions 292
conversation: conversational style 96–8, 100–1; ethnomethodology 127; gestures 85; *see also* speech
Coopersmith, Stanley 60
Copernic 142, 144
Copland, Aaron 189
Coronation Street 26, 324
Corot, Jean-Baptiste Camille 193
Cosmides, Leda 73
Coupland, Douglas 286
Crash (Ballard) 259–60
crime 235, 315
Crocker, Betty 218
Cronenberg, David 70
Cross, Charles 252
Crystal, Billy 70
Crystal, David 104
cultural capital 199, 200, 201, 208, 256–7
cultural expectations 79
cultural studies 42, 63, 131, 179, 259
cultural values 29, 138, 178, 179, 232
culture: Arnold 42, 178, 180, 182–4, 194; Bourdieu 199–201; the canon 194–8; communication across cultures 91, 95–6, 99; community socialisation 317; cultural variation in facial expressions 82, 83; definitions 41–2, 177–9; ethnicity 230; European 227; evolutionary psychology 74;

high 43, 182–6, 190, 191, 194, 199; low 184–6, 190, 194; Pinker 102, 103, 104; popular 43, 58, 184–6, 187–90, 191–4, 256–9; semiotics 25, 26, 32, 33, 35; social interaction 318–19; structuralism 166; symbols 318; technology as 294–6; Two Cultures debate 187–90; Williams 41–2, 178–9, 184–6, 187; *see also* anthropology; art; consumer culture; mass culture

Dad's Army 109
Daily Mail 110–11
Dallas 132
The Damned 218
Darwin, Charles 73, 82, 83, 103–4
Darwinism 102–3
data collection 125, 128, 129, 133
Davies, Merryl Wyn 248
Davis, Mike 233–8, 260
Dawkins, Richard 102
de Certeau, M 257–8
De Niro, Robert 70, 323
debriefing of research participants 137
deception 136
decoding: facial expressions 82, 83; Osgood and Schramm model 39; process school 25, 265
deconstruction 18, 166, 324
Defoe, Daniel 106
Deleuze, Gilles 326
democracy 5, 150; extension and control of 269, 270; public relations 167
democratic leadership styles 117–18, 119
denotation 52, 324
denotative codes 34–5
Denzin, N K 223, 224
Derrida, Jacques 326
Dervin, Brenda 131
desire 273
Destiny's Child 111
Deutsch, K 277
dialectical materialism 203
dialogic writing 224
dialogue: internalised 40; vision relationship 11
Diana, Princess of Wales 254
Dick, Philip K 255
Dickens, C 1, 4, 193
Die Hard 234
diet 263